MODERN CINÉ PHOTOGRAPHY

HOW TO SHOOT HOME MOVIES

UWE NEY

TRANSLATED FROM THE GERMAN BY
JACQUELINE WILTSHIRE

CROWN PUBLISHERS, INC., NEW YORK

Library of Congress Cataloging in Publication Data

Ney, Uwe.
How to shoot home movies.

1. Amateur moving-pictures. I. Title.
TR896.N49 778.5′3 77-27429
ISBN 0-517-53390-1

First published in the U.S.A. in 1978 by Crown Publishers, Inc., New York
Originally published under the title *Moderne Schmalfilm Praxis*
Falken-Verlag Erich Sicker KG, 6272 Niedernhausen/Ts., 1977.

Printed in Great Britain by
Hazell Watson & Viney Ltd.,
Aylesbury, Bucks.

CONTENTS

Preface vii

When Pictures Learned to Move 1

The Development of Film Material 6

Ciné Film 8

Modern Ciné Cameras: Equipment and Uses 16

Simple Cameras 18

Standard Cameras
- Film Drive 21
- Optics 23
- Automatic Lens Aperture 32
- Film Speed 35
- High-Speed Filming 35
- Automatic Release 39
- Rotary Disc Shutter/Fading Out-Fading In 40
- XL-Optics 42

Superior Cameras
- Macro-Zoom Lens 43
- Automatic 'Dissolve' 44
- Automatic Single-Frame Device 45
- Prolonged-Exposure Control 46
- Interchangeable Lens 47
- Sound-Film Cameras 48

Ciné Camera Accessories
- Universal Accessories 51
- Attachments 57
- Optical Accessories 62
- Other Accessories 63

Filming
- The Test Film 83
- The Improvised Film 88
- Directed Filming 116
- Filming with a Script 130
- Scoring 135

Special Filming
- Macro Shots 145
- Filming with Flashlight 149
- Underwater Filming 150
- Wide-Screen Filming 152
- Trick Film 153
- Educational and Commercial Films 154

Technical Faults 156

Film Titles
- Choosing the Title 160
- Title Lettering 162
- Title Shots with Close-up Lenses 165
- Work on the Title Text 165
- Title Texts 167
- Trick Titles 169
- Titlers 178
- Lighting for Title-shots 181
- Title Leaders 183
- 'Two Hours to Spare' 184

Filming Editing and Montage
- The Meaning of Film Editing 187
- The Film Viewer 188
- The Single-Frame Counting Mechanism 190
- The Splicer 191
- Other Accessories 197
- Final Observations on the Theme of Film Editing 200
- Editing Plan and Film Montage 202

Sound Film or Silent Film 211

Film Scoring: Technical Possibilities 213
- Picture and Sound Projector and Musical Equipment 213
- Coupling Picture and Sound (Synchroniser) 214
- Picture-Synchronised Sound Recording 218

The Practice of Film Scoring 226
- Sound Recording 226
- Lip-Synchronised Recording 228
- Practical Aspects of Film Scoring 230

The Sound Library
- Music Library 238
- Sound-Effects Collection 240

Film Presentation 243
- The Silent-Film Projector 244
- Equipment for Silent or Sound Film 249
- The Sound-Film Projector 249
- Projection Accessories 251
- The Projection Screen 252
- Arrangement of Equipment 257
- Compilation of a Film Programme 257

Care of the Equipment
- Camera and Accessories 260
- Projector 263
- Film Viewer and Splicer 264
- The Films 265
- Insurance Cover 265

Tables 266

Glossary 269

PREFACE

This book is an invitation - inviting you to discover the world of ciné photography. It describes the opportunities open to the amateur using modern equipment, and proves just how easy it is to make a good film.

The book serves both as a useful guide for beginners and for those who have already made films but are not yet satisfied with the results; all readers can learn how to put their technical equipment to the optimum use. A comprehensive discussion on the components of the modern camera, and the accessories that will prove the most useful, is followed by advice on the right and wrong way to hold the camera, how to take films, how to edit and mount them, and, finally, how to add sound to the film and to present it.

This book is designed to stimulate your own ideas by providing suggestions of what to film and how to choose subjects. It is obvious that for every creative person a small amount of technical skill becomes an essential requirement, and that with it much is possible. Naturally, certain limitations will still present themselves, and in a productive and creative hobby like filming it is important to recognize this; nevertheless the existing opportunities provide plenty of scope.

At the end of the book the most important technical words and phrases are listed in a glossary, providing a quick and easy explanation of any terms that may be new to you.

This book has been based on practical experience. All the examples have at some time been tested, so if you try an experiment and it fails, have another attempt - there is usually something new to be learned from mistakes.

Much of the content of my conversations with amateur film-makers has become a part of this book - ideas that are repeated almost daily in my work in the same, or in a similar, form. Not the least of these ideas was the one that prompted the writing of this book - a book, not of abstract theories, but of practical hints and advice of use to every amateur in his bid to produce better films.

WHEN PICTURES LEARNED TO MOVE

Once upon a time – all fairy stories begin like this. The subject of this book is not of course a fairy story, yet there was a time, not all that long ago, when no one thought of pictures being able to move, in other words, of films.

Scholars and historians are not agreed on the actual date when films began. Some consider the genius Leonardo da Vinci to be the inventor, as it was he who established the idea of living pictures and constructed a four-cornered box, which later served as a model for the 'photo-box'.

Self-evidently, the history of films is closely connected with photography, which is itself barely 140 years old, the initial developments dating back only as far as the beginning of the nineteenth century even though the 'camera obscura' has been in evidence since antiquity. The 'camera obscura' was originally no more than a curiosity, consisting of a small hole in the wall of a darkened room, through which an inverted, diminished image of the outside world was projected onto a white wall opposite. Not until the end of the sixteenth century did Italian scholars invent a convex lens for this hole with which brighter, sharper pictures could be produced. A century later, with the appearance of a collapsible, portable gadget with which, for example, a painter could produce copies of portraits, landscapes, or architectural structures in perfect perspective, the 'camera obscura' was at last put to practical use in the graphic arts. Thus this period saw the origins of the first 'mirror reflex camera', used by Niepce and Daguerre in their first photographic experiments.

However, in 1830, when photography was still in its initial stages, human imagination combined with technical ability led to the discovery of a method of making pictures move: so, chiefly at the annual fairs and in the conjuror's corner, the stormy success story of cinématography began. The years 1860-70 saw the first productions that can be considered as forerunners of the film as we know it. They were derived from a piece of equipment in which every single stage of movement was depicted in separate pictures on a cylinder or disc, which when viewed through a rotating slit deceived the eye into believing that the movement was continuous. This device became known as the 'Wheel of Life'. Various different pieces of equipment, all working on the same principle, were developed simultaneously in a number of places.

In 1868 J.B. Linnett produced the 'pocket-cinétamograph', a small book in which on each page the same figure appeared in a series of movements, each following on from the last, so that when the pages were quickly flicked through the pictures could be seen changing in rapid succession, giving the impression that the figure was actually moving. This principle is employed even today in objects designed to entertain young and old alike.

The 'pocket-cinématograph' was the first of a number of slightly varying modes of photography. In 1877 E. Muybridge (California) became the first person to produce a continuous set of photographs of a moving animal, and he used his pictures to demonstrate the 'wheel-of-life projection'. His subject had been a galloping horse: using thirty cameras, taking a picture with each, one after the other, he obtained his results, which he then used in the course of his scientific investigation.

The development of films made a considerable advance when, in the same year, the Frenchman Reynaud succeeded for the first time in projecting the moving pictures on the 'wonder-wheel' on to a screen. In 1882 he improved his 'praxiroscope-projection' (by means of optical adjustments), which used a strip of sheet-gelatine on which the pictures were drawn. He produced three sketched films and for the first time used perforated picture-strips to give a show. Already mechanical equipment existed that made it possible to add simple, appropriate sound-effects.

In 1887 O. Anschütz invented an electrical 'fast-motion viewer' for use with continuous pictures, the idea of this being to illuminate briefly pictures arranged in a ring or disc shape with a flash of light from a Geissler tube, so that the movement of the pictures was no longer irregular. A whole collection of new inventions appeared around this time. As early as 1877 W. Donisthorpe had published a plan for combining the 'Wheel of Life' and the phonograph, which was realised in 1893 by Edison, who introduced both the use of 35mm. film and the art of perforation, both of which are still practised today. Only a year later, in 1894, Edison made use of the phonograph to produce the first sound film ever, which showed a man talking into the phonograph, saying 'Mr. Edison, what do you think of cinématography?' However there was one great drawback to Edison's method: only one person at a time could look at the film in the viewer, a fact that remained even though the equipment was altered and greatly improved, the camera used becoming known as the 'cinématograph', and the device used for reproduction as the 'cinématoscope'. Yet it remains to Edison's credit that sound film is actually older than the silent film!

The year 1895 became one of the most important in the history of cinematography. The Lumiere brothers (Lyon), W. Lalhan (New York), Max Skladanowsky (Berlin), Oscar Messter (Berlin), and others had by this time simultaneously developed the first practical equipment for taking and reproducing films; everything that came later was based on the pioneering work of these inventors.

On 28 December the brothers Auguste and Louis Jean Lumiere showed the first ever film, in the modern sense of the word, in front of a huge audience in the Grand Café in Paris. The occasion created a reaction of shock, uproar, and amazement amongst their contempories, and to those present it became clear that the event heralded a revolution. The Lumiere brothers showed their film using a 'cinematograph', and from this time on the term cinematography became current in the story of film, our word 'cinema' being directly derived from it.

Just two months earlier, on 1 November 1895, the Skladanowsky brothers had given their first film showing as part of a programme of entertainments in the Winter Gardens in Berlin, but this had proved less spectacular than the Paris event and was not held in the same regard. Later, however, a memorial plaque was placed in the Winter Gardens in memory of the occasion. The Skladanowsky brothers used two projectors to show their films, and used film strips for the first time. As one machine projected a picture, the other switched on to the next picture in darkness, so that a picture was shown alternately from the first and second projectors. Their equipment later became known under the name 'bioscope'.

In 1896 the work of Oscar Messter, who has already been mentioned, resulted in decisive improvements being made to cinematography. Above all he invented the Maltese-cross device for the transportation of the film, which enabled the film to advance intermittently and so produce a picture free from flickering. (The Maltese cross is still included today as a part of much professional equipment.) In 1900 Messter was responsible for the construction of a hundred cameras, made in accordance with the principle that he had developed; each was equipped with film-cassettes of 30m. length. Thus Oscar Messter developed the first easily portable ciné camera, a camera that could be set up almost anywhere. It was also he who produced the first German newsreel, and the first films for dispatch were taken with the Messter cameras. Above all, however, Messter sought to combine pictures with sound, and he gave the first public demonstration of his cosmograph used in conjunction with the gramophone in Berlin in 1903.

Yet the modern film techniques at the turn of the century did little more than provide something new for the fair ground and similar places. The films were between 10m.

and 20m. long. Moving pictures seemed to provide an original way of producing simple shows – comedies or short thrillers – but the novelty soon wore off as far as the public was concerned. Filming appeared to reach its first crisis-point, and it became necessary to try to create a more engrossing type of entertainment. Messter apart, the Lumiere brothers very quickly came to appreciate the documentary value of filming and began to prefer using topical events as their subject matter. Yet the public demanded more and more variety, and, as a result, the producers, who as a rule also acted as their own directors and cameramen, were forced to produce larger and more absorbing films. Film lengths grew to about 300m. and the simple strips of the early years were replaced by works adapted from literature.

At the same time, the film pioneers were of course experimenting with new methods for adding sound to film. An absolutely silent film never in fact existed. Newspaper headlines of the times disclose that even the first films were shown with a piano accompaniment, sometimes a gramophone or even a whole orchestra was there. Edison's sound-film did not have the capacity to reach a large audience – there was still a lot of ground to be covered before the arrival of synchronised film.

Various people were responsible for an invention that eventually led to the so-called optical sound, in other words, photographed noise. At the turn of the century many physicists were concerning themselves with these photographic recordings of sound. From 1916 onwards experiments began to bear fruit, starting in 1901 with the successes of the scientist Ruhmer, and significantly developed through the work of Berghund, a Swede, and Mihaly, from Vienna. Finally a patent was established, shared by the three German scientists J. Engl, J. Massolle, and H. Vogt. for the so-called 'Tri-Ergon', a machine containing an amplifier for photographed sound. In 1922 the first ever performance was given using the Tri-Ergon method; this event was a significant one in the history of sound-film.

In the meantime, however, the silent film had reached a sufficient level of sophistication to bring it in line with the theatre in terms of artistic production. Stars like Henry Porter (discovered by O. Messter), Albert Basserman, and Paul Wagener, among others, had helped to pave the way. After the First World War Germany became the leading country in the further development of the silent film, an art form that reached its apogee in the twenties.

The invention of sound film signified a decisive turning-point in film creation, yet initially it remained chiefly an attraction at the annual fairs; by and large it was rejected as unaesthetic in comparison with the silent film. Nor did the first Klamank sound films do much to allay this impression, and it was not until 1929 that the first stage-worthy sound film was presented in Germany. However, as time passed, sound films eventually achieved the world recognition they still possess today. The 'photographed-sound' system is still used in modern feature films, albeit in a much improved form.

THE DEVELOPMENT OF FILM MATERIAL

The history of moving pictures would never have been possible without the development and improvement of film material, a subject of interest to every amateur film-maker.

As already mentioned, 35mm. film originated with Edison. Subsequently various inventors experimented with different film widths, until the introduction of 16mm. film in the 1930s. The use of this narrower and less bulky film provided a great stimulus for the amateur film industry. A short time later, 8mm. film appeared on the market, both in cassettes (Movex-film from Agfa) and 2 x 8 (Double-8) on spools. Super-8 film, the new baby in the development of ciné-film, has only been in existence since 1964.

Nowadays these three film formats are clearly differentiated. Thirty-five mm. film is used in the cinema, while 16mm. and 8mm. are collectively known as ciné film; it is 8mm. film in particular that is normally considered for amateur use.

It is well known that in the pioneering period all pictures were taken on black-and-white film, yet the desire for colour film undoubtedly dates back equally as far. Indeed, the first German patent for the making of colour photographs was taken out as early as 1912, the process having evolved in the course of scientific research by Dr Rudolf Fischer at the Agfa Film works in Wolken, Germany. His experiments showed that by means of chemical processing silver emulsion produced pigments that were not soluble in water, and on this basis the first Agfa colour film was finally developed, to be demonstrated to the world on the occasion of the Olympic Games in Berlin in 1936. Soon after this the facility of filming in colour became available to every amateur film-maker.

Just a year earlier the Kodak-Eastman company in Rochester, U.S.A., had succeeded in presenting the first full-length feature film, made with Kodachrome colour film. The story of how the world-famous Kodachrome film came to be invented has touches of the fairy-tale: it was developed by two musicians who enjoyed photography but were not content with the film commonly used. They began to experiment at home in the cellar and the bathroom, studying mathematics and physics in their spare time to equip themselves with the necessary groundwork, and were so successful in their investigations that in 1930 they were finally given the opportunity to continue their research in a Kodak laboratory.

In the very early days of film – long before the well-known Agfacolour and Kodachrome films were invented – attempts were made to heighten the expression of the pictures by colouring the film. The method most worthy of mention was the so-called hand-colouration; using this technique the Frenchman Charles Pathé hand painted colours on hundreds of metres of film– an extremely laborious task. In the early years of this century Pathé achieved sensational success with these hand-coloured films: there was after all nothing else. It was, incidentally, the same Pathé who initiated the 9.5mm. film format, which is now, however, of little more than historical value. Whereas sound film, once established, totally supplanted silent film, since the introduction of colour film both black-and-white and colour films have been produced side by side.

It is difficult to define when the distinction between amateur and professional films was first made. During the pioneering period everyone was an absolute amateur. There were no prototypes, so everything the inventors wanted to work with, they first had to invent. The 'amateurs' included musicians, mathematicians, physicists, and soldiers, who in their free time frequently stumbled across problems that they would then attempt to solve. Only in the fullness of time and with the perfecting of film techniques did the professionals finally emerge. In the history of films, as in many other fields of discovery, many an idea for innovation and improvement originated with a hobby-enthusiast and was later utilised by the industry.

With the introduction of small ciné film (9.5mm. and 8mm.), ciné cameras also became smaller and more practical, and their use rapidly extended. In addition, the new film sizes meant an ever increasing divergence between the development of amateur and professional cameras. On the market today amateur and professional equipment is usually quite separate.

CINÉ FILM

Ciné-film enthusiasts have chosen for themselves a hobby that is without a doubt one of the few really creative pursuits possible in the open air. As in every serious hobby, there are many questions to be answered anout its possibilities and its limitations, and the means by which the optimum results can be obtained. Not until everything is going well does one really experience a feeling of satisfaction or enjoyment.

Types of Cine film for Super-8 cameras
a) Normal Super-8 film
b) Super-8 sound film with additional sound track
c) Single-8 film in special cassette

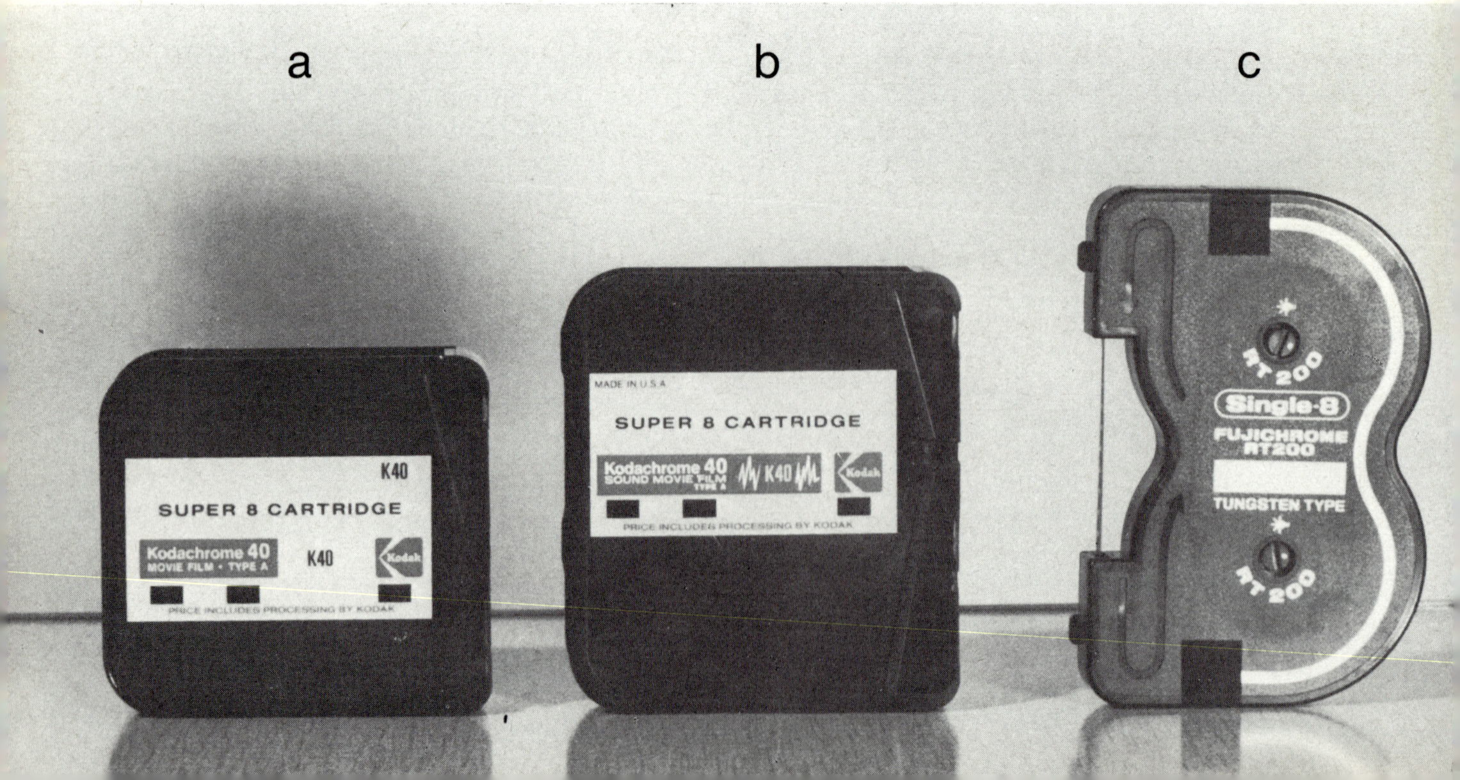

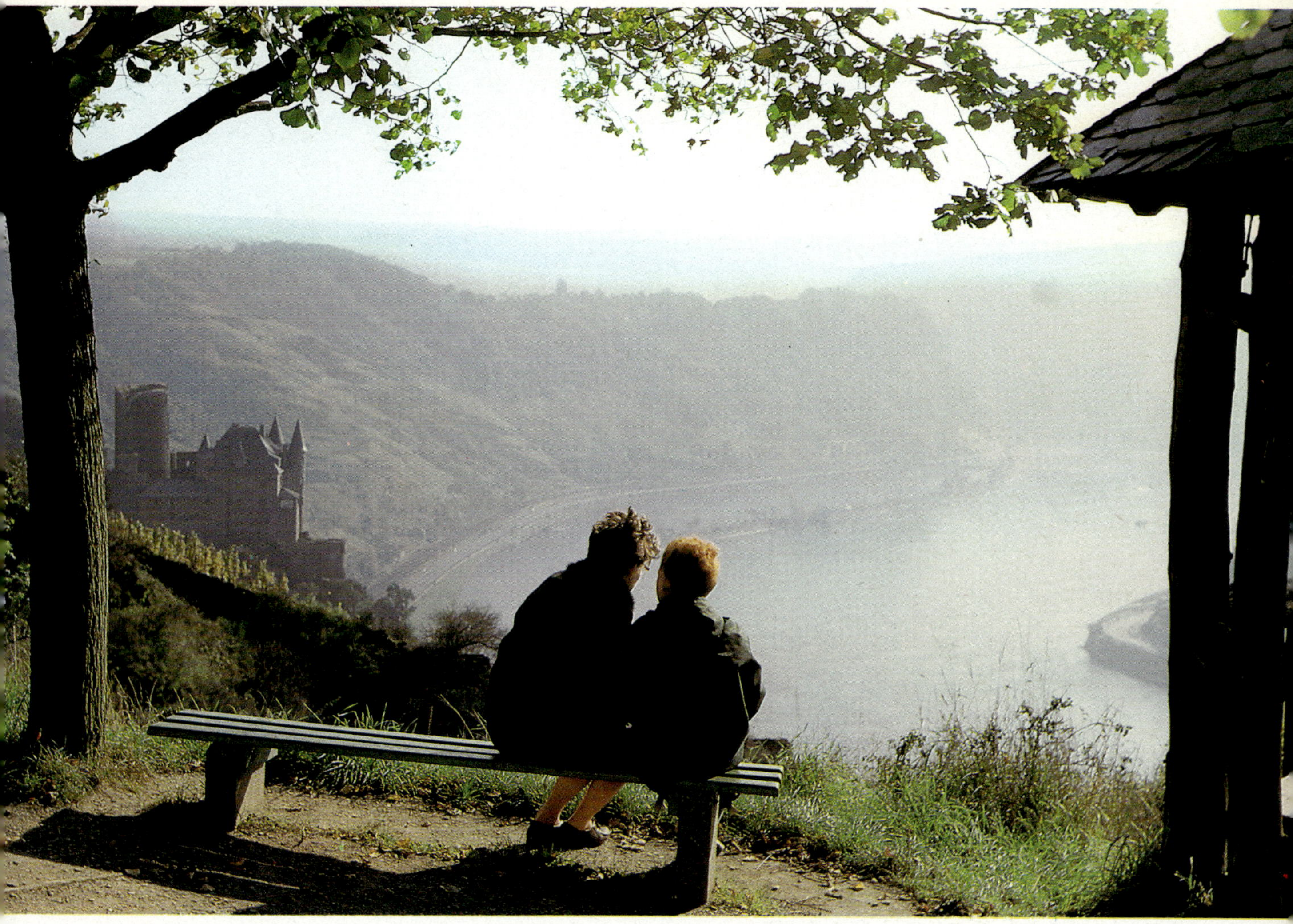

Plate 1: People in a landscape, an oft recurring film theme. The walkers in front of a mountain back-drop produce a striking impression, particularly suitable for the close of a film. The all-important movement in the film is caused by the wind in the trees.

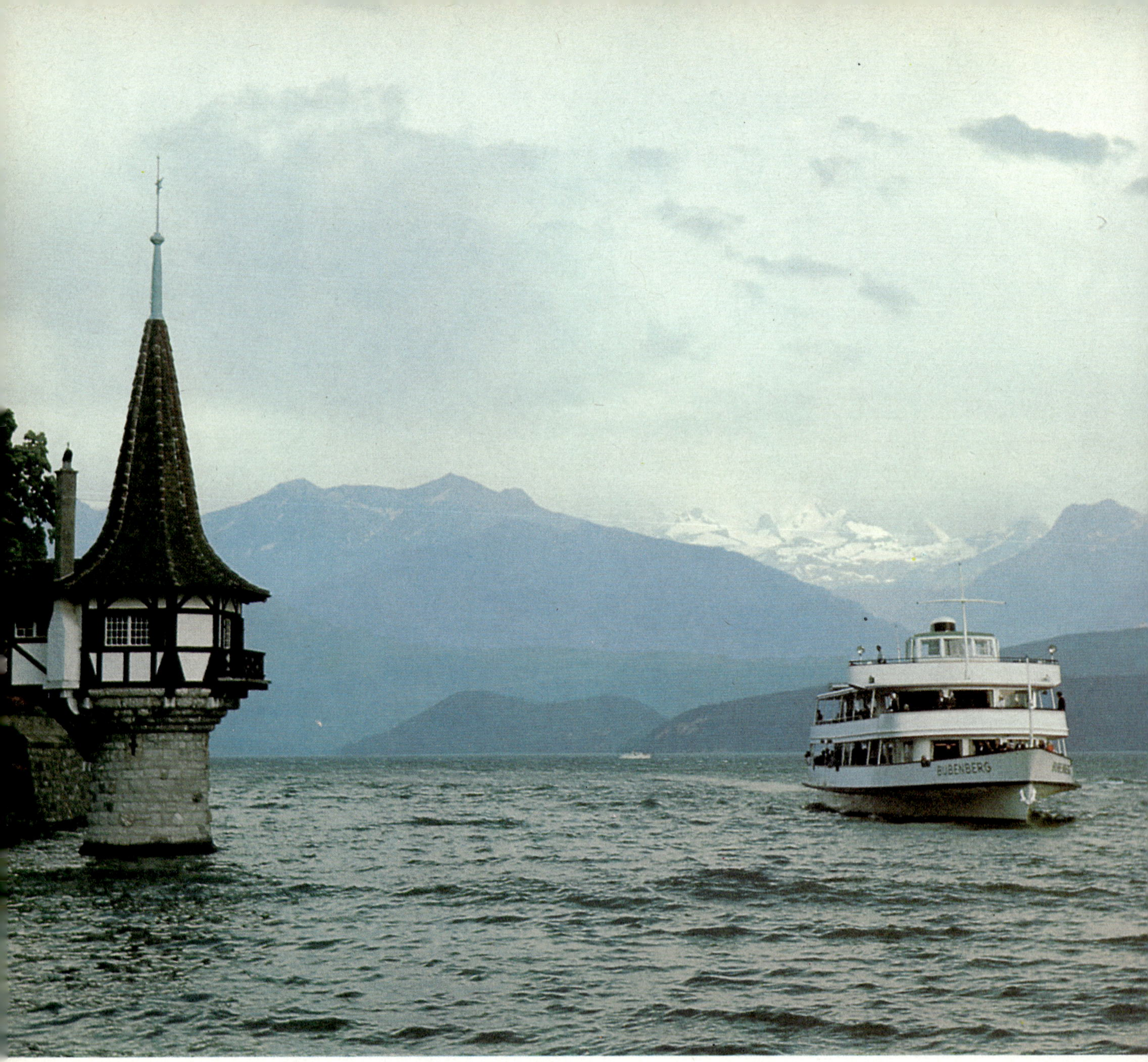

Plate 2: Even in dreary weather filming can continue. Indeed the increased movement of the water makes it more exciting than on a calm, sunny day.

Probably most ciné photographers begin with still photography, indeed many film-makers still continue with still photography at the same time. Consequently most amateur film-makers have had many years experience with photography before they turn to ciné film. Perhaps here lies the origin of an old advertising slogan:

Those who take photos have more out of life,

Those who film have life itself.

Life in this context means joy, something that can be captured with the help of a ciné camera!

The basic principles of photography and film-making are, however, very different, which means the lessons learned in photography cannot simply be reapplied in the case of ciné films, each has a separate code of practice, which must be adhered to. While a still photograph captures a snatched moment in the midst of an activity, the ciné film can reproduce a time-span, a whole sequence of movements. the single photograph can only represent a frozen expression, perhaps a laughing face, but a film enables you to hear the laughter once again. The difference between the two is immediately obvious.

In his first film the amateur photographer usually runs the risk of filming what is in effect a collection of slides, because he regards his subjects as photographs, not as part of a film, and thinks in terms of picture composition, ignoring the action. In film-making the arrangement is also of significance, indeed it may be of the utmost importance, yet in a different manner.

Embarking on ciné filming without any previous knowledge of photography is in many respects simpler, for one then remains ignorant of the laws governing choice of subject matter, picture arrangement, etc. Often the purpose of getting a camera is to film the children growing up or at play, or to record a holiday or some other special event. It is easy to feel at home with filming when the rules of photography are not allowed to intervene. The most important ingredient to be captured on film is life: movement, movement, and yet more movement! Ciné film can only be exploited to its full with moving objects, whether people or animals, leaves or clouds: precisely those things a still photograph cannot do justice to.

The way to make films will be described in the course of this book. The amateur photographer will discover how to apply his photographic knowledge to ciné photography; the beginner will learn how to go about the whole business.

To begin with, a couple of points about ciné-film itself.

The long line of events leading up to Super-8 film, ciné film as we know it today, has already been described. The term ciné film eventually emerged to cover all film that is narrower than 35mm. film (feature-film). Although theoretically this includes 16mm. film, that size of film is mentioned only in passing as it is used almost exclusively for professional filming (one of the reasons for this being that 16mm. cameras are considerably more expensive, and consequently the cameras produced for the amateur film-maker are usually of the 'shoelace' (8mm.) type).

At the beginning of the century, also the beginning of the manufacture and use of ciné film, no standard size existed; 2 x 8 film (Double-8), with a length of 7.5m. and a width of 16mm., was the most developed. This is the film best known to many film-makers, as it governed the world film market until the appearance of Super-8 film. The film had to be exposed twice, first on one side then on the other - a principle also applied to tape-recorders. Thus 7.5m. of film, equalling 2 - 3 minutes of film time, were run twice through the camera per spool, the film being turned round before the second run. The relatively short running time considerably lessened the possibility of making a continuous film of any significant length, particularly as valuable time was wasted each time the film was changed. Moreover, a certain amount of skill was necessary to insert and wind on normal Double-8 film as it was only loosely wound on to the spool; if wound on too loosely it would be exposed unintentionally. Yet another difficulty lay in the fact that most Double-8 cameras were only fitted with a spring, rather than an electric, motor to transport the film, and this spring motor had to be rewound after about 1.5m. of film had run. All in all, using Double-8 film was a pretty tedious business. Eventually further laboratory experiments resulted in the film being divided in half, making a film which was 15m. long and 8mm. wide.

Those who still use this sort of film will be aware of one particular peculiarity, almost forgotten in the mean time - there are two types of film available, one for artificial lighting and one for use in daylight. The former must be used for pictures taken with film-lamps, the latter for outdoor filming. (Artificial light is predominantly yellow, daylight predominantly blue.) The problem of varying colour sensitivities can of course be solved by using filters to modify the colour, if the prescribed lighting is not being used, but this may affect the light intensity adversely, and should be avoided if possible.

Long before the Second World War there existed, as previously described, one 8mm. cassette film - the 'Movex' cassette. In this, all 10m. of film were run through the camera in one piece, making it unnecessary to turn the film over as with Double-8 film. There were, however, only a few cameras able to take these cassettes, although technically speaking this film bore the same features as Double-8 film.

In 1924 the Pathé company in France produced a film cassette that took 9.5m.-wide film; although little used and soon forgotten in other countries, it is still used to a small extent in France. This film differed from any other make in that it had a perforation hole between each picture down the centre of the strip, the assumption being that film made in this way would be far less likely to break than film perforated at the edge, and this proved to be exactly the case. The main reason for this film being little used was, again, that there were hardly any cameras suitable for it.

For those who do not find the 7.5m. film length sufficient for their needs, there are a number of Double-8 cameras on the market that can take 30m. spools, but are otherwise used in exactly the same way as small Double-8 film cameras. Film used on the 30m. spools has a total of about 16½ minutes running time, in other words, a good eight minutes of unbroken film on each side. A very tempting proposition, but nevertheless one that is little exploited because of the high camera costs.

In 1964, to the regret of most Double-8 users and to the delight of all new film-makers, Super-8 film appeared on the market (originally developed and introduced by Kodak and now in general use). The film buffs, who had been using the Double-8 system for decades, were decidedly put out over this new creation in the amateur film world: they feared, with good reason, that the new Super-8 film would completely supercede Double-8 film. Super-8 film necessarily brought with it a new camera and a new projector. Users of Double-8 had therefore either to remain true to their past

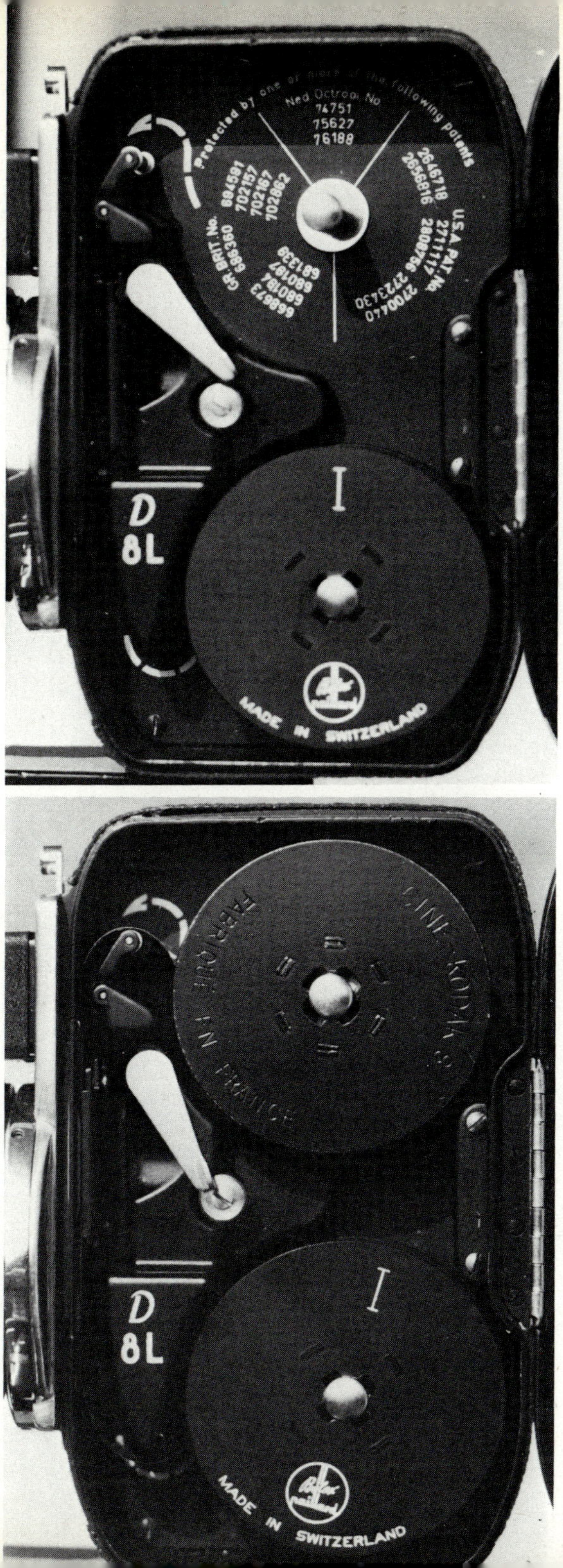

Double-8 camera

i) without film
ii) with film inserted

methods or buy an entirely new set of equipment. Such considerations were obviously going to have a great effect on the manufacturing industry, and a vigorous advertising campaign was launched to promote the new film technology.

Super-8 film, which is nowadays common everywhere, had a number of distinct advantages over all the earlier processes. Above all it provided 15m. of continuous film and did away with the necessity to turn the film over, so it became possible to take about three minutes of uninterrupted film. In addition, after a few trial runs it was easy enough to change the film in a matter of seconds, so that in practice film even longer than three minutes could be shot without any great gaps.

Another innovation, this time welcomed by those previously using Double-8, was the existence of only one type of film, which meant that swapping from artificial-light film to daylight film became a thing of the past: with Super-8 the camera merely had to be set to suit the type of light available. With 15m. film this can be altered as often as required, which makes it a great deal simpler than before, although those who have never used the Double-8 system regard it as a matter of course.

It is hardly possible to make a mistake

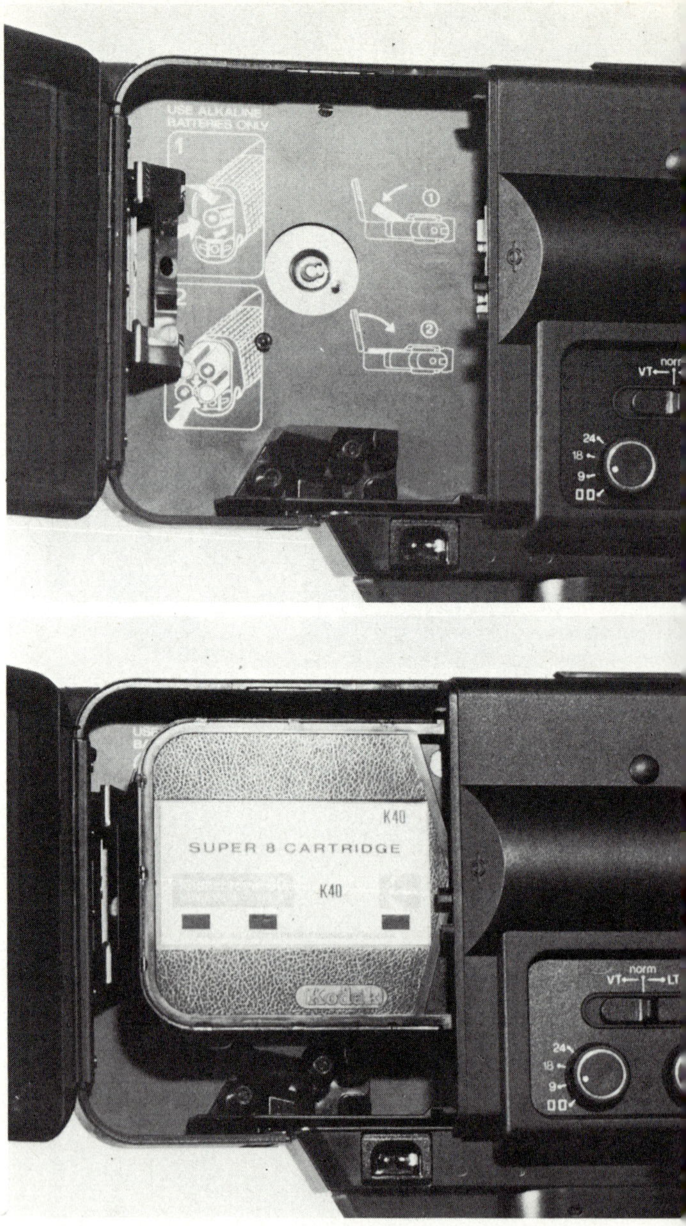

Open Super-8 camera

i) without film
ii) with cassette inserted

using Super-8 cassettes. The cassette has a number of small indentations by the film-gate that automatically set the lens aperture inside the camera (users of Double8 had to remember to do this manually). Super-8 cameras using cassettes will always adjust themselves to the correct aperture setting, even if the wrong film is put in the camera by mistake.

Occasionally a defect does appear in a Super-8 cassette and this ought to be mentioned. It sometimes happens, although extremely rarely, that a cassette will not run smoothly, but even if this does occur there is no real cause for worry: the manufacturer will replace a faulty film-cassette without hesitation.

Incidentally it is, in theory, also possible in Super-8 filming to use 30m. film, but there are very few cameras to be had which are designed for this. It is possible to get a so-called Double-Super-8 camera, the film for which is wound on a spool as with Double-8 film. As the perforations on this correspond to those on Super-8 film it is not necessary to use a different projector.

Another cassette, the Single-8 magazine, is also fitted with Super-8 film, but it is flat-shaped as the two film spools for winding off and on lay next to each other, while in the Super-8 cassette they lie on top of one another. Consequently, the Single-8 magazine is much thinner than the Super-8 cassette and the cameras themselves are narrower and easier to hold. However, like the Movex magazine in the time of Double8, this magazine system is not very widespread because it is applicable only with certain cameras; it is outside the normal range of Super-8 film.

All films are made both in colour and in black-and-white. The latter was used far more in the Double-8 system than with Super-8 because the amount of black-and-white film available was considerably more then than now. There is hardly any black-and-white film for Super-8 cameras, which is of course partly because colour film nowadays is half the price of the earlier Double-8 films. Certainly some things would make perfect subjects for black-and-white film, but time has proved colour film to be unequivocally successful in the amateur film world.

The film industry has long been using acetate as a film-base, and this base is still used today for all Double-8 film as well as most Super-8 film. Nowadays, however, Super-8 film is also made with a polyester base, particularly in the Single-8 system developed in Japan. Using a different film-base does not affect the way the film is taken, but becomes significant later when the film is processed. The sound-track, if required, must also be processed according to a different method from the one previously used, as the conventional acetate glues are ineffectual on polyester film. I will return to this later. Films made with polyester are somewhat thinner, so a Super-8 magazine can hold considerably more film. If this type of film is to be used, some adjustments to the camera counting-device will be necessary.

The story is rounded off for the time-being with a relatively new type of cine-film: Super-8 sound film. The magazine is bigger than usual as there is a second opening on the underside, and the distance between the opening and the film-gate must be exactly equal to the length of eighteen individual shots. With this film both the picture and the sound are recorded simultaneously in the camera. This process came on to the market in 1973 but, as it requires a special, and generally speaking expensive camera, is not yet very widespread. The problem of sound-film will be discussed later in more detail. The speed rating of Super-8 film is generally 15 DIN for daylight and 17 DIN for artificial lighting. The difference lies in the fact that in daylight a conversion filter is used, which cuts out some of the light, although not enough to justify a diaphragm stop (however, 3 DIN grades mean a lens-aperture value equal to double or half the light intensity). Film with a higher speed rating of 21 DIN to 23 DIN is rather expensive, but provides a wider range of possibilities, particularly in poor light conditions.

Although it is only a relatively short time since the introduction of Super-8 film, it is said that since then more people have used it than ever used all the other systems together. This in itself would appear to be a good argument in favour of using cassette-films, although the amount of effort made in recent times to introduce more people to amateur filming must of course be taken into account.

A couple more points about the size of the film: the surface area is about 40 per cent larger than normal 8mm. film. The following diagram shows the sizes of normal 8mm. and Super-8 film:

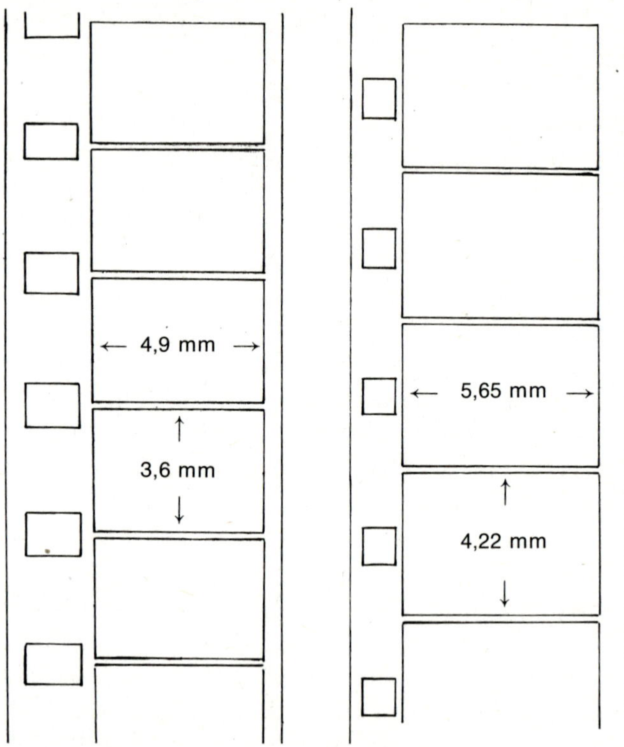

Normal	**Super-8**
4.9 x 3.6 mm.	5.65 x 4.22mm.
= 17.64 mm^2.	= 23.84 cm^2.
per frame	per frame

To compare: 16mm. film = 10.3mm. x 7.5mm. = 77.25$mm.^2$ per frame.

By now it must be clear that the only type of film of interest to the amateur film-maker today is Super-8 film. For this reason almost all cameras now in manufacture are intended for use with these cassettes; only a few are made for Single-8 cassettes, although these are not distinguishable in format from Super-8 cassettes.

Looking to the future, at the moment there do not seem to be any indications that a new film format is about to emerge. The only development that might be expected is in the field of magnetic sound and picture recordings, as used in television, but at present any such projects are frustrated by their high cost and such a system remains inaccessible to the amateur film-maker. Super-8 film will therefore be available for a long time yet, but Double-8 material is less and less sought after, and it is not easy to estimate how much longer it will remain on the market. Even those who viewed the new film format with scepticism in 1964 have in the meantime been convinced of its advantages.

It is worth noting that the introduction of film cassettes has by no means been confined to ciné film. Everyone is familiar with other cassette systems, which have been developed along parallel lines: photographic film, tape recorders, and, recently, television programmes!

Simple compact camera with correspondingly simple fittings

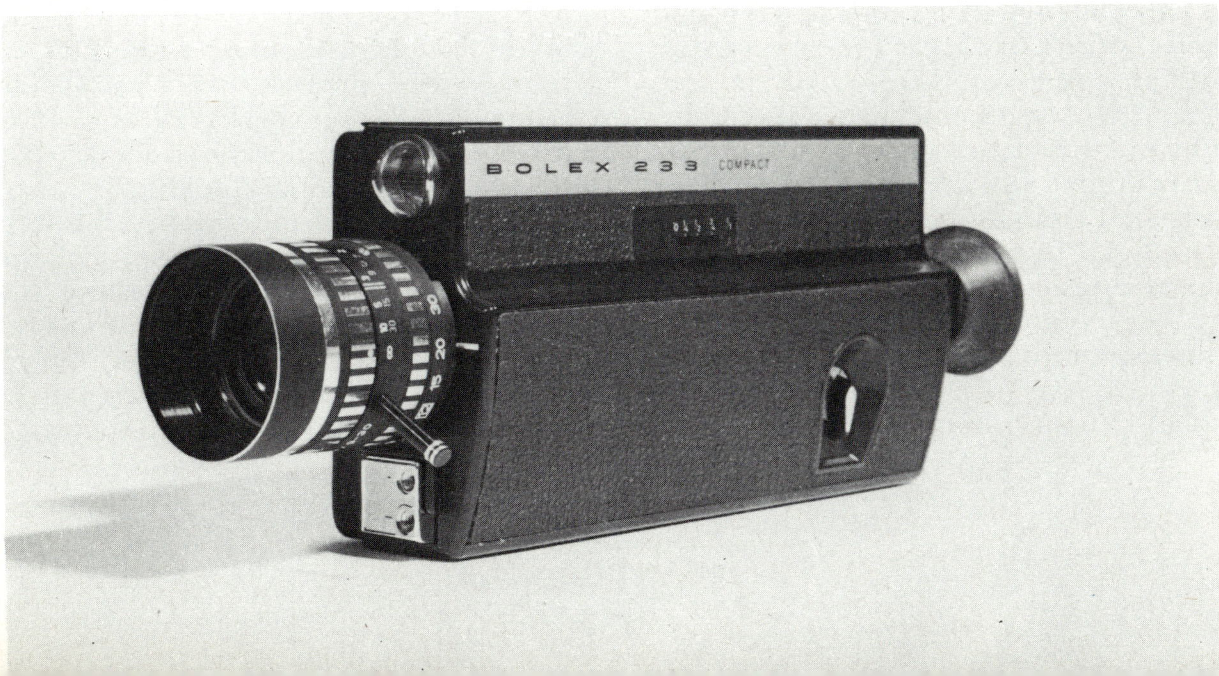

MODERN CINÉ CAMERAS: EQUIPMENT AND USES

There are a number of important aspects to be considered before buying a ciné camera, and the ultimate choice will depend upon certain deciding factors, including:

1 financial considerations
2 the intended use
3 the desire for simplicity
4 the scope for later increasing the camera's potential by the addition of accessories

Every factor requires careful consideration.

First of all, be warned against buying too small a camera! When confronted with the problem of buying a ciné camera for the first time, it is difficult to have any clear idea of the number of possibilities involved, and consequently some sound advice should be sought on the matter. The specifications initially desired will often seem unrealistic on financial grounds, yet they should not be ignored, as they will without doubt reappear, and a hasty purchase cannot only prove disappointing, it may even prove to be an expensive mistake.

Obviously everyone is limited by their personal situation, but within these limitations there will still be a wide range of choice. Experience proves that it is better to choose a camera with more features than one initially anticipates requiring, thereby allowing scope to 'grow into it'. But the deciding factor for most buyers is the price. Obviously the price is always relative to the quality of the goods. A simple camera takes films, of course, but lacks refinement. Cameras equipped for a variety of uses come in a variety of prices. When buying a ciné camera it is not the price that should be looked at first, even if it is ultimately the deciding factor: it is more important to consider and define one's personal requirements. In my experience it is obvious that a lot of people do not know exactly what they want when they start looking.

It is a laborious business wading through catalogues without being able to judge the articles recommended or understand the meaning behind the words used. We must therefore consider the things a film-camera **must** possess, together with the parts used to expand its potential, and those only required in certain situations. To begin with, cameras can be divided into three groups; though the divisions are somewhat unconventional they simplify the business of description:

1 simple cameras
2 standard cameras
3 superior cameras

It is not always easy to draw a dividing line between these groups because the criterion is not simply based on price. There can be considerable differences in price between cameras of very similar quality but of different make. But on balance these rather clumsy distinctions serve a useful purpose. In any instances in this book where details of equipment are given, it is clearly indicated which pieces of equipment fall into each category.

Reflections on the water (such reflections may be avoided with the use of a polfilter)

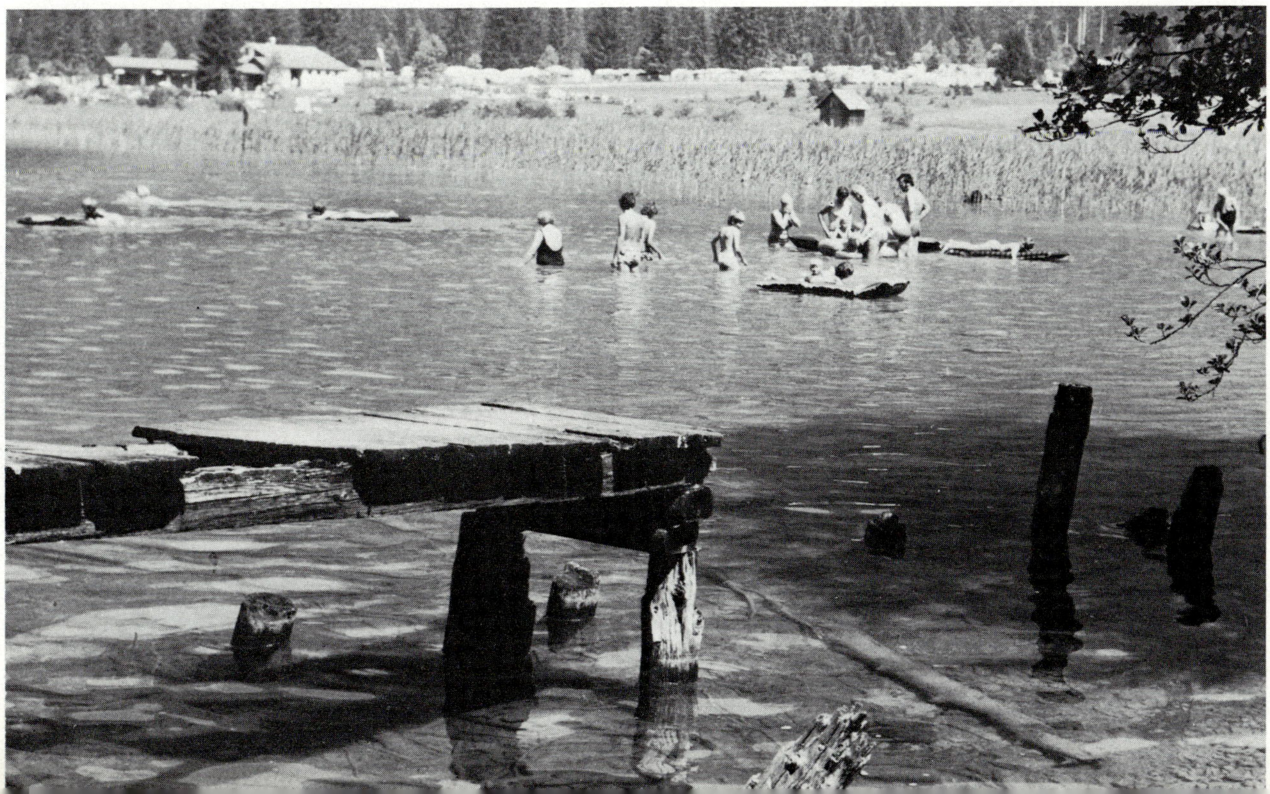

SIMPLE CAMERAS

One glance at the camera catalogues is sufficient to see that there are not a great many simple cameras on offer: cameras that are fitted with only the absolutely essential requisites for film-making.

What does the simple-camera test consist of? To begin with it must of course have a film compartment that takes Super-8 magazines. The film is then transported through the camera by means of a motor powered by two, three, or even four batteries, according to the camera model. Only batteries with a metal casing should be used, in order to avoid damaging the battery compartment. Cheap batteries are liable to leak, and the acid that runs out of them will

Simple Super-8 camera with good fittings

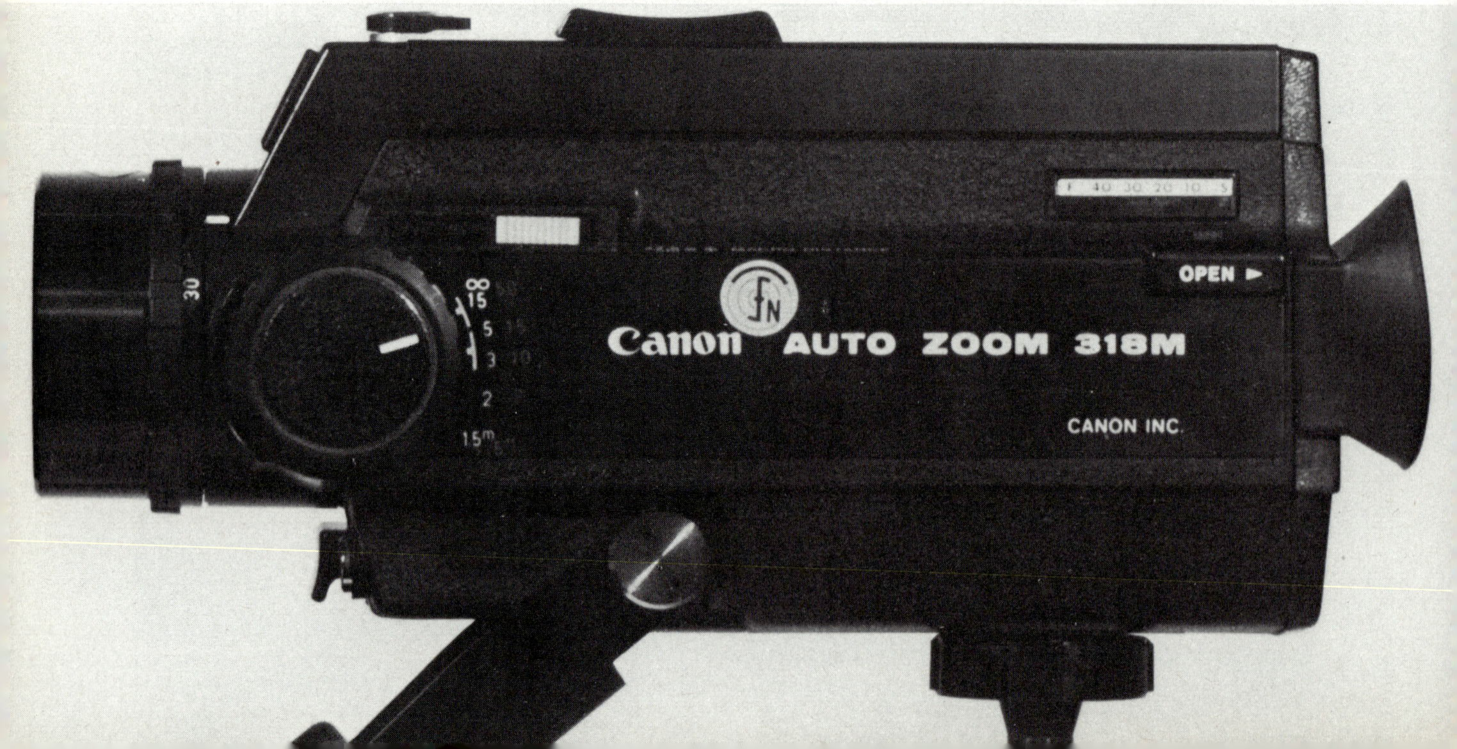

corrode the inside of the camera. Moreover, steel-coated batteries have a considerably longer life expectancy.

Obviously even the simplest camera will require a lens, but it will only be a very simple one. In most cases a fixed-focus lens is used, in other words, a lens on which nothing can be altered, neither the range nor the focal length. The lens is therefore adjusted to a middle setting, which means it has a range of about 4 - 5m., and the focal length in Super-8 cameras is 15mm. In fairly good weather it is possible to take well-defined though by no means outstanding, pictures using this type of camera.

Another component of even the most simple camera is the automatic exposure device. I know of no Super-8 camera that does not possess this. By this means the light is regulated by the diaphragm, automatically guaranteeing that the film is correctly exposed. In simple cameras this device is usually powered by the same batteries used to transport the film, although sometimes a special battery is used for this purpose, usually a very small battery with a fairly long life expectancy. Some cameras have a signal in the viewfinder to indicate when the light is too weak or too bright. Even in the simplest camera there is a setting for artificial light filming, which has the effect of displacing the filter required for filming in daylight (all Super-8 films are fundamentally designed for artificial lighting). The camera is set either by means of a key or a switch.

An equally important feature of any camera is the socket on the base designed to receive the screw of a tripod or film lamp. Yet an even more essential feature must of course be the release button, which is found on the front or in another easily accessible position. When pressed this button has the effect of switching on the motor that transports the film, and is thus used to control when filming begins and how long it lasts.

Equally obviously, every camera must possess a viewfinder, as mentioned earlier. As in a still camera, it presents the portion of the scene that is going to be represented on the film. The more precise the viewfinder, the more exactly the shots can be determined. Simple cameras, which generally speaking are not fitted with a reflex viewfinder sometimes show slight inexactitudes, but these are not usually enough to make any significant difference.

To sum up, the most simply constructed camera must possess:

1 A fixed-focus lens
2 An automatic exposure device (regulating the exposure, preferably with an indicator in the viewfinder)
3 A reasonably accurate viewfinder

With these fittings it is possible to take films, indeed, even ones of surprisingly good quality. An eye for interesting subject-matter and a bit of luck also help of course!

A lively or impressive foreground adds life to the dead building. Twigs and grass move in the wind, transforming a slide into a film scene.

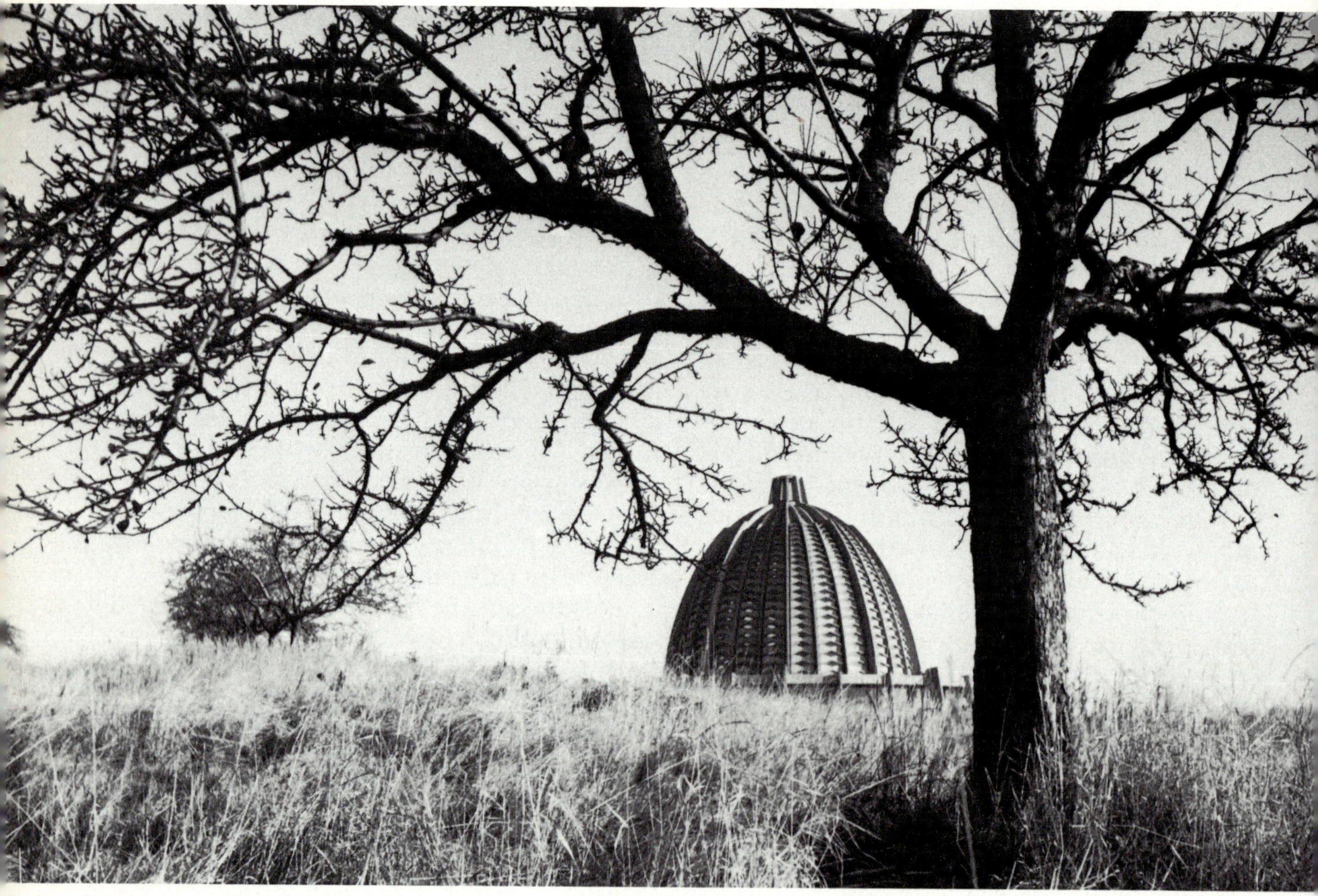

STANDARD CAMERAS

In cameras of this range all the components described in relation to simple cameras are replaced by better parts, with a correspondingly wider range of possibilities. Such cameras enable exploration of well nigh the entire field of ciné photography. The differences between the two classes of camera will become obvious in the following discussion.

FILM DRIVE

Every camera has a battery-powered motor to transport the film. Standard cameras need at least four batteries to provide the power required to keep the camera fully functional. Many models are even fitted with six. In the battery compartment of every camera it is

Super-8 camera in the standard range.

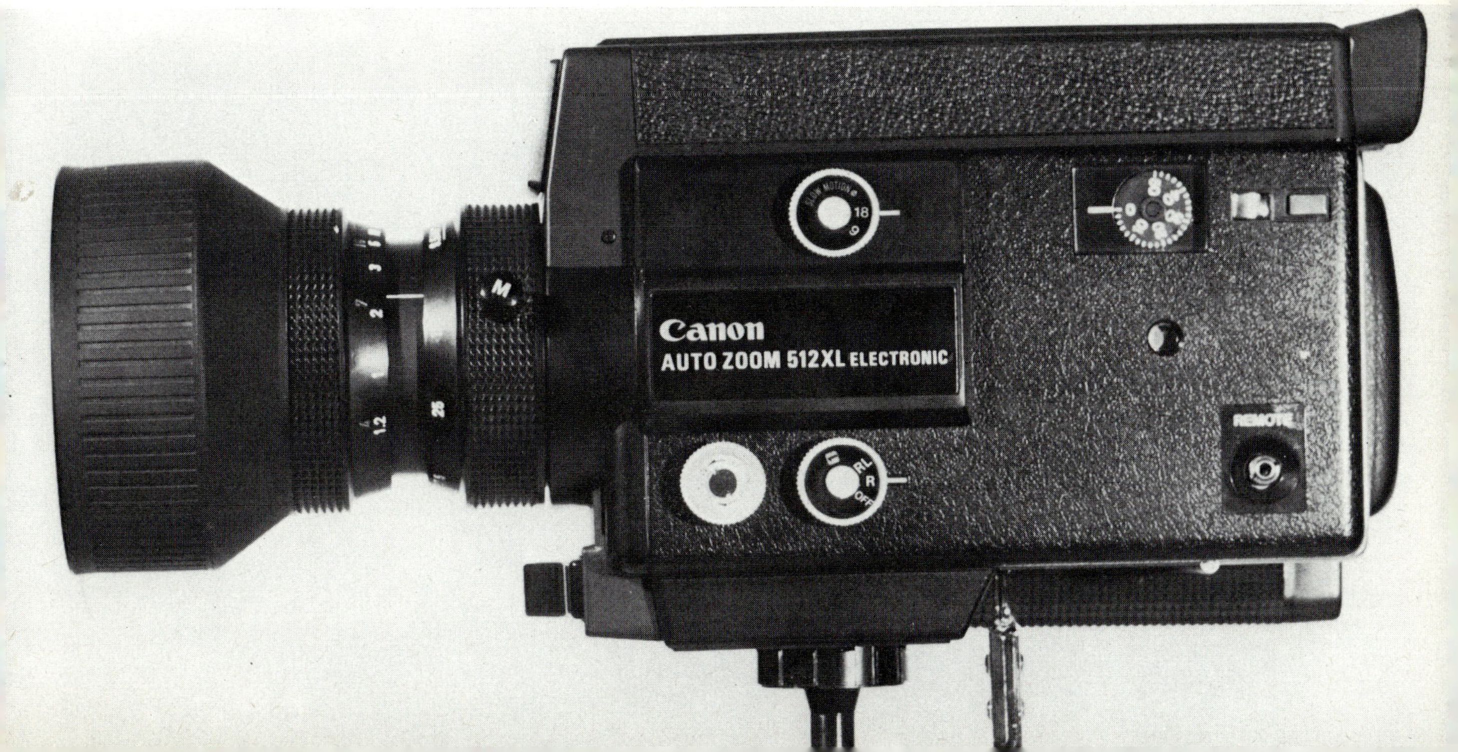

indicated exactly how the batteries are to be inserted. If the terminals are connected incorrectly due to the batteries being inadvertently placed in the wrong position, it may cause a serious camera defect: great care must be taken over the insertion of the batteries, so that they are placed in exactly the right position.

In some cameras a whole block of batteries can be inserted, in which case the batteries are placed in a case and the case is loaded into the handle of the camera. Apart from the fact that batteries can be changed quickly and easily, there is yet a further advantage. It is well known that the output of the batteries will be reduced considerably if the temperature falls below 0°C, but a battery block can be carried around in a coat or trouser pocket to keep it at body temperature, and not inserted into the camera until the last moment, so that the camera is always ready for use, even on a skiing trip, for example. Moreover two complete blocks can be used alternately, so that one of them will always be warm.

Some cameras are powered by batteries that can be recharged at the mains, and in addition can be connected directly to the mains. With these rechargeable batteries there will never be any difficulties if after every film session they are left to recharge overnight, so that the camera is always ready for use.

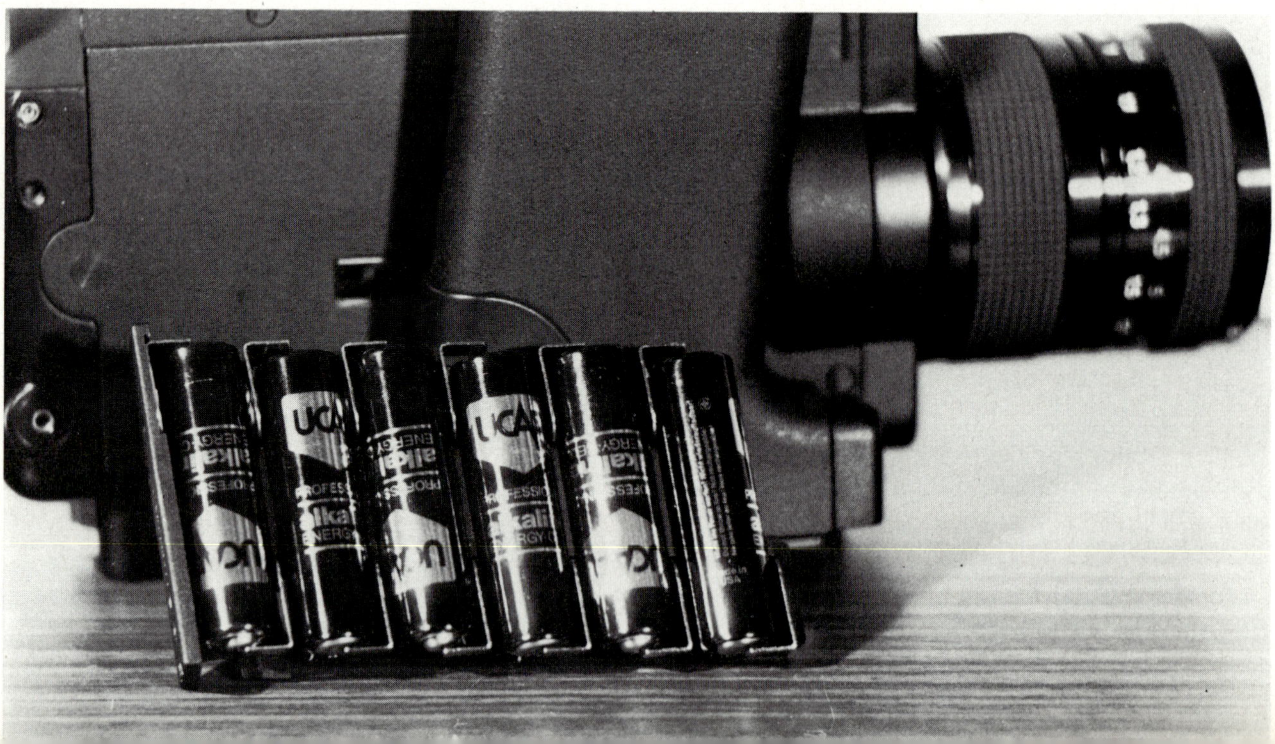

Ciné camera with open battery compartment. Here eight cells, each of 1.5 volts, are used. Most cameras require fewer cells.

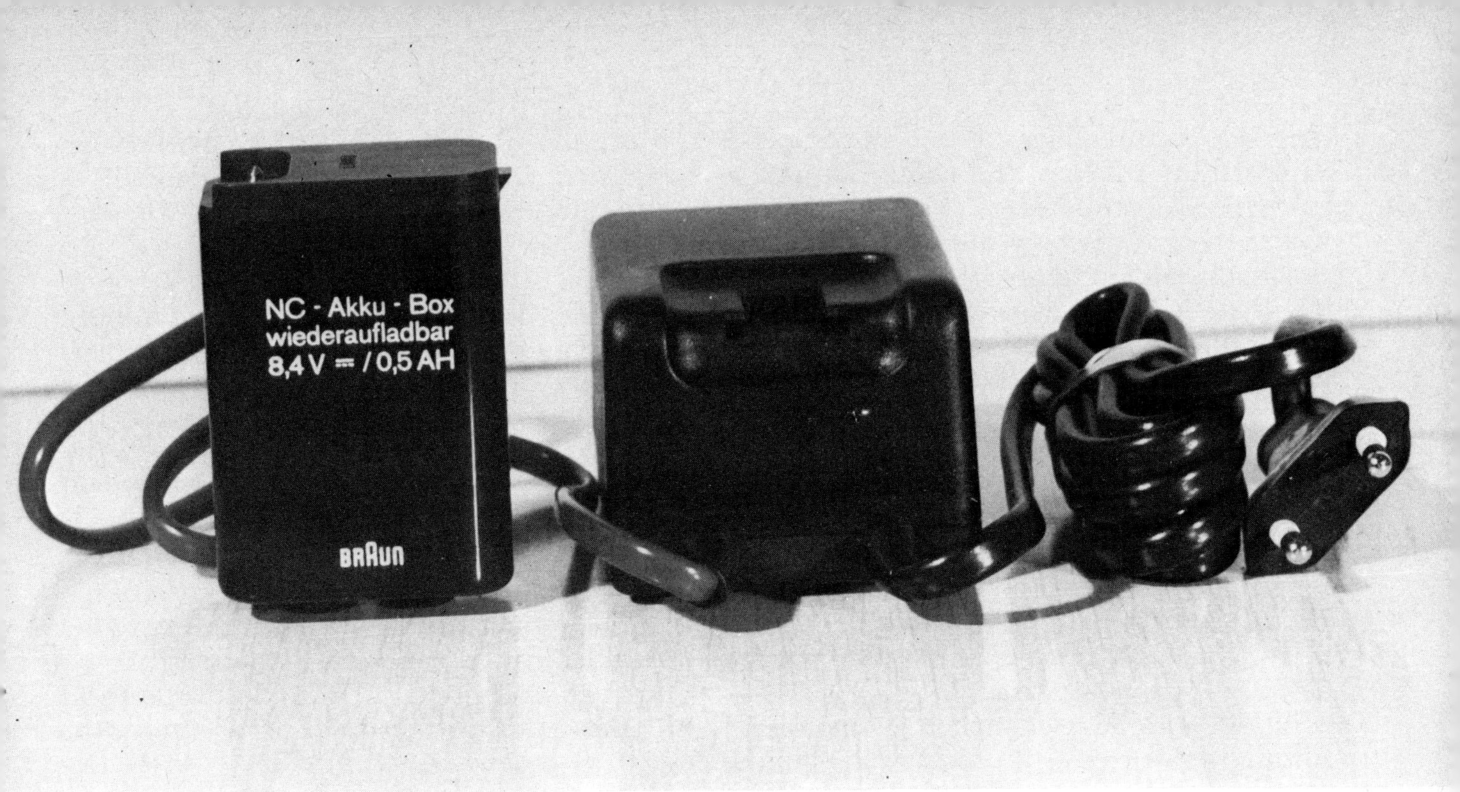

Rechargeable battery for a Super-8 camera.

OPTICS

In filming, as well as in still photography, the lens is of critical importance. It goes without saying that in order to be able to take good shots using Super-8 film, which has a small frame size, it is necessary to have a first-class lens.

Most ciné cameras are fitted with a variable lens, that is to say, a lens with an adjustable focal length. The normal focal length for Super-8 film is 15mm. (Double-8: 12.5mm.)

We know from still photography that the normal focal length should be about as great as the diagonal length of the negative, so if in a camera with a normal lens of about 50mm., we insert a film with a negative size of 24mm. x 36mm., the focal length would more or less correspond in size to the diagonal length of the picture. This rule cannot simply be transferred for use with Super-8 film. The frames in Super-8 film give a very small picture, which must be in sharp and full focus right up into the corners. The picture diagonal in Super-8 film does provide a rough guide to the focal length required, but a different formula is applied: normal focal length x picture diagonal = 2. The Super-8 film size of 4.22mm. x 5.65mm. equals a picture diagonal of 7.08mm., which multiplied by two is about 15mm., the normal focal length used with Super-8 film. Thus it becomes apparent that a normal ciné-film lens corresponds to a telephoto lens in still photography.

Computers are frequently used to collate hundreds of figures, and thereby eliminate as many optical errors as possible, to produce the optimum standard lenses that we use today. This has led to the manufacture of a lens that is both economically viable and possesses a high light intensity, excellent definition, and is well adjusted to allow colour to pass through it.

Those who have changed over from still photography to ciné filming, or who pursue both side by side, will be aware of considerable differences between the two camera types. One look in the viewfinder proves that the angular fields are not at all similar: the ciné camera takes a smaller section of the total scene than the ordinary camera. However, it does not require long to get used to this particular peculiarity of ciné lenses. The next point to notice is that the lenses in ciné cameras have a different light intensity, which is related to the fact that flashlight is practically obsolete in ciné photography. Although very popular in photography because it turns 'night into day', it is clearly quite unsuitable for filming: it only lasts for the duration of one shot. The equivalent of flash in ciné filming is usually film lamps, which we will return to later. In order to achieve as much as possible without the use of these film lamps, which are generally mains operated, the lenses must be set to the widest lens aperture possible. An aperture of 1:1.8 is common; some cameras also have 1:1.4. The wider lens aperture of 1:2.8, well known to all still photographers, does not apply to ciné cameras. Only variable lenses with the extended tele-range have a lens aperture of 2.5 – 2.8. What does the term lens aperture mean? The physical explanation is as follows: the lens aperture is the ratio of the diameter of actual aperture of the lens to the focal length, assuming the real aperture = 1. For example, in a ratio of 1:1.8 the focal length (at infinity) is 1.8 times as long as the actual aperture of the lens with the diaphragm open. The actual aperture with the diaphragm open is the diameter of the diaphragm in front of the frame, usually about the diameter of the front lens. In other words, the real aperture is the maximum aperture of the lens, the greatest diaphragm setting.

As already described, all variable-focus lenses (zoom lens,) provide the opportunity to alter the focal length and hence the picture angle for each shot. The distinction must be made between variable-focus lenses and lenses with a fixed, in other words, non-variable, focal distance; and further distinctions must be made between wide-angled, normal, and telephoto lenses.

There are then various types of variable-

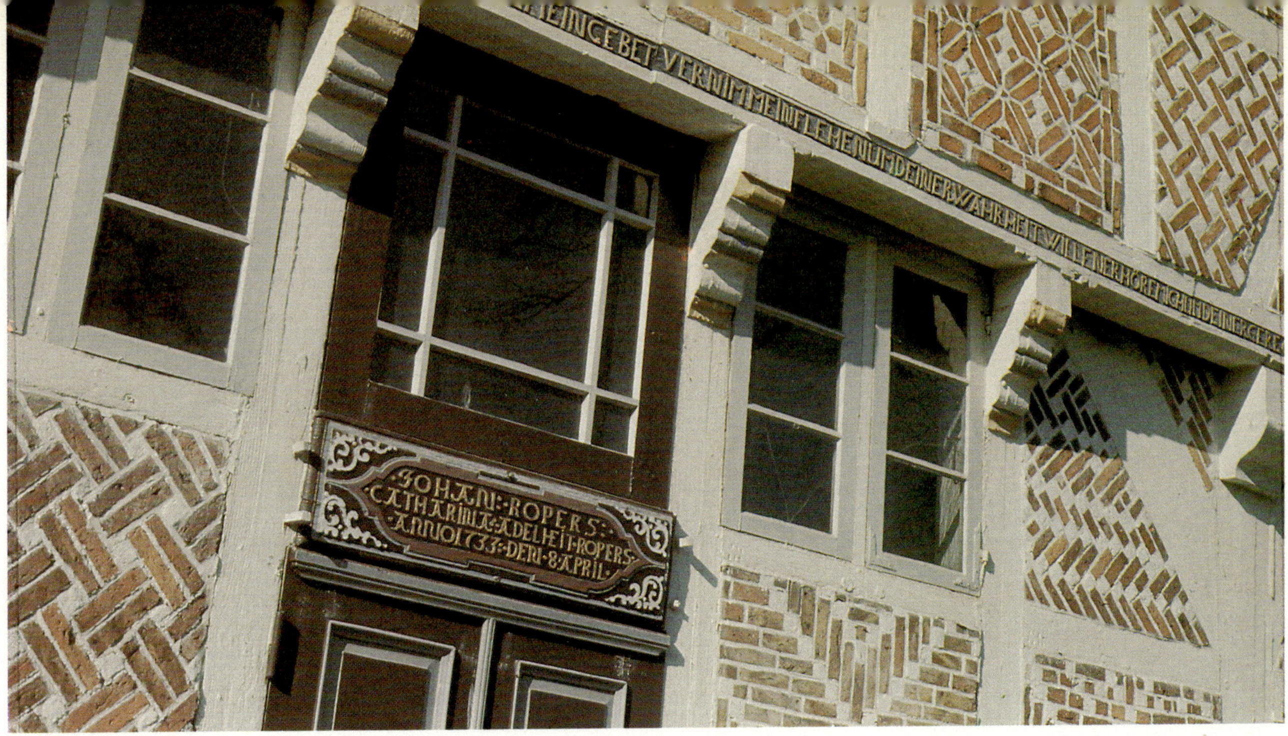

Plate 3: By using a zoom, and varying the taking distance and perspective, even a dead object is brought to life on film.

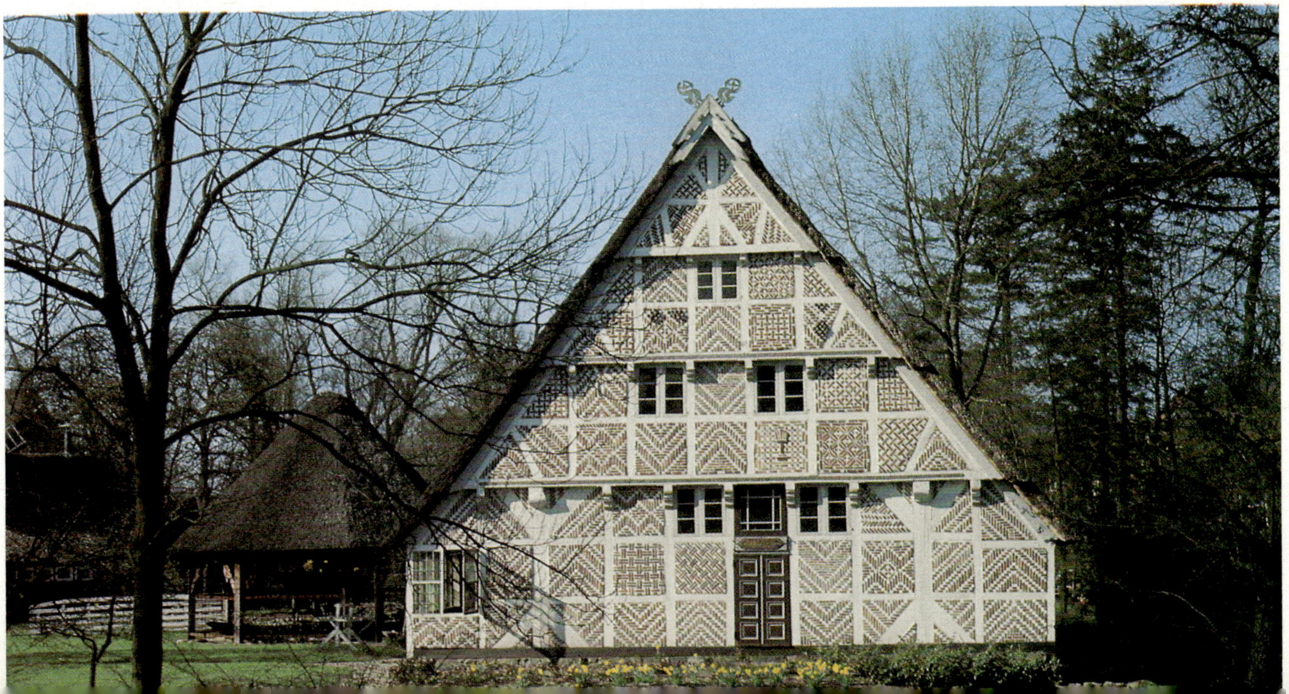

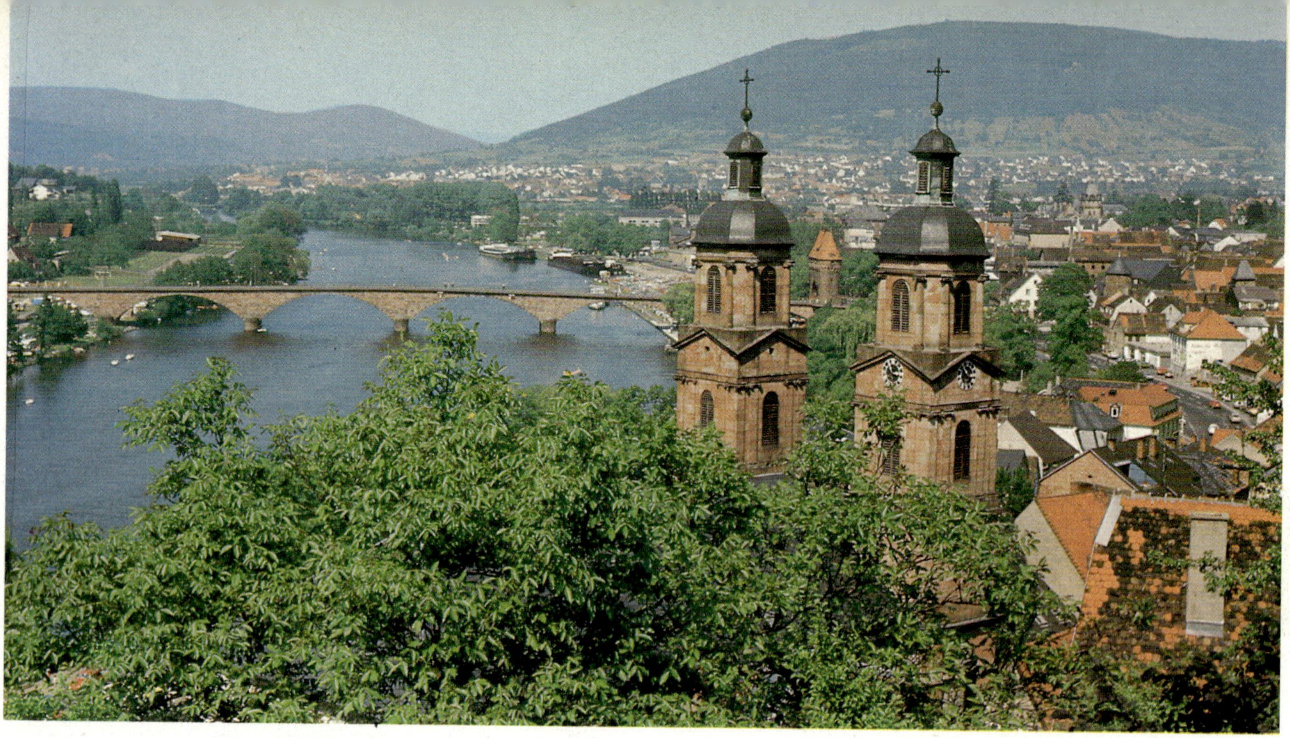

Plate 4: Miltenberg, a bird's-eye view, and a view through the bushes. The undefined foreground is caused by a breeze in the bushes.

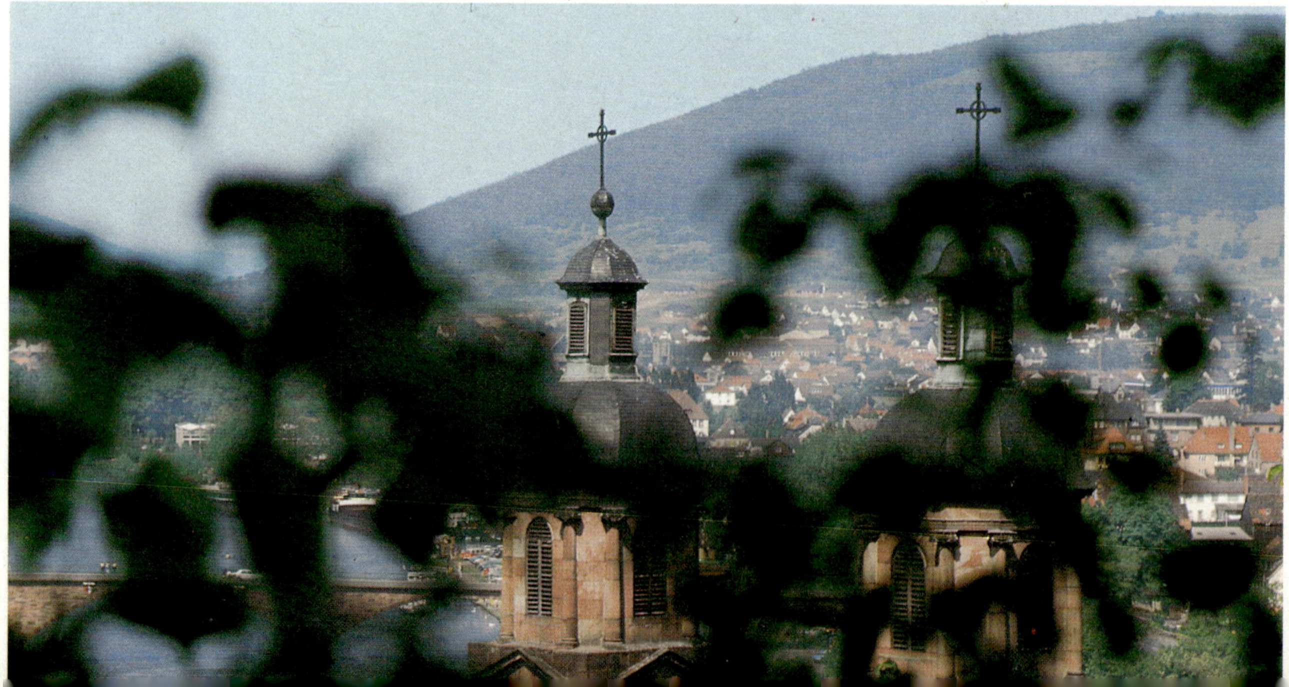

focus lenses, depending on the type of camera being used. The lens aperture and the last point on the diaphragm range is always engraved on the lens mount, figures that will already have been observed on the front ring of the lens. If it says, for instance, 1:1.8/7 - 56, the first number indicates the lens aperture and 7 - 56 describes the scope of the diaphragm, 7 being the greatest wide-angle range and 56 the greatest tele-photo range. This is called the 8 multiple zoom, as the greatest range of the lens (56) is eight times the shortest range, thus 7 x 8 = 56 or 7 -56 = 8 multiple zoom. Some more examples to help clarify this:

9 - 36 = 4 multiple zoom
8 - 48 = 6 multiple zoom
6 - 60 = 10 multiple zoom

Without doubt the numbers indicate something about the lens uses, but they reveal nothing about its optical quality. To use these numbers as a criterion for the whole camera would be a mistake: it would lead to a false evaluation. It is true that superior cameras are equipped with lenses of as great a range as possible, but it is not to say that a smaller, say a 4 multiple zoom, necessarily produces less clearly defined pictures. On the contrary, the chances of a mistake with a long zoom lens are greater by comparison.

In order to be able to insert a variable-focus lens correctly, it is necessary to be aware both of its potential and of its limitations. There are a few elementary points to be observed. To begin with, the usual focal length for nearly all pictures lies in the wide-angle range and extends to 15mm. Thus the wide-angle range covers all lenses with less than the normal focal length of 15mm. and anything above this comes into the telephoto range. This distinction is also made in still photography and in both contexts there is a distinct relationship between the focal length and the depth of field. Depth of field is the term that describes the area of the picture in sharp focus. It can be seen on any film or photograph that the focus is dispersed over a more or less large area. Depth of field should define the limits of the area in complete focus as accurately as possible. Beginners will soon notice the following: if a wide-angle lens or the wide-angle setting of a variable lens is used, there is practically no problem with focusing. The depth of field is so great there is no need to focus accurately, if at all. The following rule applies for depth of field: the shorter the focal length, the smaller the aperture and the greater the depth of field. In other words, the depth of field gets larger as the focal range gets larger and the focal length, and with it the aperture size, get smaller. Obviously the reverse also applies: the longer the focal length and the wider the aperture, the shorter is the distance setting and the smaller the depth of field.

Nevertheless, no problems will occur with depth of field when a focal length of less than 15mm. is used; using long focus is a different matter. The depth of field will get smaller as the focal length increases, with of course unfortunate results if the long focal length is set incorrectly. However, this problem can still be solved. The picture will nearly always go hazy if an attempt is made to 'close-in' on the subject, in other words, if the focal length is adjusted during filming. Often the following happens: filming starts with a focal length that provides for a large depth of field, for instance, 15mm.; the scene appears in focus from front to back: perhaps a landscape in the foreground with a church further in the distance; now, while filming an attempt is made to close in on the church by altering the setting slowly to 40mm.; thus the camera appears to move in on the church (travelling shot); the result: the landscape is in focus to start with, but at a certain point the view begins to go out of focus and at the end of the film the church is completely blurred. The problem lies in the fact that the subject was moved out of the depth of field. How can this mistake be avoided? Firstly the long focus setting on the camera is used to focus exactly on the church (this can be judged exactly through the. viewfinder as most ciné cameras have a reflex view-finder, which produces an exact register of the focus on the ground-glass screen). To begin with, the focus is concentrated on the place where the film is to end up, thus guaranteeing that at the close of the scene the church will appear in focus. Then the variable-focus lens can be used to return to the point where the film is to begin, that is, to a 15mm. focal length. Focusing in this order is a certain way of avoiding any problems.

What is to be understood by the term reflex-finder, mentioned here? It is used directly in conjunction with a variable-focus lens and is found on practically every camera. All reflex viewfinders have a focusing eye-piece, enabling every film-maker to adjust the camera to suit his own eyesight (those who wear glasses should have them on when adjusting the focus). The adjustment is of such importance that it should be undertaken with the aid of an expert when the camera is purchased. If you miss this opportunity, you can do it yourself, and there are in fact two ways of arriving at this optimum setting.

1 Point the camera at the sky or a white wall, making sure that you can see nothing whatsoever in the viewfinder. Now adjust the focus until you have the lens aperture number, or some other symbol, as sharply focused in the viewfinder as possible. In most cameras there are some numbers or symbols engraved on the setting ring. Note the point at which you find the exact setting to suit your eyes. You will now only have to alter this if your own eyes change.

2 The more long-winded, but more exact, way: spread out a sheet of newspaper on a wall and place your camera on a stable tripod in front of it, at the shortest possible distance to which the lens can be set. Measure the distance from the camera to the newspaper and set the camera optic to this value. Then look through the viewfinder and turn the ocular ring until the viewfinder image appears as well defined as possible. Now the focusing eye-piece is perfectly adjusted to your eye. Unless the viewfinder is correctly

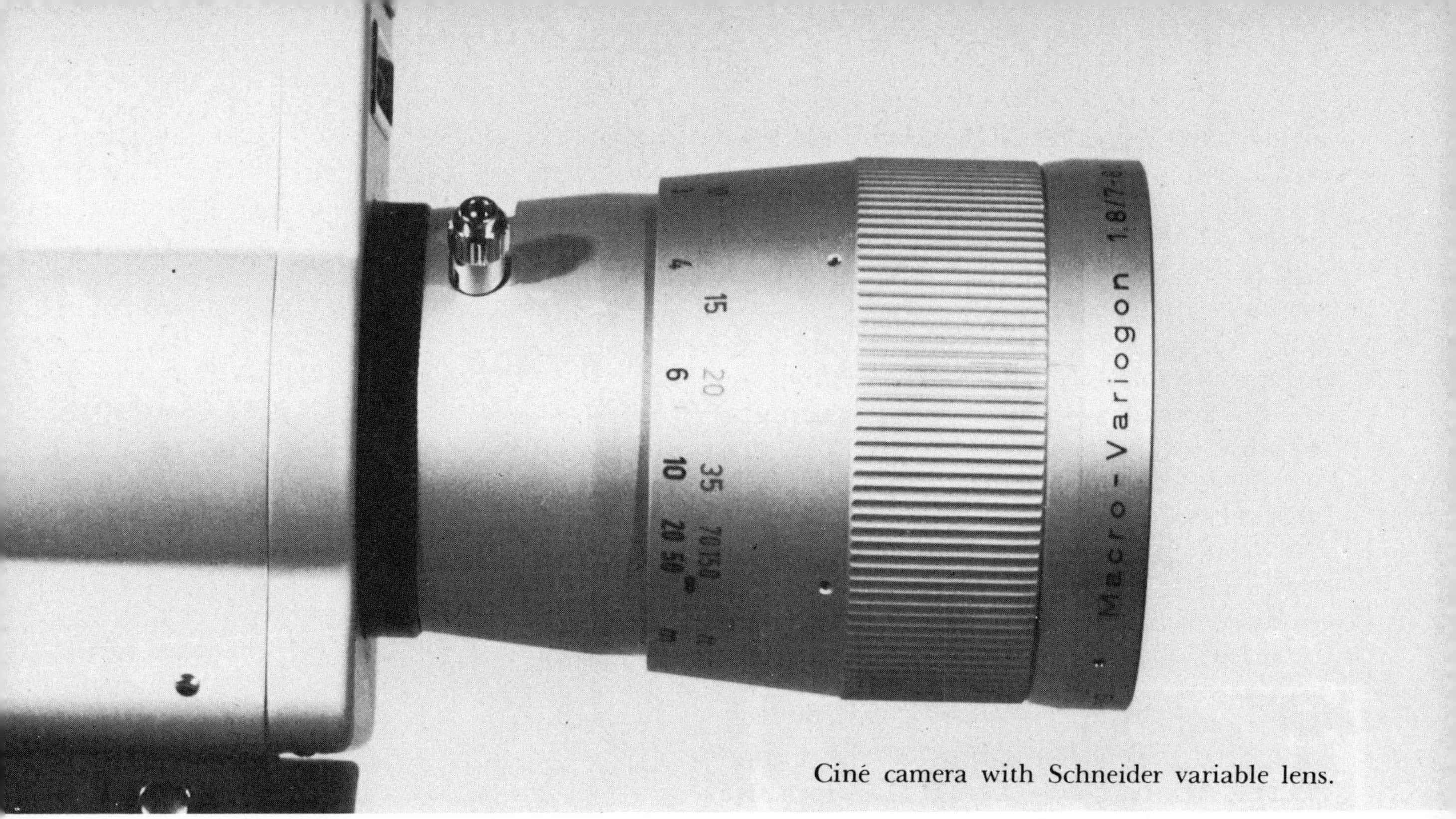

Ciné camera with Schneider variable lens.

Cross-section of a variagram lens.

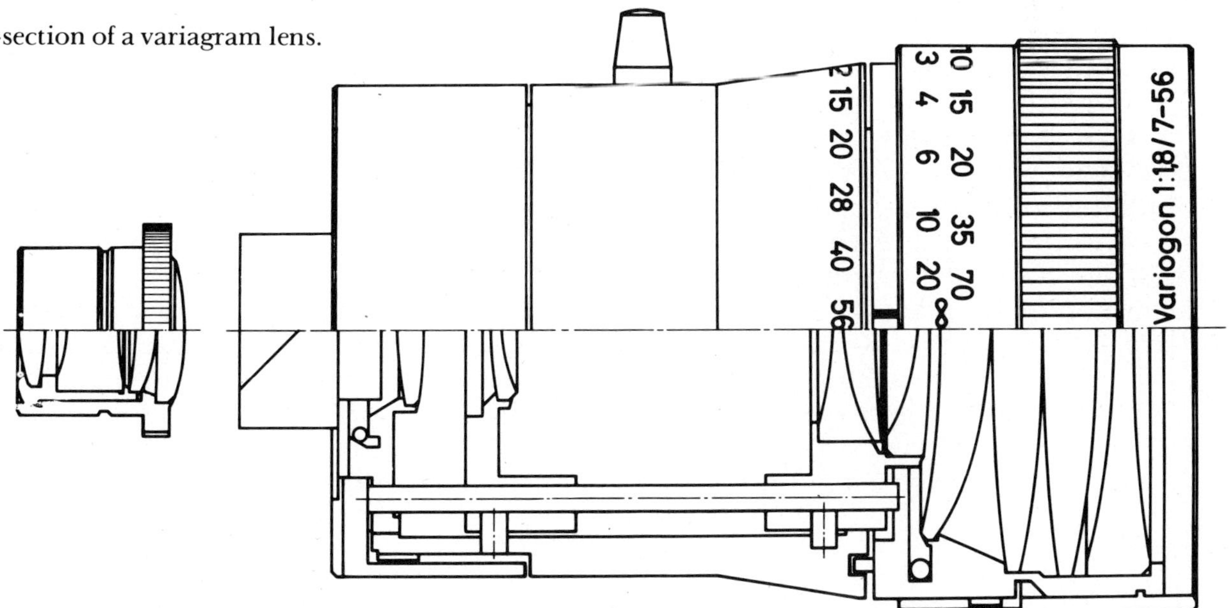

adjusted in this way it is not possible to focus exactly when using the long-focus setting of a variable-focus lens. If the focusing is done incorrectly, although a well-defined picture may be seen in the viewfinder, the film itself will nevertheless appear hazy.

With a focal length of 25 - 30mm. it is impossible to film, holding the camera by hand, a mistake often made when using a variable-focus lens. At this distance the picture is likely to be spoilt owing to the movement of the camera. Even those with a very steady hand usually come to grief when filming with a long focal length. A lens with a 4 multiple zoom **can** be used by hand, but the result will not prove very satisfactory.

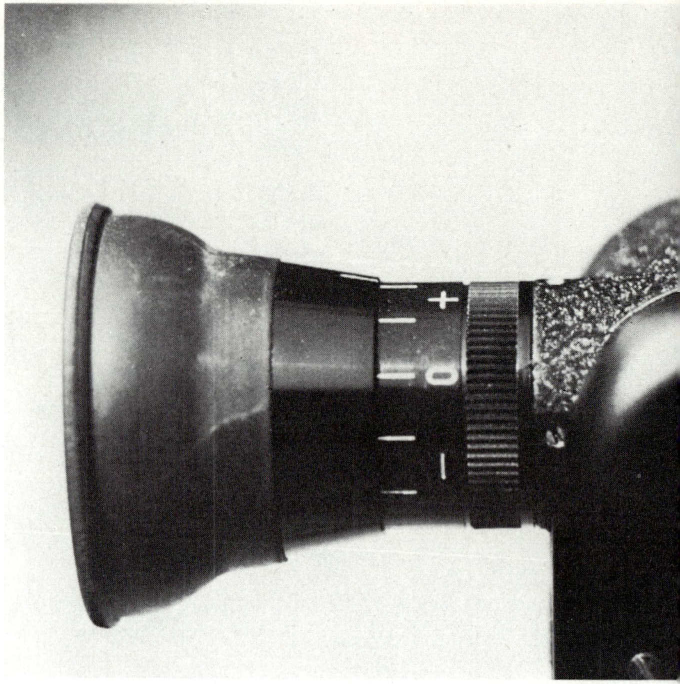

Eye-piece setting on the viewfinder of a Super-8 camera (the numbers facilitate an optical setting)

The problem of long focal lengths using ciné cameras is perhaps more obvious if compared with the situation in still photography. At first glance it might be supposed that it would be possible to film by hand with a focal length of 60mm. without blurring the film; it can after all be managed in still photography even at a distance of 135mm. Although this would certainly appear to be the case, it really only confuses the facts. Why? Ciné film has a very small surface area of 4.2mm. x 5.6mm. Let us take, for example, a common variable-focus lens, the 8 multiple. Its greatest range is ten times the length of the longest side of the frame on a ciné film. If this is applied to still photography, with a format of 24mm. by 36mm., ten times the longest side would be 360mm. Would it ever occur to anyone to take photographs using a 360mm. telephoto lens without a tripod? Certainly not. Then why should such a thing be considered possible in the case of ciné photography?

I hope this example shows how important it is to use a tripod in order to produce good results when using a zoom lens. At least a single-leg tripod should be used. The different types of tripod will be discussed in greater detail later on in this book.

There are then various points that must be

Mode of operation of an 8 x variable lens

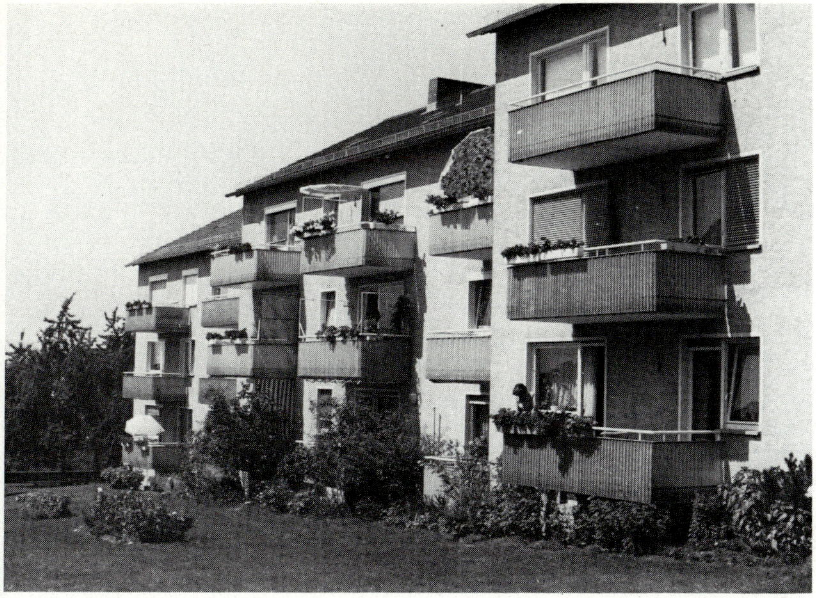

Wide-angle setting 7mm

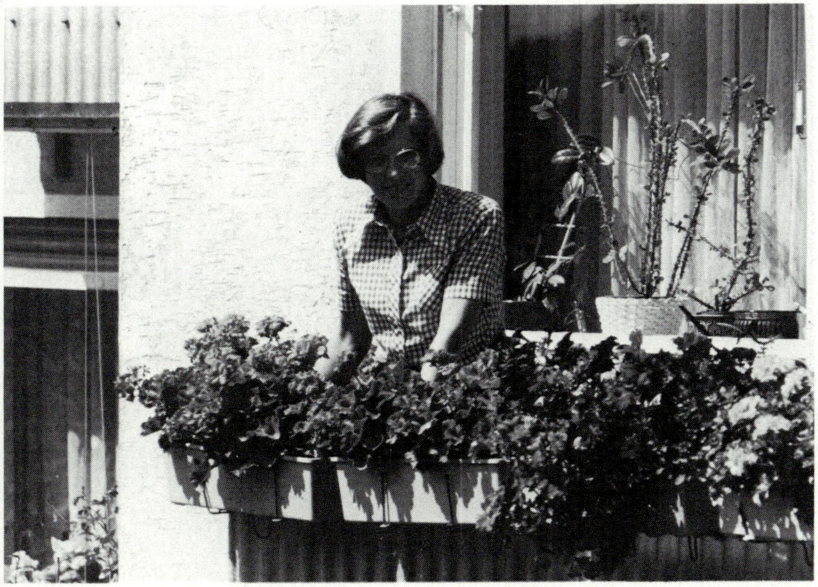

Tele-setting 56mm

Mode of operation of a 10 x variable lens

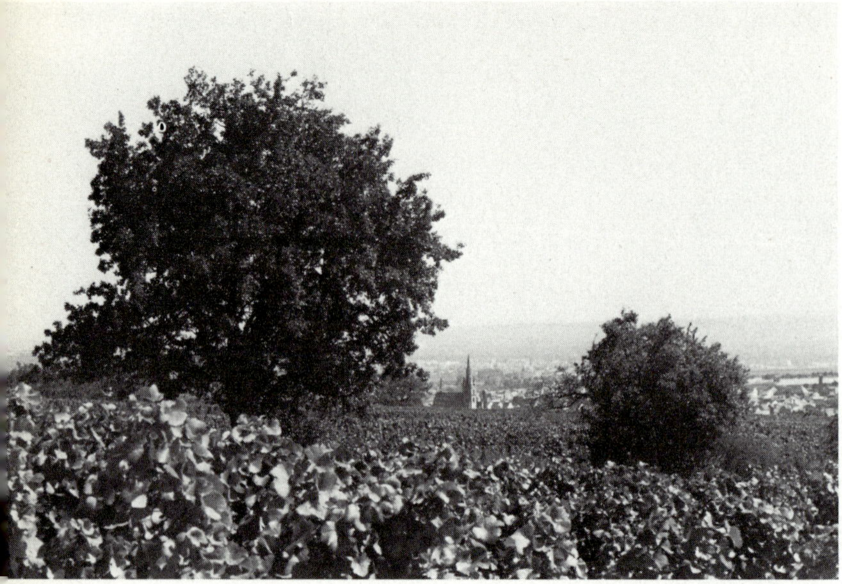

Wide-angle setting 7mm.

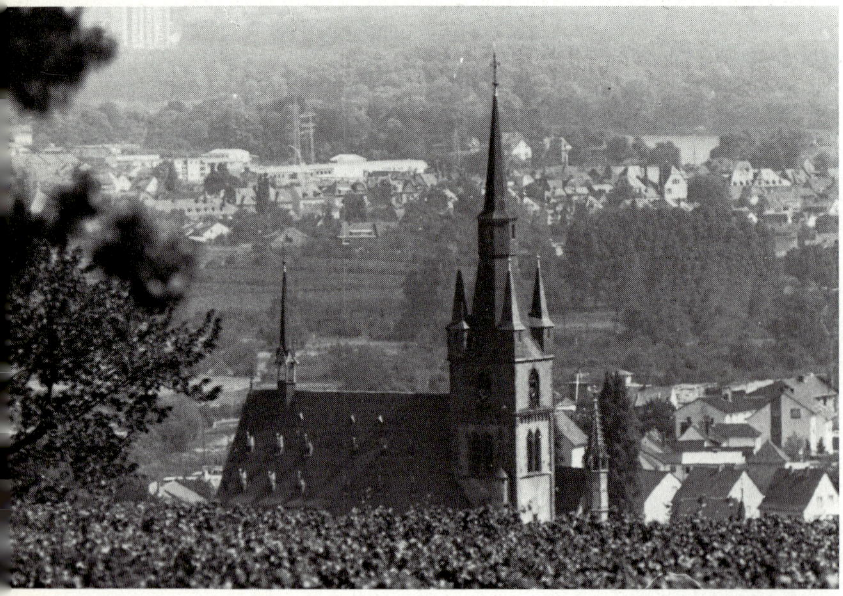

Tele-setting 70mm.

noted in order to use a variable-focus lens properly. I want to add one more piece of advice: the variable-focus lens should represent details in the distance as clearly as a telephoto lens would in still photography. Consequently, if a variable-focus lens is used as a telephoto lens would be in still photography, not much can go wrong. In filming, this means taking advantage of the adjustable focal length to achieve the angle of coverage required for the best possible picture. If the picture blurs at all at the side, or anywhere else, the focal length must be extended by a few mm. A variable-focus lens must first of all be adjusted to accommodate the right viewing angle, and then the film can be taken without it becoming necessary to alter the focal length again during filming. The movement in the scene should of course lie with the subject and not with the camera, though this does not of course rule out the occasional moving effect (with a tripod). As already explained, most pictures will be taken using a focal length of between 10mm. and 15mm., and within this range neither depth of field nor unsteady handling of the camera will present any problem. However, it is wrong to make generalisations. Everyone must discover his own limits with regard to holding the camera.

The term 'zoom' has already been mentioned several times: what does it actually mean? It is only possible with a variable-focus lens and refers to a 'travelling shot', which is achieved by means of continuous adjustment of the focal length of the lens during filming. The camera itself remains stationary, but during zooming appears to move in on the subject at a telephoto range, or, conversely, to move from the centre of the picture into the wide angle range. The adjustments to the focal length must of course be made smoothly and evenly.

In simpler cameras the variable-focus lens is only adapted for manual adjustments, but most Super-8 cameras are fitted with an additional motor (which has nothing to do with the optical effect of the zoom-lens). The motor obtains the energy required to adjust the focal length from the same block of batteries used to transport the film.

Reference can thus be made to a motor zoom lens. Modern Super-8 cameras are equipped with an electric motor that gives a movement through the entire lens range, from a wide-angle setting to a telephoto setting, and back, at the press of a button. It goes without saying that the manually operated lens cannot be adjusted nearly as smoothly. While the speed of a motor is permanently fixed on most models, variable speeds can sometimes be selected, which allows for additional possibilities.

There is only ever any point in using a zoom if the camera has to follow an action quickly, and the cameraman cannot alter his position. Zooming is often referred to as the 'beginner's disease', because most people, when they try out the variable-focus lens for the first time, are understandably so enthusiastic about the adjustable focal length that they use it with gay abandon.

We can conclude by reiterating a few points to indicate the possibilities available using a variable-focus lens and the sources of error.

1 Blurred pictures at a telephoto range
a) Cause: viewfinder lens set incorrectly
Remedy: readjust to suit your eyes
b) Cause: distance set incorrectly
Remedy: focus sharply on the most important point of the picture using the telephoto range, then move back into the desired range.

2 Wobbly pictures:
Cause: focal length too long for filming by hand
Remedy: use a tripod with focal lengths over 25mm.

3 Jerky zoom effect:
Cause: zoom movement made unevenly by hand
Remedy: use a motor zoom

AUTOMATIC LENS APERTURE

As already mentioned, all Super-8 cameras have an automatic lens aperture that guarantees that the correct amount of light is transmitted. In cinematography deliberate reference is made to lens-aperture control rather than exposure control, as only the lens aperture is used to measure the light. While in still photography both the shutter speed and the lens aperture have to be adjusted for the correct exposure, in a ciné camera the speed of exposure is regulated in accordance with the speed at which the film is transported. As this movement must be absolutely constant, it necessarily follows that the exposure time for each frame will also remain constant, from which it is only logical to conclude that only the lens aperture can be used to regulate the exposure. Hence the apparently curious term, automatic lens aperture. The diaphragm is open wider or closed further according to the measured brightness, so the film always receives the same amount of light.

Nearly all standard and superior cameras are fitted with a special battery for automatic lens-aperture control. Generally speaking, the way this functions varies greatly from model to model, although there are only two basic ways of measuring the light: through the taking lens, or through a special measuring window. Measuring through the lens is more awkward but more exact, and consequently the most widely used method. It entails the light falling on a CDS light-sensitive cell (CDS = cadmium sulphide), which converts it to a current of greater or lesser strength according to its intensity. If this current is not alone sufficient to operate the diaphragm, or the diaphragm motor, energy from a special battery must come to its aid. There are various ways in which the current is used to operate the opening and closing of the diaphragm. The current may actuate a moving-coil instrument that is connected to a fine metal blade. This instrument is not, however, likely to usurp the iris-diaphragm, which is the optimum of all the different types of automatic diaphragms. Superior cameras with iris diaphragms consequently incorporate an electric motor, as distinct from the standard system, in which the electric current provided by the light-sensitive cell is put to use. This motor automatically opens and closes the iris diaphragm according to the lighting conditions. However this system is only found in superior cameras. The implication is that even in most of the simpler cameras the automatic lens aperture satisfies all the necessary optical requirements, but one must remember that while it will of course function adequately, it is often an inferior way of dealing with the problem. In the simplest cameras a slit diaphragm is employed: the camera is fitted only with a moving and a fixed blade. Those cameras that operate with two moving blades are more advantageous. This system is known as the 'swing diaphragm' system: both diaphragm blades move in contra-rotation, locking into a small square. Both blades are lightly mounted, so less energy is needed to set them in motion than is required for the iris diaphragm. The automatic lens aperture in most cameras works in this, or a very similar, way.

Sometimes one comes across the so-called pendulum effect, which would appear to indicate the limitations of automatic lens aperture control: the exposure oscillates. The apparent effect of this is that the first couple of shots on the film will be too light or too dark. On closer examination the cause is usually found to be the considerable discrepancy between exposures. To take an extreme case, if one scene was shot in a dark room and the next in very light surroundings, it is obvious that in darkness the lens aperture will be wide open, and so at one optical extreme, yet in the light it has to close completely or very considerably in order to avoid over-exposure of the film. However, this type of device requires the space of two or three frames to change from the widest to the smallest aperture, which means of course that these intermediate shots will be either under- or over-exposed. Such an occurrence is not really the fault of the device, but a problem of timing. In cases where the scene changes noticeably, poorly exposed film can be avoided by pressing the release button briefly, which allows time for alteration of the lens aperture before the film transport is activated. If small bright places still appear on the film, they can be easily eliminated during editing.

On most cameras it is possible to take a reading of the position of the diaphragm. There is a central control point in the viewfinder that gives a lens aperture reading, indicating whether or not there is sufficient light for the planned shot, in short, whether the picture will be successful. The controls vary from camera to camera. The simplest method consists of a green signal, visible in the viewfinder when all the conditions are satisfactory, and a red signal, visible when there is excessive or insufficient light. A more reliable method includes the lens-aperture scale in the camera's viewfinder. A clearly visible pointer indicates the size of the lens aperture, set automatically, in use at any one time. At both ends of the scale are red markings, which the pointer should not normally cross, as this means that the exposure needed is too long or too short for the picture being taken. Cameras possessing this equipment reveal at a glance the lens aperture, from which the depth of field can also be inferred. When the pointer persistently proves that it is too dark to film, but a particular scene must be filmed at all costs, a more sensitive film can be inserted. The automatic exposure control must be adjusted to the sensitivity of the film material being used, which can be done in several ways. A Super-8 camera adjusts itself automatically. Sometimes the automatic device can be switched off and the adjustment made by hand.

Mistakes may be made in the measurements if the battery used is getting old: they have a life expectancy of about 1½ years. As in nearly all cameras it is possible to test the batteries, it is worth taking the trouble to do so from time to time. A useful tip with reference to this: by noting the position at which the diaphragm is automatically set in certain typical recurrent light conditions, and knowing its value exactly, the difficulties that will arise should the battery fade will not be insurmountable. In any case, as already stated, it is possible to operate the lens aperture by hand in many cameras. Relatively few cameras possess a lens-aperture correction knob with which to correct the automatic process. As in still photography, it is possible to vary the exposure within 2 stop values during filming without affecting the automatic lens aperture. So with a back-lighted shot, for example, the diaphragm can be opened one stop to compensate for the number of dark shadows. On cameras without this control, the automatic device is constructed in a way that allows the exposure to be automatically extended when necessary, which is also an entirely satisfactory method. However, this supplementary manual aperture setting should not be over-estimated. Nearly all pictures are taken with the automatic device, and in the final judgement no one can measure as exactly as this in-built equipment.

Finally, a comment about an oft-made mistake. Many film-makers (usually beginners) think that as long as the diaphragm point lies in the red area, on account of the bad light conditions, the only cure is to make a manual adjustment. This is not true. The diaphragm is already set automatically at maximum aperture before the point gets into the red area. Even adjusting it by hand will not result in any wider opening, so any manual interference with the lens aperture is quite useless.

FILM SPEED (IMAGE FREQUENCY)
To film successfully the film must travel through the camera at a constant rate, which is normally the same speed at which the film will run in the projector. The film speed ± image frequency is shown in a numerical value, which represents the number of frames exposed per second.

Modern ciné cameras can nearly always be operated at several speeds, increasing or reducing the number of frames exposed per second, so a slow-motion or speeded-up effect can be produced. Cameras in which the running speed of the film cannot be altered are set at 'normal speed'. In Double-8 and Super-8 cameras this is equal to 18 f/s (frames per second). Of course the term 'normal' is relative. In the Double-8 era the norm was considered to be 16 f/s. This is because when the film is projected at less than 16 or 17 f/s the human eye cannot distinguish movement, the change from light to dark, or the dark pauses between shots. During filming any sequence of movement is reduced to a number of individual pictures, with a small pause between each; if the picture changes less than 16 times a second, to the human eye the film appears to flicker, while at a frequency of more than 16 f/s the pictures seem to run on smoothly.

A speed of 18 f/s, the normal speed for Super-8 cameras and, correspondingly, for projectors, implies that in every second eighteen individual pictures will be exposed on the film. This means that for every second there will be eighteen exposure processes and eighteen transport processes, half the available amount of time being given to each. As this equals thirty-six processes, it follows that the exposure time for every single small frame is 1/36 second. In comparison with a still camera - on which 1/125 second is the most frequently used speed – this appears to be a surprisingly long time. But, as the previous discussion on automatic lens aperture has explained, in ciné photography lens aperture can be adjusted to gauge the light, the exposure time of course remaining the same for each frame.

As already mentioned, many cameras can be set to other speeds besides normal speed. As a rule, all the important switches are positioned near each other.

Why should anyone want to alter the speed, if the normal speed of 18 f/s is the optimum in any case? Deviating from the normal speed allows special effects when the film is shown. If we assume that the projector runs the film at a constant speed of 18 f/s, a filming speed of less than 18 f/s will produce a speeded-up effect, conversely anything taken at more than 18 f/s will appear in slow-motion. Cinema and television have aquainted us with both effects.

HIGH-SPEED FILMING (slow motion)
The slow-motion speed is frequently used, and to this end many cameras are fitted with varying speeds, ranging up to 70 f/s in

superior cameras, though 24, 36, 48 and 52 f/s are typical. The greater the number of frames exposed per second, the slower the movement will be when the film is projected.

Professional cameras can film at more than 1,000 f/s to capture every quick movement. Naturally, amateur cameras do not possess this potential, nor would it be of any use with 15mm. film. We are well acquainted with the cases where the technique might be used – a shot flies through a pane of glass, yet with a camera filming at 1,000 f/s it hovers towards it. This method is used alike in television and in scientific research.

The most frequent use of the slow-motion technique is found in the field of sport. Everyone has seen slow-motion sequences during coverage of a league match or an athletics competition. Most film reports use slow motion shots to add clarity as a goal is attempted or the finishing line is approached.

Amateur film-makers will be well advised to keep slow-motion sequences as short as possible, as the audience easily becomes bored with them. The exceptions to this are of course teaching and study films, which allow a study of sequences of movement that cannot otherwise be clearly distinguished. In performance sports, for instance, the performers use such films for self-appraisal and to enable them to correct their style.

The slow-motion setting on a camera serves, then, to film a greater number of frames per second than will actually be projected. Consequently the movement will be considerably slowed down, and each phase can be carefully scrutinised as the film is projected. The increased number of frames per second means of course that each picture is allotted a shorter exposure-time, so more

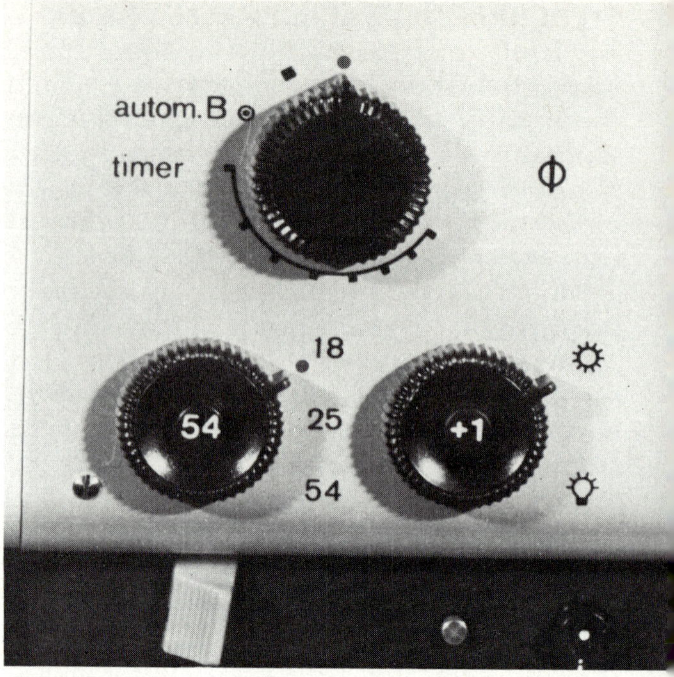

All the essential controls on a 'superior' camera are positioned near each other and are easily accessible
above: dial for setting the running of the film, i.e. normal running, single-frame setting, exposure, and timer
below left: film-speed switch
below right: switch for setting to daylight or artificial light, with a stop correction button in the middle

light than normal is required for the duration of the scene. Before switching to a slow-motion speed it is advisable to have a look at the aperture control. The lens aperture control will however adjust itself to the correct aperture setting when the film speed is altered.

The film speeds most frequently considered for slow-motion filming, together with the corresponding exposure settings, are as follows:

24 f/s: single exposure time about 1/50 sec
36 f/s: single exposure time about 1/70 sec
48 f/s: single exposure time about 1/100 sec
52 f/s: single exposure time about 1/125 sec
72 f/s: single exposure time about 1/150 sec

The frequencies vary slightly in different models, so it may prove to be 32 f/s instead of 36 f/s or 50 f/s instead of 52 f/s. Hardly any amateur cameras would extend above this limit. Some go up to 36 f/s, others to 52 f/s. A movement stretched to three times the normal speed (48 – 52 f/s) already produces a remarkable effect, quite sufficient for an amateur film.

Next to 18 f/s, 24 f/s is the most frequently used speed, not just for slow-motion pictures. The difference in effect at this speed is quite small. If it is employed as the normal speed in conjunction with a projector that also runs at 24 f/s, it provides a flowing movement and better defined pictures (due to the shorter exposure time). Many film-makers who aspire to sound-film use principally 24 f/s speed to achieve better sound quality. (We will return to this in more detail in the section on sound.) Moreover, the 24 f/s film speed allows for a smoother film, for instance when filming from a moving car: the jolts from an uneven road are stretched to such an extent that they become barely noticeable. The projector must of course remain at 18 f/s.

Even when turning the camera on to its longer axis, in other words, panning it, it is advisable to use the 24 f/s speed, as few film-makers are capable of making a smooth swing by hand at 18 f/s. More will be said about panning the camera, with all its restrictions and uses, in the chapter on 'taking film'.

A few cameras possess a 25 f/s film speed. This is not of any significance in amateur filming, as there is practically no difference between using 24 f/s and 25 f/s. However, anyone making a film for television – depending of course on country – may have to use 25 f/s, a common television broadcasting frequency.

Time Lapse

All film frequencies of less than 16 – 18 f/s can be classified as time lapse speeds. The use of time-lapse in ciné filming is less feasible than slow-motion. Many of the cameras fitted with various slow-motion speeds have no capacity for speeded-up filming. This applies even to superior cameras. What is a time-lapse picture? The frame frequency means that the sequence of movement is taken with less frames per second than at normal speed, but the film is run at normal speed in the projector. The movement is thus accelerated, the time snatched away. It would take, for example, two seconds for a projector to show something that actually lasted three seconds but was shot at 12 f/s. In three seconds 12 x 3 = 36 pictures would be taken, which the projector would show in two seconds: 18 x 2 = 36. In other words, very slow movements are made visible by being speeded up – but this actually happens extremely rarely, which is one reason why so many cameras lack a time-lapse speed. The effect of speeded-up pictures is seen on films, from the era of the 'flicks' that have been touched up for television, that is to say, given a musical accompaniment. The classic films of Stan Laurel and Oliver Hardy or Charlie Chaplin are by far the most well-known examples. The movements of the characters are jerky and faster than normal. The 'Charlie Chaplin effect' can be achieved by filming at a speed of 12, 9, or 8 f/s. While we are on the subject, it is important to mention how the time-lapse setting can be used to widen the scope and so enrich the quality of one's filming. According to the same principle by which the exposure time of each frame is shortened during slow-motion filming, it can be lengthened by adjusting the camera to a time-lapse setting. This makes filming possible, at a low film speed, in rooms or in evening light conditions, when there would not be sufficient light to film in normal circumstances. However, scenes taken in this way should not include any people, as the technique would then produce quite unsuitable 'silent-film' effect.

The following settings should be used for frequency and frame exposure during time-lapse filming:
12 f/s – about 1/25 sec.
9 f/s – about 1/20 sec.
The amount of light allowed in is equivalent to up to one stop more than at the normal speed. When using a time-lapse setting the following point should not be overlooked: 9 pictures per second require double the filming time (the projector runs at 18). If the scene is too short it cannot be used, on the other hand scenes that are too long can be shortened.

Single-Shot

As a rule cameras have a single-shot setting, which is not to make the film serve for still photography, but to enable a single frame to be exposed for a chosen time span. This might sound at first a rather abstract idea, but is in fact quite logical. The setting can be used to take cartoon film, trick titles, or for extreme time-lapse sequences. Used appropriately, such shots can help considerably to enliven the film. Cartoon films and film titles will be considered in a separate chapter; for the moment we will confine ourselves to considering exaggerated time-lapse film.

Nature films often contain shots that show a flower opening, apparently in the space of a few seconds: a process that takes hours according to nature happens in a moment before our very eyes. Such an effect is achieved when single pictures are taken with long time intervals between – about every 30 seconds a very slight alteration has occurred in the flower, barely visible to the naked eye. The exposure is repeated 18 times in all, so producing 18 pictures to be projected. At 18 f/s this is equivalent to a projection time of 18 x 30 seconds (= 9 minutes film time). Consequently whatever occured in 9 minutes is seen in one second. The result can be varied by altering the length of the time intervals, according to the subject being filmed and the effect desired. 'Lay-yourself-a-table' sequences made on a single shot set are also delightful. To begin with, a shot is taken of the empty table, and then single shots are made as it is laid: laying the tablecloth = 9 frames, one plate being put down in position = 9 frames, etc. The person who actually laid the table is not visible on the film, only the individual parts involved.

For individual shots the exposure is usually the same as at 18 f/s, which amounts to about 1/40 second. Only when the single-shot setting and the speed setting are operated by different switches on the camera can the exposure time be altered for single shots. An example will make this clearer: if the camera is set to single shot and the speed is set to 24 f/s, the individual picture will be exposed for 1/50 second, which is shorter than usual.

The film exposure continues otherwise to be controlled by the automatic lens-aperture control, even when the camera is on the single-shot setting. As long as there is enough light, the exposure cannot go wrong.

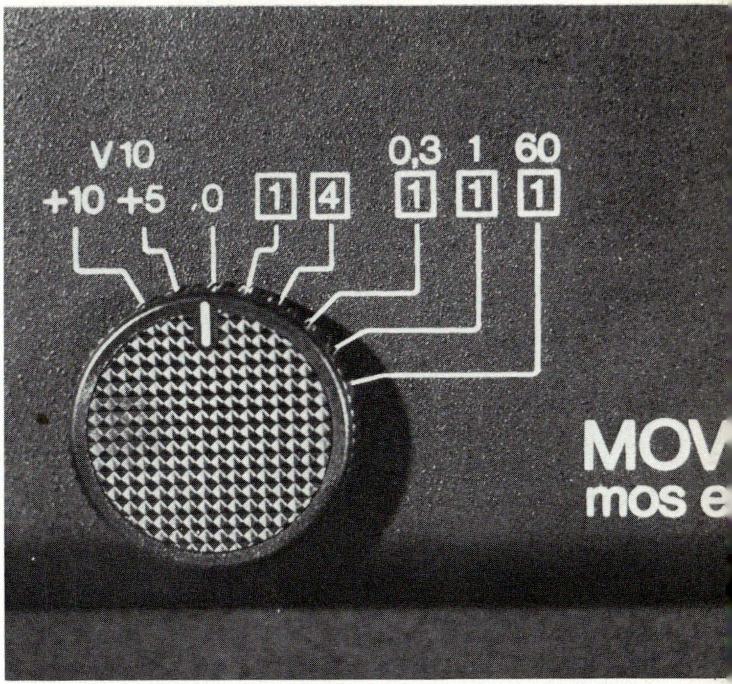

Timer and in-built automatic release on a modern ciné camera

AUTOMATIC RELEASE

Until fairly recently automatic release buttons were only to be found on still cameras; their appearance in ciné cameras is relatively new.

The automatic release functions as follows: the length of time during which the scene is to run is set by a switch on the camera. The pre-running is usually constant, about 10 to 12 seconds, after which exposure of the film begins. When it has run for the set time the camera automatically switches itself off again. The only difference from still cameras is that instead of being set for a chosen exposure time, the film runs for the length of scene set. It is of course of no consequence which speed the film is set at, as the automatic release setting can be used for film at any speed. Opinion is divided about the desirability of such a technique. It is without doubt pleasant to have all members of the family together on film, but on the other hand the film-maker has no control over the positioning, behaviour, or expressions of those filmed at the crucial moment, because he cannot of course stand by the camera. If the intention is to film ad hoc movements, its success just depends on luck.

We return to this topic in the section on the various types of release button.

ROTARY DISC SHUTTER/FADING OUT – FADING IN

Part of the established repertoire of standard cameras is the ability to produce fade-in and fade-out effects. In order to understand how this happens, it is important to clarify the following:

In any ciné camera the film is transported by means of a motor, not absolutely continuously, but with slight rhythmic jerks. A rotary disc shutter is used to cover up the film at the point of transportation, to avoid exposure (as there would otherwise be no division made between the individual frames on the film). In most 16mm. cameras, but only a few Double-8 or Super-8 cameras this is achieved by a sector shutter. Strictly speaking, neither one nor the other has anything to do with the diaphragm; it is however a closure device.

Rotary disc and Sector Shutter

The construction details vary from model to model. Cameras without a sector shutter possess a rotary disc closure, which usually consists of a half-disc that rotates at a speed corresponding to the frame frequency, alternately allowing exposure of the film and covering up the opening while the film is transported. The closure may also be in the form of a round disc, which opens and closes to 180°. The principle is the same. If the open sector is in front of the film gate, the film will be exposed; if the closed section is in position, the film is being transported on to the next frame. By looking inside a camera, operated without a film in it, the movement of the rotary disc shutter, constantly changing from light to dark, can be observed.

Cameras with a sector shutter work on the same principle. The arrangement here consists of two half-discs positioned opposite each other: if the device is completely open they lie one behind the other, if it is closed both discs alter their position until they together form a round disc. While with a rotary disc shutter the light and dark phases are normally of equal length, with a sector shutter it is possible to differentiate between them. It can move within an angle of 270° instead of 180°, so that individual exposure can be altered while the speeds remain constant. While at 18 f/s each frame is exposed for 1/40 second, with the sector closure being opened to 180°, at the same speed the open sector can be halfed to 90° and the closed sector can be increased to 270°, so that the dark sector is three times as long as the light sector. Shortening the effective exposure time is however a technique that will only interest the 'expert' in new filming possibilities; perhaps more interesting is the use of this device as a 'dark curtain' during filming. With it it is possible to achieve successful fading-in and fading-out and dissolve techniques. However, this is not of chief importance here.

Fading Out - Fading In

The previous explanation makes it clear that without a rotary disc or sector shutter fading-in and fading-out would not be possible. The lens aperture remains unaffected, that is to say the lens aperture in use at any given time is not altered during fading-in or fading-out processes. The sector shutter can be closed quickly or slowly as desired, in order to vary the effect. As mentioned earlier, certain cameras have variable discs, which in order to fade-out can be gradually closed completely, so that it is dark throughout 360°. The effect created by this method when the film is projected is a slow darkening of the film, until at the end it is completely black; in other words, the picture, quite normal and 'correctly' exposed at the beginning, gets darker at a chosen pace until it finally disappears completely.

Fading-out is particularly suitable for closing a scene or the entire film. At the end of a film, the slower it is done, the more effective it is, as the film just dies away very gradually. On the other hand during changes of scene within the film the fading-out should not last long. It is possible to regulate the tempo. Fading-out and fading-in are generally operated by means of a lever or small hand wheel.

In some cameras fading-out and fading-in is controlled automatically, which means that the sector shutter opens and closes at a constant speed and the rate at which the process occurs cannot be affected. While its smoothness is an advantage, it may not be that a constant movement is always desired. This is one of the problems to be taken into consideration when buying a camera.

It goes without saying that fading-in works on the converse principle. The sector or rotary disc shutter is initially completely closed, then the picture is slowly allowed to emerge from the darkness, in other words the shutter is gradually opened. This technique can be used to create an impressive beginning to a film or a scene within it. In addition, harsh scene changes can be avoided or tempered down by following a fade-out with a fade-in, which gives the film a more harmonious, flowing quality.

XL-OPTICS

The term XL comes from the words existing light, also called low-light. As this innovation is concerned with the sector shutter, specific reference should be made to it here.

XL-cameras were only introduced a short time ago. They contain a lens of great light intensity, and are particularly suitable for filming in unfavourable lighting conditions. In all such cameras the light sector of the rotary closure is increased from 180° to 220°-230°, which results in about 40 per cent more light being given access to the film during exposure. It might be supposed that this is achieved via the lens aperture, but in fact the optics are not altered at all. XLcameras offer new opportunities: with them it is possible to film in conditions that would be too dark for a conventional sector shutter, particularly in conjunction with highly sensitive film. As the exposure time oversteps the normal limits, the image definition of fast-moving objects may be impaired.

XL-cameras are not exclusively high-class cameras, as some can be found even in the lowest price range. Some quite simple cameras are equipped for filming in dark or badly lit areas, although they are otherwise not technically sophisticated. This applies moreover for all facets of camera equipment: hardly any standard camera would combine all the elements described here. Everyone has to seek out for himself from the wealth of equipment on offer the camera that will come nearest to satisfying his requirements.

Hard back or side light is very formative. The exposure must be lengthened on account of the marked shadows, which run in the direction of the camera (back-light correction!)

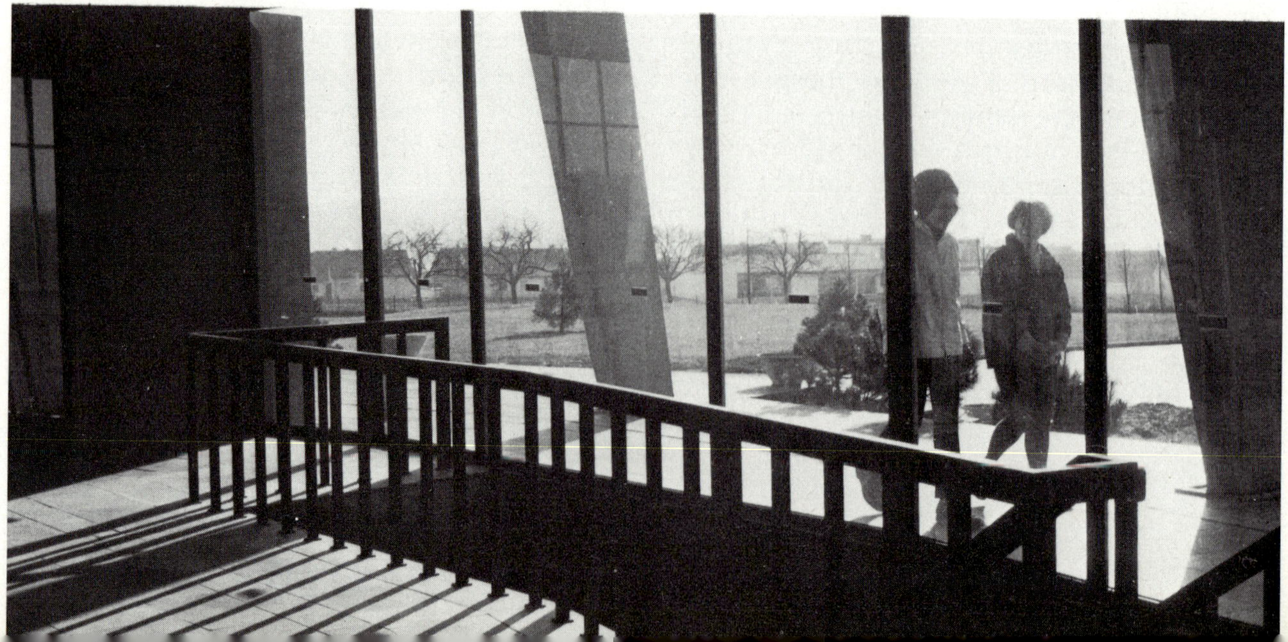

SUPERIOR CAMERAS

Those fittings that are considered extras in standard cameras generally form part of the basic equipment in superior cameras. Moreover, in superior cameras all the devices already described are of optimum quality: they will have a zoom lens of the greatest possible scope, the maximum number of different speeds, and excellent fading-in and fading-out processes. Such cameras are usually made to the latest technical standards.

MACRO-ZOOM LENS

As already stated, many standard - and superior-class cameras possess a macro-zoom lens, or simply, zoom-lens, which makes it possible, without any other additional parts, to move almost right up to the object, in order to film at the closest proximity possible, in other words, in macro-scope.

What does this lens look like, and what happens? A zoom lens usually consists of a basic optical part situated as close as possible to the film surface, which remains unaltered during zooming, and a central part in the lens that is displaced when the focal length is adjusted, thereby changing the angle of view. The front lens element on all cameras remains fixed, its function being to regulate the focus. By looking into the front lens, it is possible to see how the middle element moves as the focal length is adjusted.

On a macro-range setting the following changes occur: the base lens is pushed out of its normal position and nearer to the film

Macro setting on a Nizo camera

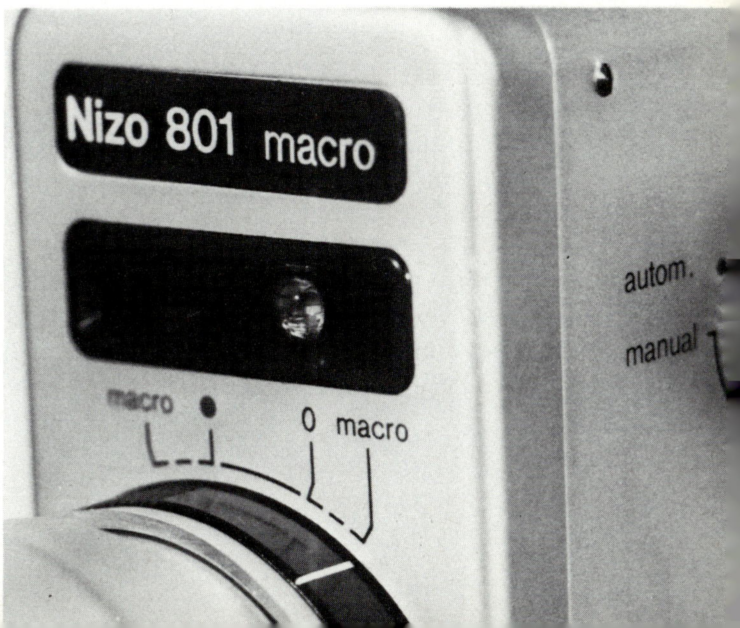

surface. The distance to the film gate is increased, so the optical composition is totally altered, without however affecting the image definition. The zoom part (the middle piece) is now used to adjust the focus, which is always controlled on the focusing screen in the view-finder. Pushing the base-lens forward brings the taking distance into macro-range (analogous with the intermediate ring or bellows attachment on a still reflex camera, which likewise shifts the lens forward).

The macro-setting opens up completely new opportunities to nature-lovers (flowers, insects etc.) which without macro have been until now almost, if not completely, beyond their grasp, for close-up lenses are nearly always handicapped by optical deficiencies, which do not arise in macro-lenses. The depth of field in macro-shots is naturally extremely small; it must therefore be finely adjusted to limit the margin of error as much as possible. Macro-shots are explained in further detail in a later chapter.

AUTOMATIC 'DISSOLVE'

All superior cameras are distinguishable by their automatic dissolve facility. A dissolve is nothing more than an overlapping of a fade-out and a fade-in, which allows one scene to flow very gently into the next, as the previous shot very slowly disappears and the subsequent one emerges equally slowly. It is none other than a seamless gliding from one scene to another. This particularly attractive effect is so well known from feature films that we cease to notice it.

Technically the following occurs during a dissolve: a film is shot, the content of which is considered suitable for a dissolve technique; when the end of the normal running time is reached, the camera is set to 'dissolve'; as a result the film is auto-automatically faded out during the course of a set number of frames (this number cannot be altered; according to the camera model it will be between 50 and 70 frames, which means that the fade-out will last about 3½ seconds); when the fading-out process is completed, the camera automatically shuts itself off and winds the film back to the point at which the fading-out began, in other words, over exactly 50 or 70 frames. The device is so precise that the exact position is always found, although a difference of a few frames would be of no consequence. When the film is wound back the camera stops automatically and the next scene begins with a fade-in, which overlays the fade-out just made and equals it in length, in other words, it overlaps the fade-out exactly.

The process is therefore fully automatic and it is not possible to influence the amount of time needed for the dissolve. By implication, only a camera with a backwind mechanism coupled with a numerical counter can effect a dissolve. Achieving a dissolve with a Super-8 camera is a very complicated matter, as the cassette does not allow for a winding back of the exposed film and so a storage device becomes necessary to catch the partially exposed film and make it possible to rerun it by a double-exposure method.

The problem is without doubt far more easily and more satisfactorily solved in a Super Double-8 camera than in a Super-8, as the two spools in a 2 x 8 film allow a backwind of the desired length. It is thus possible to double-expose a whole film and to produce dissolves of a chosen time span. Despite this the Double-8 camera should not be over-estimated, because a dissolve of 3½ seconds is adequate for a normal scene.

The complete automation of the dissolve lens has another great advantage: it is so exact that no mistake can be made in the double exposure. Without fail it complements the fading-out and fading-in so exactly that every single frame matches. In the time of Double-8 this could only be achieved by careful calculation. Making dissolves with a modern Super-8 camera is now a fail-safe process.

To make dissolves requires some experience and a minimal amount of planning, which is mentioned here only in passing. The scenes that are to overlap should of course be suited to each other, both in subject matter and in their colours or even their shape, in order to ensure that the film runs on harmoniously. When the colours mingle well or whole areas blend into each other the filmed result is a very attractive scene change.

In some camera models problems occur when a dissolve is used at the beginning or end of a film cassette. For safety reasons it is therefore advisable with all cameras to avoid dissolve techniques wherever possible on the first and last quarter of the film. If the first side of the film is nearly at an end, an attempt at a dissolve can end up a mess.

Dissolves by no means make simple fading-in and fading-out superfluous. A combination of both techniques, used sparingly and at the right moment, creates a harmony of interesting and impressive scene connections.

AUTOMATIC SINGLE-FRAME DEVICE (TIMER)

Nearly all cameras have a single-frame setting; the opportunities it allows have already been discussed. In superior cameras, as in standard camera models with an additional automatic control, yet another variant is added in the form of the automatic single-frame device. (It is true that the results that the device achieves can also be accomplished by hand, but this sometimes requires great patience.) The automatic control, also called a timer, makes it possible to establish in advance the interval at which the pictures are to be taken, the operative settings varying from about five frames a second to one picture a minute, according to the type of camera. The device can be pre-set anywhere within this range.

In the section on film speed the example of a flower blossoming was used to describe single-frame filming. When an automatic device is used, the process functions completely smoothly, the shots are absolutely uniform and no further adjustments are required. The length of the interval between exposures depends on how long the event is to last when projected; however the whole time-lapse sequence can be planned out exactly beforehand. For example, a flower takes three hours to open; the procedure is to be represented in the film within the space of ten seconds; for ten seconds projection time 10 x 18 single frames will be necessary; so these 180 pictures must be equally divided over three hours, which means that in three hours (180 minutes) one exposure must be taken every minute. The camera is now set to this time interval, and everything else happens automatically. Only the initial setting must be made manually, and after three hours the camera must be switched off again. It goes without saying that such shots could **never** succeed without a tripod. The camera must not be moved a single millimetre while the automatic device is in action.

PROLONGED-EXPOSURE CONTROL

Amongst all the superb automatic and electronic devices to be found in a high-class camera is the automatic prolongedexposure control. It is one of the newest additions to amateur cameras and is, quite frankly, only of very limited use.

The prolonged-exposure control allows an extremely long exposure-time for single-frame exposures. It is slightly similar to the setting on a still camera used to set the exposure time at any desired length. Each frame will be exposed for the required length of time; in other words, the ciné camera measures out each shot, frame for frame, and automatically moves on to the next frame when the appropriate exposure is complete. This technique differs considerably from the single-frame device, in that the exposure time can be varied from shot to shot and the film is transported automatically.

Another practical example will clarify the way in which this technique works: a scene is to be filmed inside a fairly dark church. There is not sufficient light to film normally; artificial lighting is ruled out on technical grounds. Usually this would mean the shot cannot be managed, but this is no longer so if a prolonged-exposure device is put to use. The camera is set up in front of the subject, supported of course on a tripod, and set to automatic prolonged exposure. Now the camera will automatically expose each frame for the required length of time.

The number of frames to be exposed depends on how long the scene is to last when projected. Some cameras even have a programme control that switches off the process when the desired number of frames has been taken. It is only necessary to operate the first shot.

The dissolve setting is the most frequently used of the automatic techniques mentioned: the prolonged-exposure control and single-frame device are considered superfluous by most amateur film-makers. Their greatest significance lies in the field of science, where extreme conditions frequently demand new technical developments.

INTERCHANGEABLE LENS

Only in a few models within the high-class camera range can the original lens be replaced by another. Anyone possessing a still-camera system can use the lenses belonging to this equipment on a ciné camera that allows interchange with the aid of suitable connecting rings. As this involves entirely different focal lengths, it presents a whole new range of possibilities. The long lens distances of a still camera, about 135 to 200mm., produce a strange effect on ciné film. In film terms, this means that the focal length is thirty times as long as the longest side of the frame, which would be equivalent to using a lens with a focal length of 110cm. on a still camera. It is true that such lenses do exist for still cameras, but they are seldom seen.

Such long focal lengths are most frequently used to film animals, particularly shy creatures that can only be filmed at great distance. Again, it is without doubt mostly scientific films that take advantage of this opportunity.

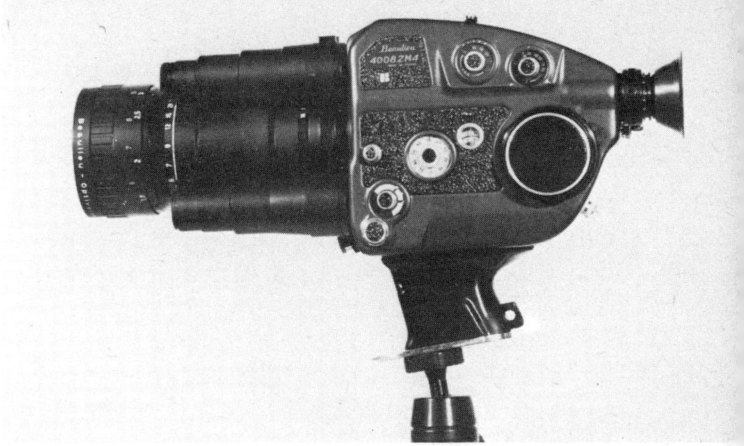

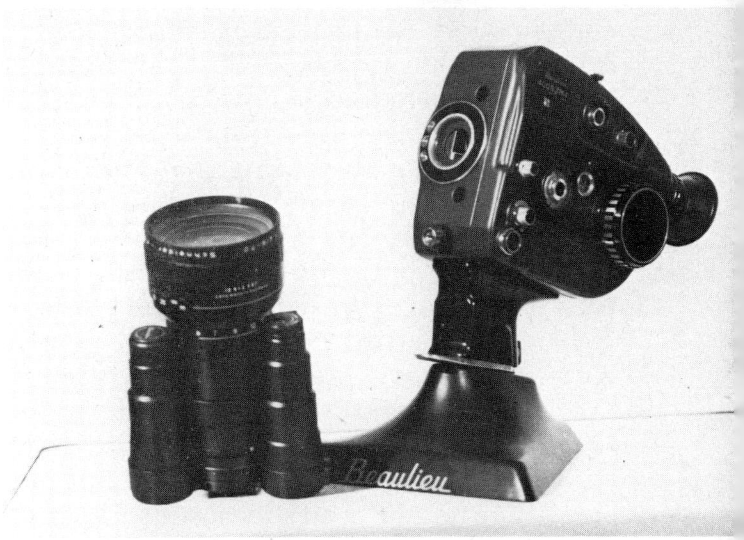

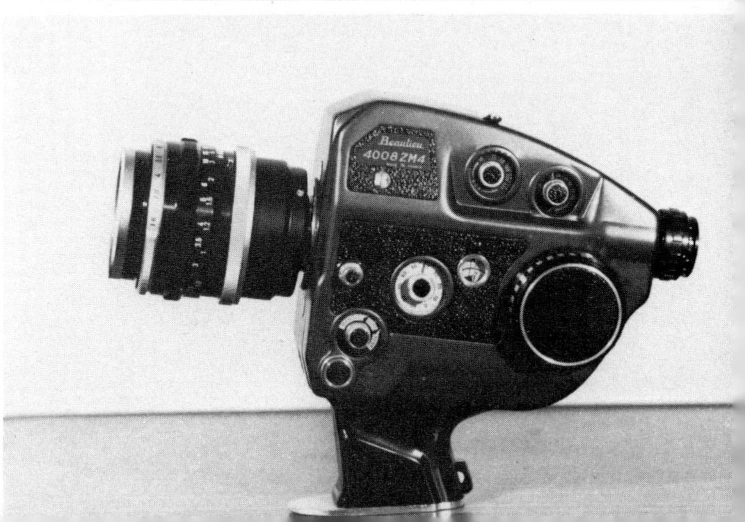

Superior camera with inset lens and diaphragm motor
Superior camera with screw-on lens
Superior camera with inset lens from a still camera

As only a few cameras can take an interchangeable lens, this short digression is sufficient comment on the topic.

SOUND-FILM CAMERAS

Recently there has been yet another technical innovation: the sound-film camera. For this, special Super-8 film with a sound track is required: the sound is directly recorded as the film is being taken, a technique that incidentally is not exclusive to high-class cameras. Sound-film cameras are included throughout the standard camera range. Sound filming is therefore not only available to those who can afford a superior camera, But to anyone who wishes to make use of the opportunity.

However, not everything that applies to silent film can be transferred to sound-filming. Fade-ins and fade-outs, for example, are optically extremely effective, but not on a sound recording. As the introductory and closing music is not usually recorded as the film itself is being taken, there is no problem with fades at the beginning and end. Some sound film cameras have a dissolve setting, but the sound must be added to these scenes afterwards. An attempt to dissolve with sound could go quite awry.

Many trick shots, e.g. time lapse and slow motion, can of course be filmed with a sound film camera, but, again in each the sound recording must be switched off. Obviously every recording, whether on spools or cassettes, must run absolutely evenly both when being made and when being replayed, otherwise it is bound to sound distorted.

The points just mentioned help justify the fact that most sound-film cameras are not as richly adorned with technical equipment as comparable models without sound potential. There are in fact some particularly simple cameras, with no speed, distance, or lens aperture settings, that allow filming and sound recording to be made simultaneously. Pictures and sound belong after all together, and these cameras are made purely to that end.

However, by far the majority of sound-film cameras are found in the standard range. It may be that in the foreseeable future sound filming will overtake present conventional filming methods, and become the method in common use.

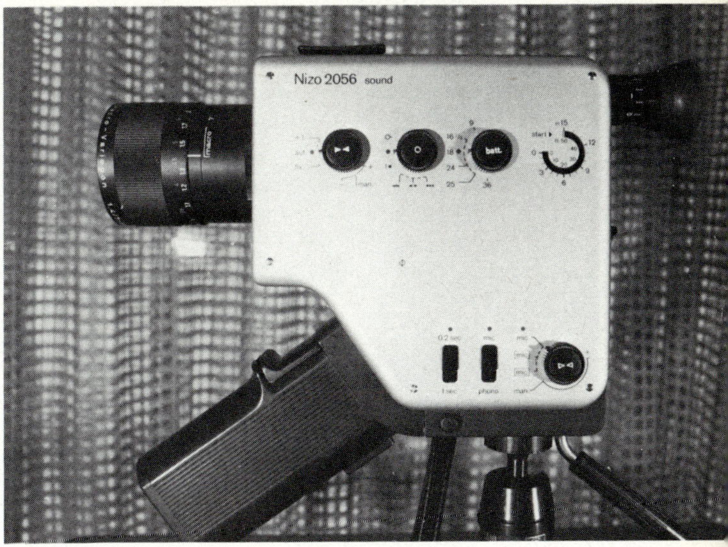

Life-sound camera in the superior range

Life-sound camera in the standard range

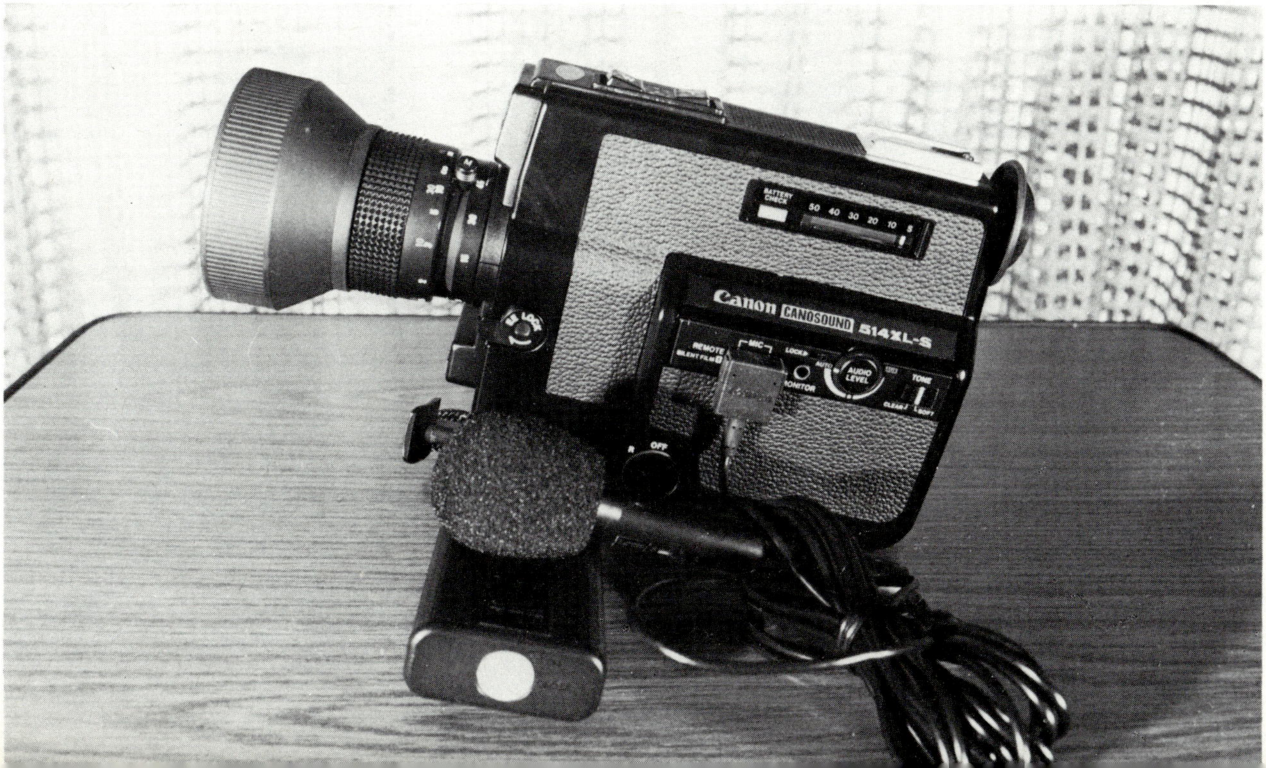

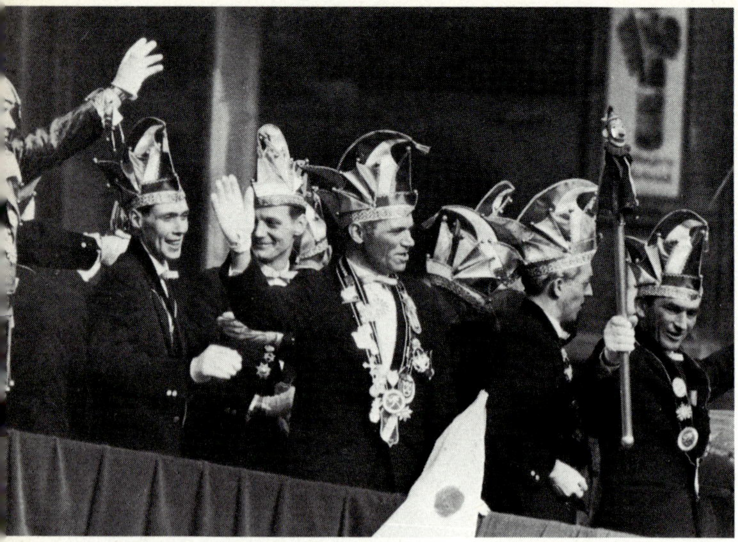

Crowds make good filming!

Festivities lend themselves well to ciné treatment

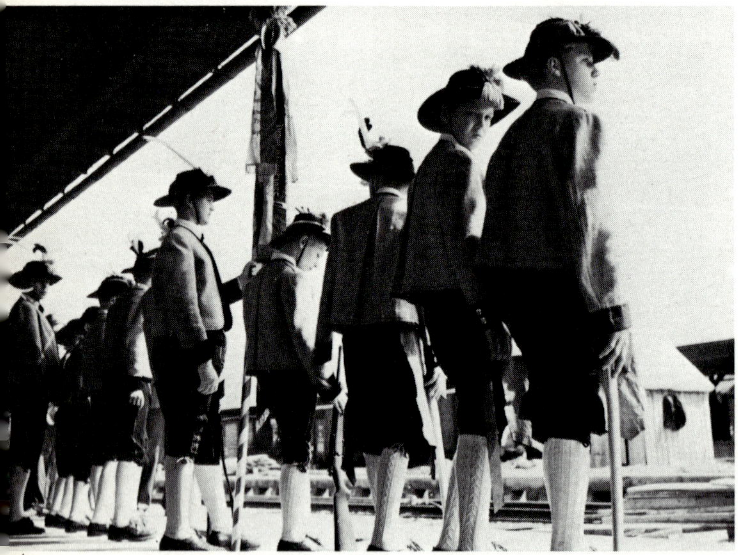

Equipment of the Different Types of Camera

	Simple Camera	Standard Camera	Superior Camera
Lenses			
Transmitting power	1:2.8	1:2.8	Up to 1:1.0
Variable-focus lens	—	4x to 8x	over 8x
Setting	Fix focus	1m - ∞	all ranges
Macro setting	—	yes	yes
XL lens	—	yes	yes
Motor zoom	—	yes	yes
Variable speeds	—	yes	yes
Interchangeable lens	—	—	yes
Ocular compensation	—	yes	yes
Automatic devices			
Integral measurement	yes	yes	yes
Disconnectable	—	yes	yes
Back-light correction	—	—	yes
Energy Source			
Dry battery	yes	yes	yes
Rechargeable battery	—	—	yes
Separate measuring cell	—	yes	yes
Trick Settings			
Film speed	18, 1	18, 24, 36, 1	all possibilities
Fade-in	—	yes	yes
Fade-out	—	yes	yes
Dissolve	—	—	yes
Timer	—	yes	yes
Automatic prolonged exposure	—	—	yes
Automatic release	—	yes	yes
Remote release	—	yes	yes
Sound			
Live sound recording	—	yes	yes
Synchro socket	—	yes	yes
Pilot giver	—	—	yes

CINÉ-CAMERA ACCESSORIES

The range of ciné-camera accessories is so vast that whole branches of industry thrive on it. The range includes both those attachments that are used only very occasionally and those that are the film-maker's 'daily bread'.

As a rule, all the essential components are included in the basic equipment of a camera. Where this is not the case, parts for any model of camera can be acquired later.

Our intention here is to describe some of these accessories and, in doing so, to explain how and when to use them. To simplify matters we can make a distinction between optical accessories – which for the sake of convenience may also include lens shades and filters – and other pieces of equipment.

In its narrowest sense 'optical accessories' refers only to lens designs that alter the angle of coverage: interchangeable (wide-angle, tele) lenses and lens converters. A wider understanding of the term would include close-up and 'trick' lenses.

UNIVERSAL ACCESSORIES

We will begin with the simple things, by describing the lens-hood and filters, and follow this with an explanation of lens designs (wide-angle, tele-lens, etc.).

Lens-hood

There are hardly any filming conditions where a lens-hood would not be in place. It consists of a round tube, made of rubber or an elastic type of plastic, which is screwed in front of the lens, preventing the infiltration of unnecessary light, which might cause disruptive reflections.

A lens-hood should always be used. It is usually unnecessary to unscrew it from the camera, as it will probably be collapsible and will fit into any case.

Lens-hoods come in varying sizes, narrower and wider, the so-called tele- and wide-angle hoods. The use of a wide-angle hood is to be recommended on a ciné camera, otherwise a movement into the wide-angle range using a variable-focus lens could result in the corners being darkened.

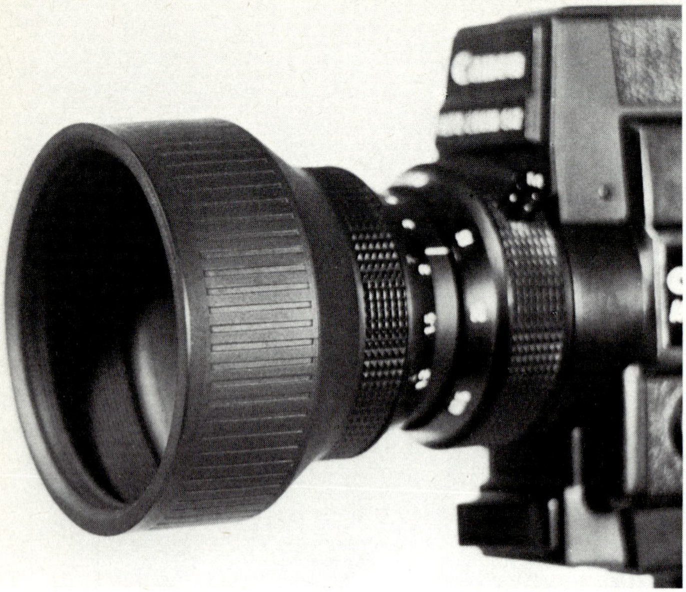

Lens hood in position. Not particularly elegant, but useful everywhere

Something of this nature always happens when the angular field of the lens is greater than the opening of the lens hood. Of course when the lens-hood forms part of the camera's basic outfitting, this problem does not exist.

Filters

There are a number of different filters, usually suitable for use with both still and ciné cameras. However, still-camera filters often do not fit the ciné camera, because the diameters of the lenses vary in size. This can be remedied by using filter adapting rings. There is one important point to note when purchasing a filter: the filter should be bought to fit the greater of the mountings and adapted to fit the smaller. Otherwise the filter mountings may cause vignetting, as happens with lens-hoods that are too narrow.

Skylight, UV, and Colour Filters

The most widely used is the skylight filter, which is suitable for any type of film. It has a very slight pink colouring, which absorbs the surplus blue in the atmosphere and is particularly advantageous for filming mountains and sea, in other words any setting where the ultra-violet (UV) rays are particularly strong. We have all seen pictures of mountains with an extremely blue background: this is caused by UV rays, which have the most concentrated effect over a height of approximately 1,500m. The skylight filter should not only absorb these UV rays, but also improve the picture definition, which is adversely affected by the different wavelength of UV rays.

The UV filter is known to everyone. Strictly speaking, it stems from the time when colour film was only rarely used, and is the forerunner of the skylight filter. UV filters have the same effect on black-and-white film, but because they lack the pink colouration they do not subtract any blue light from the subject. They have now been more or less superseded by the skylight filter.

The terms CR 1.5, skylight filter, or pink filter are various names for the same filter. As with many other products, different films occasionally use different terms of reference. Apart from the effect that a skylight filter has on colour and definition, it has a useful side-effect: it protects the surface of the lens from mechanical damage, finger prints, etc. The filter should be left permanently on the camera in order to take advantage of this protective function.

There are, of course, a vast number of other familiar and commonly used filters. Those people concerned with black-and-white photography use them in a variety of colours: yellow, yellow-green, green, orange, and red. However, they are filters for special photographic effects, only for use with black-and-white material, for if used with colour film the whole film would be coloured by the shading of the filters used.

All colour filters have the potential to change the colour spectrum on the film, and every filter makes its complementary colours appear more powerful. The extent of the contrast will consequently appear all the greater. A yellow filter will make a landscape look more impressive, by adding emphasis to the cloud formations. If an orange filter is employed, a sunny summer scene with fine-weather clouds is practically transformed into a storm scene, and a red filter can conjure up out of a sunny landscape pictures that almost appear to have been taken by night. However, to repeat, this applies only to black-and-white films.

Incidentally, all filters have a thread on the outside of the mounting, which is screwed into the lens, and a thread on the inner side (identical with the camera thread) into which the lens-hood can be screwed. It is always a good idea to use a filter and a lens hood together. As most filters (apart from skylight filters) are used predominantly in fine weather, this usually occurs anyway. In bad weather the lens-hood serves to protect the front lens or the filter against raindrops.

Grey Filter

Anybody who has tried filming on a winter holiday will have experienced the incredible brightness that can emanate from the sun and snow; there are hardly any brighter situations in which to film. In this setting many film-makers might conclude that the automatic exposure device in the camera has suddenly reached its limit, as the pointer on the lens aperture control remains permanently in the red area, indicating that it is too bright to film.

In a similar situation, the amateur still-photographer can shorten the exposure time to up to 1/1000 second. What can the film-maker do? He can also continue filming, although the exposure time is not shortened (indeed the exposure time will be largely dictated by the film speed). But there is a solution: the grey filter. A grey filter is a normal filter in varying shades of grey; when used with colour film it is completely neutral in its effect on colours and has the task of dimming the light by one, two, or three stops. Cameras where the light is measured automatically through the lens make this correction themselves, in all others the lens aperture must be adjusted manually.

With a grey filter in front of the lens it is possible to film anywhere where filming could otherwise only have been carried out with difficulty, if at all, because of bright-light conditions. The most commonly used filter is the multiple-4 grey filter; if the automatic device in the camera reaches an aperture of f16, for example, a 4-multiple grey filter would achieve a lens aperture of f8 to f11, in other words a normal value. Incidentally this filter can be used in conjunction with both colour and black-and-white film.

Polarising filter

The polarising filter has quite different qualities, and serves to prevent or minimise reflections, One particular feature of these filters is that they only allow the light to travel in one direction, which means that all rays from directions outside the scope of the filter are absorbed.

Reflections are usually caused by interfering side light, and are to a great extent eliminated by a polarising filter. They are used, typically, when filming through a pane of glass or taking shots of water. With the aid of a polarising filter it becomes possible to see through the water surface, which would otherwise be overlaid by reflections from the sky. The absorption of certain rays of light when such a filter is used means extending the exposure by one or two stops, depending on the setting.

A polarising filter can also be used to eliminate reflected colours, which sometimes disturb the picture, although they are always naturally caused. For example: a family is filmed sitting under a red sun shade. The light bears red strains from the red shade, so everybody takes on a slightly red tinge. As long as the sun shade is included in the picture this is of no consequence, but if the focal length is extended, so that only the faces are visible, the red light of the sunshade will adversely affect the picture. In a shot of this type a polarising filter would filter the red light out of the picture, returning the world to optical order.

A polarising filter is easy to handle: like any other filter it is screwed on to the lens, but it can be turned within its mount. The best effect for any subject can be sought by turning the filter and checking the results in the reflex viewfinder.

Conversion Filters

Film-makers with Double-8 cameras require conversion filters to compensate for daylight and artificial lighting, when the wrong film is in the camera. The filters necessary to accomplish this compensation are the blue-converter, strength 12, and the red-converter, strength 12.

As is commonly known, daylight contains a predominant amount of red, and artificial lighting is predominantly blue. The films, as described elsewhere, are specially attuned to these colours. To undertake filming in artificial light while there is daylight film in the camera, a conversion blue 12 is employed, to transform the red-bearing artificial light into the correct colour value. Conversely, a conversion red 12 filter is used with artificial-light film for filming in daylight.

Skylight filters in fact also count as conversion filters, but are the weakest of the collection.

Notably, conversion filters are only discussed with reference to Double-8 cameras. Colour-correction filters form an integral part of Super-8 cameras, and thus the problem is solved simply by setting the camera to the type of lighting being used at the time.

Hence all conversion filters are transforming or colour-correction filters, which serve to filter the correct light or light colouring when differing sources of light are being used, or when the light has the wrong composition from the outset for the type of film in use.

Every amateur knows the false colours that ensue when film is taken at home using artificial lighting while at the same time the sun is streaming in through the window, or the colouring that appears on films taken in the early morning or late afternoon. Conversion filters can be used to partially or completely compensate for this. Such colour correction is by no means a matter of taste; on the contrary, it should result in the correct representation of every colour.

Admittedly there are limitations in all areas of photography and of filming, which naturally includes colouring. It may indeed be the case that we prefer the 'false colours' to the strictly correct ones. For example, everyone knows that snow is white and white it has to be. However, sunshine and clear-blue skies give the snow a tinge of blue, which is quite natural and correct, because the blue sky is reflected. Therefore on close observation the snow is also found to be blue. However we want snow to be pure white, because snow **is** white, because, as Christian Morgenstern said, nothing can be what it must not be. Colours, or colour perception, is entirely a subjective matter. Hardly anyone is in the position to recall a colour exactly as seen. All colour perception is affected by 'sight-desire', in other words, we see colours as they appear in pleasant memories, even though the memory does not usually exactly coincide with the original, if viewed objectively.

Hence any evaluation of colour exaggeration or of colour film poses great difficulties. Whether or not it is advisable to transform pictures into absolute colours by means of a conversion filter is bound to remain a matter of dispute.

Yet another example: colour pictures filmed in the midday sun can, or rather must, have a blue tinge to them, which can be compensated for by means of a 1.5 or 3 conversion filter. In fact, this renders the shots untrue, as the daylight at midday is always blue. However, something more nearly approaching red appeals to us more as we generally prefer warm tones of colour. Most people experience blue colours as being too cold - yet further proof of the subjectivity of colours.

Transformation filters in the form of conversion red and conversion blue come in graduations of 1.5 to 20. The higher the density of the filter, the greater the intensity of that particular colour on the film. Any desired density can be acquired by combining the available filters. If for instance a conversion red 7 filter is required this can be achieved by combining conversion 3 and 4 filters. The given densities of the filters are therefore added together in order to obtain the appropriate filtering.

The two filters R12 and B12 have already been mentioned. When using them it must be borne in mind that normal electric lamps, halogen burners, head lights, flash equipment, or other sources of light can have greatly differing effects on colour. In order to attain the normal colour when filming it is therefore necessary to use varying conversion filters (we need say no more about what is considered 'normal' with reference to amateur ciné filming). Those who work with conversion filters should discover for themselves the densities that are generally suited to their taste, independent of scientifically established colour correctness. As conversion filters are obsolete in the case of Super-8 cameras, other remaining uses in ciné filming are relatively small. In extreme circumstances, such as night filming or theatre filming, slight filtering is sometimes possible. However, conversion filters are of chief significance within the scope of diaphotography, mostly in the scientific field. Here it is of course of prime importance to establish correct filtering objectively, to produce absolute colours.

It has already been noted that both artificial light and daylight film exist. Both are gauged to quite definite, established colour temperatures. The colour is generally measured on the Kelvin scale and is lower the greater the amount of red light present (artificial light = 3200°K., daylight = 5600°K). These values are, however, as everyone knows from his own experience, in no way constant or the same at all times; but the given colour sensitivity of the film remains unchanged. Special measuring instruments have been developed for this purpose: they work in a similar way to an exposure meter and show the exact filtering necessary to produce absolute colour correctness on any given film.

As stated, this is of no consequence in amateur filming, but is of significance for film used for the purpose of study, for instance the study of plant growth, which would continue over a long period. During fertilisation peak efficiency must be maintained at all times, as even the smallest alteration in the plant colour might be of great importance and must be recorded objectively. For recording experiments, both

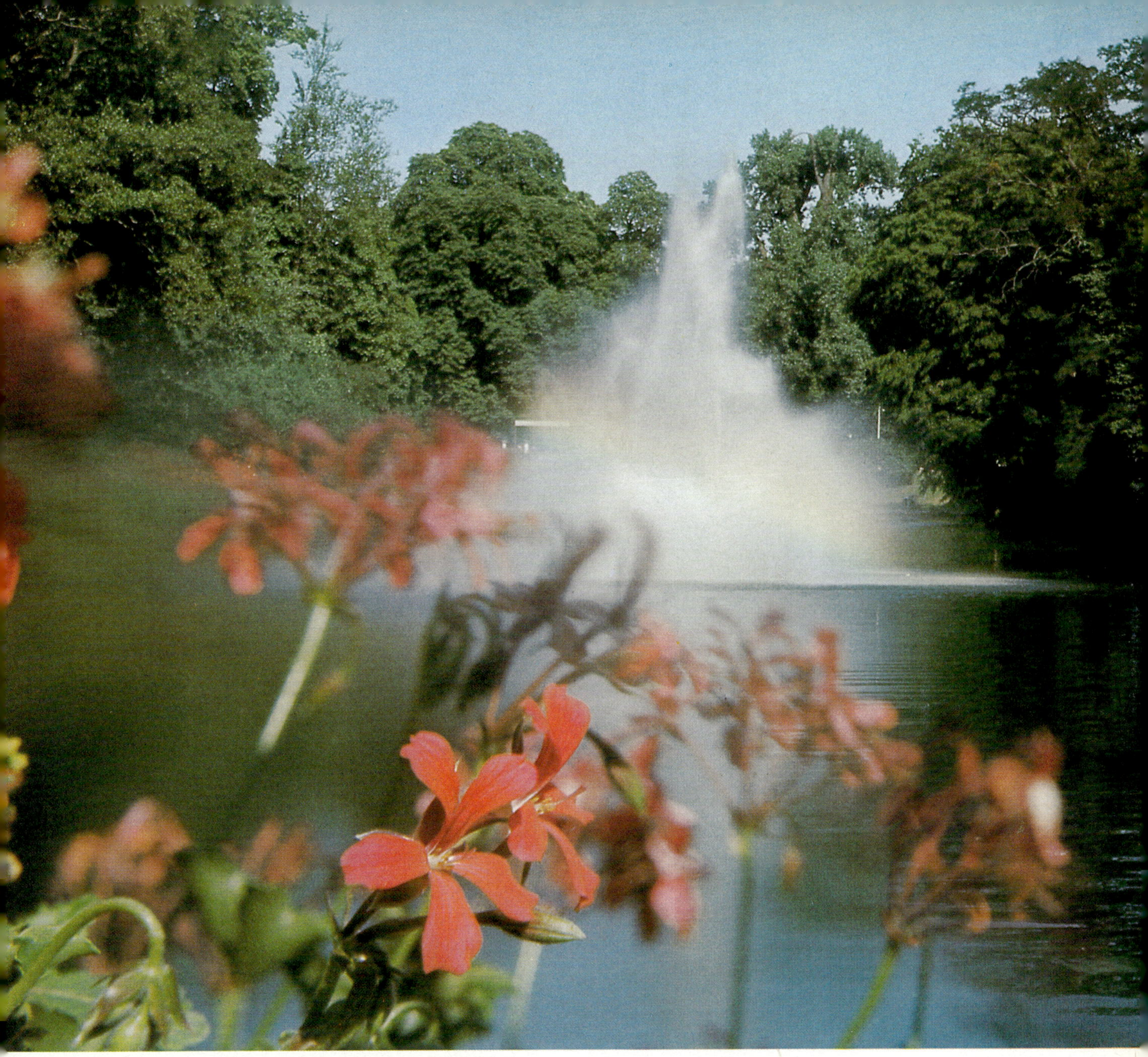

Plate 5: This shows clearly the effect of a bi-fo lens, producing images on two levels. The flowers in the foreground are at a distance of 30cm. from the camera, the landscape behind is at the normal taking distance

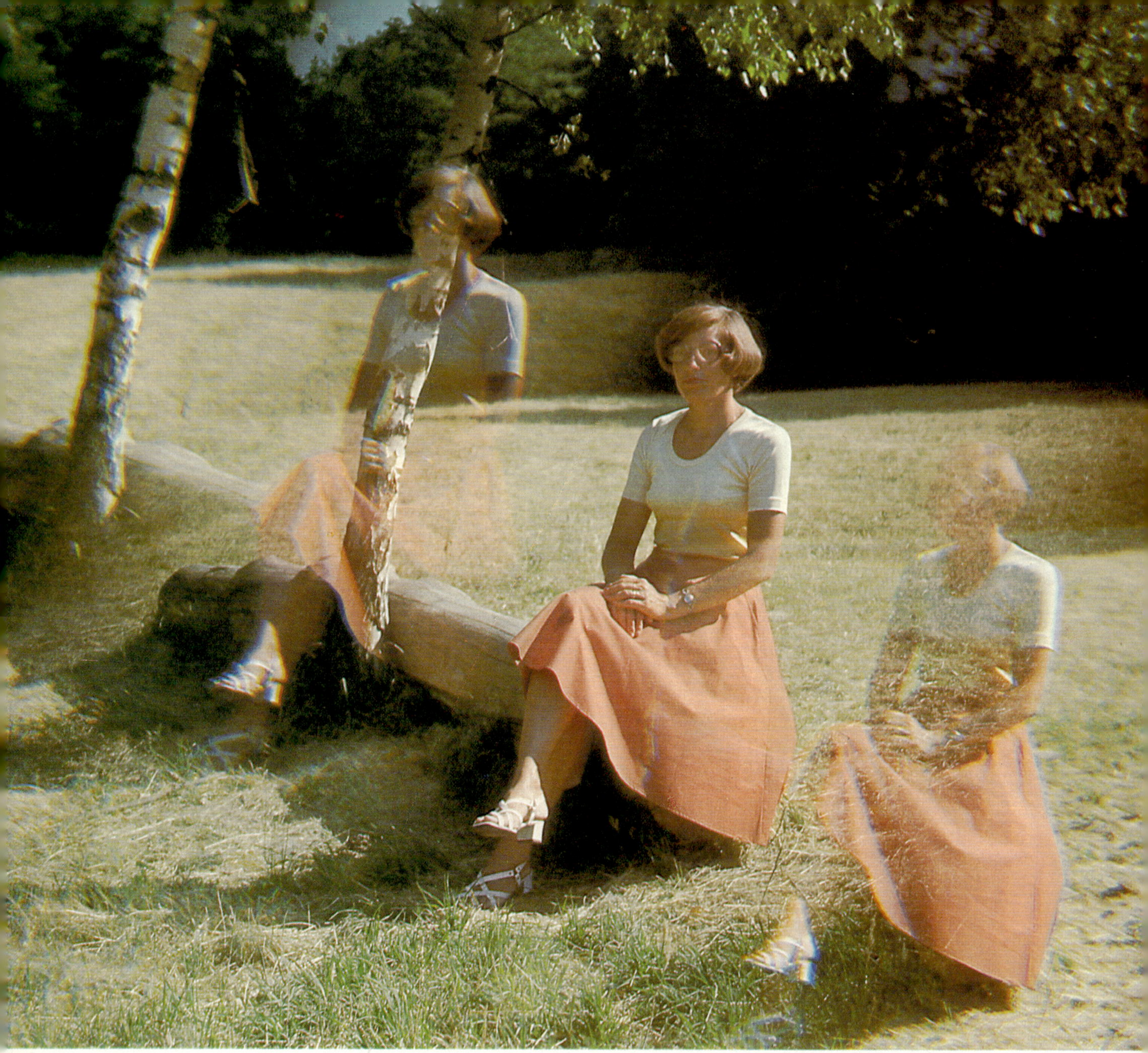

Plate 6: With a 3 x multiple prism the subject is represented by three images. The positioning of the images in relation to each other may be varied by rotating the whole filter.

transparencies and film may be used with equal success. The above remarks will suffice as an indication of the possible range of uses of conversion filters.

Pop filters
Finally, there is yet another group of special effect filters to be mentioned, which come in the most diverse colours: pop filters. The colour of the filter is superimposed over the entire picture, giving it a very strange character.

Thus a completely artificial colouring, which chemists have been seeking to eliminate for years in normal circumstances, is in this case deliberately contrived.

The name pop filter indicates its association with the 'pop-art' style. Film scenes with this pop-colouring must be considered as exceptional cases. This type of filter is without doubt more suitable for use in still photographic work.

ATTACHMENTS

Trick lenses

Trick lenses are often counted as filters, although they are in fact quite different. They are not used for corrective purposes, indeed they always produce somewhat bizarre effects.

There is a large assortment of trick lenses, and new ones are constantly appearing. It is quite possible that by the time this book is published, there will already be some new varieties on the market.

All trick lenses are intended solely for creating special effects. Used sparingly, they can enrich one's filming no end and give it a quite personal flavour. Trick lenses should on no account however be used at every available opportunity: the less the better!

The best-known group of lenses is multiple prisms. I will try to explain these lenses with the aid of the following pictures.

We can differentiate between two-, three-, five-, and six-faceted prisms, all of which are included in the term multiple prisms. The effects they produce are so varied that the lenses must be described individually.

All trick-lenses, like polarising filters, can be rotated in their mounting in order to find the most effective positioning.

The two-faceted prism is a lens with a line cut into it, so it appears to be divided into two equal parts. The effect of this line is to produce two images of the subject in question. The positioning of the prism in front of the lens dictates whether the images lie side by side or one in front of the other. Three-faceted prisms are of two types: in one the circular area is divided into three sections of 120° each, in the other there are three parallel cuts, giving three side-by-side images. In the former, there will be three triangularly positioned images.

The five-sided prism possesses a completely different appearance. In the middle lies a square, in which the image remains unchanged. Lines from the corner of each square to the edge of the lens divide the area

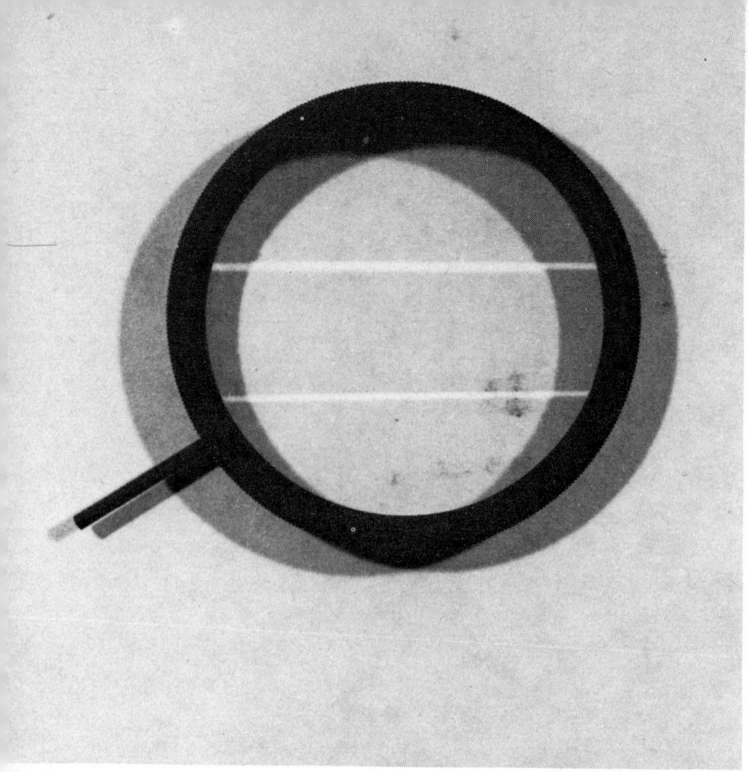

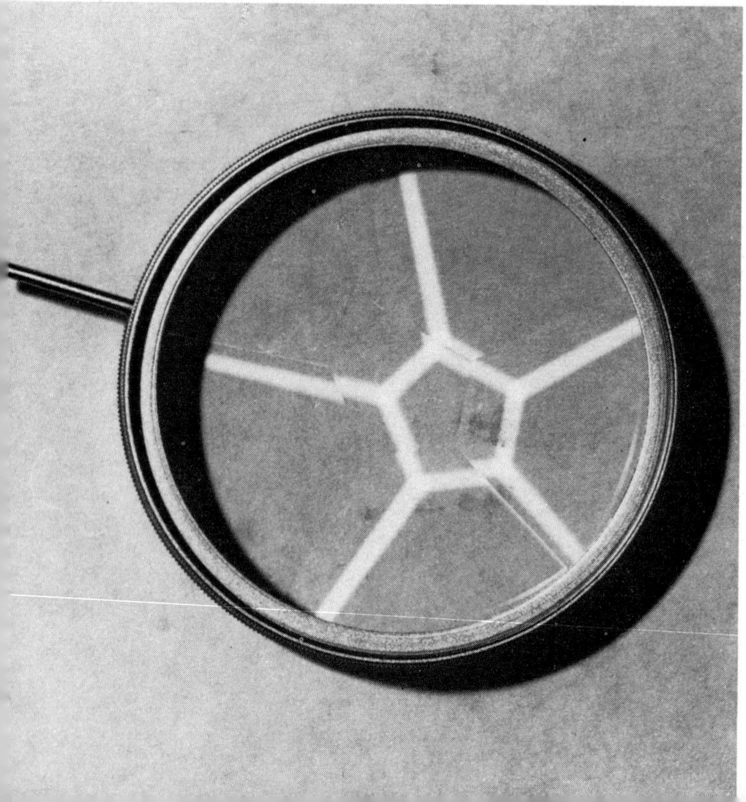

surrounding the middle square into four parts and the image is thus presented another four times. Consequently five images of the subject are produced in all.

The six-sided prism works in a similar way. The central area consists of a pentagon, with five separate areas around the outside, as in a honeycomb, producing six images of the same subject.

The effectiveness of the trick lens in a film is achieved by virtue of the fact that it can be turned during filming, creating an unexpected effect on the film. If, for instance, a six-sided prism is rotated while taking a portrait, the following happens: the image appears as normal in the middle of the picture, but five other impressions of it revolve round the outside. It produces a novel effect, though one that can only be impressive when it does not appear too often.

To this description must be added the note that three-sided and six-sided prisms are also available in varying colours. Each sector of the lens has a different colour from the others, so that an effect of blurring colour is added to that of the multiple image. These coloured trick devices necessarily imply that the exposure time must be increased. Incidentally, the colour has hardly any effect on black-and-white film.

3 x multiple parallel prism

6 x multiple prism

An original effect is produced when two of the trick lenses mentioned are combined and counter-rotated as the shot is being taken. In this way the world becomes completely unreal. You may of course be in two minds about this type of filming – but give it a try!

Some trick devices still remain to be mentioned. Firstly, there are the point or dream lenses, which produce very similar effects. In both cases the image appears quite normal in the middle of the picture, but becomes less defined towards the edges, thereby accentuating the central details. With other subjects the outer area can be submerged in a dream-like haze (hence 'dream lens'). Such effects can be used in varying fields, according to one's personal wants and taste.

Another type is the star-effect filter, with 4 or 6 lines across it. These are engraved in the filter and act as dividing lines, radiating four or six reflections from all the bright points in the picture (lamps, candles etc.). The lines run across the lens, all meeting at a central point.

A variation of this is the star-lattice filter, which has a lattice engraved over the entire surface area. This creates a very soft image of the subject, which stretches over the entire picture area, and produces stars at all the illuminated points. This effect is particularly valuable for back-lighted shots, in sea and snow. Every reflection is broken into a star-like shape.

The spectral-star device produces a similar effect, except that the reflections are additionally coloured. Many millions of tiny crystals disperse the light in its spectrum, the result being similar to that of the star-lattice filter but with the rays appearing in the colours of the spectrum.

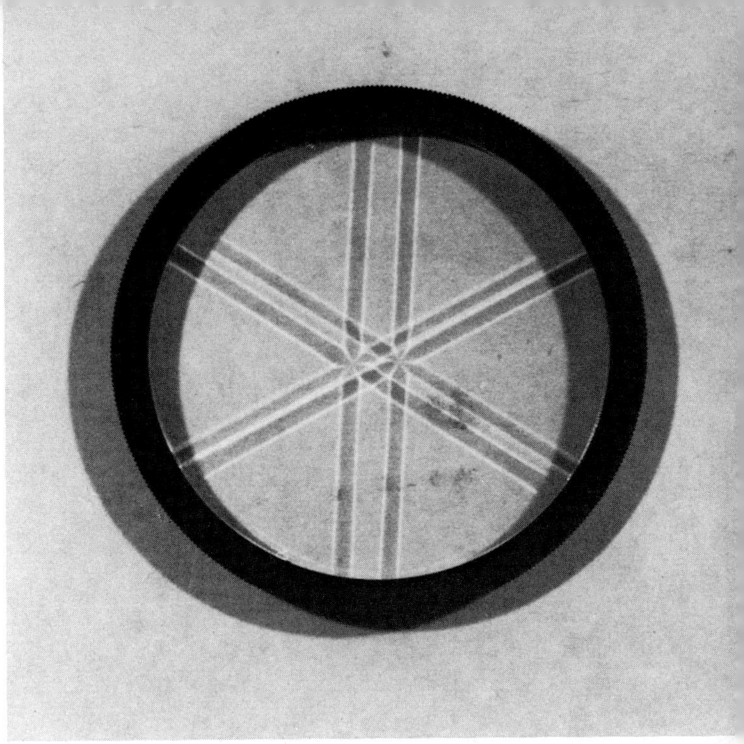

6 x multiple star filter

Common to all trick devices, then, is the fact that they produce quite particular effects, and moreover they should be used for a particular purpose and within the recommended limits. Their success can only be guaranteed if they are used sparingly.

As with filters and lens shades, special-effect and trick devices are available in all the popular sizes. Consequently, the components mentioned here may be used in conjunction with all cameras, if necessary with the aid of an adapting ring, as previously described.

Close-up lenses

Close-up lenses allow for optical modification of the basic on all equipment. As the name implies, the taking distance is shortened as much as possible, in other words, it enables one to move closer in on the subject. The occasions for this are numerous, for instance, for filming flowers, insects, in short, anything at all that is small.

However, even films that are not exclusively concerned with small o bjects can make use of an occasional shot of this type to add variety and thereby improve overall impression.

Close-up lenses have one definite disadvantage, which applies to close-ups in general: the nearer one moves towards the object, the smaller the depth of field becomes. For all shots, whether films or photographs, this means that the distance must be set exactly, in order to obtain the clearest possible image of a small object. In fine weather the depth of field can be improved by using a small lens aperture; in bad-light conditions even greater accuracy becomes necessary.

Close-up lenses come in varying strengths, usually three or four variations to cope with different distances. Lens 1 is a direct continuation of the lens scale, which means that if the closest distance possible without a close-up lens is 1 m. it becomes possible to film at a distance of 1m. to 50cm. Close-up 1 is the most frequently used lens, as with most subjects it is sufficient to film at a distance of 50cm. In addition, the zoom lens can be used to dictate the field of view. The effects produced by zoom and close-up lenses can complement each other very successfully.

The close-up lenses 2, 3, and 4 – size 4 does not exist for all cameras – follow in succession after lens 1 in the optical lens scale, that is to say, if the effective scope of lens 1 extends to 50cm., it would be replaced here by lens 2 and so on until lens 4.

If even lens 4 does not serve for the desired distance, the lenses can be combined at will. The distance thus achieved will be even smaller and can be ascertained with absolute accuracy using the reflecting plane in the viewfinder. If several lenses are combined, it is always advisable not to open the diaphragm completely, otherwise the edges may lack definition due to the optical modification. This can be avoided by fading out on a middle value (about 5.5 to 8).

On account of the unfavourable effect filming at extremely close proximity has on the depth of field, it is advisable to use a tripod. The slightest movement could cause the camera to deviate outside the depth of field: in such shots it is only a matter of a mm.

A lens hood should always be used in conjunction with close-up shots. Close-up lenses just like a filter have a coil into which the lens hood can be screwed.

An important note: if a close-up lens and a filter are used together, which is readily achieved, the close-up lens must always be the first screwed into the lens. It is a component of the lens and must be in the closest possible contact with the front lents. Filters, trick lenses, and the like must therefore always be screwed on in second place.

The closest setting that can be achieved with a close-up lens always depends on how near the camera may approach the object without the use of lens attachments. Any calculation is determined by this closest setting, but it is not uniform for all cameras. In any case, and this applies to all models, the definition can be adjusted exactly using the reflex viewfinder, whether or not a close-up lens is entailed. The enormous advantage of the reflex viewfinder on modern Super-8 cameras is proved yet again. In older equipment, making an adjustment manually is not always so easy: sometimes it cannot be done without tables and a measuring tape. Ultimately it produces the same result, but the method is more tedious and demands great care.

The reflex viewfinder has yet another advantage when taking close-ups: there is no discrepancy between the field of view in the viewfinder and in the lens: both are identical. Such a discrepancy - called parallax - commonly occurs when the viewfinder and the lens are separate, but can be compensated for with prisms or with compensatory slides on the tripod. This problem is again a relic of the Double-8 era; it does not exist in modern cameras.

Bi-fo lenses

Another special lens belonging under the heading close-ups is the bi-fo lens (bifo = bifocal). This lens can be compared with spectacles for long-sight and near-sight. The bi-fo lens serves the same purpose. It divides the focus of the film shot on to two levels simultaneously. The smaller section of a bi-fo lens can be equated to a close-up lens. It should focus sharply on a near object, perhaps a text for a film title, while the remainder of the lens behaves normally, producing an unchanged image of whatever is in the camera's field of view.

Bi-fo lens

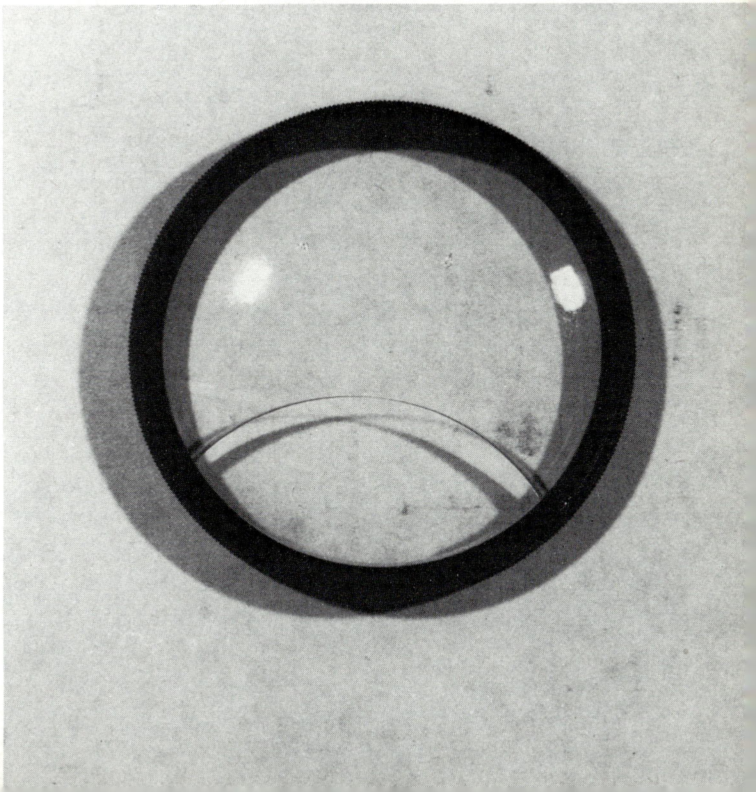

A bi-focal lens makes it relatively easy to film titles as the actual film is being made, which could not be achieved without the aid of such a lens.

OPTICAL ACCESSORIES

Wide-angle and tele-range

A problem that many people come across when filming at home is that the shortest focal length is still too long, and the wide-angle field is not wide enough. Any deviation outside the field of view, as is usual with a wide-angle lens in photography, will mean that the shot is not successful.

The greatest wide-angle range of most Super-8 cameras implies a focal length of between 6.5mm and 7mm, which is about equal to a 'normal' viewing angle, but not a wide-angle, of a still camera. Wide-angle accessories can be used to provide filming conditions comparable to those in still photography by considerably increasing the view. If the tele focal length is too short, the problem can be solved in the same way. Tele-accessories can extend the focal length to allow double the scope.

Wide-angle and tele devices can be screwed into the filter thread on the lens. The other functions of the camera, above all the automatic light measurement, remain unaffected. With some devices, however, if the diaphragm is completely open, the edges of the picture may not be in perfect focus. In good light there is no problem, as the lens aperture is then on a central setting, and no hazy edges appear.

Interchangeable Lenses

Lenses can only be interchanged on a few of the top-quality Super-8 cameras, which are without exception all in the high price range. These interchangeable lenses provide new opportunities, particularly insofar as it means that lenses used on still cameras can be employed in a ciné camera. The camera manufacturers provide the necessary adaptors to fit all conventional lens mounts. Thus the film amateur is offered an abundance of new prospects: the longest photographic focal length can be used to film extremely small objects over an enormous distance – using a tripod, of course.

However, in practice, the use of a still-camera lens in filming is not often possible. As explained in the chapter on optics, focal lengths that are frequently used in photography (e.g. 135mm.) are extremely long for a cine camera. However, cameras that possess an interchangeable lens have, as already described, an almost limitless range of applications.

One can say without exaggeration that modern Super-8 cameras are made to comply with very high technical standards, so that it only rarely becomes necessary to consider optical accessories. The technical possibilities are so diverse that nearly anything can be accomplished with complete success.

OTHER ACCESSORIES

Film Lamps

Film lamps are necessary for indoor shots. In the past, intraphoto lamps were used almost exclusively, often being used in combination, in order to produce a sufficient amount of light. Such combinations were also mockingly called 'antlers' due to their form. They emitted about 1500 to 2000 watts and sufficed for the lighting of rooms about 3-4m. high.

Not only was the weight of these lamp collections a hindrance, but the heat radiated by each of the 500W. bulbs was more than a little irksome for all involved. For these reasons considerably less filming was undertaken indoors in the Double-8 era than nowadays, for in the meantime film and camera techniques together have considerably reduced the problem of filming using artificial light.

Modern amateur film lamps are exclusively halogen lamps. There are numerous types: it would be impossible to enumerate them all here. Basically they are all substantially smaller and lighter, mostly about 1000W., yet considerably more powerful than two 500W. tungsten lamps, as the halogen light has a completely different

(cont. on p. 66)

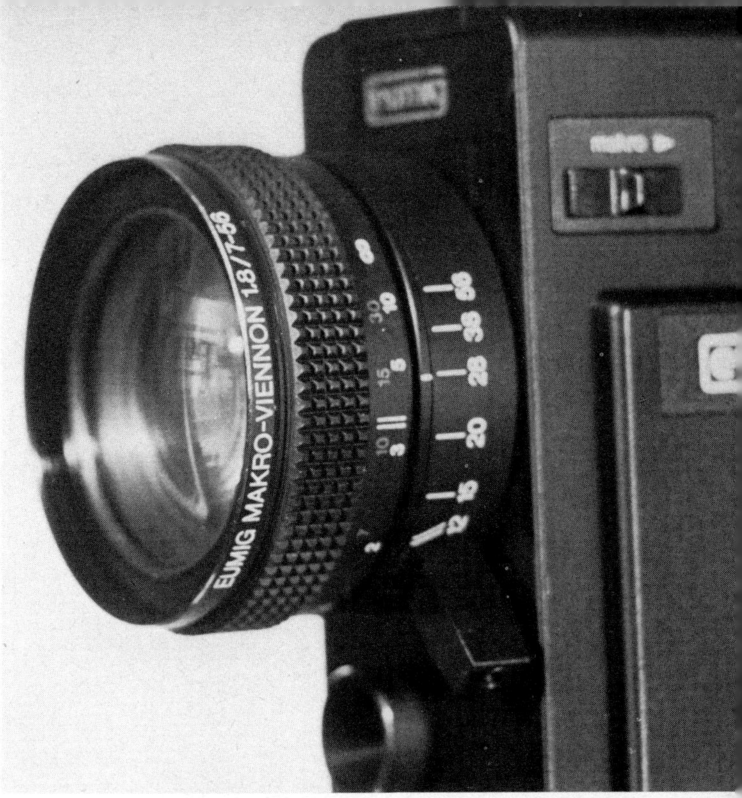

Vario lens on an Eumic ciné camera

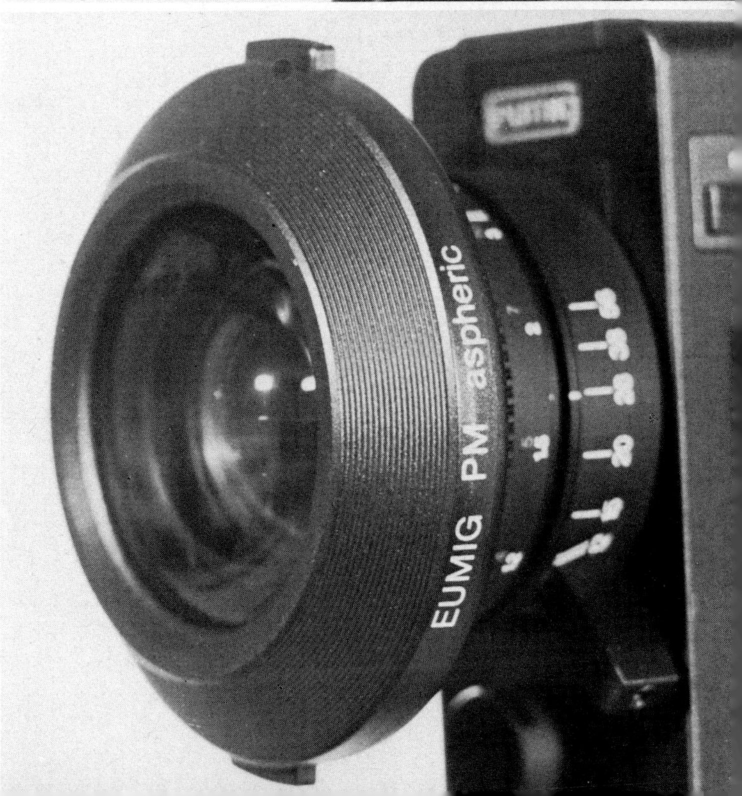

The same lens with a wide-angle adaptor placed in front of it, approximately doubling the field of view

ZOOM LENS (variable lens)

The five pictures show the effect of a variable lens. All the shots are taken from the same camera position

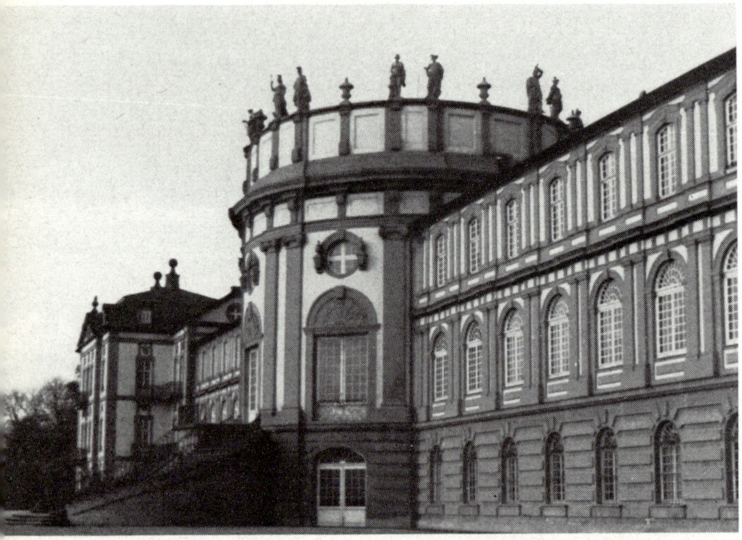

Starting-point
Focal length 7mm. (wide-angle)

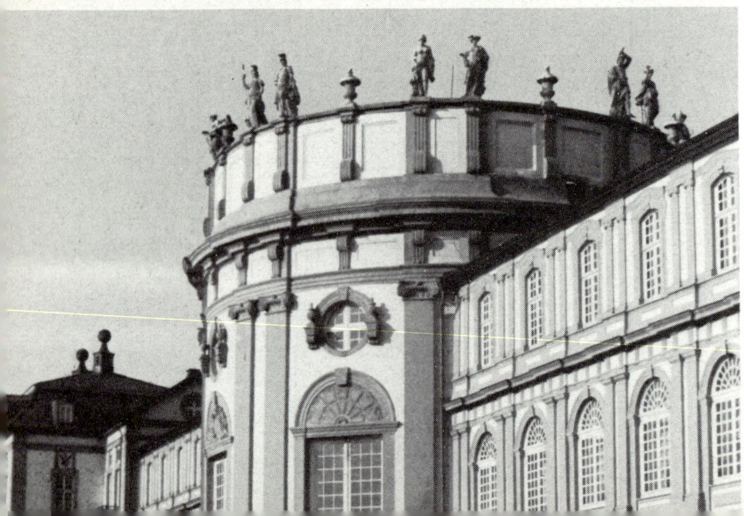

Focal length 15mm. = 2 x zoom

Focal length 35mm. = 5 x zoom

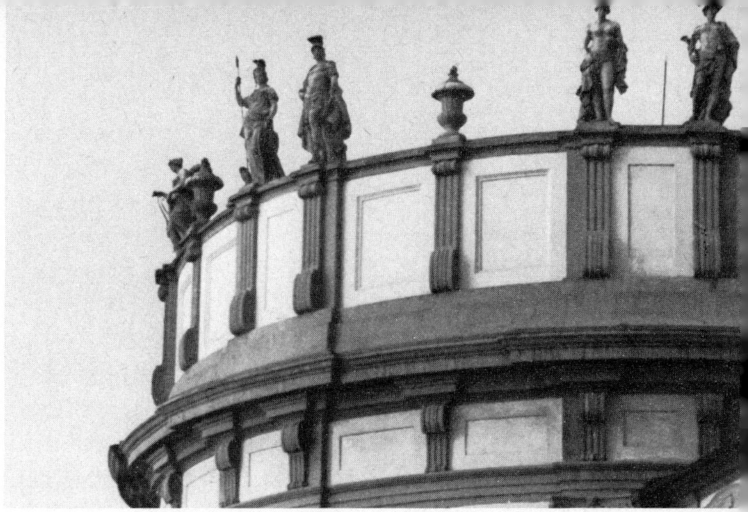

Focal length 56mm. = 8 x zoom

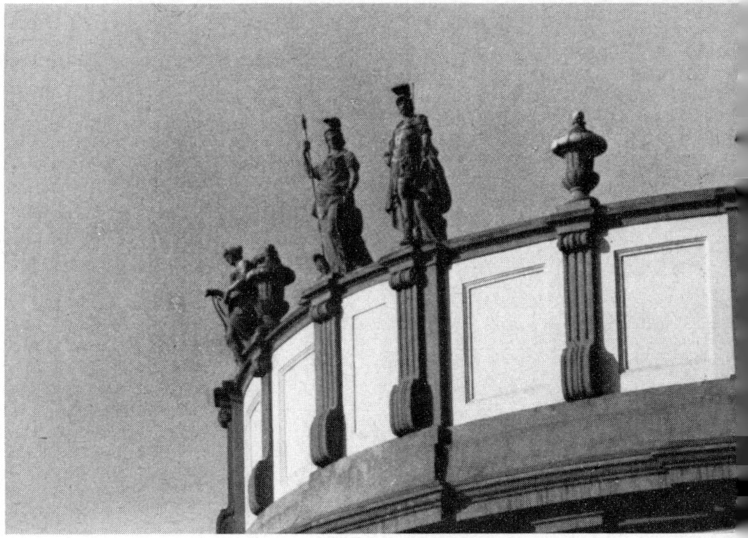

Focal length 70mm. = 10 x zoom

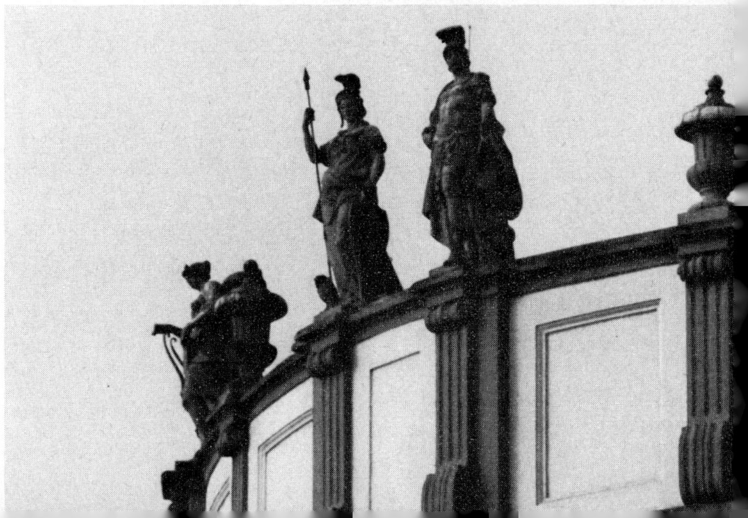

construction. Both lamp types however produce artificial light equivalent to 3,200 on the Kelvin scale, all Super-8 cameras being made in accordance with this. For 2 x 8 films a Type A artificial light film is necessary.

As a rule halogen lights are secured to the camera by means of a bracket (in the tripod screw thread). Consequently if they are screwed on correctly, the light angle of the lamps conform to the viewing angle of the camera.

Any film lamp may of course be screwed on to the tripod, allowing free movement around a room. However, if the room is to be evenly lit, several lamps are needed.

Nearly all film lamps are powered by mains electricity, so require a lead to the wall-socket. When using a number of lights, it is necessary to establish how much current they can take. The values can easily calculated with the following formula:

$$\frac{\text{Watt}}{\text{Volt}} = \text{Amp}$$

which related to film lamps means:

$$\frac{\text{Watt} = 1{,}000 \text{ Watt}}{\text{Volt} = 220 \text{ Volt}} = \text{approx. } 4.5 \text{ amps}$$

The number of amps the circuit can stand can be judged according to the fuse. If you possess a 6A. fuse, which was previously the norm, you can use a lamp of 1,000W. quite safely, but a second such lamp would overload the circuit: it would require a 10A fuse. It is always wise to calculate ratios exactly. In modern homes, the circuit usually includes 15A. fuses, so that there would be no difficulty with the example given.

Some film lamps are equipped with 2,000W. from the start. For this, two lamps of 1,000W. each are combined in one unit, so that they can be used independently of each other or both together. The basis of this idea stems from the fact that a 1,000W. light gives a coverage of about 3m., which is insufficient for large rooms. There is no straightforward answer as to when it is better to use one lamp with 2 x 1,000W. or when instead to use two separate lamps with 1,000W. each. Without doubt the 2,000W. lamp is easier to handle, as the camera and film lamp together form one unit and the lighting is precisely correct. Taking into consideration the need for the room to be evenly lit, I would personally prefer two individual lights, as their positions can be staggered, so that the whole depth of the room is illuminated. According to the law of physics, which states that the light is reduced to the square of its distance, one must reckon when filming that it is darker in the depths of the room than it is in the correctly illuminated foreground, even if this does not appear to be so. A second lamp placed in the room will remedy this to some extent. Incidentally, this is fundamentally the same for all film lamps whether tungsten or haolgen.

As such apparatus becomes very hot in a

small space of time, the lamps should be switched off to cool after about every five or six minutes. In normal use the halogen burner has an average life expectancy of about 15 working hours. Considering that a Super-8 film lasts for about three minutes, fifteen hours equals a vast amount of artificially lit film.

Some halogen lights are fitted with flaps in front of the burner, which condense the light slightly, but above all protect the person filming from being blinded. Another and more important reason for these flaps is to protect the burner from mechanical damage. Any touching of the tube, particularly with fingers, should be absolutely avoided. It is extremely sensitive to tracs of sweat and grease, which not only discolour the burner, but also adversely affect both the power and the life expectancy of the lamp.

Lamps that are powered by accumulators rather than by the mains have been developed by the manufacturers for use in the garden or on a camp-site. The accumulator is about the same size as one found in a car and recharged from the mains after use. One charging is sufficient for about six or seven minutes, after which its performance declines very rapidly and it must be recharged. The relatively short duration time is conditioned by the great demands made by these lamps, which extract vast amounts of energy from the accumulator in a short space of time. Moreover, the initial outlay required for this equipment is still very high, so it has been little used up until now.

To repeat, when using film lamps, Super-8 cameras must be adjusted to the artificial-light setting, while in Double-8 systems, special artificial-light film must be used.

Tripods

Which tripod for which camera? A question frequently asked. There are many mistakes that can be made just in buying a tripod.

Often tripods are bought which are more than a size too small. The tripod should provide the camera, though the actual model is not significant, with a firm support, a function which can only be fulfilled by a stable tripod. The tripod will only be stable if it is designed to accommodate the weight of the camera for which it is intended, and to suit the stature of the person filming. Both these factors form criteria by which our question can be answered.

Halogen film lamp: 1,000 watt

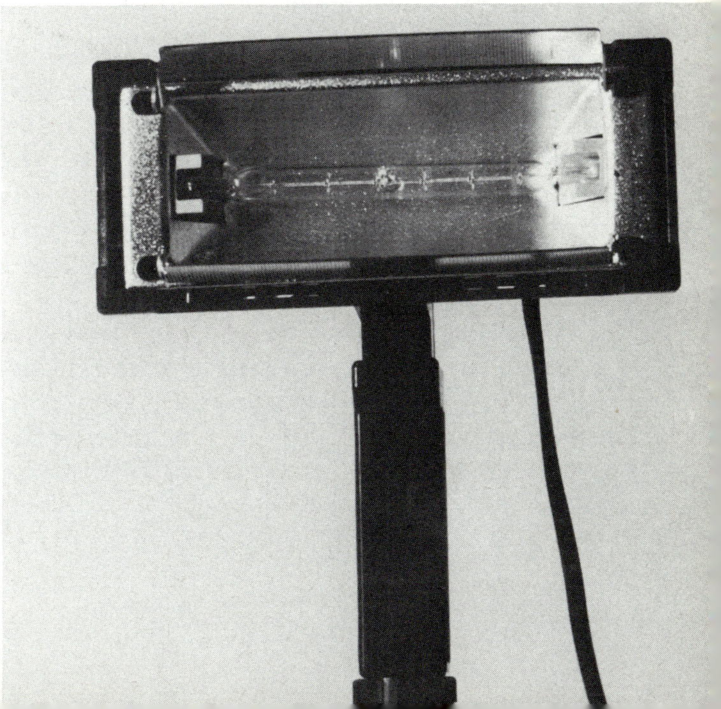

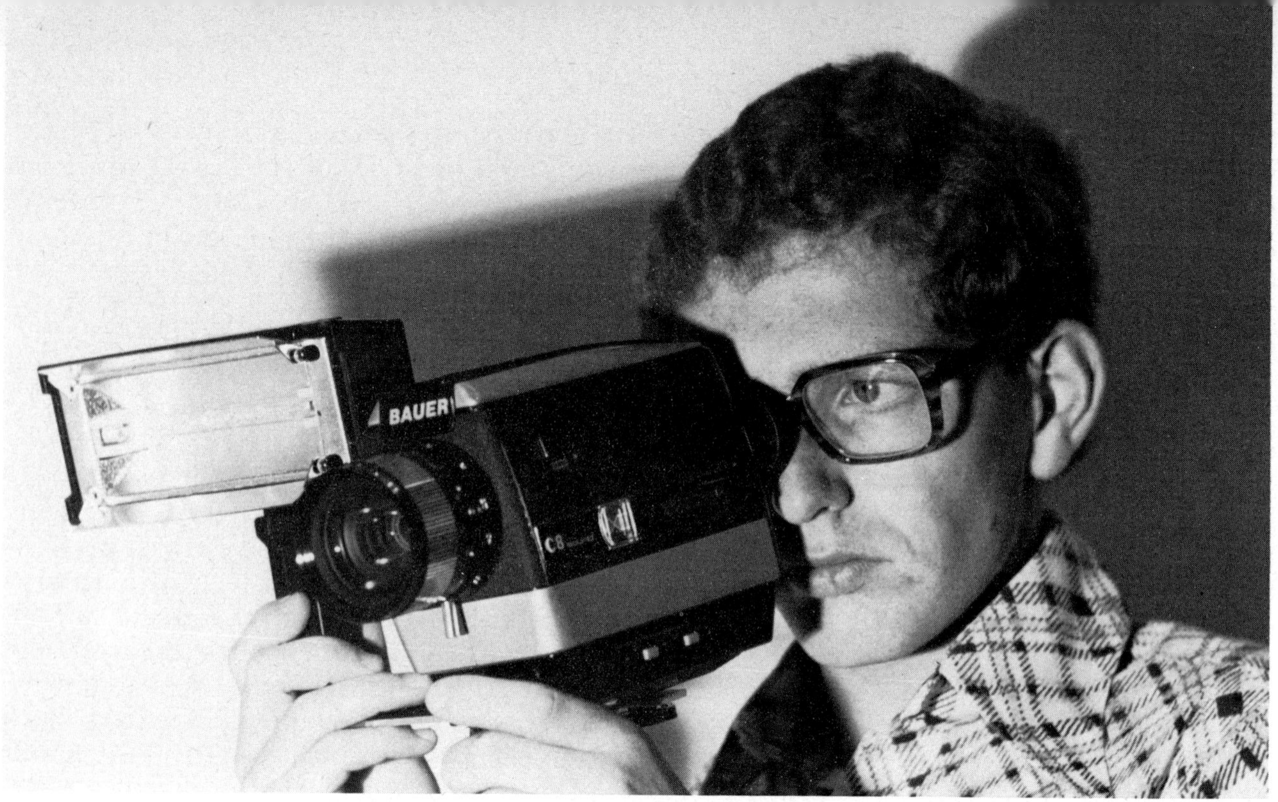

Ciné camera with halogen lamp attached

Occasionally of course it becomes extremely tedious to carry around a tripod that answers these requirements, as it is too big and heavy. However, anyone who resigns himself to this will see a positive effect on his filming that will compare favourably with many other films: no one can hold a camera as steadily as a good tripod!

It has already been stated that a tripod is absolutely necessary for single-frame shooting, with or without an automatic device. In this case it is particularly important that the position does not alter even a millimetre between the individual shots. The same applies for all trick shots and especially for filming titles, which cannot be achieved successfully without a tripod.

What does a suitable film tripod look like? The choice is vast, but not everything on the market is equally suitable for any camera. As already mentioned, the weight of the camera is a deciding factor, plus the length of the zoom lens. The further that the zoom lens can and will extend, the steadier the tripod should be.

We can begin with very small tripods,

which are certainly adequate for small, light ciné cameras. Often, however, they are so low that even an average-sized person has to bend in order to be able to film, although in itself this presents no problem, other than being rather uncomfortable. These small tripods correspondingly have thin legs, and are not suited for moving the camera during filming, as they would certainly rock. A shaky tripod is even worse than none at all!

Tripods of this type do not usually possess any special fittings. It is unusual to find a small tripod furnished with a tilt top. A tilt top makes possible the camera movements necessary during filming: horizontally and vertically. For this careful handling is necessary, which can only be guaranteed with a film tripod. Occasionally still-photo tripods with ball joints are used for filming. The purpose of this ball and socket joint is to allow the still camera to be turned in any direction and arrested in any position: it becomes a necessity when taking high or diagonal shots with a still camera.

Different rules apply for ciné cameras. Consequently a film tripod with a tilt top is preferable, and the photo tripod just mentioned is only of optimum use if the ball head can be replaced by a tilt top.

In good tripods the tilt top forms an integral part of the equipment. It must possess a fairly long guiding arm, so that the movement made is smooth and without jerks.

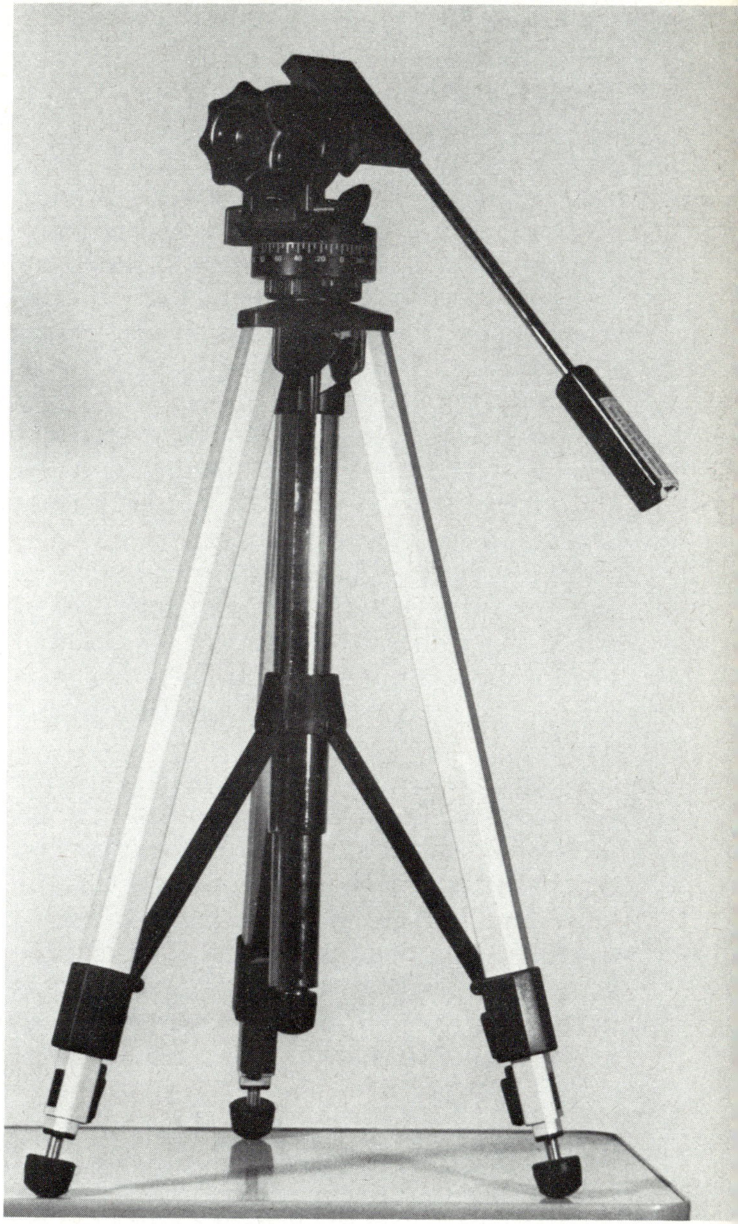

Three-legged tripod with tilt top

Another important requirement of a tilt top is that the supporting surface must be large enough to provide a satisfactory hold for the camera. The heavier the camera the greater the area of contact should be. The plate must be of rubber or some synthetic product similar to rubber to avoid any displacement of the camera once in position. Experience also proves that the holding screw must not be too short. It is not sufficient to fix the camera with one turn of the screw.

The swing arm, used to make smooth, even movements with the tilt top, is in all good tripods hollow so that a cable release can be passed through it. In this way, the camera is released by the arm of the tripod, and the film-maker has both hands free to guide the camera. Besides this the camera cannot be operated as gently by its own release as by the longest possible cable release.

Larger tripods are of course more luxuriously equipped. What must a tripod include in order to satisfy all the criteria? The height must be such that the camera is at the same level as the eye of the film-maker, or slightly lower. It must be possible to fix the legs at any height to account for unevenness in the floor surface, and they must be braced to each other so that the apparatus will not slide sideways.

Many tripods have a middle support, which helps compensate for difference in height, but to some extent detracts from the general stability. Normally the right height can be achieved without using the middle support.

The mid-support is however of great benefit for title and close-up shots. With such shots it is very tiresome or time-wasting to have to adjust the height or positioning of the camera on all three legs, and this can be done considerably faster with the mid-support.

When buying a tripod it is essential to check that the mid-support, whether fitted with a winch or with a winding-screw, can be fastened absolutely securely. It can happen that the support subsides due to the weight of the camera. Be careful!

The 'spreader' is, as already suggested, of great significance in respect of the stress and steadiness of the tripod. It not only prevents the legs from sliding sideways, but also provides additional support for the middle prop. Adjustable feet on the tripod are also an important feature. Normally tripods have rubber feet, which can make a firm grip on smooth wooden floors, carpets, or similar surfaces. On nearly all tripods these rubber feet can be screwed or pulled off, revealing metal points, which are eminently suitable for use on stone floors or soft earth. A pointed foot will provide a particularly secure hold on flag-stones, if it can be placed in the gaps between the paving.

Various methods are used for adjusting the height of the tripod. Even today this is sometimes done by screws that are screwed up tight to fix the length of the legs. Usually a clamp is used, which when compressed

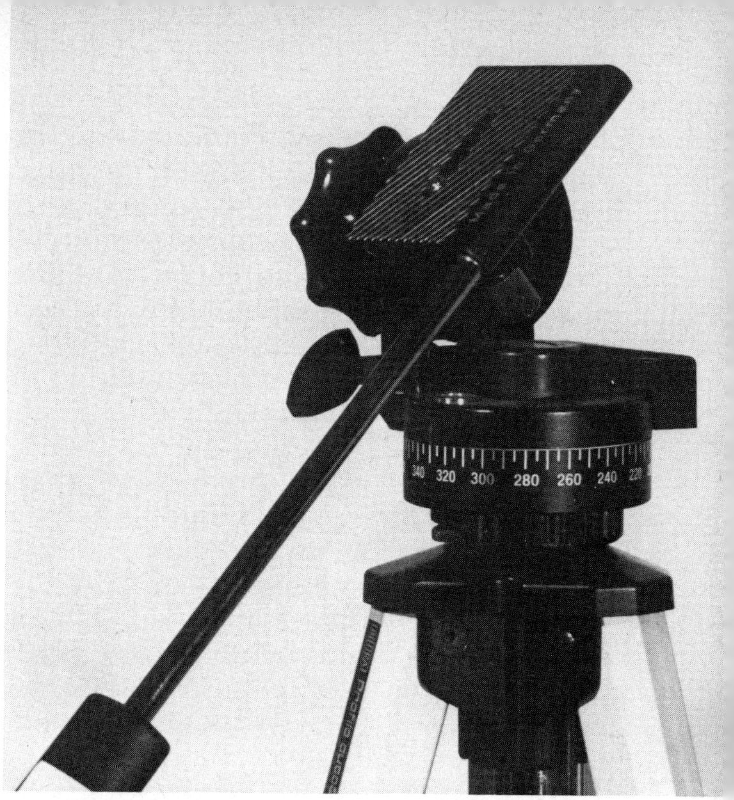

The tilt top possesses a sufficiently large surface area to accommodate the camera and a long guiding lever

prevents the legs from being further extended. The process is quicker when using tripods with clamps of this type. Moreover, the clamps are barely sensitive to external influences and accessible for easy cleaning, while a screw thread can easily be contaminated by sand or similar substances, which are difficult to remove. Above all, however, the clamp functions more speedily, a particularly valuable feature in the cold months when gloves may have to be worn while the tripod is being set up.

Some tripods include a spirit level in the top part, which can certainly be useful, but should not be considered a deciding factor when choosing your equipment. The picture to be taken can be seen clearly in the camera's viewfinder, and it is seldom critical that it is set absolutely vertically. In any case the spirit levels incorporated in a tripod are usually so small that they do not allow an exact adjustment.

The colour of the tripod is of no significance. Most tripods are chrome coloured or black anodized. Sometimes, however, a whole range of colours is offered. Black tripods do not create any reflecting surfaces, which may be a distinct advantage if they are to be set up in hiding, for instance for taking animal shots. Anything else is more or less a question of taste or fashion. There is not always an answer to the complaint that a tripod is too heavy for one or another purpose. For those film-makers who on the one hand must not be too weighed down, mountaineers and hikers for example, but on the other hand recognise the limitations of filming by hand and do not want to forgo use of a tripod, the answer is a single-leg tripod. It is surprising how many film-makers do not seem to be aware of the existence of this light and extraordinarily useful gadget. A single-leg tripod cannot of course supplant a more robust tripod, but may provide an indispensable alternative on certain occasions.

The single-leg tripod consists of one extendable support, with a coil on the upper end in which to screw the camera, and can be extended enough for the camera to be at eye-level during filming. Of course it is then necessary to hold the tripod steady, but even so the gadget is sufficiently stable to allow, after a certain amount of practice, the person filming to use even long focal lengths without the horizon beginning to waver.

From my own experience I can say that I have always been able to find room for a single-leg tripod in my rucksack. It weighs very little and takes up hardly any space.

In some circumstances it is not possible to accomplish anything with a three-legged tripod, as it curtails mobility. Every new arrangement takes so long that spontaneity is lost. The simple, 'quick' single-leg tripod also lends itself well to these situations.

Some tripods are constructed in such a way that the middle support can be taken out and used as a single-leg tripod. However, for this it is important that the mid-support can be adjusted firmly and smoothly. If such a support is to be used as a single-leg tripod, it is necessary to guard against possible mechanical damage, for instance a burr or something similar could form which would severely affect the smooth adjustment of the mid-support. Thus the scheme obviously implies a compromise, which should be considered carefully.

As most film-makers are also car drivers, how to manage filming from a car is a recurrent question. The manufacturers have produced a special car tripod for this purpose. The construction varies: not every tripod can be used in every car, as the differing windscreen shapes require differing fixtures. However, all models are based on a similar principle: almost always one, two, or three suction pads are stuck to the inside of the windscreen. The suction pads hold a support for the camera which is thus positioned right up against the windscreen in front of the passenger seat. With a long cable release the driver can operate the camera whenever he wishes without any trouble. Some models are additionally supported by a pole similar to a single-leg tripod, although this has little significant effect on the stability of the camera.

Film from a car is best taken at speed 24, which takes into account the unevenness of the road.

There are yet many more tripods on the market: pocket tripods, clamp tripods and other similar small gadgets of varying descriptions. However, they are too small to use with most ciné cameras, although eminently suitable for some still cameras, in which the exposure lasts only a split second; during filming of course a steady support is necessary for the whole film length of 6 to 8 seconds.

There is another little-known type of tripod yet to mention: the shoulder tripod, which can be used for still photography and for filming with a lens of a long focal length. This tripod also comes in a variety of designs, but all have a shoulder rest to allow

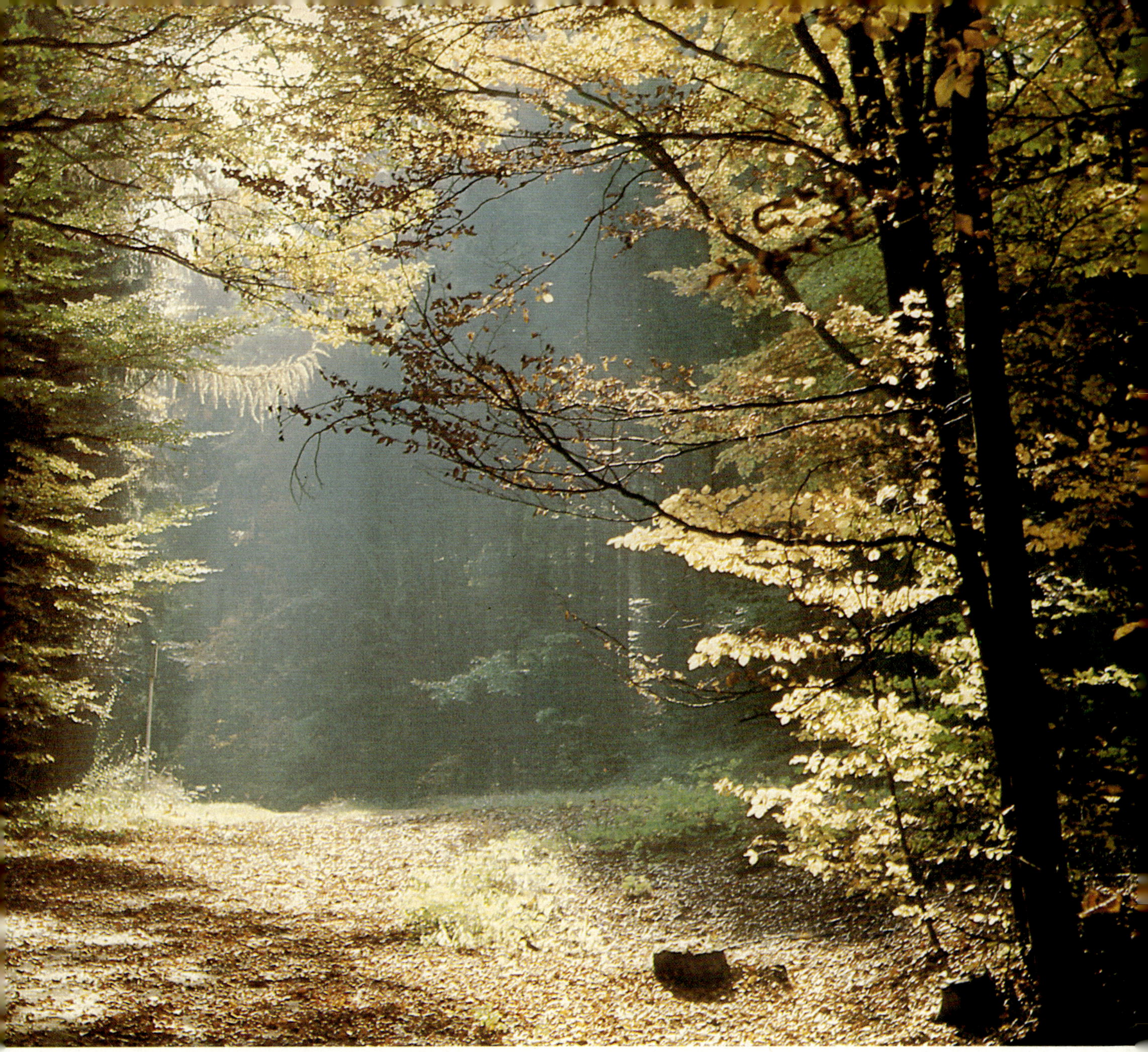

Plate 7: Opening scene over a bridle-path. The autumn stillness constrasts effectively with the movement of the horse-riders appearing later

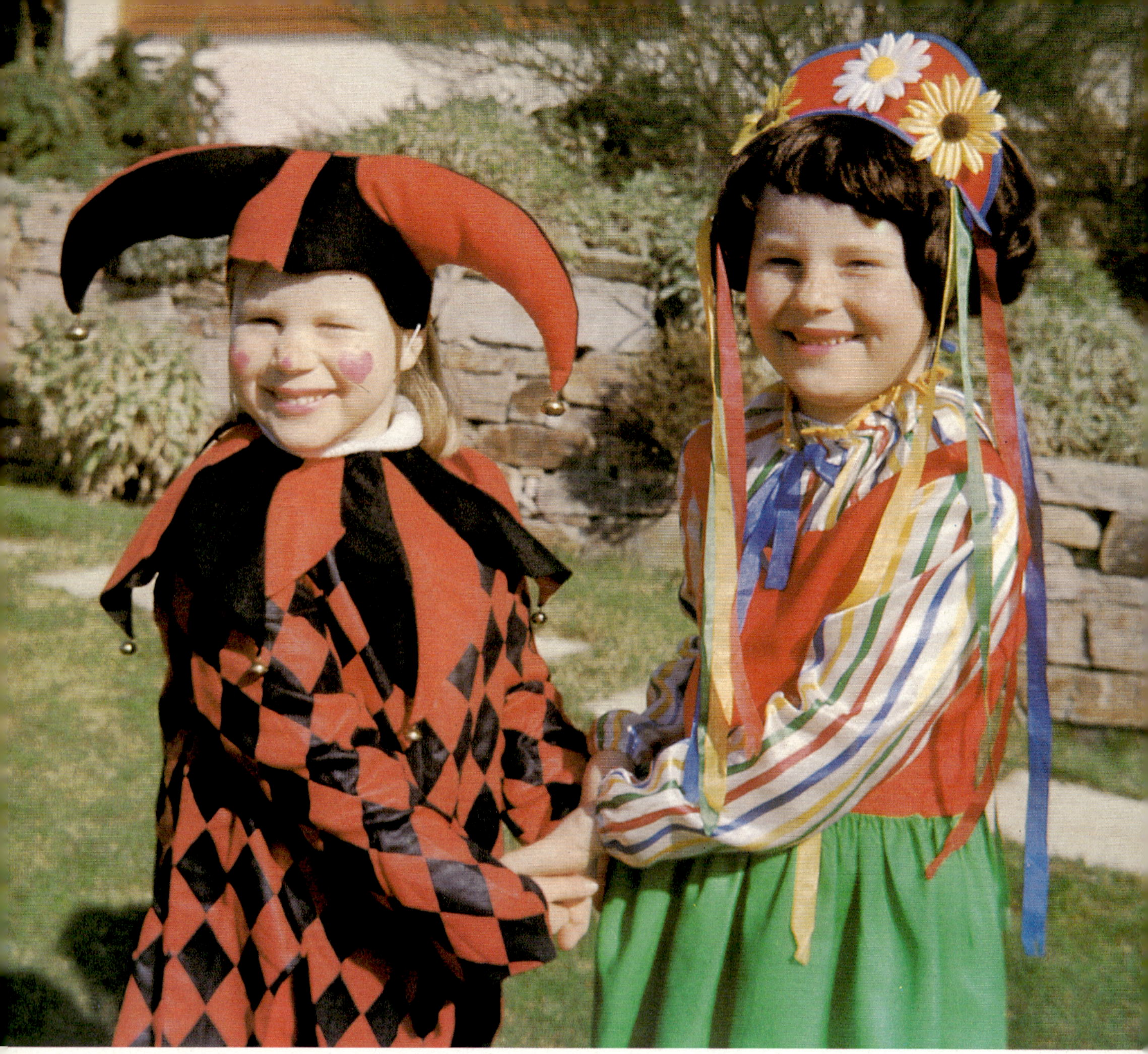

Plate 8: Children in gaily coloured costumes at carnival time are an excellent and very popular film theme

smooth picture taking. Frequently a release cable leads from the shoulder pad to the camera, so that you can release the film very gently. The rule here is press the button and release it gently.

One limitation of the shoulder tripod should be mentioned: if faster breathing is caused by physical exertion, the chest movements will affect the shoulder rest and endanger smooth running of the film. In this case it is preferable to use a single-leg tripod, but otherwise a shoulder pad is a good idea and moreover can be folded up small.

Tripod dollies

For those who like filming indoors, the manufacturers have developed a very interesting accessory in the form of the tripod dolly. This is a moveable base to which almost any tripod may be attached, the three feet of the tripod being held by clamps, so that the tripod plus camera may be moved around the room. On suitable floors this provides a quick and easy way of turning the camera in different directions.

Tripod dollies are still little known, especially as their range of uses is relatively limited, although they are an important feature of indoor filming.

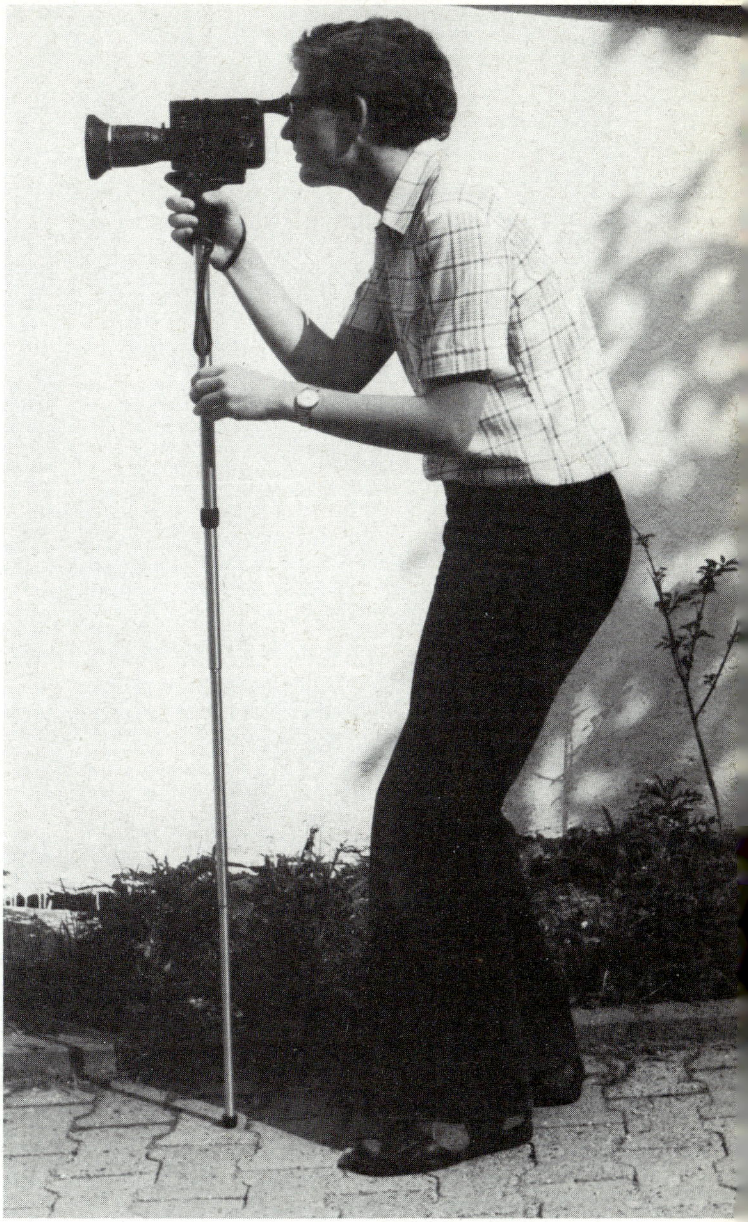

Camera with light and practical single-leg tripod

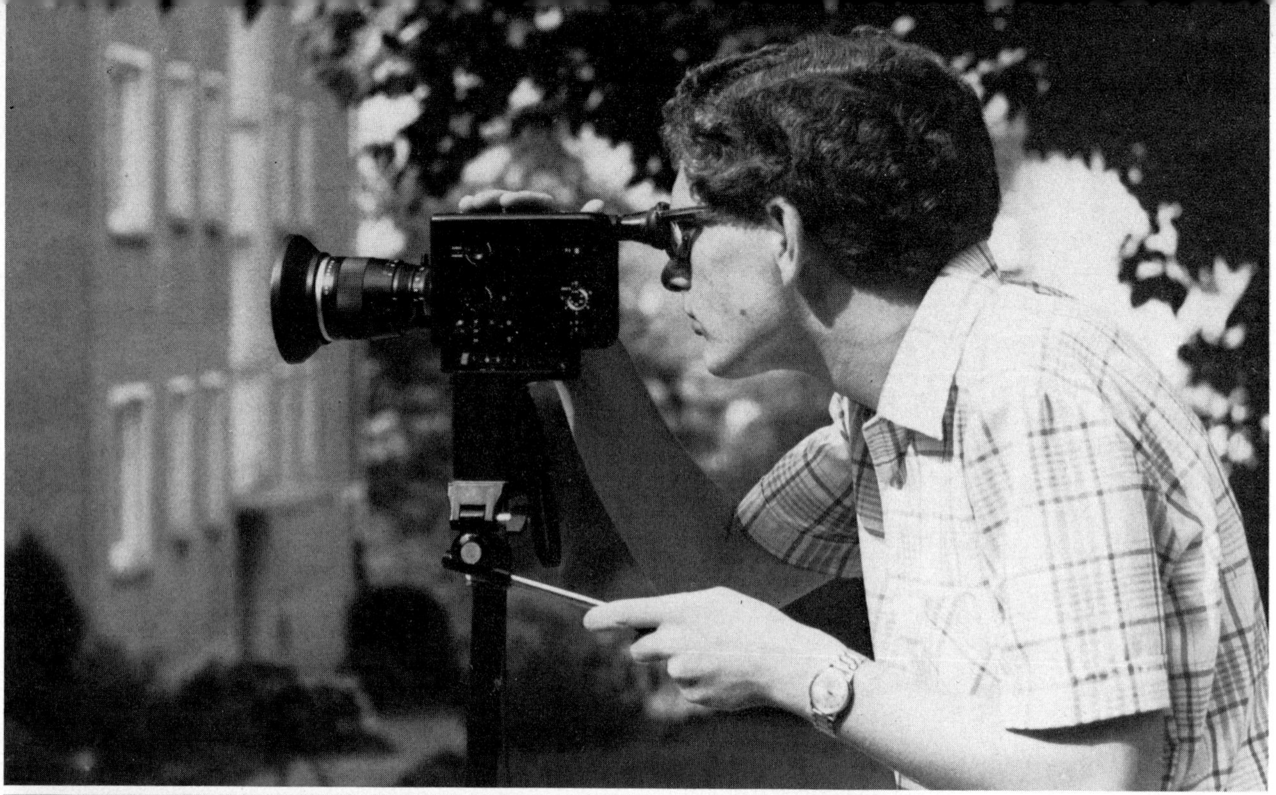

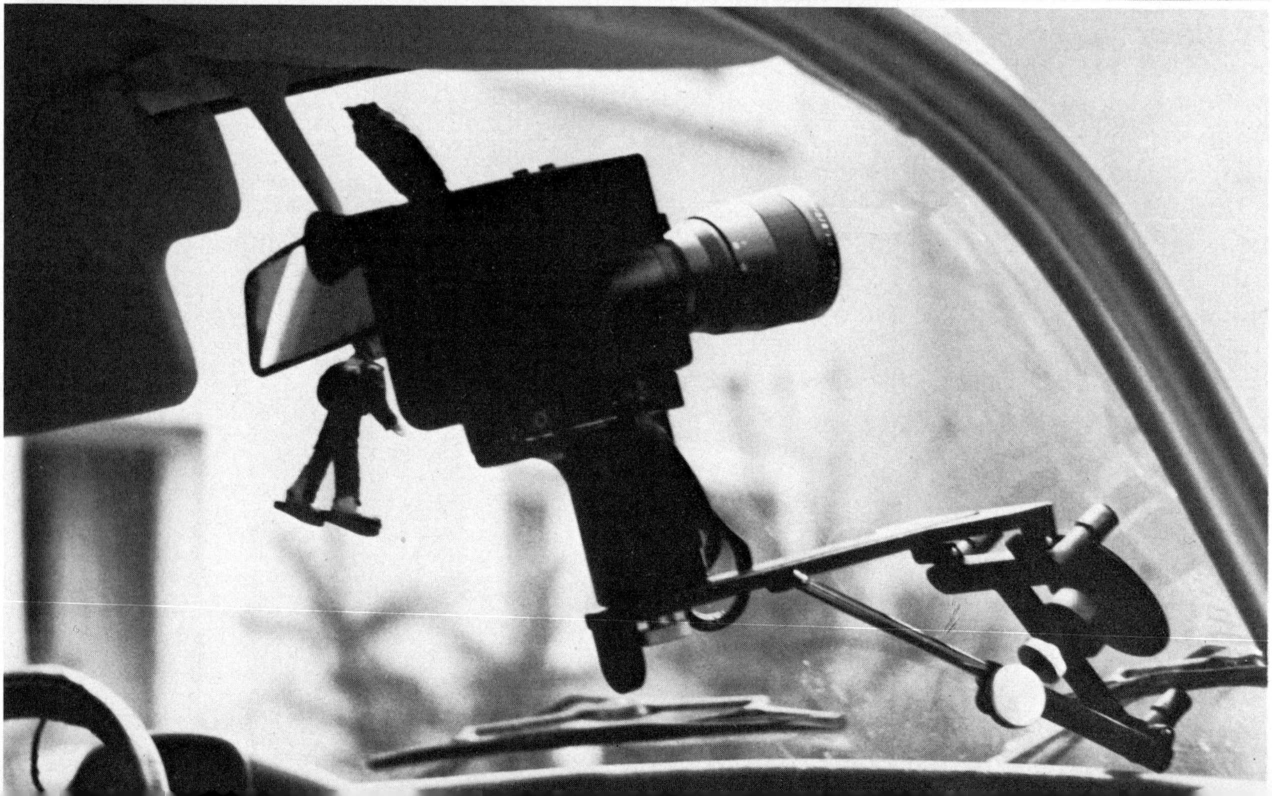

The object of the tripod, namely to prevent the camera wobbling or swaying during filming, must be borne in mind when deciding on a purchase. A light tripod, in other words one not sufficiently stable, cannot satisfy these requirements. Moreover, a larger tripod is more suitably matched to body size.

Release

The camera should of course be released as smoothly and gently as possible, and all release buttons are designed with this in mind. The cable-release, already mentioned in connection with the tilt top, is the most frequently used. It is screwed into the camera contact or another contact point provided for this purpose. This eliminates the possibility of spoiling the picture by jerky movements. Film should never be taken without a cable release when using a tripod, whether it is large or small. The most stable of tripods is of no use if poor picture taking makes everything vibrate. In addition the cable-release should be longer than normal.

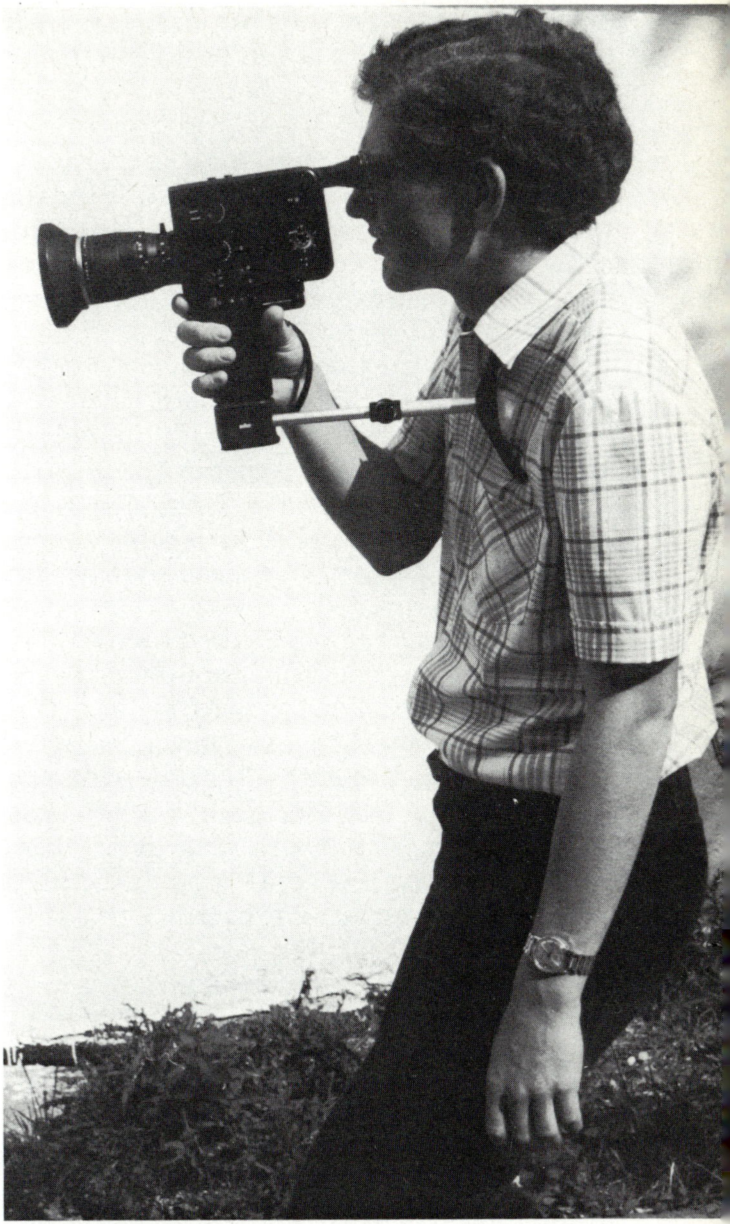

A shoulder tripod is useful for shots with long focal lengths

Camera at eye-level on a single-leg tripod, for which the mid-support of a cinema tripod was used

A car tripod mounted on the car windscreen. It is fixed to the glass by suction pads

Sometimes it is only 10cm. long, which is totally pointless; it should be at least 25cm. long; the longer the better. There are cable-releases up to 10m. long. Pressure of the hand should not affect the camera, so the longer the cable-release the better. If the tilt top has no provision for pulling the cable-release through the arm, it can be fastened to the arm by means of a rubber ring, so that the end result is the same.

A very long cable-release also becomes necessary if a considerable distance between the film-maker and the camera is unavoidable. This then requires quite a lot of pressure if its impact is to be carried over a long distance, perhaps 10m. of cable. There is, however, a better and more economical way of doing this.

All ciné cameras possess their own battery for transporting the film and operating the automatic lens-aperture control, and this may also be used in association with an electrical remote release. This type of release is considerably smaller than a 10m. long cable release. It comes in lengths of up to 15m.; moreover several may be joined together to cover a total distance of about 100m. Any great length would pose problems insofar as the resistance in a long cable would be too great for the energy passing through.

An electrical remote release may of course be used in place of a cable-release in normal circumstances, in which case the whole length of it need not be unravelled. On every electrical release there is a switch, which the film-maker holds in his hand, to release the shots. The scene length may be dictated at will and without involving a time-lag even at a great distance.

In which circumstances is it advisable to have a very long release? To take an example, filming a bird-table in the garden. Perhaps an otherwise shy creature regularly visits here and the intention is to film it. To do this the camera is set up near the table, concealed as well as possible, and connected to a remote release of the required length. The camera must naturally be on exactly the right setting. When the bird arrives the film-maker can operate the release from his observation point without being noticed. This is only one example of the way in which a remote release can be used – it is not difficult to think of others.

It rarely happens that the length of the electro-release is inadequate. In such exceptional circumstances the answer is a radio-controlled release, which consists of two completely independent parts: the transmitter, placed with the film-maker or photographer, and the receiver, which is connected via a release button to the camera, positioned on a steady tripod; both transmitter and receiver are fitted with an antenna. With this arrangement the camera can be operated at a great distance, up to about two miles. The filming of extremely shy wild animals is a good example of when such a method might be put into practice. Howerver, this relates mostly to professional filming, as there are without doubt few amateur film-makers who would pursue a hobby on this grand scale.

The 'blimp-box' should also be mentioned in this connection. This is a casing that is fitted round the whole camera and provides for noiseless work. It is always used with the wireless release if the person filming is to remain both invisible and inaudible.

The term automatic release is already known in relation to still photography, where it is normally used for all group shots. In filming it may occur that the whole family wants to be filmed, at the tea-table, for instance. Even if the automatic release is not inbuilt, there is still a solution to the problem for ciné cameras.

An automatic film release works in quite a different way, however, to an automatic photo release. In a ciné camera it functions as follows: the spring mechanism is wound up and runs down over a time span of about 12 seconds. The length of the shot released can be decided, usually within a range of one to thirty seconds. When the prescribed time has run out the camera switches itself off automatically via the release mechanism. This additional circuit is fixed to the cable release coil in the camera or in the plug for the electro-release.

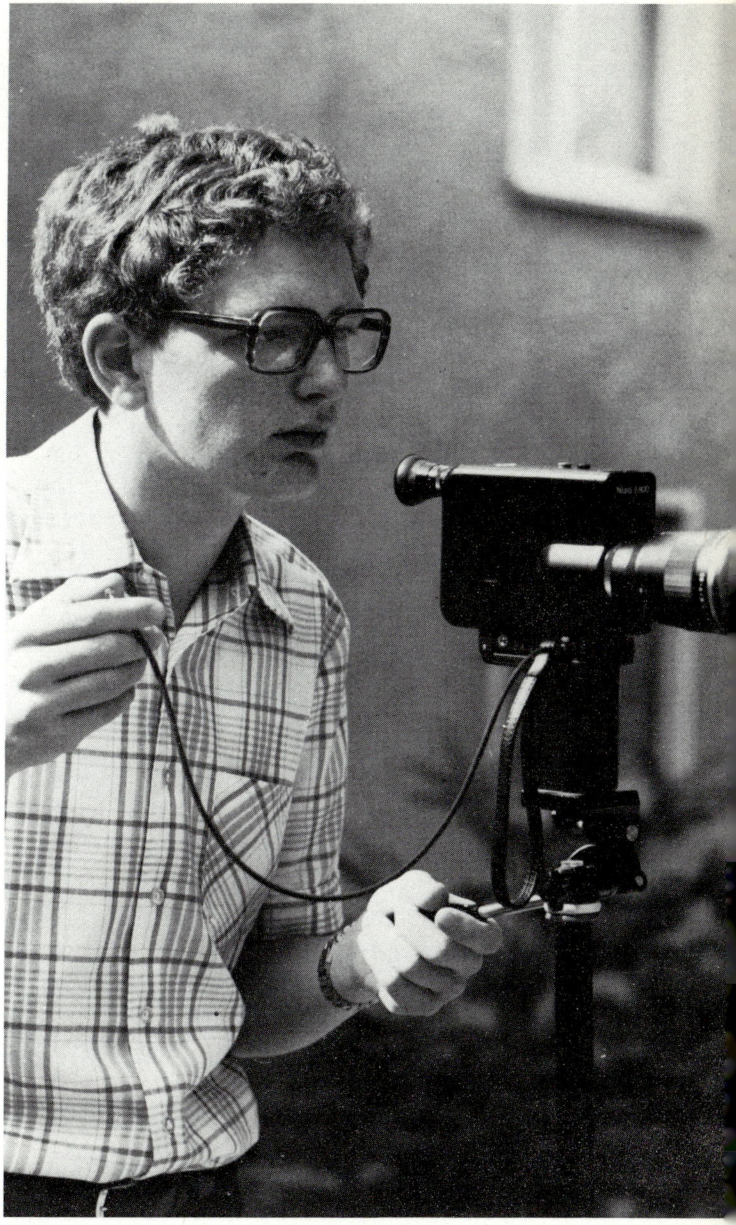

A long cable release allows for smooth operation of the camera

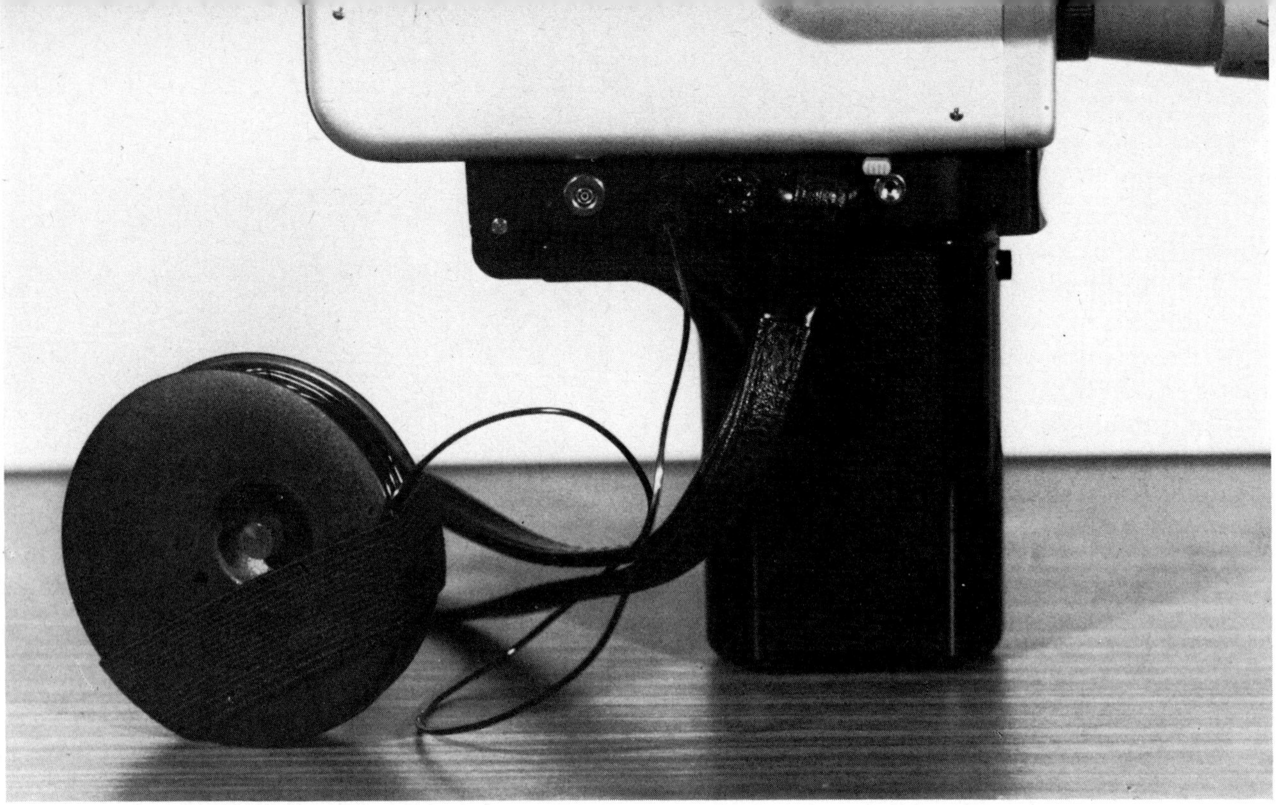

Electromagnetic remote release with a length of 15m. Several connected together give a maximum length of up to 100m.

In the section on 'superior cameras' the automatic single-frame device has already been mentioned. Only a few cameras include this as an integral part, as it is relatively little used. This circuit may also be built on subsequently by means of an additional interval-timer.

An interval switch is powered electronically by several batteries. It automatically gives the camera a switch-impulse. The interval can be set at will within certain limits – for instance, for three shots a second or for one change in thirty seconds. The interval switch is normally connected to the case for the electric cable. With additional grips it may also be fixed to the tripod screw thread on the camera. It can also be screwed directly on to a separate tripod.

It requires careful consideration to work out which of the many types of film-release on offer will be best suited to one's individual film-work. Certainly hardly anyone makes use of all the methods, but a cable-release is certainly a necessity.

Bags and Cases

Sooner or later every film-maker has to face the problem of what to do with his equipment and accessories. Although it is easy enough to buy a bag into which everything will go, this is not a complete solution to the problem. Rarely are all the accessories required for filming. It is usually possible to judge from time to time which accessories will be required, and thus to assemble only the necessary equipment.

Without doubt the carrying case provided by the manufacturers is the most useful. To film on a family ramble, for instance, nothing is required except for a lens hood and a spare film. Experience proves that in the majority of situations only the basic equipment is necessary.

The original bag has room for the camera, plus filters and a hood, several films, and perhaps a close-up lens. This comprises the basic equipment and is as a rule sufficient. Generally, most amateurs do not possess any further accessories anyway, and consequently a larger accessory case would be superfluous.

In order to carry optical attachments, trick lenses, and other extras another case becomes necessary. In this case the divisions are nearly always adjustable, so that it can be made to suit individual requirements exactly. For those keen on water sports, aluminium cases are ideal. When closed they are entirely waterproof, protecting the valuable equipment inside from splashes, particularly of salt-water. Moreover, aluminium cases come in a wide variety of sizes, and have the advantage of a small net weight.

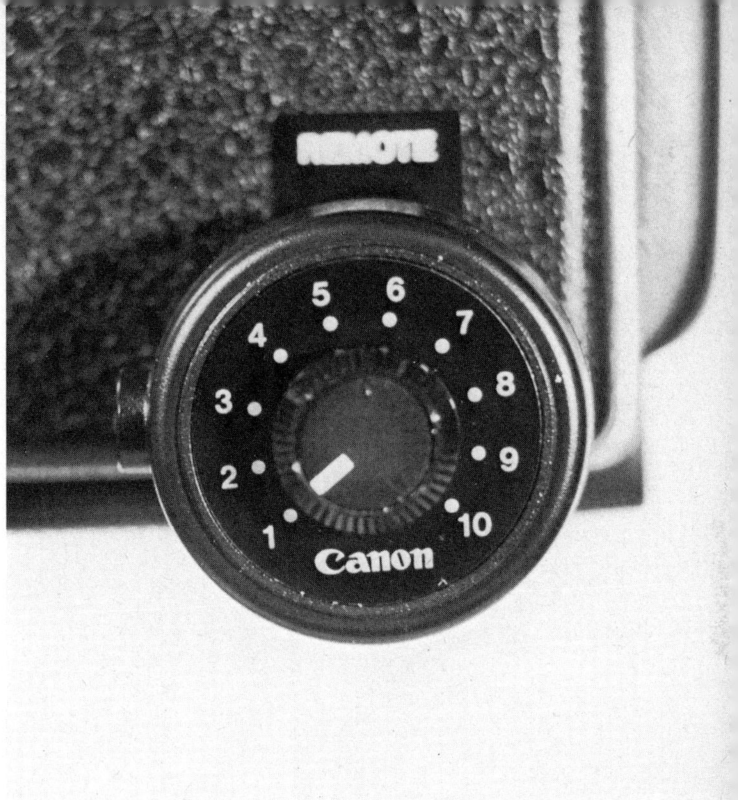

Timer on a camera, added at a later date

Sometimes it is thought desirable to be able to carry both film and photographic equipment in one big bag, which would seem initially to be logical and sensible. Yet think how big a bag you would need to accommodate everything and, more important, how heavy it would be. Optical equipment is heavy, above all lenses. Normally the idea of such a bag is best abandoned.

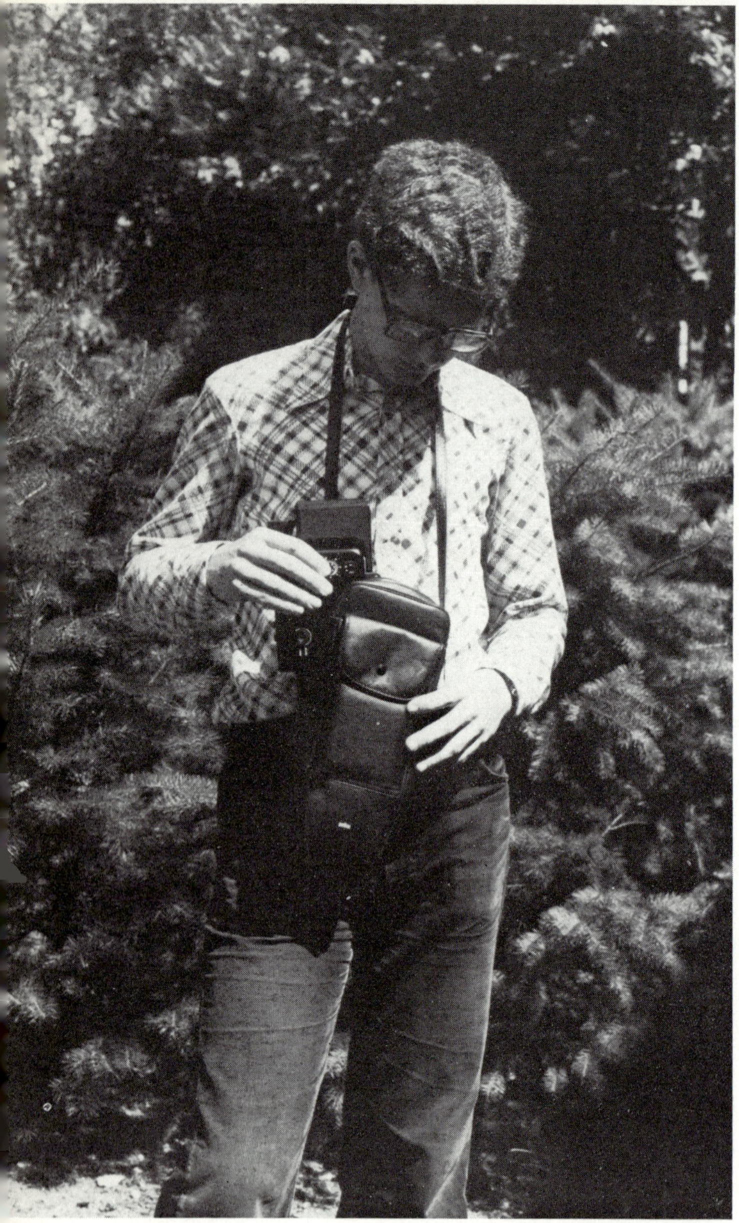

An exception would be on a car journey, where an enormous bag can be very useful, as it is only necessary to take out the actual parts required each time. The bag can be used as a storehouse.

Lenses, filters, and trick devices are made of optical glass, which is considerably softer than window glass and consequently appreciably more sensitive to mechanical damage. Because of this most optical components are sold in small leather purses, and it is highly recommended that they remain in these purses when put in a holdall or case. It is worth taking this additional care.

Anyone often on the move with his film equipment should buy a bag with two straps on the outside, either at the side or at the bottom, that will hold a single-leg tripod. There are several models of bags with this design. It is very tiresome to have to carry a tripod in the hand for very long, yet it is so light that it will not noticeably weight down a bag. It is most important that it is handy.

For larger tripods, bags are available that can be carried over the shoulder like a rifle, so that the weight causes as little hindrance as possible. Judging from experience, without a bag the three-leg tripod stays mostly at home or in the car.

A bag designed for the camera: small and handy

Aluminium cases often have one particular speciality, in that both the case and the lid are completely lined with foam rubber. With a small knife, which is included, holes can be made in the foam rubber to fit exactly the equipment, so the bag is exactly made-to-measure. If changes are made - a new camera or additional equipment is bought - a new lining can be obtained and the divisions can be recut to fit the new pieces. Incidentally, foam is also useful for filling gaps in the bag or providing extra padding.

Some bags are made in a soft material such as deerskin, and some have stiff sides, sometimes incorporating plywood. Softer bags wear better, and look to some extent more elegant, while hard bags on the other hand provide more protection against bumps and falls. Of course personal taste features above all, but it is also worth paying attention to expert advice and considering whether or not a soft bag is going to provide adequate protection.

Large bags usually have a firm frame, while among the smaller bags there are both firm and soft styles. The material used for the bag determines both the price and how it is made. Leather is without doubt the most expensive raw material, but nearly always makes up into the best-quality bag. Cheaper bags sometimes consist merely of cardboard covered in plastic. Naturally, the same standard of workmanship cannot be expected of them. As a rule, they do not last long, and so it is cheaper in the long run to buy a good leather bag.

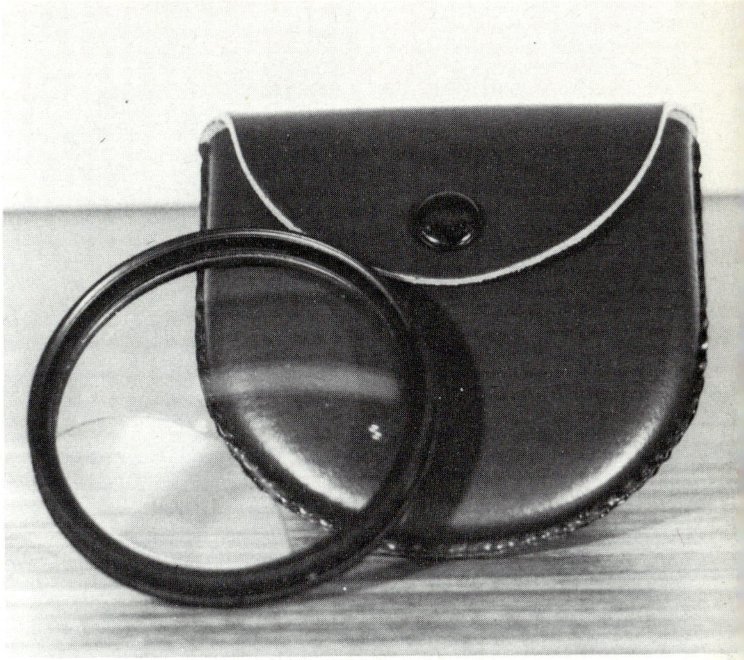

Purses for filters, lenses etc. The relatively soft glass cracks easily if not protected

Even bags for film equipment are subject to the whim of fashion. This is most obvious in the colours, which usually change again after a short time.

Colours are dictated by fashion in all fields but a long-lasting product like a good leather bag should be bought independently of such considerations, which means choosing the most neutral colour possible. The only point of importance is that it is appropriate for its intended use. All bags must be designed to prevent the rain getting in. There are also bag lids that shut so badly that the contents are not sufficiently protected. At best, the bags should be fitted with a throw-over lid, so that the rain can run off around it.

Clasps or buckles are particularly suitable for fastening the bag, as they can be quickly opened and closed. Moreover, nothing can be stuck in the way, as often happens with zips. If there are small children in the family, the bag must in any case be locked to stop them unpacking everything possible out of curiosity. In actual fact that is the main reason for buying a bag that can be locked, rather than fear of the equipment being stolen: a thief would certainly take the locked bag as well, and thereby get the contents.

It is important that bags be colour fast. That it must not be soaked in the rain goes without saying, but neither should the colour come off on clothes etc.

There are, then, a number of points to be considered just in buying a bag to hold the film equipment. As already said, the original bag should still be used. If a bag for accessories is chosen according to individual needs, every film trip should be made easy and comfortable.

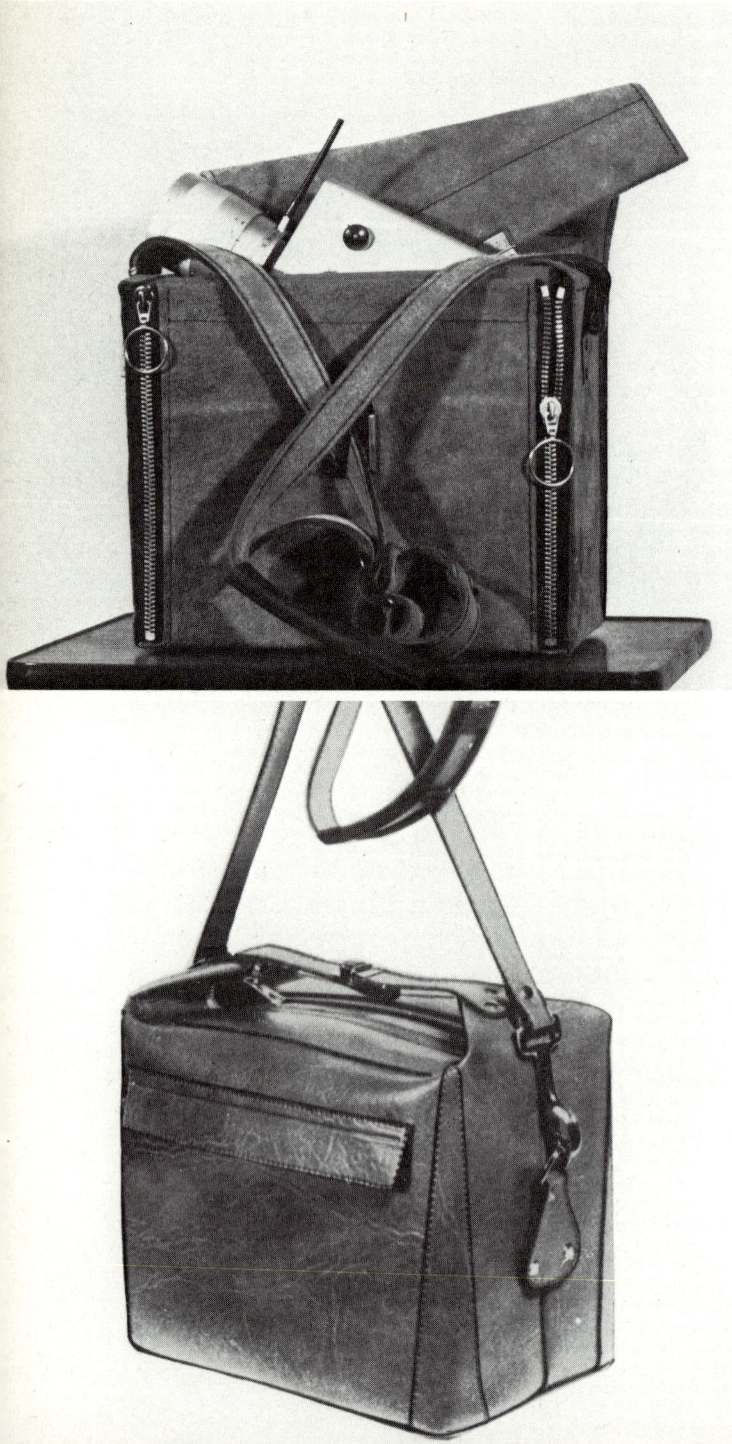

Hold-alls, providing plenty of space for the camera plus necessary accessories

FILMING

We now turn from a discussion of the theoretical possibilities of the camera, including its composition and accessories, in the first part of the book, to a discussion of filming itself.

Those now embarking on the following chapters have probably long since sought out the right camera with the aid of an expert or an experienced friend.

Now you must be itching to get to work and make your first film, and can hardly wait to give a 'performance'. However, you should first of all prepare a test film, to get everything right from the outset.

THE TEST FILM

Everything learnt so far about the wonderful potential of the new camera has come from books or catalogues, and is all theoretical. As with all things, the theory sounds impressive, but it is now time to put it to the test.

It is quite normal for a lot of things not to turn out as hoped or expected, to begin with, and this need not cause undue concern. Indeed, I hope that the first film will contain as many mistakes as possible, so that you can recognise them and learn how to improve in the second film.

Ciné cameras and still cameras are two fundamentally different things, something you will, at the latest, establish with your first film. Should the new camera have been bought especially for a holiday, it is absolutely essential to have the test film back before starting the journey, so that you can not only make a critical appraisal of the results, but also become as accustomed as possible to handling the equipment. This is very important to avoid unnecessary worrying on holiday.

Every ciné camera is accompanied by detailed instructions for use, providing comprehensive information about the techniques and handling particular to that equipment. As even those who are old hands at filming will discover something new somewhere on any new camera, the novice must without fail read all he can about his camera, although usually plenty of information is supplied when the camera is chosen in the shop.

Now to the test film. With the first film you produce you become the producer, director, lighting controller, cameraman, and production manager rolled into one - positions that in professional filming would be filled by skilled specialists. Even if you discuss your plans with the family or friends, the actual conception of it is yours: you alone decide.

First of all let it be said that when the first developed 15m. lay before you, the expectations of the first presentation are enormous. However, the first film should not be criticised as a whole as either good or bad; in practice it will have both its good and bad points.

I want to indicate from the outset which mistakes will arise and how they can be avoided. Be very critical about your test film in this respect. Do not allow sheer joy over the first production to cause you to overlook the weak points, which will without doubt exist. If amongst your friends you happen to know another cine photographer who could offer an opinion on your test film, discuss it with him. The more you do this, the better it will be for your filming.

It is now time to focus our attention in particular on any exposure failures, which the first film might possibly show. In the following paragraph I discuss the mistakes that most often occur. They will of course not all be combined in the first film: the film's errors and weaknesses depend on the individual film-maker. One film-maker produces one mistake, another film-maker produces other mistakes. Which mistakes might these be?

Tracking shot

One mistake that is often made, and not just by beginners, is caused by incorrect use of the zoom lens. This has already been discussed in detail. Can you still remember the correct procedure? 1. Adjust the viewing lens to your eye. 2. Adjust to the longest possible focal length. 3. Focus on the main object in the reflex viewfinder. 4. Re-adjust the focal length to the setting which is to be used for the shot. Now the picture will be in focus, even if a tracking effect is included during the shot. If a mistake is made somewhere along the line the subject will go out of focus during 'tracking', i.e. out of the depth-of-field area, which results in the picture being partially or completely blurred. Many films, not only test films, possess such zoom errors.

It is essential to test and to witness the effect of a zoom lens. To this end you will need to make travelling shots, back and forth. When the film is projected you will be able to establish whether the effect is too uneven. What causes this? When we look, our eyes are permanently moving, and consequently they take in a lot more of the surroundings than a camera lens is able to do. For this reason the tracking effect of the camera can not be compared with eye

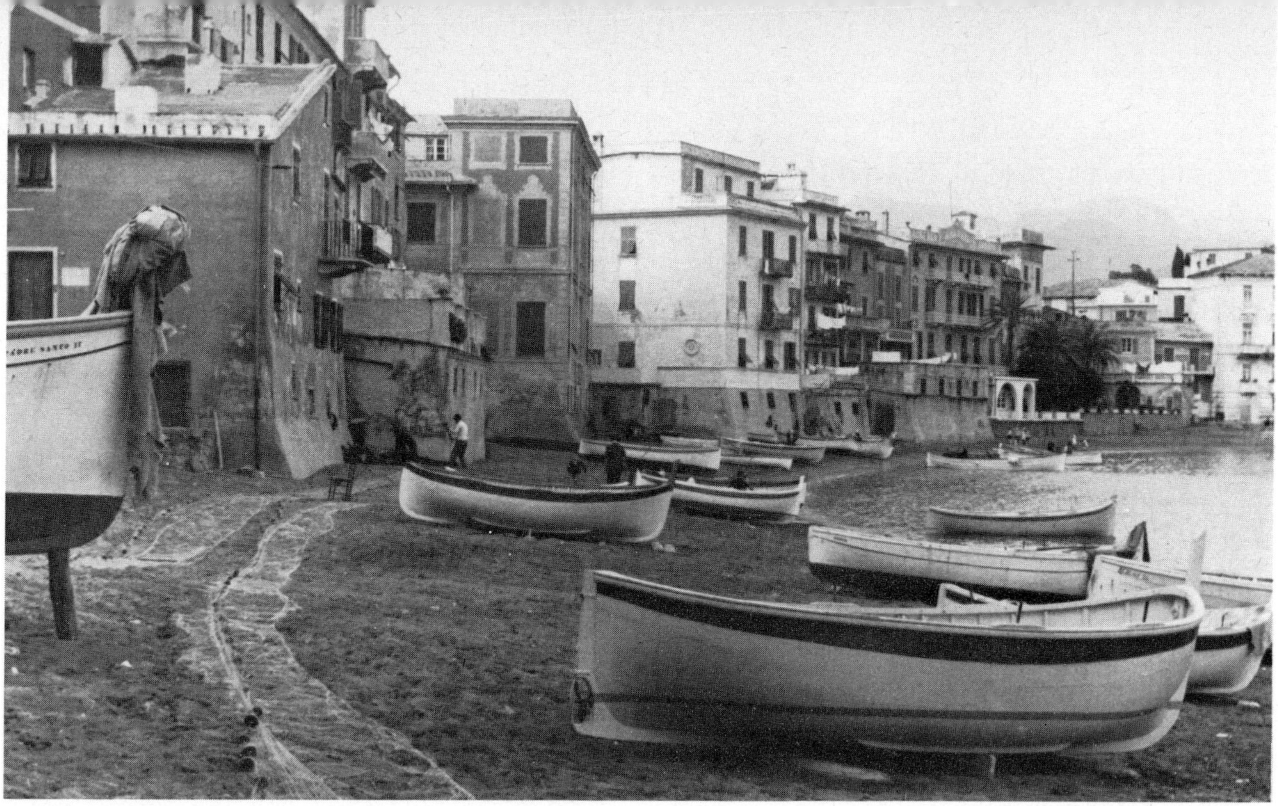

A wide-angle shot in preparation of a travelling shot. The camera finally arrives at the people in the boat. The travelling shot concentrates on the most important features of the picture

movement. The film shot represents only that segment of the surroundings which the camera is able to grasp.

For a correct tracking shot the following rule should be applied: Still-Movement-Still. Position the camera at the starting point and film for two or three seconds before beginning a tracking movement. Then move up to your target – which will by no means always take advantage of the entire focal range – and at that point let the camera run on for another two or three seconds. Example: the subject is a mountainous landscape and a village with a prominent church spire. The idea is to film the landscape and concentrate on the spire by means of a tracking shot. In order to achieve this, proceed in the following way: use the longest focal length to focus on the spire, then determine the focal length that shows the right section of landscape (wide-angle). Firstly, capture a shot of the landscape for about three seconds, then move in on the church spire (tele), until it becomes the dominating feature of the picture. At this end point the camera again, run on for another three seconds, directed at the spire and moving as little as possible. The travelling shot lasts about eight to ten seconds, which corresponds to the usual length of this type of scene.

When the film is projected such a process allows the audience time to grasp the whole panorama, experience the 'travelling' and take a calm look at the ultimate goal.

What has gone wrong when a shot misses the mark? Several things!

Above all the initial stillness is often not observed and instead the shot begins immediately with the tracking movement. Filming of this type, with no 'framework', will always appear disjointed.

Secondly, the camera must remain still during filming. An unsteady hold may otherwise cause the horizon to waver when using a long focal length. When a tripod is not available, the search for some sort of support to lean or rest on is usually forgotten. This results in a wobbly and uneven tracking effect, as two movements are at work here.

Thirdly, the scene is often stopped short at the end of the tracking movement. The eye, however, requires a stationary point at the end of the movement. The tracking shot should bring the scene nearer to the audience, and it is important to allow adequate time for this. After the movement, in other words after the tracking, a second still phase, likewise of two or three seconds, is essential. Those who make travelling shots by this logical process, prove in so doing that they have a basic understanding of the facts.

Something else: the less the travelling shot is used in film-work, the greater its effect will be. It is sufficient for this type of shot to appear three or four times in a 15 minute film. Enough is as good as a feast: this also applies to special effects in cine photography!

Pan shot

Back to the test film. Often the mistake is made of turning the camera to take in a panorama, because the desired segment does not fit in the angular field of the lens. You are without doubt aware of this problem and have attempted to make such turns. And what happens when the film is projected? In most cases the beautiful landscape trembles disappointingly past the viewer.

The fault lies with the rotation of the camera, in film terms referred to as a pan shot. Panning is a risky business as it usually goes awry. A rotation throughout 180° would need to take about two minutes to ensure a smooth effect when the film is projected. A pan shot is accomplished over the correct length of time appears quite still on the screen, rather than wavering, so that everyone can contemplate the scene and enjoy it without feeling 'sea sick'.

You will soon realise that it is hardly possible to make a panoramic movement by hand and achieve the amount of steadiness required. Even with a tripod it is not always successful. A special tripod adaptor exists for this purpose, but is used almost only by professionals due to its high cost. With this adaptor correct turning of the camera is guaranteed.

Normally a tripod will possess a tilt-top, but even if you turn its long lever quite slowly, the pan is still nearly always too fast. It is, however, practically impossible by hand, and requires a great deal of practice before it approaches success.

Something else you will realise: when the filmed panorama is so extensive, the small 8mm. film cannot portray the many details, at least not sufficiently well. There is always the tendency to compare the result with a slide, but as the size and taking conditions are quite different, such a comparison should be resisted.

In order to be able to pan, it is important to test out the way in which this can be done most smoothly. Be critical about your attempts to achieve this without a tripod.

Independently of this, however, the same rule applies for the pan shot as for the tracking shot: the camera should be stationary at the beginning and end. With regard to the limitations already expressed, the pan shot may be compared to the tracking shot: it begins at a stationary point, then comes the movement, then another rest – and always with a tripod. The pan shot however requires even greater consideration, as an excessively fast movement would cause trembling, whereas this does not occur with tracking shots.

In my own filming, I hardly ever use the pan shot. However, should you be determined to make one at all cost, the following points should be noted:

1 Pan in the scene in only one direction and do not return to the starting point or any particularly prominent object.

2 Hold the camera to your eye and practice the pan shot before you begin filming, in order to establish the position of the two end points. In the viewfinder of the camera you can see the section in isolation and can judge it better when it is split off from the whole.

3 Never 'fidget' during a pan shot, in other words, never move forward and back. In this instance even the slowest pan would be of no use – the great amount of movement would mean as a rule that the scene would have to remain unused. Nearly every film-maker makes this mistake once before he realises that shots made in this way do not work.

There is a trick to smooth panning: the use of a greater film speed! This means that speed 24 is employed instead of speed 18, and consequently the smoothness of the pan is accentuated, as the pan movement is automatically extended by a third of its running time. However, one limitation must be imposed even here: the foreground must not contain or consist of any people, as their movements would be protracted at speed 24. Nevertheless, for landscapes, panoramas, and similar shots, speed 24 can only have a positive effect.

Scene Length

The last point to have to criticise in your first film will be the length of the film scenes. This is a controversial subject between experienced film-makers. There are no general sayings about this as there are many factors affecting the case. Above all the length of the scene is dependent on the nature of its subject: obviously the more detail there is in the scene, the longer it must be, as more time is required to appreciate everything when the film is projected, whereas a close-up, for instance, will correspondingly require a shorter time.

If a sequence of movement is to be filmed, one has to consider whether it is necessary to represent every phase or whether a part of it would be sufficient. If the entire movement would demand a long time span, it could become monotonous. Possibly it could be divided into two sections filmed from different positions, which is at least worth considering.

You are of course primarily responsible for the length of your scenes. A vivacious person who is quick and sure about everything he does, will no doubt produce a film which consists of a larger number of shorter scenes than a film produced by someone who cares for peace and contemplation. Consequently every film style will be dictated by the mentality of its maker.

The choice of scenes, the scene length, and everything which contributes to a quiet, calm style, or conversely to a hectic and restless style is entirely dependent on the person filming. This point must be taken into account with all films. The difference becomes abundantly clear if two people are asked to film the same event: the result is two completely different films.

Basic Rules

There are still a few basic rules which apply, irrespective of the drift or style of the film or film-maker: a normal film scene should last about 6 to 8 seconds, or 4 to 6 seconds for close-ups. Tracking and pan shots of course require more time. The first film serves as a test-run and should contain the following three basic elements:

1 Tracking shot
2 Pan shot
3 Scene length

Projection of the first film provides an opportunity for careful examination of the points to be altered or improved in the next film.

THE IMPROVISED FILM

Nearly all films are improvised, and there are abundant reasons for this. Even people who are old hands at filming usually start without any preconceived ideas. They improvise and hope that some good will come of it - and usually it does! Thanks to their wide experience the elementary mistakes no longer appear. Anyone well acquainted with the basics may certainly dispense with any minute preparations for his next film.

There are naturally a few 'rules' with regard to ciné film, and film composition, which form the basis for a film which otherwise is, or has to be, improvised. The points concerning scene length, pan, and tracking shots, discussed in relation to the test film, obviously apply equally to any other film, regardless of whether these elements are planned or happen spontaneously. After a few films everyone will soon find their own style.

Film Motifs

The accentuated foreground has the effect of greatly enlivening the film. It has already been said that the depth of field is so great when the wide-angle setting is used, that focusing problems hardly ever present themselves. This is a great advantage that filming has over still photography, and should be exploited to the full in the shots. As the subject is entirely in focus from front to back, anything in front of the lens system, within a radius of about 1m. to infinity (∞) may be considered as part of the shot – an extremely enticing potential.

Landscape shots are always very popular, and their composition varied. For instance, overhanging branches moving at a close proximity to the camera can be used to provide an interesting foreground. The effect lies chiefly in the fact that a live foreground where the leaves move in the wind, which looks remarkably effective on film, is placed in front of a static landscape. Movements of this type – rustling leaves, swaying grasses, flowing water – exist in profusion as foregrounds and bring the landscape to life.

If you extend the focal length of the camera, you can play about with definition. As is well known, the depth of field decreases as the tele focal length is extended, revealing the subject's centre of gravity. It can be extended far enough to concentrate on one point of focus, whereby one point is selected and focused on, and all the rest becomes a hazy blurr: in this way the most significant feature can be emphasised. For instance, two people at a distance of 10 to 15m. can appear in focus in the midst of totally hazy surroundings. The effect is singularly impressive, and with appropriate lighting – perhaps an oblique side-light – it can be used to induce an extremely romantic atmosphere.

Most shots are filmed on the wide-angle setting, partly on account of its problem-free depth of field, and also because a tripod is nearly always superfluous. It is a fact that although the advantages of a tripod are commonly known, most filming is practised without their use.

On a journey, in the company of non film-makers, and in other circumstances, one is often pressed for time. Accordingly the camera should remain set on the wide-angle setting for problem-free filming. In addition, many cameras possess a focal range scale and distance setting ring, with a coloured marking indicating the most favourable depth of field. Generally, this

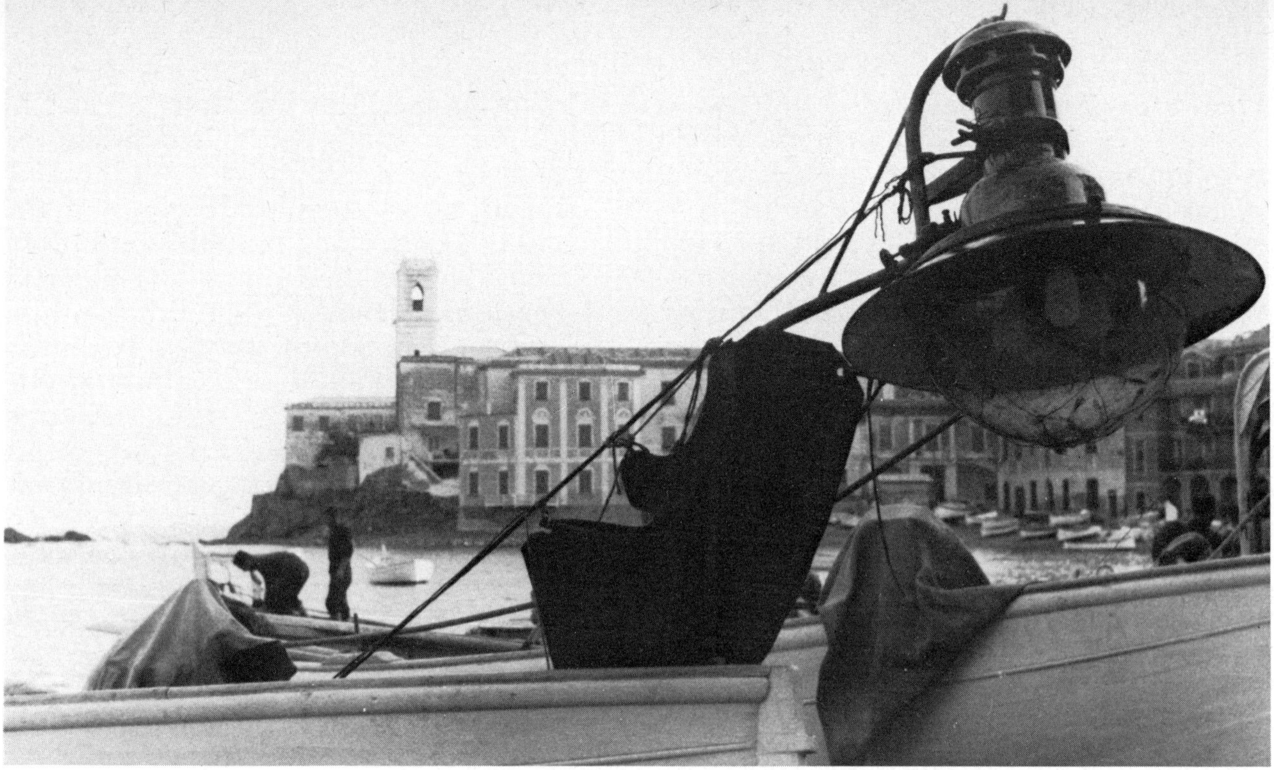

The chosen theme here is a striking foreground and water

implies a focal length of 12–15mm., and a distance range of about 5m. If this 'snapshot setting' on the camera is used, there is practically nothing else to worry about.

Shot, counter-shot

An important rule of thumb in filming is: 'shot, counter-shot'. This means that the film-maker must alter his position and the taking direction of the shot. An example will clarify this.

While on holiday with your family you go and visit a castle: the first picture is the 'shot', and shows the family entering the gateway. For this the people can either approach the gate closely, passing the camera, or they can disappear through the gate one after the other. Now the countershot follows. You run quickly past your family and film each one as he emerges again on the other side of the gateway. So to begin with the people walk away from the camera, then they come towards it. Shot and counter-shot – an important principle.

Obviously this type of filming may be used at every conceivable opportunity, and even in professional filming it is one of the most frequently occurring direction notes. Keep this in mind during the next feature film you watch. The rule 'shot, counter-shot' is not limited to one direction. For instance, you could film a tower from bottom to top, then from the top down – the method can be used everywhere.

Perspective

It is a truism that the effect of the shot depends on the perspective. The same subject viewed from below and from a high plane produces two entirely different impressions. In filming, as in other areas, these types of view are termed worm's-eye view and bird's-eye view, even though the camera rarely needs to be as low as a worm or as high as a bird. The implications of the terms are obvious.

It is easier to film from a worm's-eye view – from below upwards. The camera makes the objects appear larger and more substantial. This perspective serves particularly well for many shots of children, as it corresponds exactly to what they see. Have an attempt at filming the world from a child's view: everything seems quite different.

Incidentally, even near the ground there are objects which serve as good foregrounds, and can be fully integrated in the picture if the depth of field is exploited to its full extent: above all flowers, grasses, and similar things. With the camera in hand you will find many objects that beg to be taken from a worm's-eye view.

The bird's-eye view is not as easily arranged. It occasionally demands an elevated stand point, sometimes so high that you can stand above the activity, in order to be able to look over the heads of your fellow-creatures. Whenever a large number of people gather together (at annual fairs, sports events, and ambling through the town) you will obviously achieve the most favourable field of view from an elevated position. Not only will you obtain the best overall view, but, most important, you will be able to provide the viewer of your film with a clear impression of the site of the action. This is particularly effective at the beginning of a film. Many full-length shots can only be filmed from a bird's-eye view.

If you decide on varying perspectives for the same subject, you can play about with the size ratios. From above much seems squat and everything seems smaller, while from below small objects become large and powerful. The use of varying perspectives can considerably enliven a film, particularly when familiar objects are filmed from unusual viewpoints. For instance: kneel down instead of filming from the normal eye-level; then commonplace surroundings take on a completely new appearance on film.

As already mentioned, when filming the children, film may be taken from the child's own viewpoint. This can also be applied when your pets are to become film-stars, by

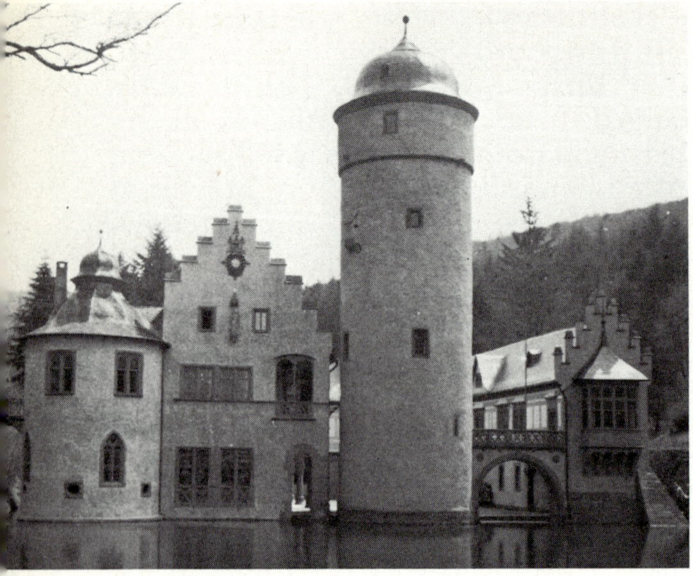

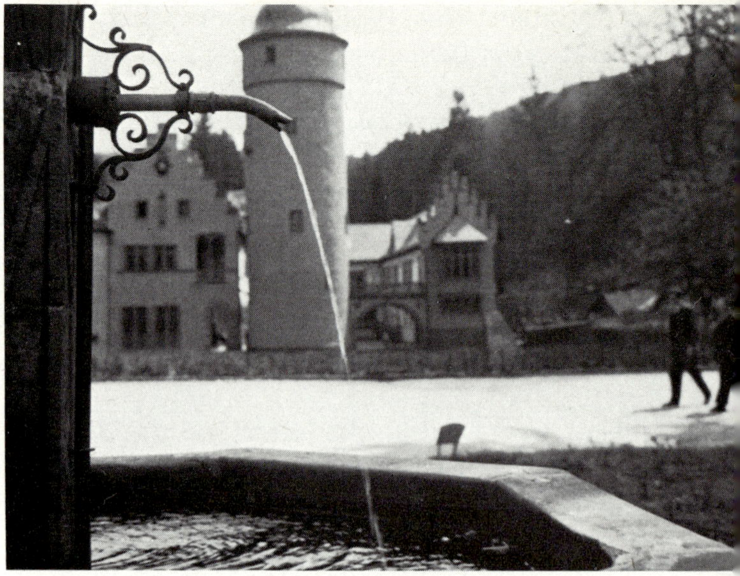

These three shots show how the film subject is altered by filming from different directions and with different perspectives. Yet further variants arise from altering the focus

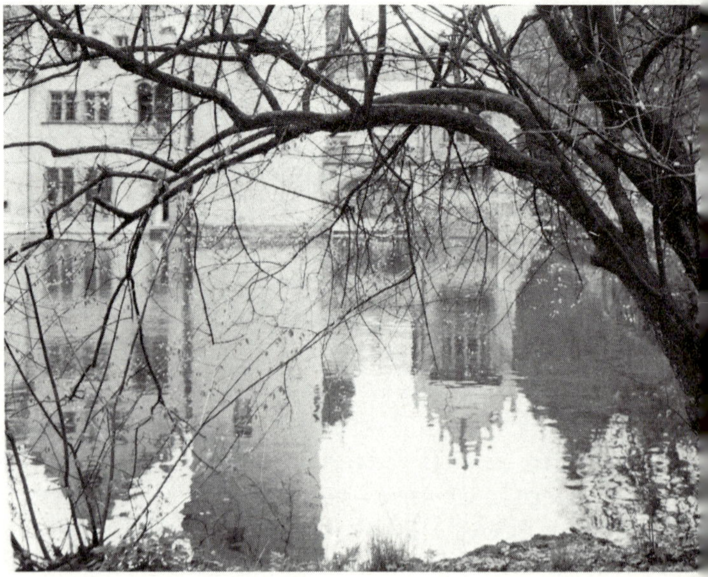

adopting the low position of the animal with your camera.

Thus perspective plays a very important role in every film. However varied the composition possibilities also are, the two cannot be entirely separated, but rather they flow into each other. For instance the 'shot' may be taken from a different perspective from the 'counter-shot', which not only augments but to some extent even overlaps the compositional choice.

Full-length and Close-up shots

A critical viewing of a feature film would reveal that a significant portion of the scenes consist of close-ups, sometimes far more than half of all the shots. That films live on close ups, so to speak, is nothing new. The nearer you move towards your subject, the more effective the projected result will be. This is based on the fact that the tiny film frames are more suitable for close-ups, which generally consist of expansive colours, than for large panoramas. Incidentally, the same applies to still photography.

Anyone who has already had a film script in his hand will perhaps remember that film subjects can be divided into the following categories:

1 Close-up shots
2 Medium close-ups
3 Full length

Those are the three basic settings, but you are not limited to these three. However, they should be used interchangeably in a film. For instance: to begin with you show a full-length shot, possibly a bird's-eye view, of the place of the action, perhaps your family in the garden. A full-length shot must normally continue for a while if it it is not to appear hasty when projected. Sufficient time must be allowed to appreciate the scene. Following this, the next setting might be planned as a medium close-up, e.g. the mother standing by the flower bed with her little girl, showing her a particularly pretty flower. Finally a close-up of the flower would be a logical continuation.

The principle must be, from all the activities, to pick out those which will prove most effective on film, which may mean that time gaps will occur between the shots: it is of critical importance that the action is of a coherent and logical composition.

To return once more to the feature film: the action here is of a logical construction, even though years or even decades may elapse between the individual parts of it, an idea which may also be conveyed in amateur filming. One need have no fear of exchanging the action in one scene for something entirely different, as long as a sense of continuity is preserved.

Lighting

Lighting is an important factor in any film, and the question concerning daylight or artificial lighting has two levels of meaning here. If one and the same subject is viewed in varying lighting, it becomes obvious that back-light, side-light, and front lighting will produce entirely different results. The true beauty of some objects is only revealed by means of back-lighting. Thus back-lighted shots of water are numbered amongst the most attractive that a landscape has to offer, and shining twigs, made translucent by the sun, take on an almost unreal transparency. The curls of the little – or even the big – daughter possess a golden glow when the sun conjures up a back-lighted effect. Generally, the close-up is more suitable than the full-length shot for filming with back-light.

If the film is to portray architectural subjects, an oblique side light rather than a back light is best used. Irregularities in the stonework, window openings, and ledges thus acquire slanting shadows, and a façade becomes remarkably alive and expressive. With the use of interesting lighting effects, inanimate objects will at last reveal their charm, and can be fully appreciated for the first time, particularly when enhanced by a lively foreground, which transforms the static architecture of the background into a film scene, instead of a filmed slide.

Front lighting exists when the sun or other sources of light are positioned exactly behind the camera, and results in flat lighting, without the enlivening effect of shadows. Of course this lighting should not always be avoided, particularly when taking indoor shots with only one film lamp, although the constant alteration of filming positions will qualify the effect. With the 'shot, counter-shot' method, for instance, the lighting will necessarily change from scene to scene. Lighting for indoor filming is discussed in more detail in the next chapter.

Film Composition

En route from the test film to the improvised film you will have accumulated a considerable amount of practical knowledge. Above all, you now know that even in an improvised film a rational ordering of the scenes, good composition, and the correct filming positions are conducive to the optimum results. Nevertheless you will increasingly realise that in all respects the various elements of film composition have very flexible limits. Rarely will you apply one without touching on another.

At this point you can substitute another effective method for the pan shot and all its problems. The necessity for a pan shot always emerges when the camera cannot take in the desired subject all at once. While a pan shot will achieve this, it possesses both advantages and disadvantages, and in my opinion the latter outweigh the former. Consequently you should try out the following suggestion.

Divide the panorama into several small sections, and with each section change the focal length and the camera position. For instance: a mountainous landscape, unbelievably beautiful, with a stream flowing towards you; the background is framed by a line of mountains. You stand in a field with gentle side-lighting, in front of all this. Filming conditions are ideal – a picture-book holiday. The panorama alone could fill an entire film. Begin filming on a wide-angle setting. The stream flows through the picture, and the view is directed towards the mountains in the background. Follow up with a medium close-up of the stream and the tall grasses growing up on the bank. In the next shot, gazing up at the mountains from a worm's-eye view, the grasses can be used as a foreground.

In this way you can show the panorama from three settings, without having to pan the camera. Moreover you have changed the

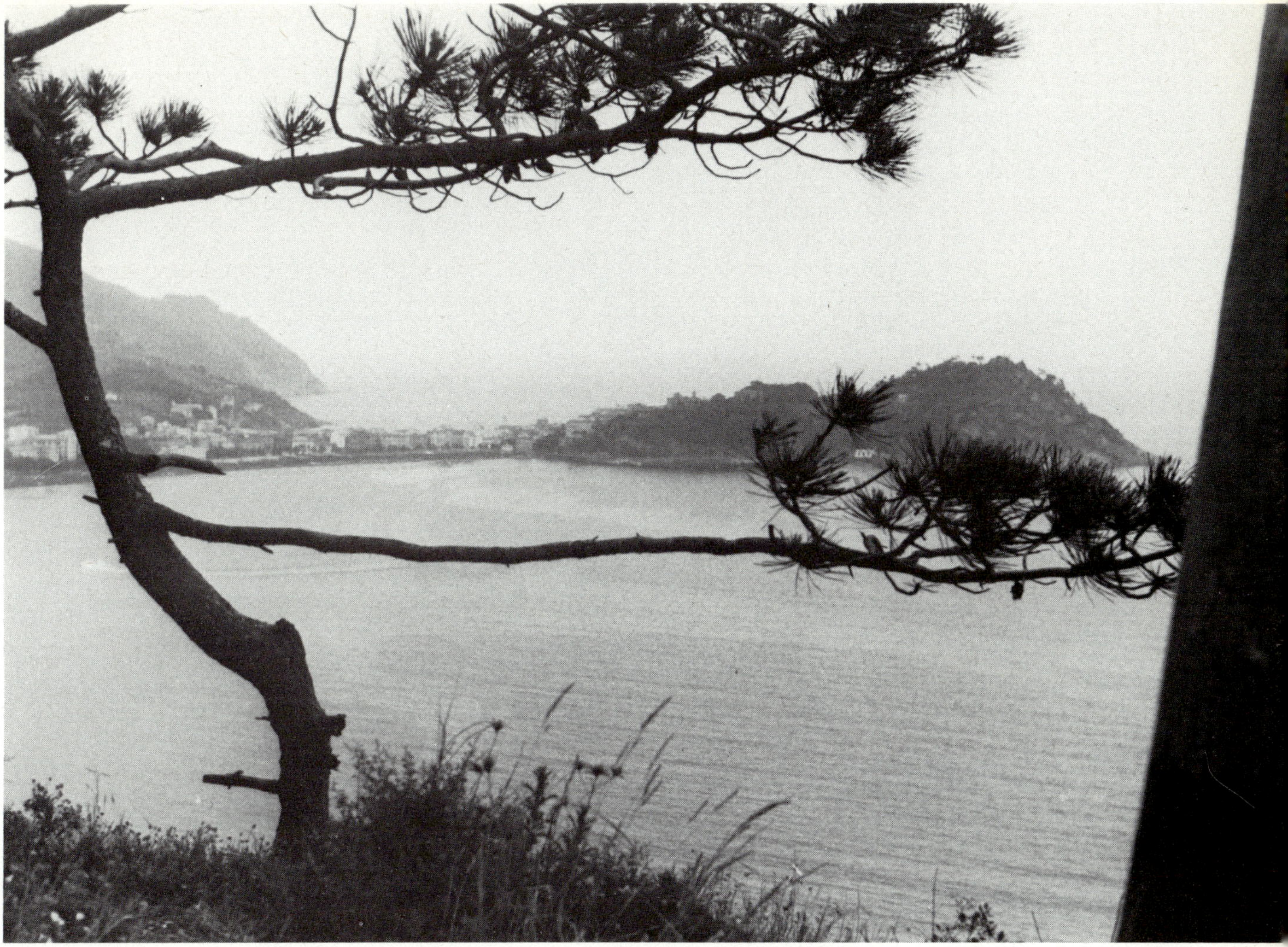

Panorama scene
At the beginning of a film or scene, this type of shot provides a good overall view. The foreground is striking, and the gentle movement of the waves is also effective

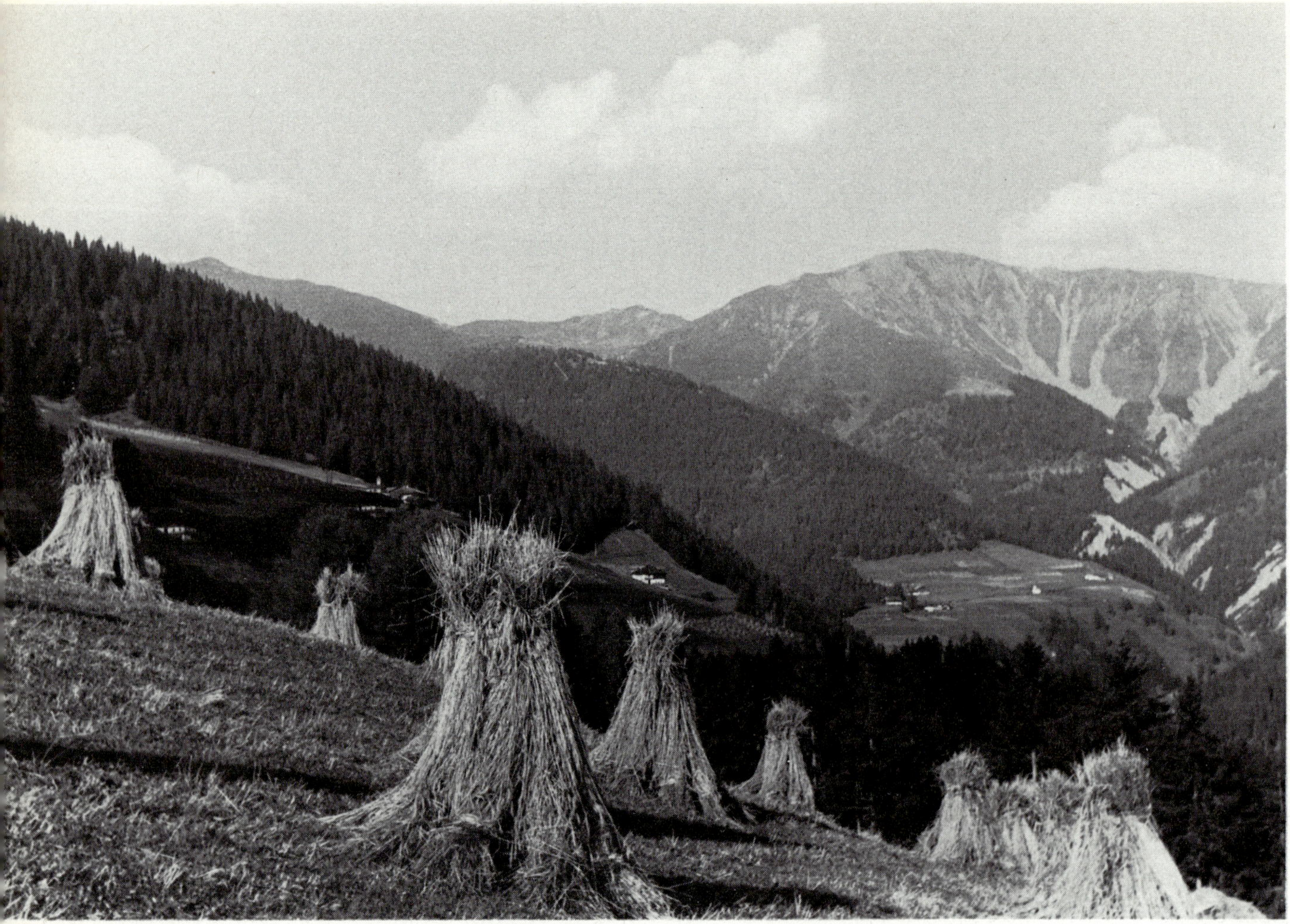

Filming a landscape is not always without its problems. Concentrate above all on a striking foreground

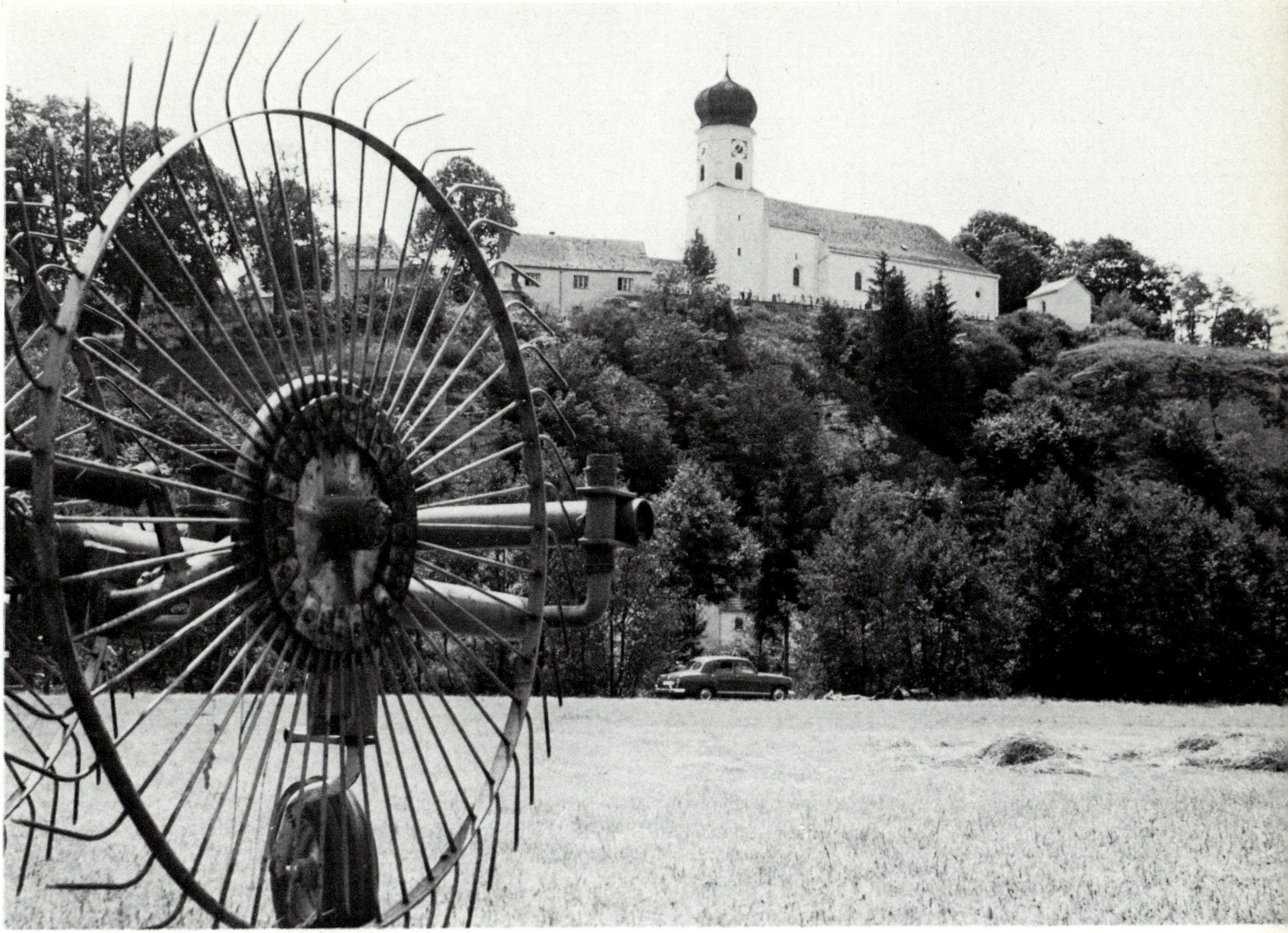

The foreground takes up almost half of this picture. A gentle pan in association with a travelling shot concentrates the view on the village church

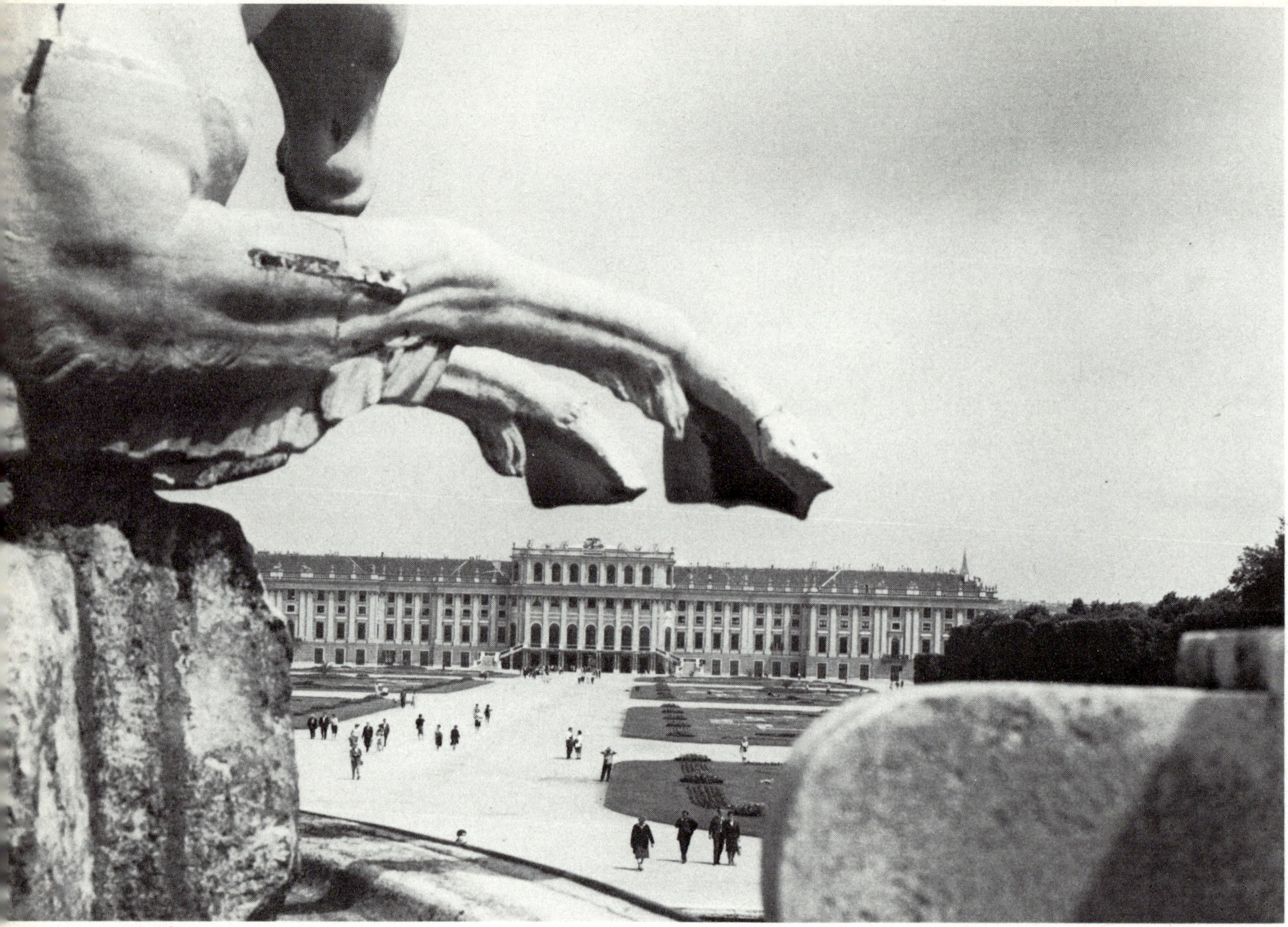

The unusual foreground gives the shot of the palace an interesting perspective. The people contribute movement

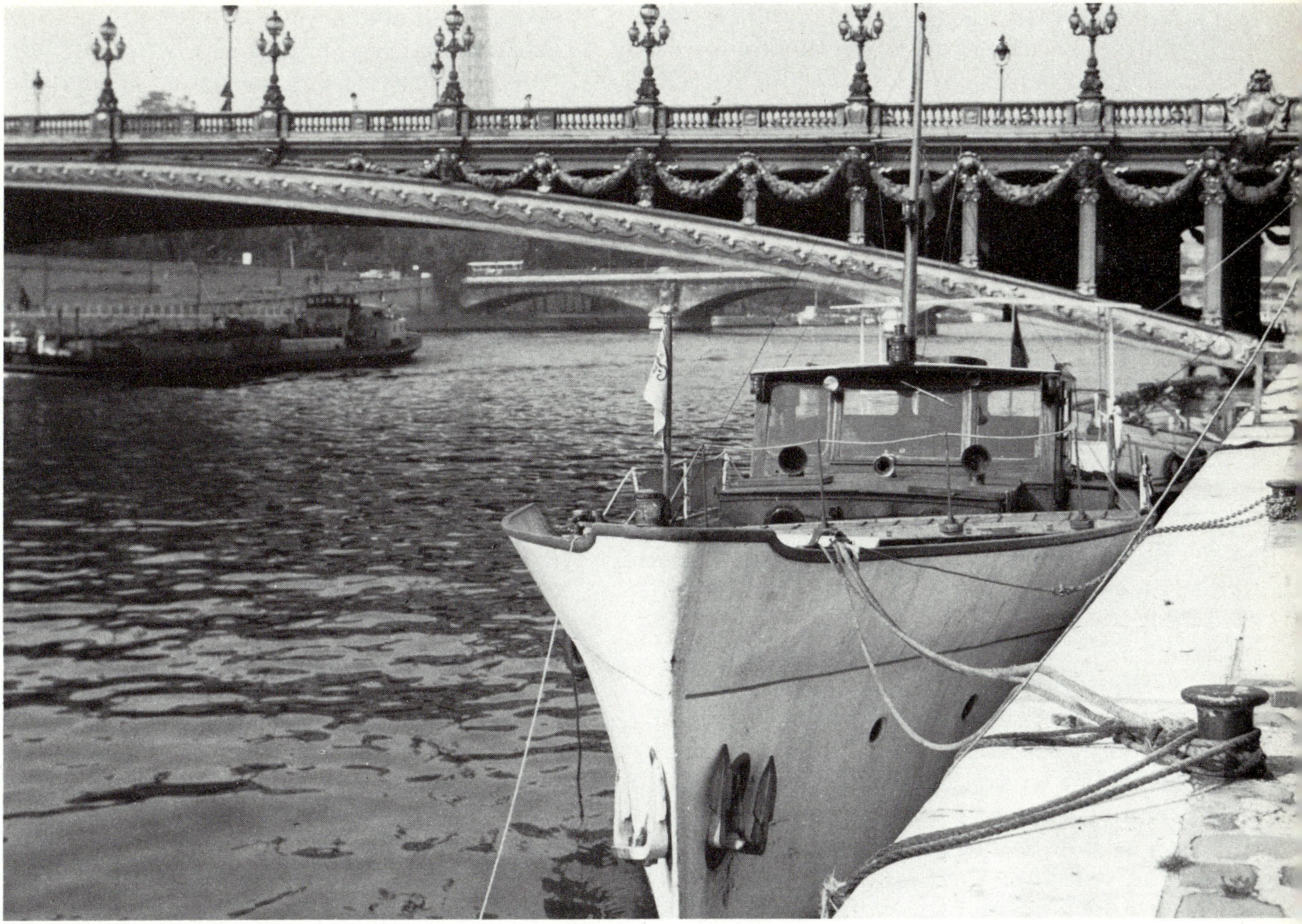

Water is a popular film theme. The scene guarantees life and movement and provides attractive lighting effects

filming position three times and used three different perspectives. All this then instead of a pan, which would possibly proceed too quickly anyway.

To sum up, we can list the various possible methods used to produce an effective improvised film.

1 Shot, counter-shot
2 Worm's-eye view – bird's-eye view
3 Close-ups – full-length shots
4 Backlight – side-light

Contrast forms a part of every method of composition, and enlivens every film. It is the constant changing of lighting, positioning, and perspective that brings life to the film, and of course it is in this way that ciné film differs from a row of filmed transparencies. Put this to the test in your first film. Filming rich in contrast is fun!

Film Ideas

At the beginning there is always the deciding question: what do I film? It would be simplest to say 'everything', although this would at once be both right and wrong. The choice of theme depends very much on the individual, so there is no common answer. It would be possible to distinguish between film reportage, documentaries, and feature films. In this respect the amateur film-maker may apply the same principles of composition as in professional filming, although admittedly on a smaller scale. Numerous possibilities exist, and there are few occasions when the amateur cannot produce an effect comparable to that of the professional, given the aid of a trick device.

It is, however, possible to film quite simply and yet achieve very interesting results. To begin with, filming usually remains within the small family circle.

In many families, the birth of the first child occasions the purchase of a ciné camera, and an interest in ciné photography. In this case there is no problem with ideas or themes for filming – there is the child! Indeed films of children make up a significant proportion of all ciné filming, and consequently this is worth discussing in some detail.

With little children, particularly, it is important that the mother can also handle the camera – the business of filming should not only concern the husband, but the whole family. The mother normally has considerably more time and more opportunities than the father to occupy herself with the child. She is, after all, usually with the child all day.

Films of children

Films of the children growing up become increasingly valuable as time goes by. They capture occurrences and phases of life that can never be repeated or replaced.

I even know an old man who during the last war carried films of his children in his air-raid kit, which is a supreme indication of how valuable and irreplaceable a living family record can be.

Hence filming for a family record should begin as early as possible. Since big events are always anticipated in advance, and the preparations are included amongst the most important concerns of the young family, film should commence even before the child is born.

At least after the birth you should begin filming as soon as possible, at best, even in the hospital. Admittedly in general these will not be the most attractive pictures, but they belong without fail in the record. At home new themes will occur every day. The most striking opportunities, always chosen for filming, present themselves at meal-times and bathtime.

Filming at home will necessitate the use of a film lamp. Many young parents fear that a 1,000W. lamp might damage the child's eyes, but this has been proven totally unfounded. A baby's eyes accustom themselves rapidly to the light, quicker than an adult's. Many adults would find unbearable the light in a child's eyes, as he looks at the sky from his pram while on a walk.

Anyone who intends to make films of children should note the following: at least one complete film should be exposed at each film session. There is little point in keeping one film in the camera for weeks, and filming single scenes at great intervals. The result will be a motley collection of scenes, which lack any sense of continuity. If film is only taken at fairly long intervals, a complete film should be shot each time. If the entire event is recorded, the overall impression is correspondingly far more harmonious.

When the children are older and no longer develop quite so rapidly, the intervals from one film to another will increase automatically. However, we have not yet reached that point. Filming is particularly fun when the child is learning to walk. Until now, filming will have been limited to certain settings - bath, bed, pram, playpen, lap, etc., and the shots could only be varied by altering the perspective. From now on you can also change your position, which will reveal quite new opportunities.

Never forget the close-up - even in the first few months. Film, for instance, the child's unaided hand as he turns over bricks, or capture his big eyes, staring curiously at the world. A film of him learning to walk must naturally include a close-up of the first steps.

For the first films of the child, variety exists everywhere - nowhere more so, however, than in the playroom.

A problem usually arises when the child is at the age when he becomes conscious of the camera, and it is one that can only be overcome with patience. However, it can be put to positive use, for the child's inquisitiveness is so natural that it can and should become a part of the film. The next move is to play with the camera together with the child. The child sees you looking through the viewfinder - let him also have a look. When the child is included in the activity he will soon adopt the right attitude to the camera, and the use of a shoulder strap will avoid any risk of the camera being dropped on the floor. Most important of all, the child will lose his shyness of the camera when he knows what can be seen in it.

Now let the game continue – the child looks in the viewfinder, then you look, and so on. Of course every time you look in, you film! In this way you will capture shots of an unusual naturalness – in play.

Films of the children seem particularly charming when their toys are also included. If Teddy is always taken to bed at night, then he must of course be included in the film – the same with a doll. You know best what is important to your child: portray it all in the film.

Children's birthdays provide a particularly attractive film subject. If the party can be shifted to the garden, there is every opportunity to make a first-class film. There are no lighting problems, space is plentiful, and the atmosphere is one of gaiety and excitement. In this situation a tripod should be used, set up at an adequate distance from the little group, which enables you to zoom in on individual faces. Hardly anything will please parents more than a full-sized picture of a laughing face on the screen.

There is much activity to be filmed at a visit to the fair or when the children romp about in the open-air pool. Have you tried filming a shower with back-lighting? Or the splashing and tomfoolery in the paddling pool, not forgetting the dazzlingly coloured bath toys? Numerous subjects exist – more than you can film.

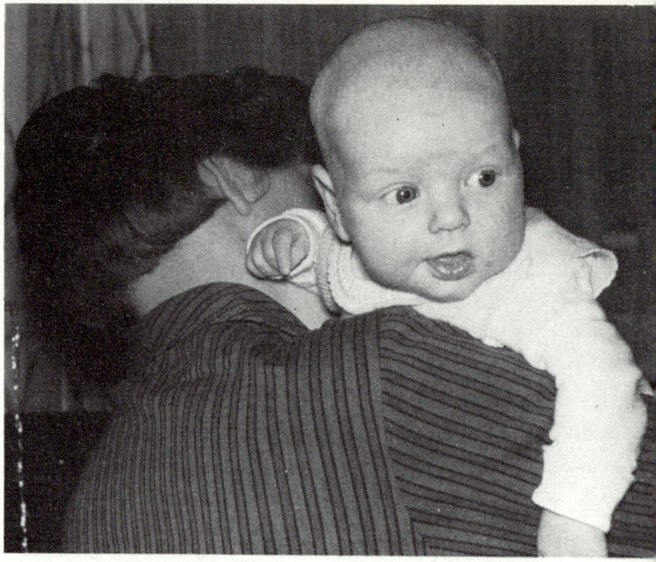

The baby of the family is film theme number one! The earlier filming begins, the more valuable the family record

Snow and sledging – light and life on film

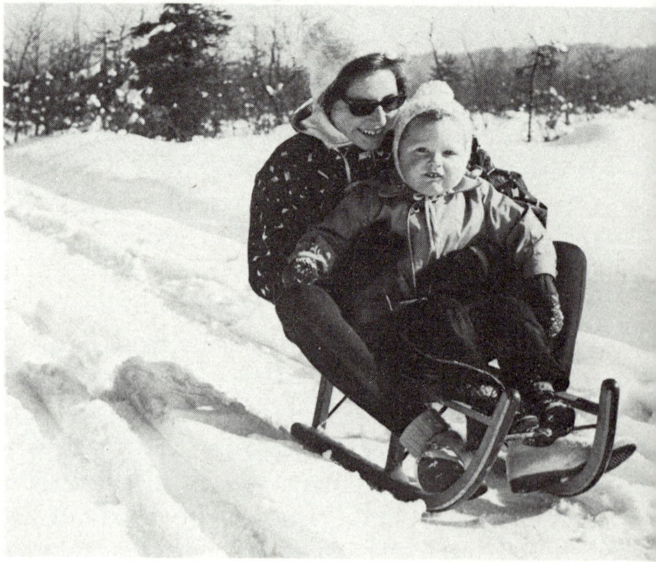

In the fullness of time, the children's games are replaced by the rather more serious activities of older children. The fascination of electric train-sets exists on film as well, and in this case all the various facets of composition should be put to effect: full-length shots, macro-shots, overall views, movement, perspective, etc. The small, seemingly insignificant, things should not be forgotten: the boy's hand on the engine, the model signal that allows the train to continue its journey, the signs on the station, and much more, which you will realise for yourself.

A railway film might even begin with father and son planning the track lay-out, filmed by the mother. Then the construction of the layout can be filmed in several phases. Introductions of this sort provide a good way into a film which, though short, should still appear as a united whole.

By going a step further, the model railway could be skillfully juxtaposed with the real one. Such a contrast, though it will naturally demand more time, will produce something quite out of the ordinary.

Growing daughters also have their typical activities, which are particularly suited to filming; the dolls, the dolls' house. Here, as with the model railway, the amateur film-maker is presented with all he could wish for in terms of film composition. Starting school is another important moment in the life of the child, and should not be omitted from any family chronicle. Few teachers would object to a couple of scenes being shot in the classroom. These 'life-recordings' of the first visit to school increase the documentary value of the children's story.

The time-intervals between each film of 'interesting happenings' will ever increase, as the further development of the child is, at least to the eye, much slower than in the baby-stages: the child's growth continues at a much smoother pace, and frequent film comparisons are no longer so worthwhile. These may well be the reasons for the fact that many families discontinue an individual film record of the child when he begins school. At least as far as filming is concerned, his further development is almost exclusively contained within family life. This seems sensible, since films that deal solely with the growth and development of the child are no longer necessary. The film themes increasingly represent joint activities, for instance holidays, visits, and outings. As the family will undertake most things together, the child will become an integral part of family films, and from then on actual films of the child will cease.

Filming with artificial lighting

It is at this point timely to make some further comment about the use of film lamps, since the child will very often be filmed at home.

With a normal film and a 1000W. halogen lamp you can adequately cover a distance of about 3m. Within this scope, the child and surroundings will be correctly illuminated, anything outside it will generally be too dark.

When film lamps are utilised, the problem can be lessened by using highly sensitive film in conjunction with artificial lighting. You thereby benefit by two stops, which can be translated into a greater depth of field or a longer taking distance.

When filming children, in particular, a great degree of care is required with the film-lamps. On no account must the child be allowed to approach the lamps out of curiosity. The tube has an operative temperature of about 300°C. and takes a fairly long time to cool down: even after the lamp has been disconnected, touching it could result in serious burns.

Those who only possess a 1000W. lamp have hardly any lighting problems, as the lamp can be affixed to the camera and illuminates the image field of the lens exactly. However, the availability of two film-lamps is a different matter, as a bright light source will without fail produce shadows. If the light shines directly on the subject, a very definite shadow cast behind it is unavoidable, but if the second light shines from about the same distance from the side, the shadow can be diminished or altogether eliminated. In contrast to flashlight, the effect can be gauged exactly in advance, and can be altered, as the occasion requires.

Obviously it is advantageous to enlist the aid of an assistant to guide the second lamp, particularly for filming children, as the light must follow the child's movements exactly. The second lamp might also be mounted on a tripod, but then you must take care that the child does not alter his position too considerably, which could be quite difficult with children at play. Nor should the area be so confined that it restricts the child's normal movements; if possible the playroom should remain as usual. Try to solve the problem of lighting with this in mind.

Various lighting effects can be achieved with just one film lamp. To this end the lamp must function separately from the camera, so that light can emerge from different directions according to the various scenes. If an assistant is on hand, this presents no difficulties; he must light the subject from the front, the left, the right, above, or below, depending on what the setting demands. Variable lighting of this sort will considerably enliven the playroom, even when the room itself, being generally quite small, does not facilitate a vast amount of alteration. Large cast shadows are incidentally only visible with front lighting: with side-lighting they fall right outside the picture and are therefore in no way disruptive. According to this method, even a gentle back-light with one lamp can be used. Insofar as lighting with one lamp is constantly alterable, it is possible to achieve a very interesting film by virtue of its light and shadow effects. Many lighting principles from the field of artificial-light still photography can be applied, practically unchanged, to filming. Have you already

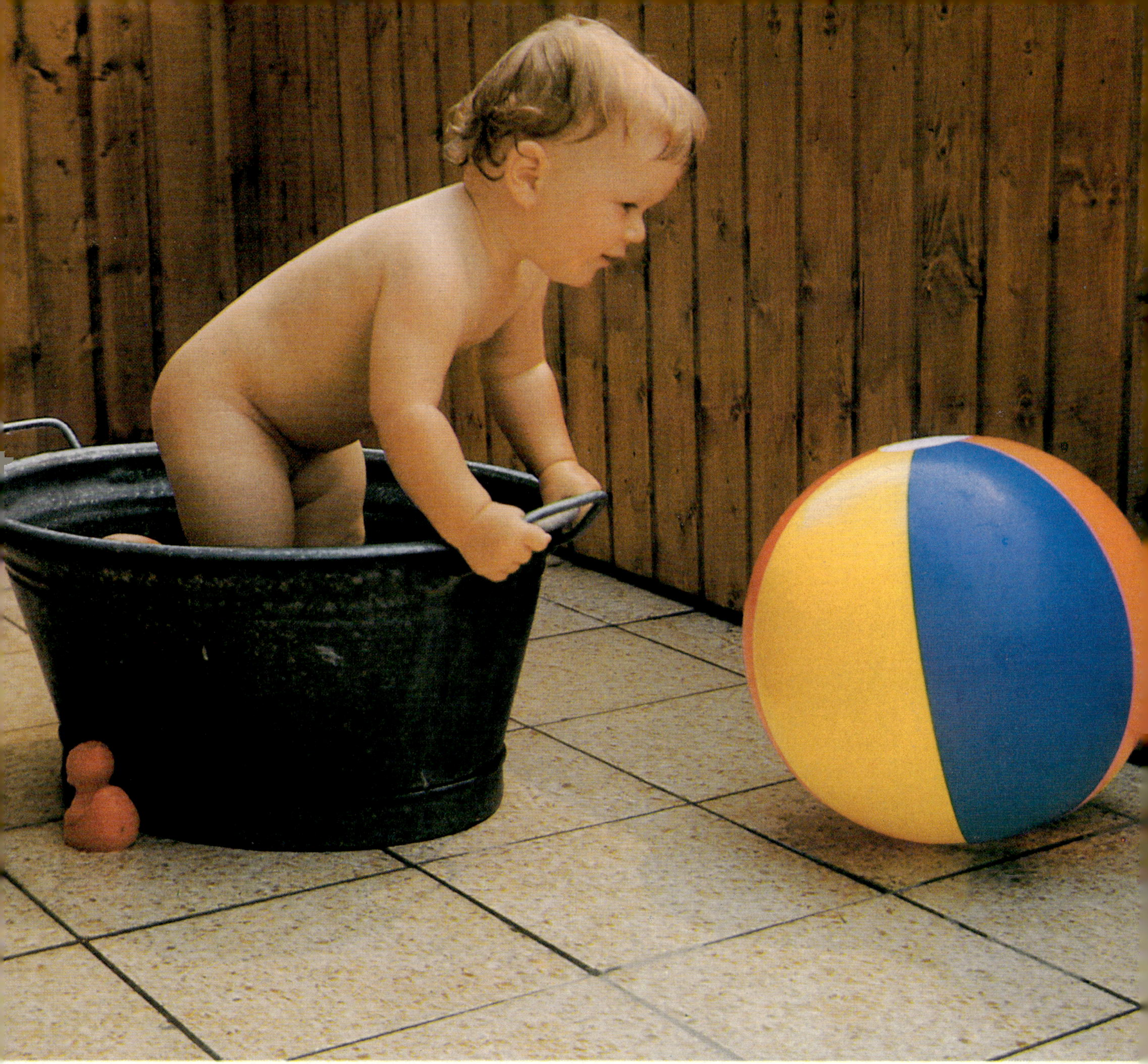

Plate 9: The development of the children must be recorded on film, as they grow up so quickly. After a time they will play quite naturally in front of the camera (E. Richter)

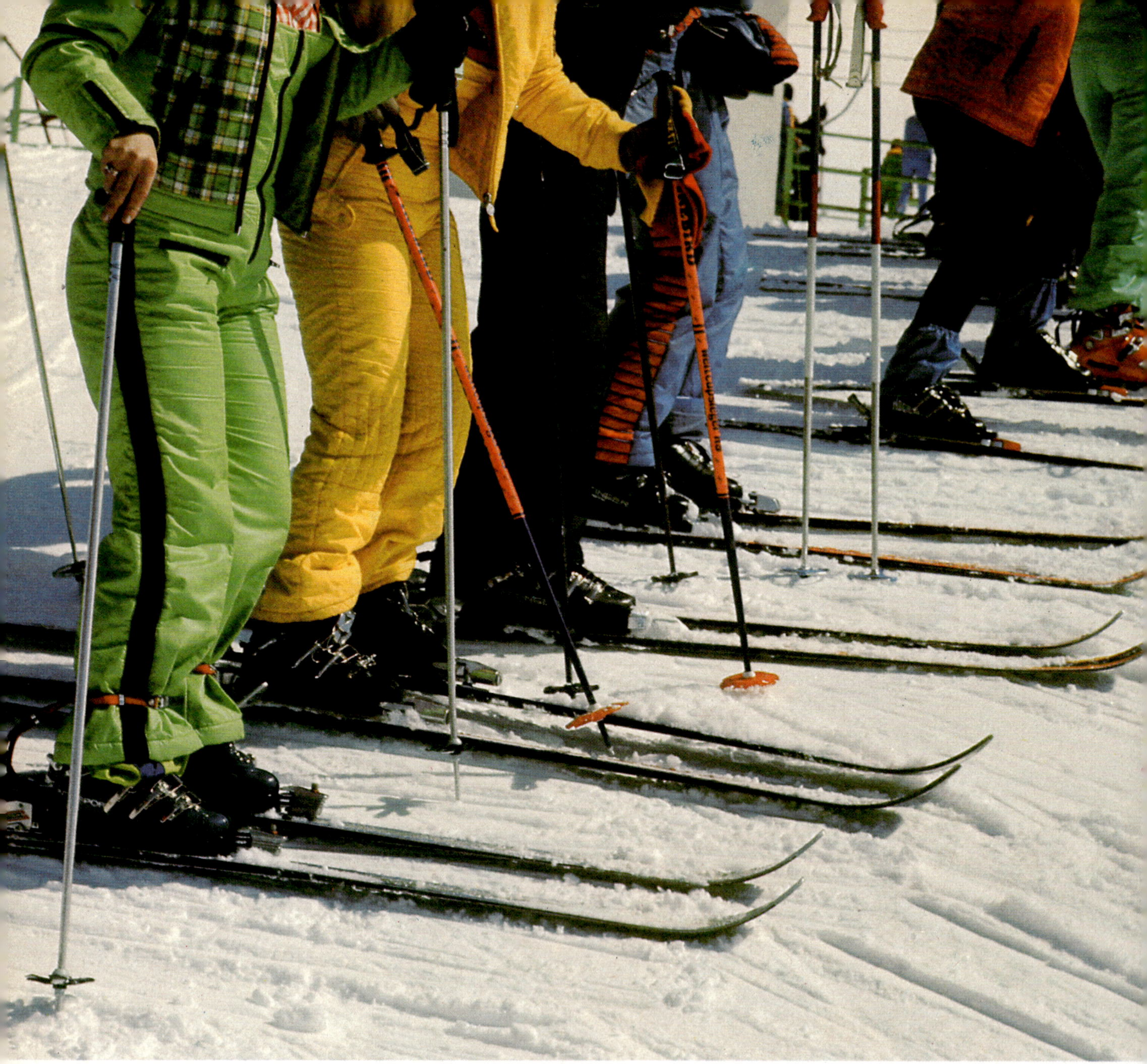

Plate 10: Besides the skiers and panoramic views of the mountains, waiting for the lift and tramping up and down the slopes also belongs in a winter film

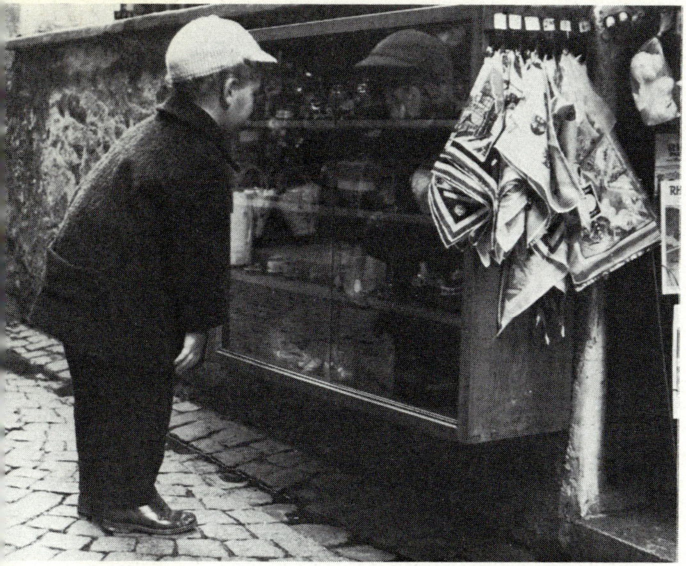

There is so much to explore!
Ice-cream! Scenes of this sort are a must in all family films

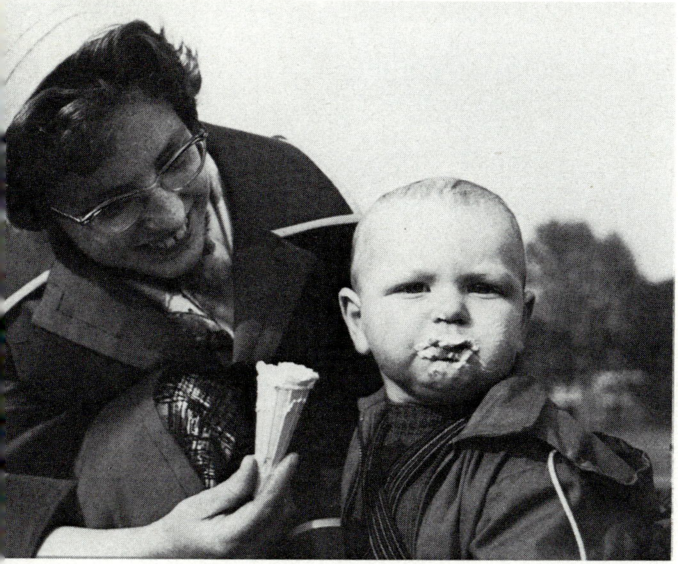

tried filming with indirect lighting? For this a 1000W. lamp is, as a rule, insufficient.

In order to obtain indirect light, the film-lamp should be pointed at the ceiling, so that the reflected light can be used for filming. The prerequisite is that your 'film studio' possesses a white or at least a pale ceiling, since coloured ceilings would naturally produce coloured reflections, resulting in a shading of the film. Moreover, it also implies a loss of light.

Indirect light is by nature very similar to daylight, as it is even and almost free from shadows. For filming, one will either need a brighter lamp, or several film lamps, since not only does the light have a greater distance to cover, but also a certain amount of light is lost in each reflection. With a room of normal height, i.e. about 2.5m., and a ceiling of a pale colour, one can generally reckon on the equivalent of two stops loss of light. Two stops are, however, a considerable amount: you will no doubt have come to realise that in artificial light filming you rarely go above stop 4, except for close-ups. With a 1000W. lamp you would soon come to a halt. In its place, 2000W. film-lamps would be eminently suitable, though in my estimation they are considerably less useful for direct lighting than they are here for indirect lighting. With them you achieve something around stop 4, which is exactly right.

You may perhaps have reservations about the use of stop 4 for artificial-light filming, since such an aperture is not willingly used in still photography on account of its all too small depth of field. However, in filming, the facts are not the same. Most artificial-light film-shots exist in the wide-angle range, so even with stop 4 no difficulties arise about depth of field.

Indirect light need not only be employed from above, it might equally well emerge from the side. In this case the lamp is directed not at the ceiling, but at a reflecting surface on the wall, which may consist of white card or of a projection screen. This method provides for a wealth of variations, since it becomes possible to work with artificial light from two directions, one lamp being pointed at the ceiling, the other, at the reflecting surface on the wall. Indeed this type of lighting can be contrived with the simplest means, yet can produce an effect similar to being in a film studio. Such an effect could not be accomplished, however, without the aid of an assistant.

No artificial-light filming should be undertaken without the use of a lens hood, otherwise you quickly discover how full of light reflections the world is. If the lamp is affixed to the camera make sure that the lens hood is not positioned too near the film-lamp, as it could begin to disintegrate with the heat.

Theme: Family holiday

In any healthy family, holidaying together is the highpoint of the year, and it is often a foregone conclusion that filming will be undertaken.

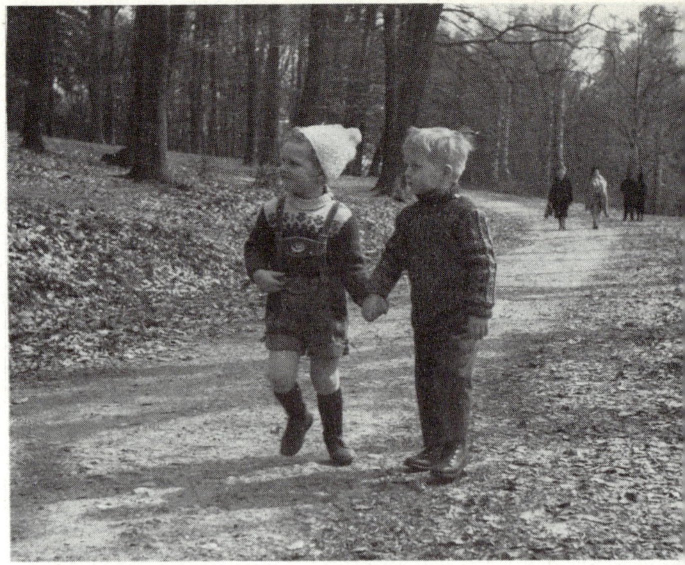

A first outing into the wide world
Children's toys belong in any film about children. The macro-shot adds a quite new dimension

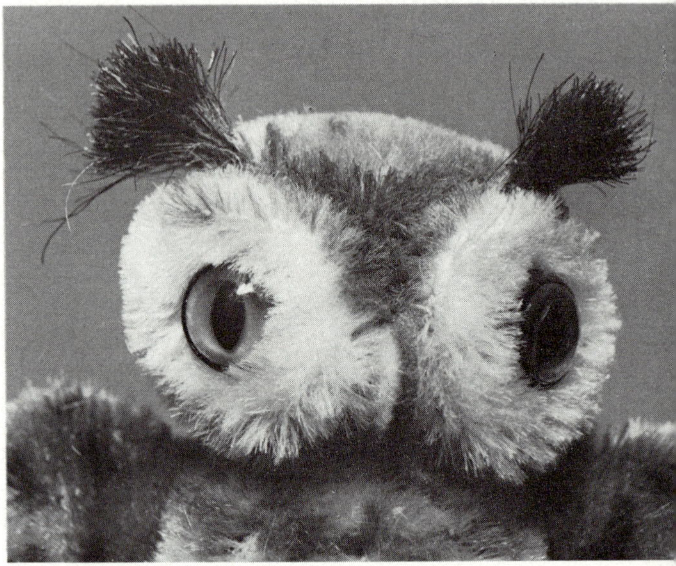

Up until now the focus has been on filming children; now we turn our attention to holiday films, where the basic requirements are quite different.

While most films of children are taken in the familiar setting of the home, the holiday is normally spent in new, totally unknown, surroundings, and the 'film director' is confronted with many new aspects. Holiday films are best considered as an individual entity, and not combined with other films in more homely surroundings. Imagine it as if a red thread ran through all the work, so that the end result does not consist of a collection of totally disconnected scenes. A red thread joins all the individual pieces together, and it is not after all, that difficult to find the appropriate scenes. The next requirement is that one person should be responsible for deciding what is to be filmed, and how it should be filmed. Everyone has their own style of composition and will make their individual mark on the film. If two or three people are involved in one continuous film, it can easily happen that it fails to suggest an impression of being a collective whole. There should therefore be only one director per film.

If several members of the family are equally enthusiastic about filming, it would be sensible to agree on who is going to make the holiday film. In certain situations it might be possible to change day by day, so that all the parts that belong together stem from the same person. It would be better still if each person could produce an entire film.

Holiday films are very much dependent on chance. Frequently the setting and surroundings are unknown, and the weather is sometimes an unstable factor. The principle that it is better to exploit fully one fine day than to take shots of a lesser quality every day applies even on holiday.

In most cases there will be definite holiday accomodation, whether it is a hotel, a guest house, or a camp-site. The next thing the amateur film-maker has to do is quietly get to know the area - the surroundings and the people - and consider what would look good on a film. Every experienced ciné photographer will recognise the rule: get acquainted with the area before beginning to take any films.

The following is a tried and true method: on a walk, mentally divide the surroundings into film scenes, establishing an idea for the 'red thread'. Spend the first couple of days or week of the holiday walking with this in mind, discovering the best settings for your film. When you have spent a while cataloguing the best points in your head, then you can begin to film. Of course with the camera to your eye you can probably find even better settings.

There are several advantages to working in this way: firstly it is not necessary to carry the camera about with you every day. By and large you make the same presuppostions for all your shots, and avoid the superfluous repetition of scenes which always occurs when you do some filming every day. If the holiday film is loosely planned, this ultimately results in the most successful filming and gives the whole a sense of harmony.

No holidays are without variety! Most excursions are planned, whether near the holiday resort or further afield, and allow for very effective use of the camera. The application, for instance, of fade-ins, fade-outs, and dissolves can produce impressive film transitions. The last film scene of one day might be faded out, and the first shot the next day faded in. This not only results in a gentle transition, but also shows quite clearly that a new section is beginning. Scene changes effected with a dissolve can be particularly absorbing, but for this the shape and colour of both subjects must be atuned to each other. For instance, a dissolve would be possible if one day ended with a sunset and the next began with a sunrise. With fade-ins and fade-outs there are in addition several possible variants: since the process is operated manually, it can also be influenced time-wise. According to each subject, you are able to decide whether the sector shutter should be closed quickly or slowly. However, when filming involves the fairly long application of the sector shutter plus fading-in or fading-out, the tripod becomes absolutely essential, since the camera cannot possibly remain still when two elements

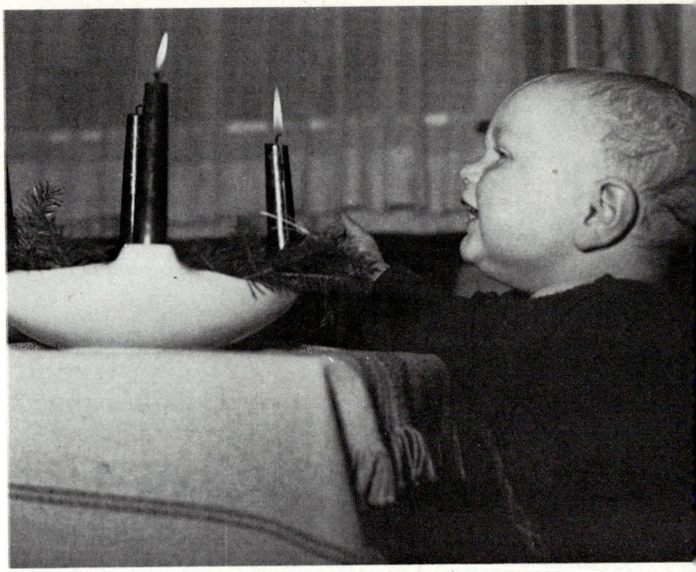

The first advent candles. A contrasting shot should follow – the candles in the foreground, with the child's face behind (looking towards the camera)

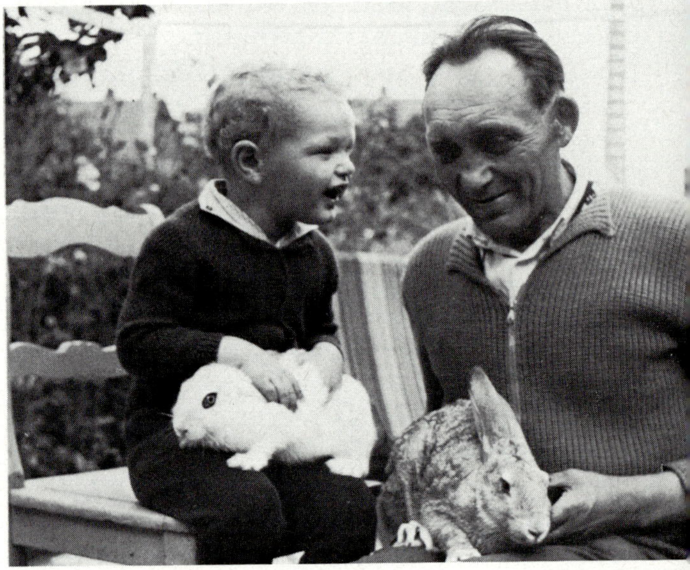

Children and animals – a charming and popular film theme, full of life

must be operated simultaneously: the release button and the fade-out lever. If your camera does not possess a fade-out adjustment, this effect can be simulated by means of a wipe. The procedure here is as follows: firstly, the final scene of a topic or of the day is filmed in the normal way. Then an object as dark as possible (wallet or similar) is brought in front of the lens from above, until the lens is entirely covered. The next scene begins, again with the lens blocked by the object, then, the camera in operation, this is gradually removed, downwards. When projected, this produces the following effect: the scene is wiped away from top to bottom by a black blind, then the blind is removed, revealing the picture down to the bottom and the next film subject remains. Thus this is an uncomplicated yet effective method of scene transition, which can be achieved even with the simplest of cameras.

Yet another method of scene transition can be accommodated by any camera. It entails a very rapid movement made in the following way: the last scene is filmed as normal, but should run as smoothly as possible – a tracking or pan shot would not be suitable. Then the camera, still running, is quickly turned throughout 180° or more on to a horizontal plane, for a length of about 1½ seconds. The next scene then continues quite smoothly and in the normal way.

Subsequent projection of the film will show the following: after the end of the first scene a wild wiping appears on the screen. The rapid movement of the camera means that the subject is no longer recognisable, only the colours flash by. Then the next scene joins on smoothly.

This wipe effect is by no means a substitute for fading-out and fading-in, and is merely designed to produce an exciting transition. This method of connecting scenes is not to everybody's taste.

It will have become clear that the two methods of scene transition latterly described require no technical accessories, which is perhaps part of their particular attraction, and consequently they can be achieved with the simplest camera. However, as with all film tricks, they should be used sparingly. Such effects can only benefit the film if they are isolated and well-mixed occurrences.

This is not to deny the fact that you can employ fade-in, fade-out, and wipe effects, particularly in holiday films, more often than will ultimately appear on the edited film, for not until the holiday is over will you be able to see how much of your film material is usable. Not until the film is developed will you know whether the shots taken live up to your expectations. In the chapter on film-editing and montage, we will discuss in further detail what can be done with the available film material. It is sometimes beneficial to have made several shots too many, as this then allows for generous cutting.

Sport

For many, going on holiday also means

sport. In the first place, of course, winter sports should be mentioned: numerous families go skiing every year, and the ciné camera goes too.

Skiing is something very dynamic and particularly suitable for filming. A landscape covered in deep snow, plenty of sun, and gaily-clad, happy holiday makers - these are the prime requirements for a very lively film.

Filming in winter rarely poses difficulties on account of the weather. Indeed, sometimes it is too bright, in which case a grey filter must be used, but this will be indicated automatically at the time in the viewfinder of the camera. A grey filter, as previously discussed in the section on 'optical accessories,' has no effect on the colour. It subdues the light by two or three stops and makes it possible to continue filming.

Winter sports can, then, be filmed without any particular difficulties, except that special attention should be paid to finding an interesting foreground, since the white landscape provides little variety of colour; blue skies, white snow, and bare trees should be qualified on film by brightly-coloured life. For the foreground, look for some colour to contrast with the snow. It need not always be the bright ski-wear or the coloured skis: there are many other colourful objects: the markings on the ski-slope, the chair-lift, the green fir trees, or a brightly painted house. One need only look around to find suitable objects.

Above all, the run down the ski-slope is the topic most favoured in films of skiing, but if this is constantly repeated it will eventually lose its attraction. As with any holiday activity, it is better for the camera to capture the entire day's events.

How does it start? After breakfast the ski-clothes are put on - as a rule the boots make interesting filming. Then the family collect their skis from the shed and carry them on their shoulders to the chair-lift, where it is amusing to record the stamping and stumbling to the lift in heavy ski-boots. Then the tickets for the cable car are bought. If this is a drag-lift, next might come the buckling on of the skis, in close-up: the cold hands or the thick gloves are also a part of skiing. The next scenes more or less run themselves, but it remains important that a sense of continuity is preserved from scene to scene, otherwise you again fall into the trap of the 'filmed transparency'.

Summer sports, water sports for instance, can be filmed along the same lines. For all sports films, not only skiing, the same is true: the movements here are faster in contrast to other themes and demand a different filming technique. A sportsman is in and out of the field of view in a moment, and so a pan shot becomes a necessity, although fulfilling a different function here to the one earlier described. The camera has to move with the sportsman in order to keep him in the picture.

This should be tried out, initially, several times without film. The object is to keep the sportsman, or any other fast-moving object,

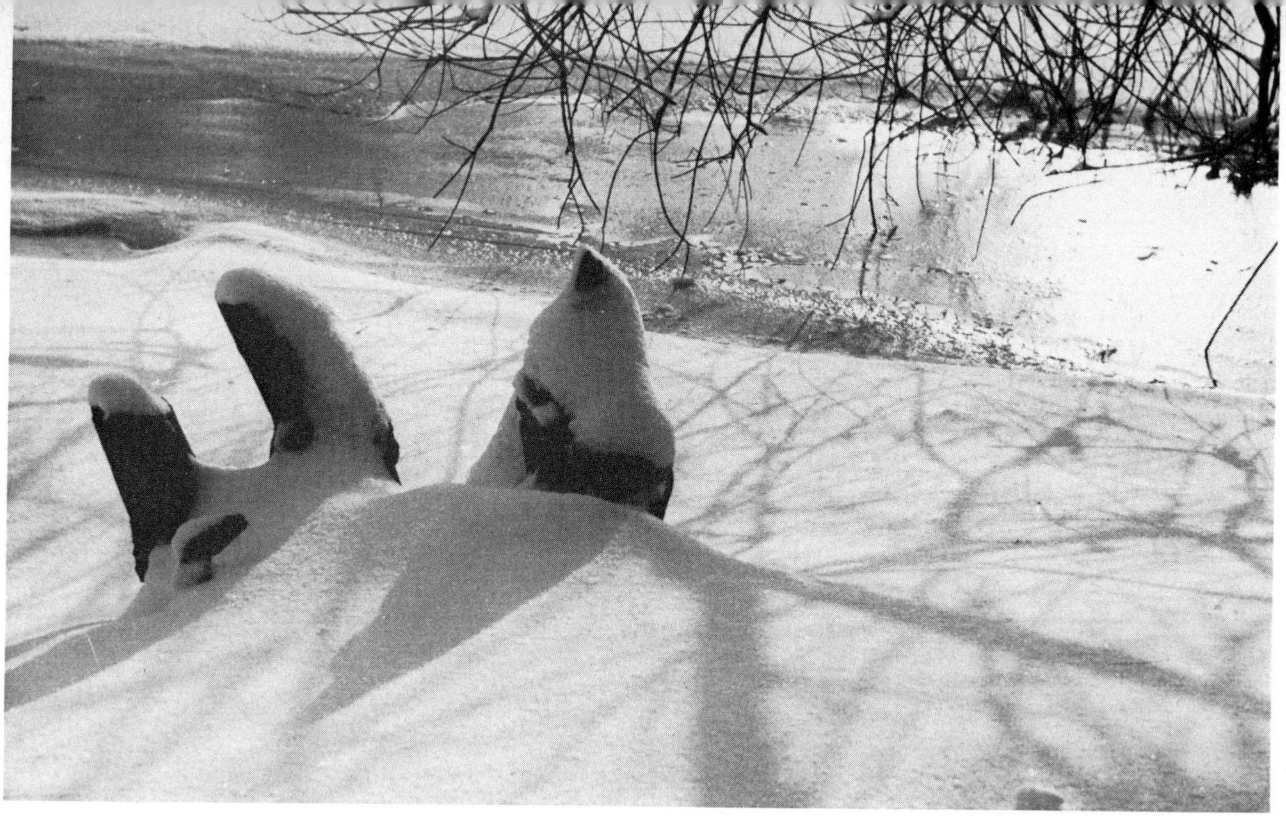

A small, 'unfilmworthy' subject: the snow-covered landscape. It can be used to indicate cold in a film

constantly in the same position in the viewfinder, as far as it is possible: in other words, the camera has to move at a corresponding rate to the object being filmed. This is not a pan shot, in the previously described sense of the word, since the background is totally deranged, and only the central object remains in focus in the picture. Everyone should practise the camera movement a few times, until they are sure of success. Even then, it should not be reckoned that every shot of this type will be successful.

Water and Rain

Everyone knows the fascinating effect produced by objects reflected in water. Holiday films in particular offer many opportunities for exploiting this effect, a point to be remembered when it rains on holiday – as far as filming is concerned, reflections are a way of making the best of it!

It is not true to say that films are always more successful in sunlight, since the light shadows enliven the subject. While it is somewhat more difficult to film in rainy weather, it is not less effective. The most important rule is equally the most obvious: it must be possible to see in the film that it is

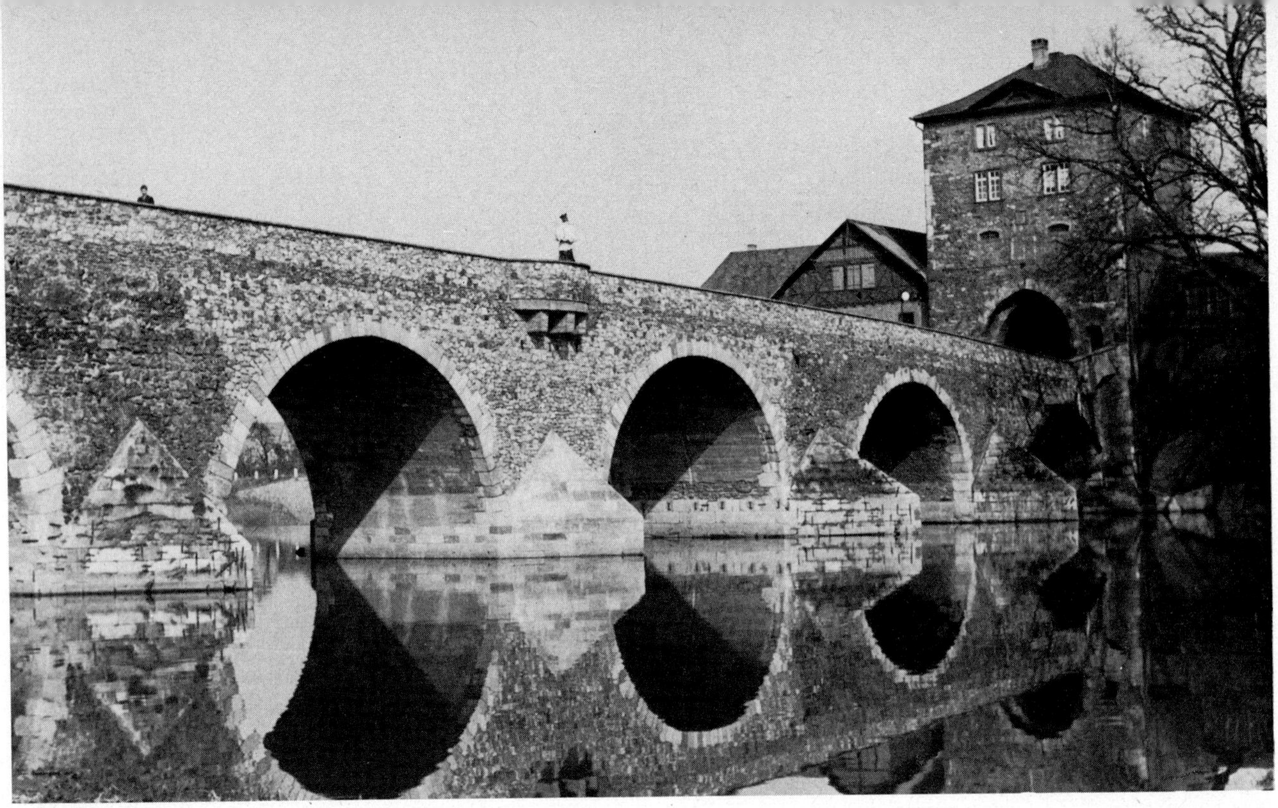

Reflections are often very attractive. Many special opportunities for this present themselves in holiday films

raining. The abundant reflections of the light on wet streets, for example, provide for interesting shots. The relatively small aperture value set by the automatic device is usually surprising, but you should believe the device!

The 'red thread' is again important for a filmed outing in the rain. Do not forget the puddles, with the raindrops splashing into them, or the façade of a house – as far as the gutter. Both the drains and people with colourful umbrellas belong in the film.

Film of a rainy holiday resort is nearly always exceptionally full of life. On rainy days everbody gathers in both large and small towns, since, to judge from experience, when the weather prevents walking and swimming, our attention is turned to other sights and amusements. The inclusion of a rainy day, with all its interesting details, can serve to enrich any holiday film.

Night Sketches

Filming at night is often found particularly effective, and is very interesting when undertaken at the fairground. Many film-makers shy away from it for no apparent reason, which is quite unnecessary.

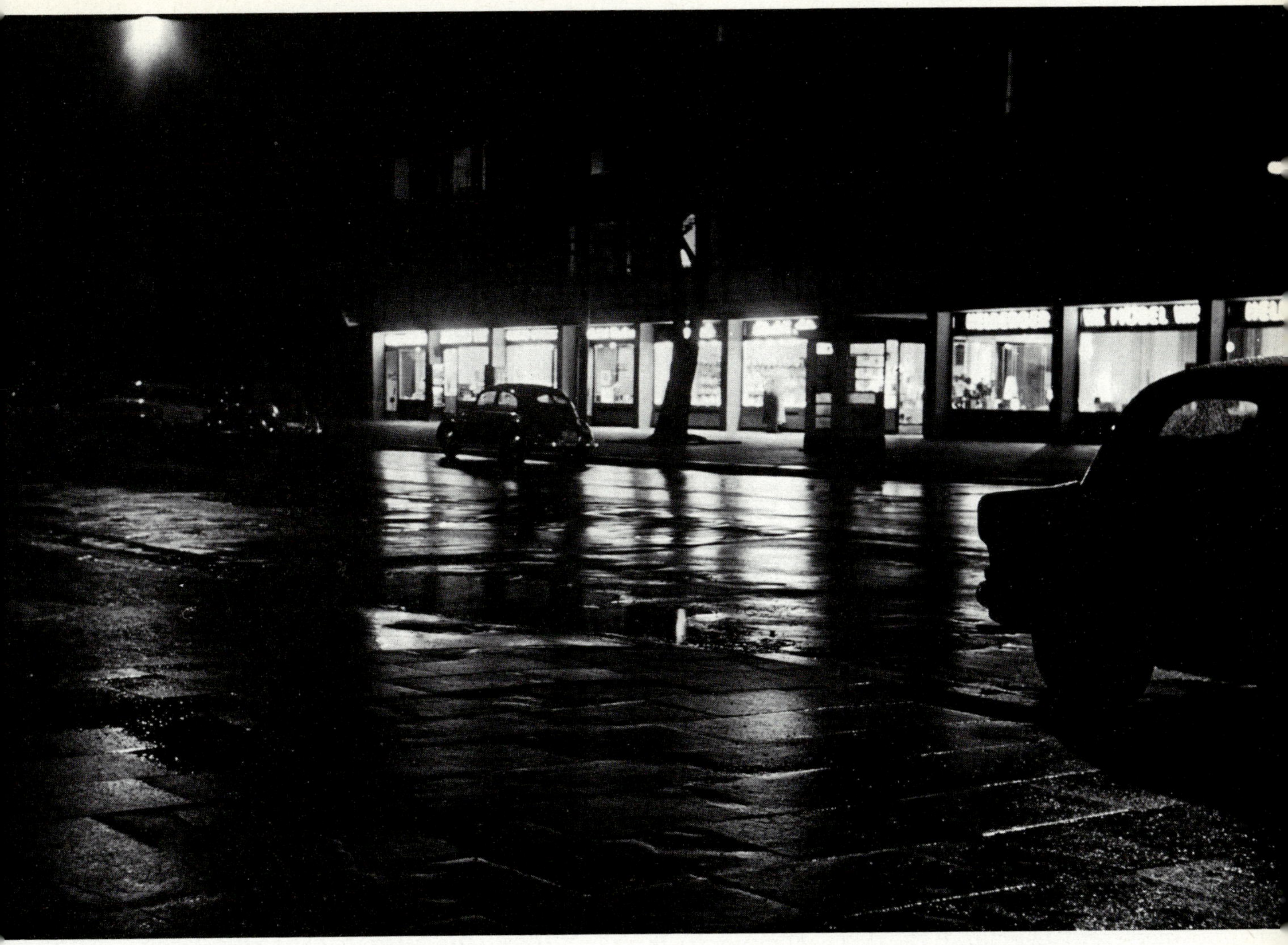

The town at night is also worth filming. When it rains, hundreds of reflections provide enough light for a ciné camera, even with normal film

Firstly, a small tip: film at the fairground in twilight, rather than in darkness. The hour between day and night is the most suitable of all: the sky is not yet black, the background not yet completely dark, yet the lights on the stalls are already burning. When projected, this creates a perfect impression of night, although there is still some light available during filming.

The fair is incidentally an inexhaustible film theme – for films of the children as well. In bright daylight you can film the young ones on the merry-go-round, or take a close-up of them with candy floss in front of their faces. Then there are the lotteries and hundreds of other things. Don't forget the smoke from the hot-dog stand! With back-lighting this can be one of the most attractive shots on the filmstrip, and is easily found at any fair or show.

You could of course set up a tripod for all this, if it were not likely to be knocked over. However, with a colourful activity of this sort, a certain amount of unrest in the camera-work can only add to the overall effect.

Colourful activity at the marketplace

Particularly on holidays in southern European countries, the markets, above all the fruit and vegetable markets, are not to be missed. Here the camera is in the very heart of the town, and the life and activity that exists is full of surprises. Opportunities for close-ups will present themselves again and again. The old native folk are found especially at the markets, and the lively traders are often wonderful actors, although they are not often willing to be filmed.

Film plenty of faces full-size. Since many southerners are camera-shy, you will often need a long focal length in order to be able to capture everything without offending. The details should also be considered: the various colourful piles of fruit and vegetables, the live fish, the vividly coloured flowers, the colourful textiles, and much more – above all, the life around the stalls. Ideal for an enchanting film!

Summary

It is of no matter where you take your holiday: films can be taken anywhere. Everywhere you find subjects which can be combined in your holiday film. The basic rules, already explained, which transform a collection of filmed transparencies into a film, are of general application, not just for certain groups of subjects. Above all, when it becomes necessary to improvise, remember the various ways of altering the setting, the lighting, and the taking positions. Improvisation need not necessarily be a disadvantage.

Once the question of scene-for-scene composition has been consciously considered for a few films, it will become second nature. Indeed, it requires only a short, although an intense, involvement with filming.

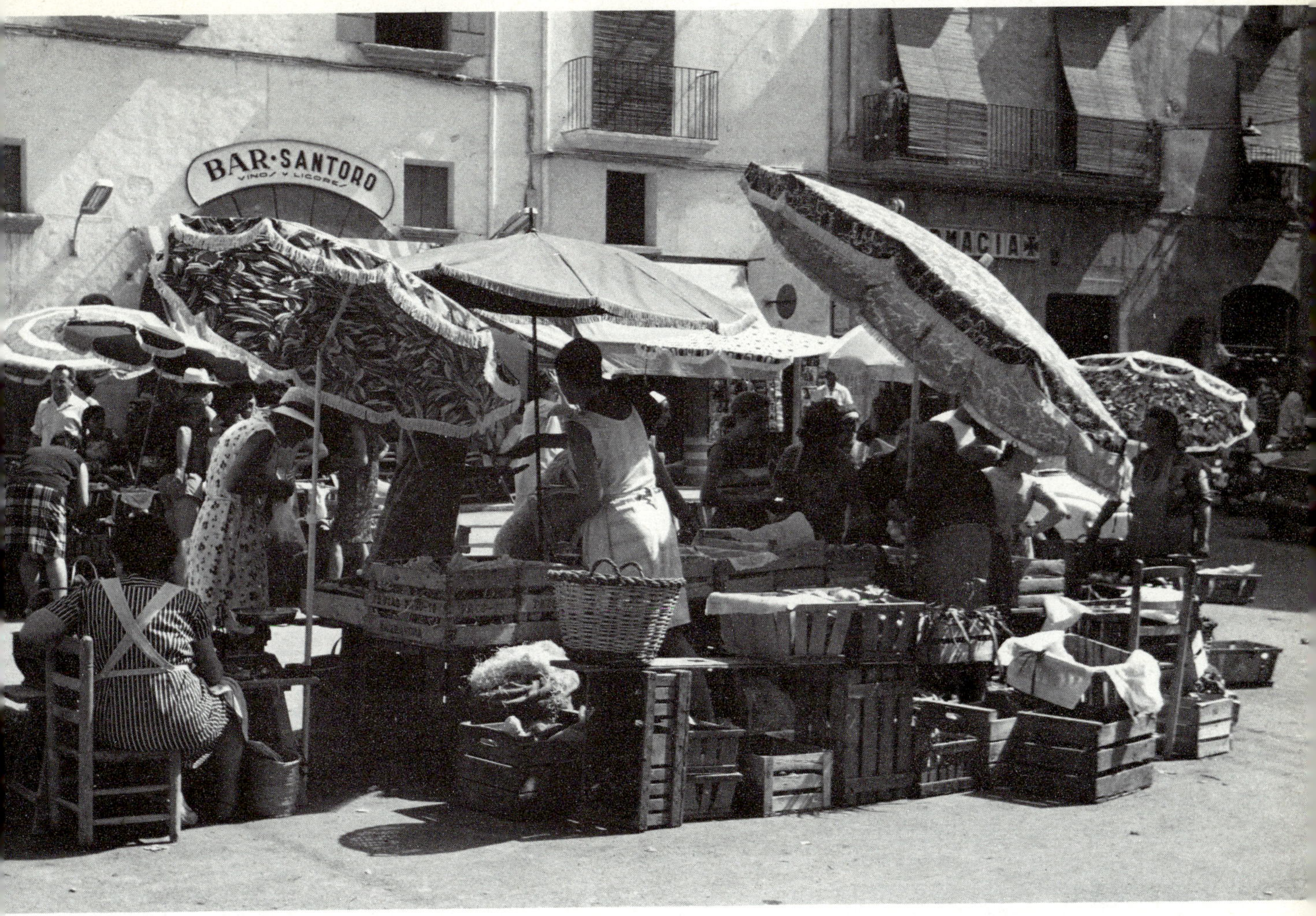

The hustle and bustle of the marketplace is always colourful and attractive. It suggests filming that includes the interchange of full-length and zoom shots

DIRECTED FILMING

Even with relatively little cine-film experience it is possible to begin directed filming: you will soon realise that many films cannot work in any other way. When it is said in relation to holiday films that no beginning should be made until the best settings have been established, or until the correct time for optimal lighting has been awaited, this is also in a certain sense a type of direction. In filming, everything that cannot be left to chance, is, if in part inconsciously, governed by direction.

Direction is above all important to every film, in order not to lose the 'red thread'. A film is a collection of pictures which must be constructed in such a way that every scene becomes a part of the whole, and so the connection between one shot and the next is easily comprehensible. Creating a film-plan of this kind can be very enjoyable without immediately inducing a desire to make a script. With travel films, every day brings changing stages, and it is therefore impossible to plan, since one never knows what there is going to be to film. In this case it is necessary to rely on improvisation. On the other hand, if you choose a familiar area for your travel film, you can produce a small 'draft'.

Perhaps you are numbered among those holidaymakers who frequently return to the same place, in which case you will be adequately acquainted with it to be able to start thinking about your filming while still at home. Should you even have photographs from an earlier trip, these might equally be employed as standpoints for your film-shots. From these already known factors, plus what is additionally discovered at the place, it is possible to construct a perfect film plan. This not only makes the whole business easier, since everything will succeed better, but also saves on a considerable amount of film material. The main objective is a loose structuring of the planned film.

By contemplating the film shots, you should be able to establish at which points to use 'shot and counter-shot', where the best effects will be achieved by back-lighting, or which passages are to be purely documentary. That this incorporates the great pleasure of anticipating the holiday goes without saying.

The Framework

Subsequent filming of a framework for an improvised film made without a plan produces the same effect as having a definite plan of direction. Of course the framework could be established before the filming begins, but I consider it better to do it afterwards.

There are many examples for this, but to remain with the holiday film: someone is sitting at a desk, with brochures concerning various holiday resorts in front of him, completely absorbed by the tempting offers. A particularly interesting picture catches his eye. His eyes light up, and he begins to dream.

The picture is allowed to melt away gradually, to represent the dream. For this, a simple trick can be used: firstly a pane of glass is needed, about 30cm. long and wide enough to cover completely the lens. The glass is smeared with Vaseline, or a similar substance, so that the first 10cm. are left free, and the grease becomes thicker towards the edge of the glass. Then while the emphasis is on the dream scene, the glass, greased side out, is moved slowly past the lens, beginning with the ungreased end. The clear ointment has the effect of blurring the contours: the thicker it is, the more ill-defined the effect. Consequently by the time the thickly smeared end is positioned right in front of the lens, the dreamer at his desk is barely recognisable and the scene has fully died away. At the same time you can gradually fade out. The next scene can then begin with a fade-in, thereby producing a perfect transition from the dream to the holiday landscape.

Should you want to begin your film in a similar way, it is important that a suitable opening shot of the holiday begins with a fade-in. If necessary you could take several and sort out the best at home. A superfluous fade-in can always be cut out, without affecting the scene adversely.

Often it is subsequently evident that a framework is essential, as once happened to me. A journey was filmed, consisting of several segments that were in themselves faultless but bore no relation to each other. It was not possible to separate the various parts from each other – on its own, each was too short to exist as an individual film. Only a suitable framework could remedy the problem, by connecting the sections together. After considerable thought and discussion with friends, the chosen theme was finally the contents of a letter.

Obviously the story had to be filmed at home afterwards. The title was 'A letter from Tarragona', and the film ran as follows: a man goes to the front door to pick up his letters, and as he sorts them out he is pleased to find a letter from Tarragona amongst them, which he opens and begins to read. As he reads the letter half aloud (obviously sound has been added), the first of the old scenes is blended in with the spoken text, text and picture corresponding to each other exactly. The first film section comes to a close, and as the transition to a new part begins, a connection is blended in via the letter-reader, and while he reads the film continues. However, the framework, blended in each time, makes the previously disjointed transitions seem natural and comprehensible. Finally we return to the reader of the letter. He reads the last sentence and folds the letter up again. The film is faded-out – end.

In this way, it is simple to create a film framework and to film it at a later date, independent of the actual film. It took barely an afternoon to shoot the letter scenes and splice them into the main film.

Obviously there are many other possibilities. A photograph album might be used in the same way as the letter to form a framework, a page being turned, as each new section appears, or there might be a group of people sitting round a table, having a discussion about the holiday, with a finger pointing at the route on the map, and lingering at the places filmed.

Since on holiday one often cannot tell whether a framework will be necessary, or how it should appear, it is advisable, as already mentioned, to film more fade-ins and fade-outs than you anticipate requiring. Particularly when you are uncertain as to whether or not it might be necessary to have such an effect, it is better to have sufficient material to answer any requirement.

Yet another tip for the holiday film: a short piece could be prepared in advance or made subsequently showing the cases being packed or the car being loaded up. There are also other things that might belong in such a scene: giving the canary to the neighbour to look after, or handing over the keys of the house.

If the journey is to be undertaken by train a similar type of introduction can be filmed, perhaps including some rather amusing shots of the station: fade-in at the station – close-up of the station clock – close-up of the ticket office and the time-table of departures – the difference between the time on the clock and the departure time of the train is only two minutes. Now the camera is directed at the travellers as they race to the platform with their luggage (film at 12 frames per second), and up to the train. Hardly are they on the train when the next scene shows the train's red tail light disappearing. Dissolve: the holidaymakers sit in the train, wiping the sweat from their brows with relief. Then the picture is slowly dissolved into the first holiday scene.

Such excitement presents hardly any difficulties and merely demands a certain amount of directing. Whether the scene is filmed before or after the holiday depends both on your choice and the opportunities that arise. If you should perchance discover an ideal film framework, you can always preserve it for another film at a later date. Frameworks of this type can never be accomplished without some direction details, but are very enjoyable if you enlist the help of a friend, or above all, the family. You need not fear that the result will not seem convincing. Once you have experienced the difficulty of having to piece together unconnected sections of film, you will never want to make another undirected film. Even the shot, counter-shot technique can only be perfectly devised with some pre-arrangement. For instance, our example of the family entering the park (shot) and approaching the camera afterwards (countershot) could hardly have been filmed without some advance direction. Either the family must stand still for a moment while the film-maker goes past them with his camera, or the action must take place twice, once for the shot, once for the counter-shot. However, these problems are always easily solved, for the family is after all also concerned that the film should be successful. Although only one person can actually direct and shoot the film, it remains as a constant memory for the whole family.

The right choice of foreground is also rarely possible without some planning. Some shots need to be filmed twice, because a much more attractive place is subsequently discovered, whether it is because the trees make more impact in the picture, or because a little stream sparkles in the back-lighting. In this case the family has to be brought on to the new stage, and again given clear instructions.

Films made over a long period of time

Many film projects are drawn out over a long time-span, which allows an opportunity for careful consideration about the shots to be taken.

A year in the garden, for instance, is a film theme which any keen gardener would find pleasure in preparing. Since the four seasons will always repeat themselves in a similar way, one can have a fairly accurate idea of what will be important to film.

Begin in late winter, when the last snow is melting and the first snowdrops are starting to appear. Don't forget the birds at the bird-table. As the last snow melts, it makes way for filming the first insects, the earthworms, the spiders, and the first appearance of greenery. This is followed by springtime in the garden, and so on. In this way you can continue the film throughout the whole year, finally ending with the first snow covering the garden once more. The year's cycle, as represented in your garden, is then at a close.

Many films which are suitable for filming over a long time span can be handled in a similar way, particularly with the use of contrasts, perhaps depicting the same region in winter and in summer. This possibility would exist if you visit the same place in the summer for walking on the mountains as you do in the winter for skiing. The contrast from one scene to the next can also be very interesting, although this is more difficult to achieve. It is created by beginning the comparable sections from the same standpoint, changing the subjects correspondingly with the season. A number of scenes of similar type are essential to the montage of such a film, in order for the transition to be made as logically as possible. The finishing touch is given to the film by means of the addition of skilful sound texts, perhaps even with two voices: one for summer and one for winter.

It is simpler to contrast two complete sections of film, each showing one season. In this case each section might be complete in itself, and then furnished with an appropriate introduction, a connecting section in the middle, and a suitable ending. Several prominent scenes could be repeated in both sections, showing each time the typical seasonal features of the landscape.

Example of a scene sequence

With the following sequence of scenes, my intention is to provide you with an example of how to present a section of film of a special occurrence.

Every film-maker has experienced a situation on holiday or on a walk of being fascinated by something which catches the eye unexpectedly. Whatever it may be, the desire of the amateur film-maker is to capture the event spontaneously with the camera: animals, children, a landscape, a church etc.

If the intention is to film several scenes, this must be done in such a way as will allow the scene sequence to be integrated into another film. If such an occurence happens on holiday, the shots must have the capacity to be included in the completed holiday film.

Judging from experience, one often finds subjects, or groups of subjects, which seem to be compulsive filming. Then the first rule is: self-discipline, for the subjects will not appear as impressive if they are added to the other scenes in a disjointed manner.

Firstly, the object to be filmed must be viewed from all sides, insofar as this is possible. In our example it is a church in the mountains. In order to elucidate the scene sequence, I have produced a photograph for each film shot, which shows, as far as was technically feasible, the same segment as seen by the ciné camera.

Obviously the scenes need not be taken in the same order as they will eventually be screened.

Now to the example: the decision concerning subject-matter has been made. The church, its surroundings, and the possibilities it entails, the dead building to be brought to life, have all been considered with regard to filming. Since my family were also present, they were of course also included.

There was not time to write a script, but with some experience one develops the capacity to form a plan of the scenes in one's mind. Keeping the basic rules of film composition in mind, there is actually very little that can go wrong.

The final polish can then be added later when the film is developed, but good film montage naturally demands the availability of adequate material.

Film theme: church in the mountains. The family have been given some instructions about when they will be needed for the shots. Since the church itself is static, the other scenes must contain life, so that the resulting impression is not of a row of filmed transparencies, an impression that can be created particularly easily in shots of this type. Seek out standpoints where the trees, twigs, people, or animals can be used to enliven the scenery (the pictures will clarify what is to be understood by this).

The following scene sequence can be similarly applied to many subjects of a similar nature.

The section of film represented in this example consists of twenty scenes. All detailed shots can be short, about three seconds. The fade-in and fade-out at the beginning and end of the film must be longer than this.

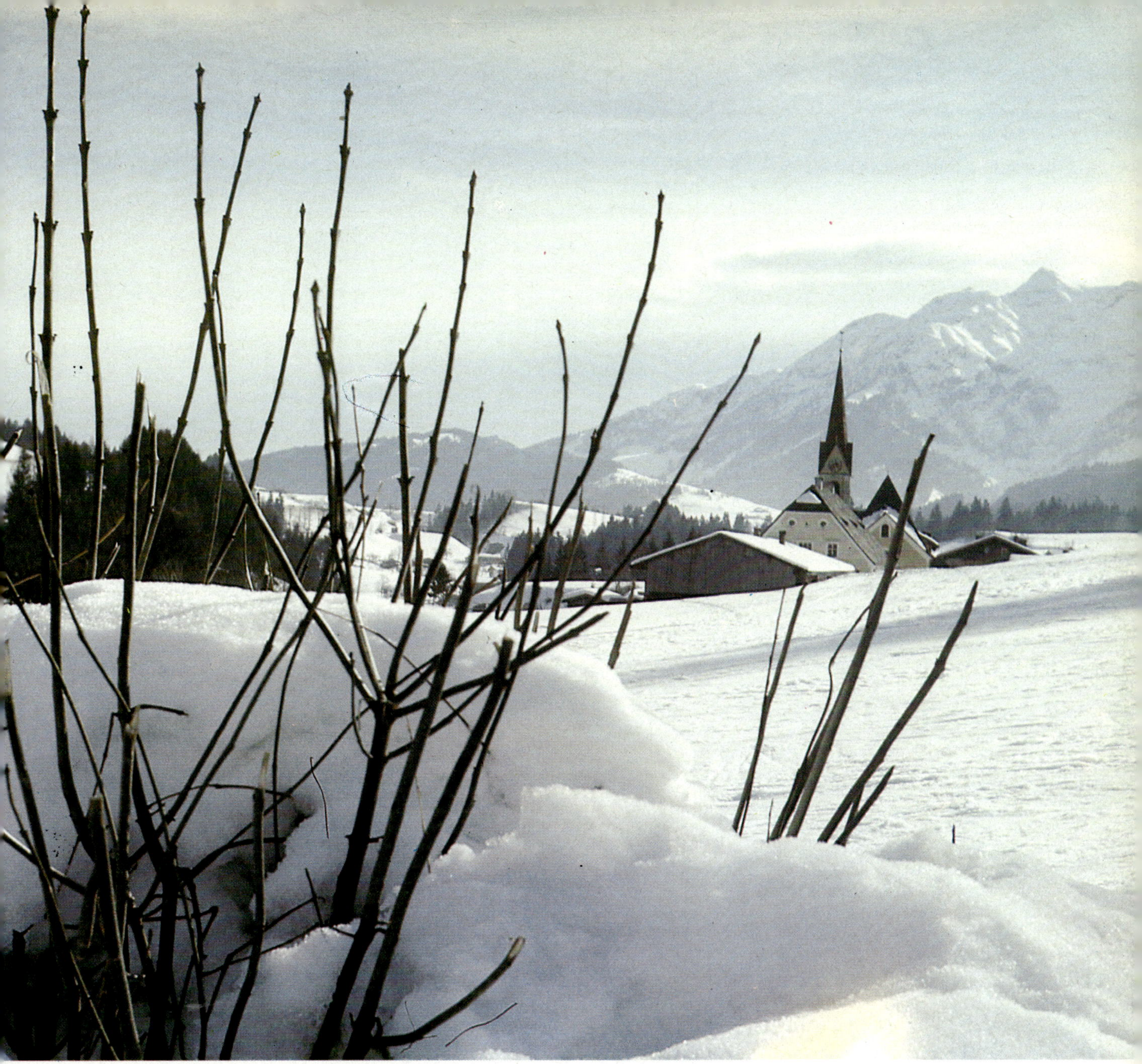

Plate 11: A snow bedecked village, starting point for wintry tours and for filming during the holidays

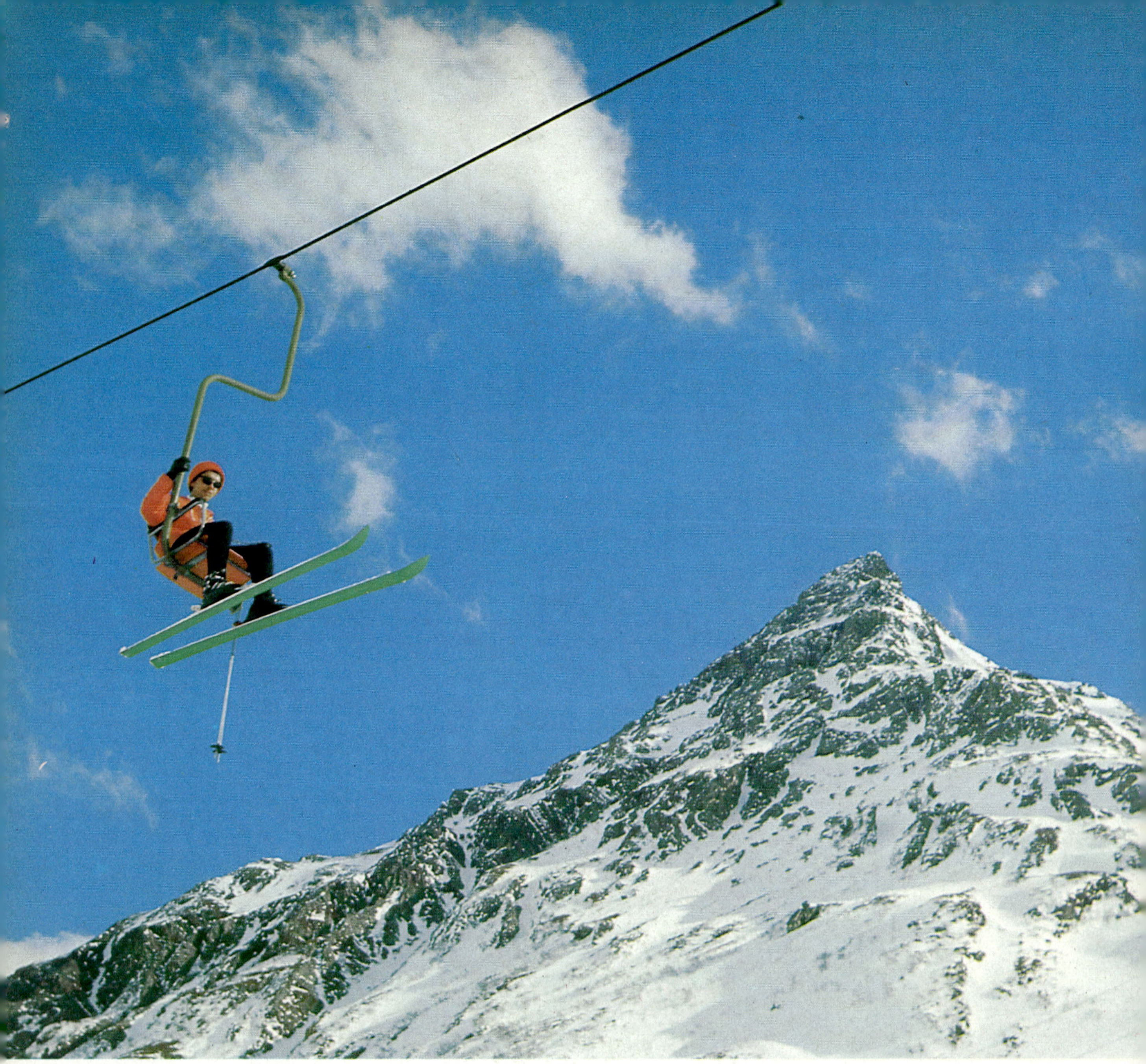

Plate 12: No ski-film should be without the coloured chair lift: the skier swinging up the mountain, and the snow-covered peaks in front of bright-blue sky

Scene A Fade-in
The first shot of the church is taken from a fairly long distance, the overhanging branches providing movement.

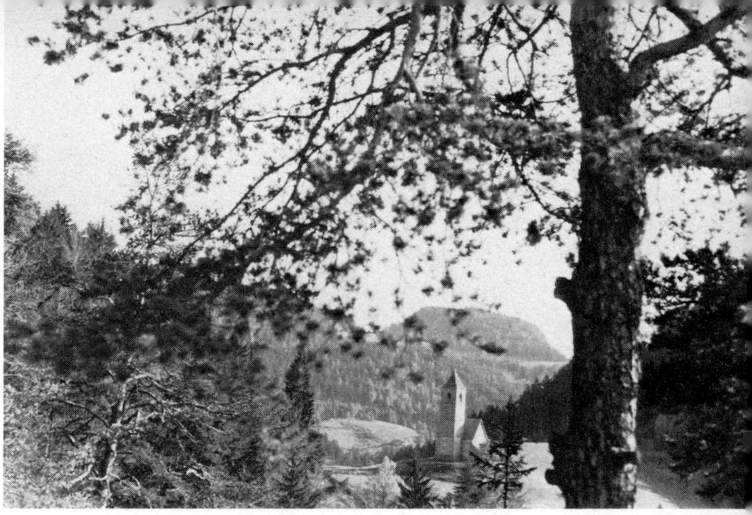

Scene B A shot of the church is taken from the other side, rather nearer this time. The changing lighting adds variety.

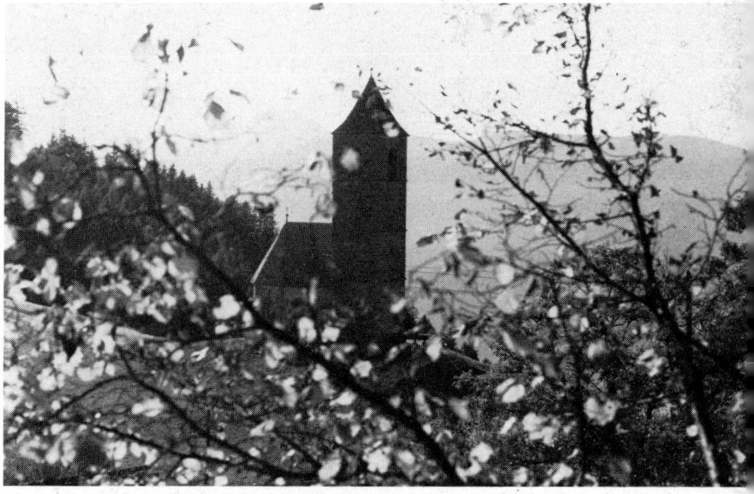

Scene C Two hikers, walking toward the camera.

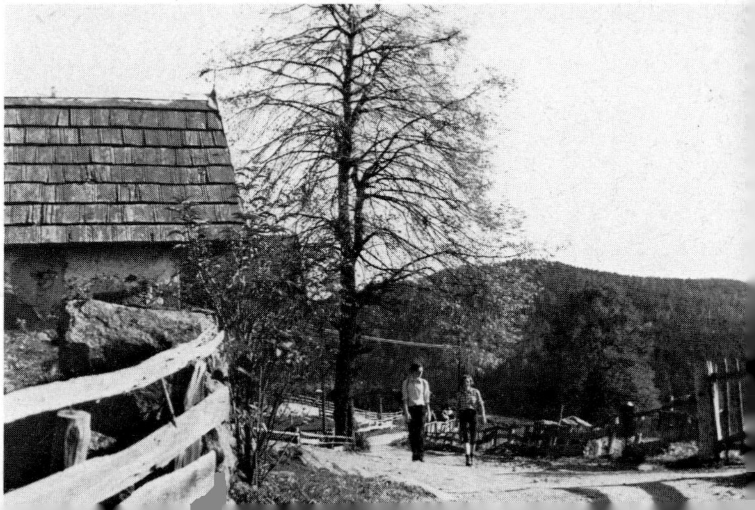

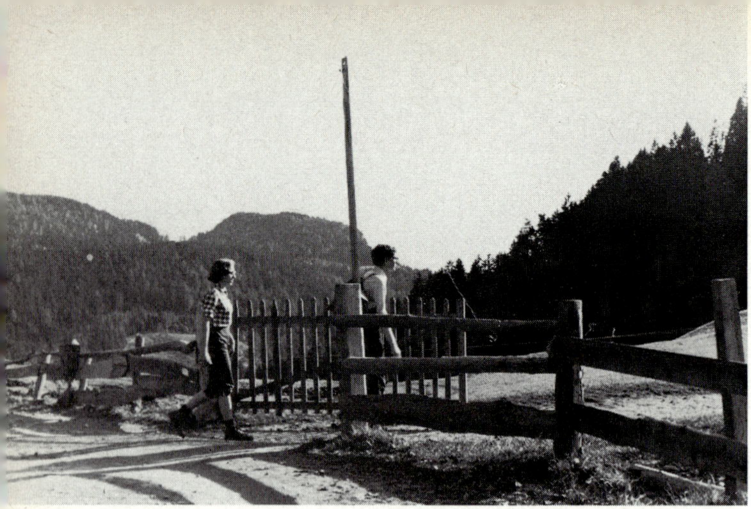

Scene D Counter shot of C, as they go through a gate.

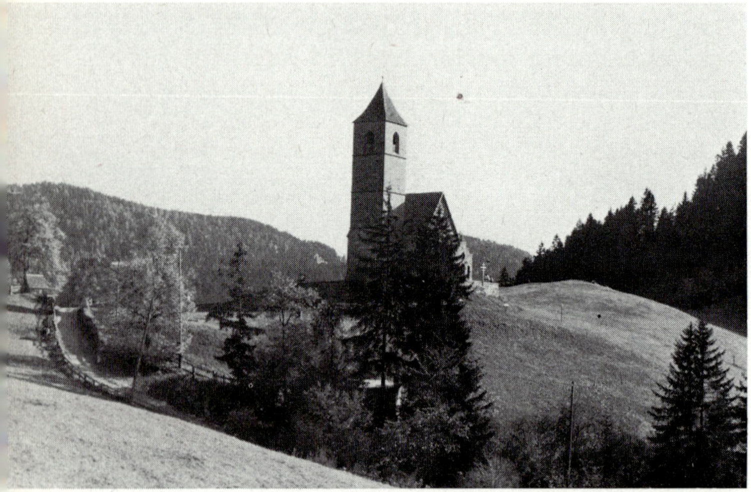

Scene E New perspective: the shot from church, as seen by the two hikers.

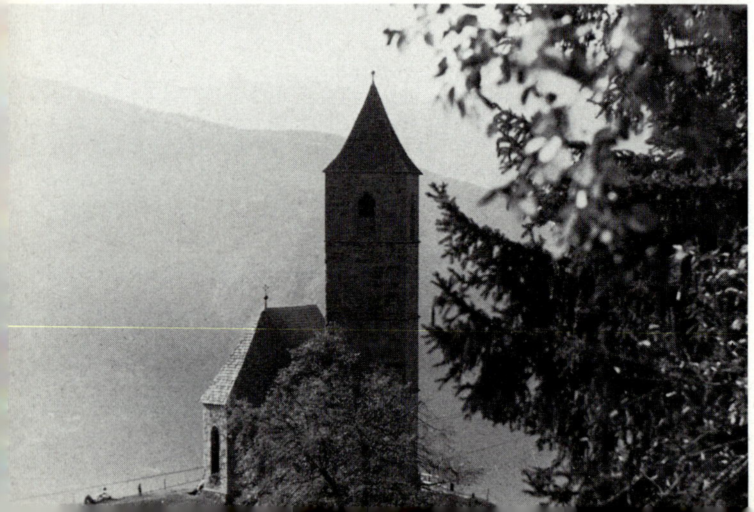

Scene F Change of camera direction: another view of the church, having moved in closer.

(Scenes E and F could be combined by means of a dissolve, if the camera is equipped for this.)

Scene G The hikers continue up the mountain to the church, walking towards the camera and moving out of the picture on the right.

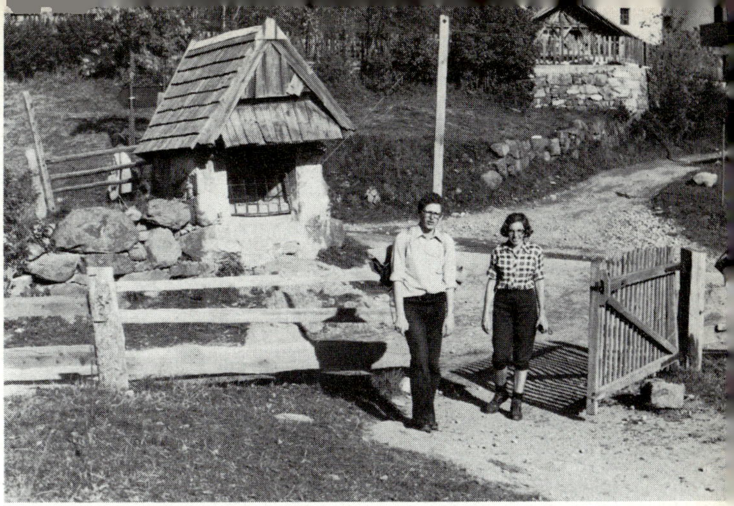

Scene H–I Tracking shot: in the first the lens is pointed at the church spire, if it is technically feasible, one then moves back into the wide-angle setting by means of a zoom-lens, until the surroundings of the church are completely in the picture (shot I).

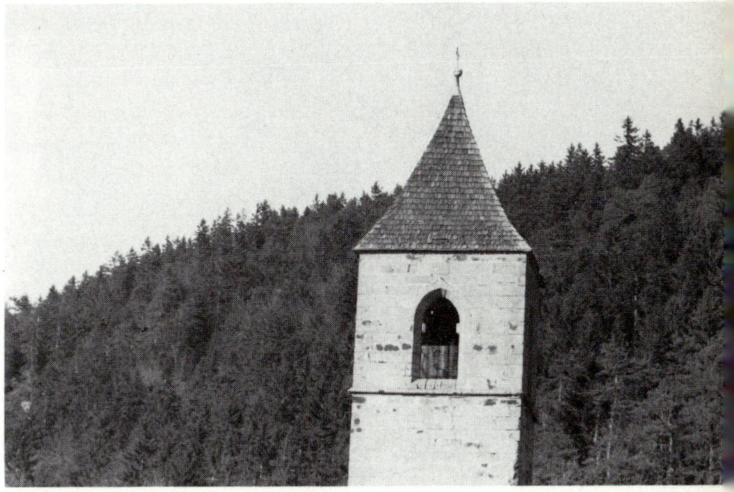

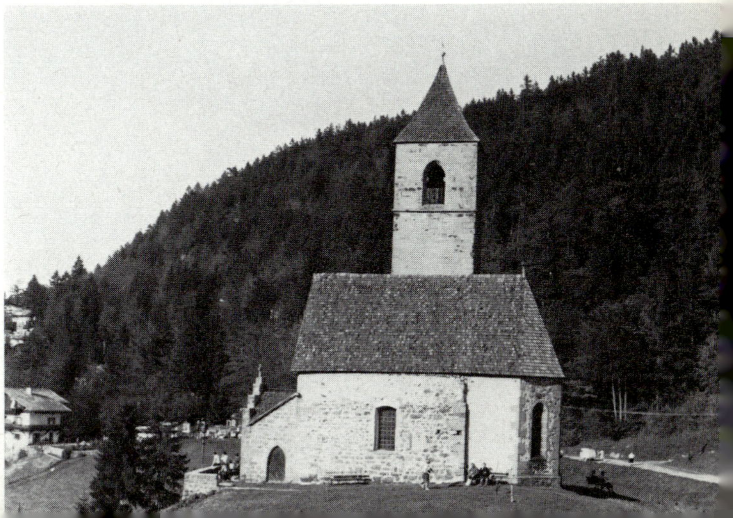

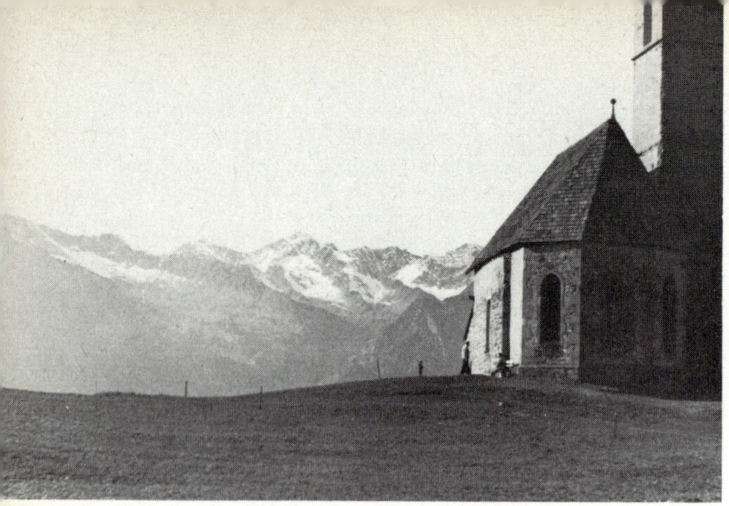

Scene K Counter shot to I. The church remains at the edge and cut off to some extent, since the mountains 'in the wings' add emphasis to the picture.

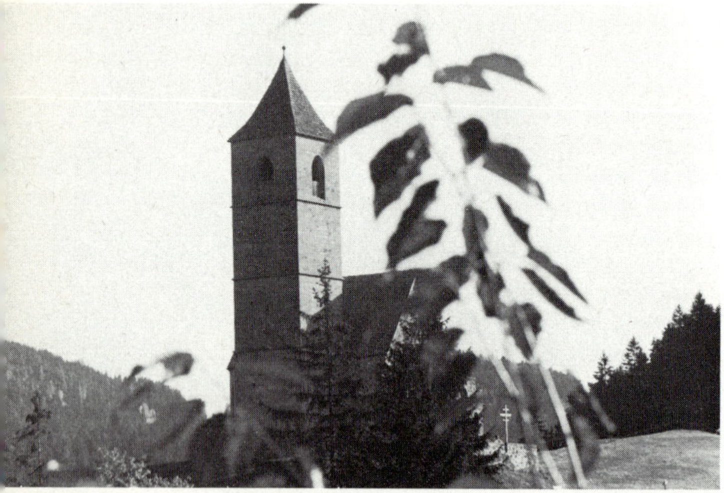

Scene L The central part of the picture, i.e. the church, is accentuated by a moving, ill-defined foreground. (Scenes of this type add life to any film.)

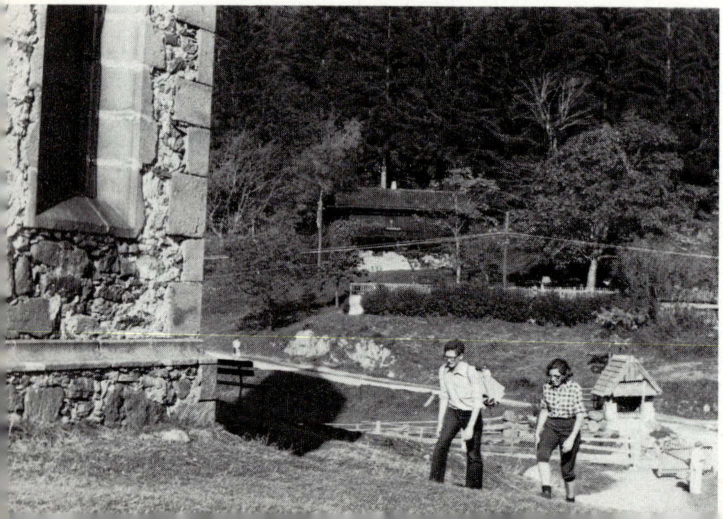

Scene M In the meantime the hikers approach the church, going out of the picture to the left.

Scene N They have reached the top of the hill and have gone to a viewing terrace. (The camera can make a pan to the left to show the impressive view, finally becoming stationary in the valley or at the mountain peaks. Move very slowly!)

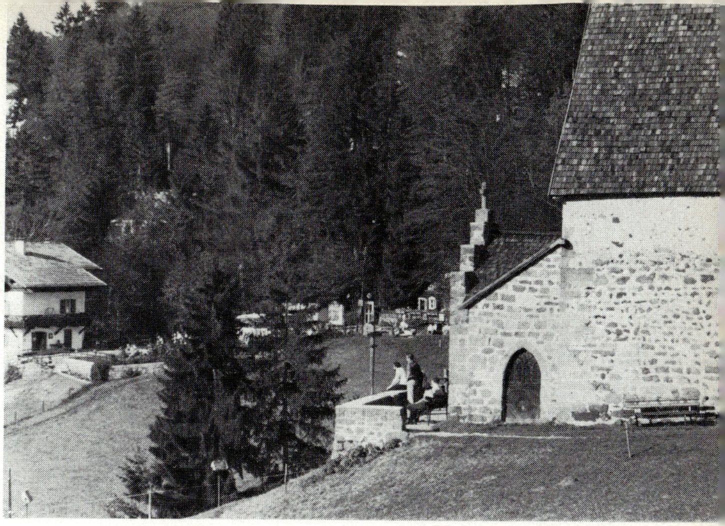

Scene O Counter shot to N: the camera films up the mountain to the two hikers.

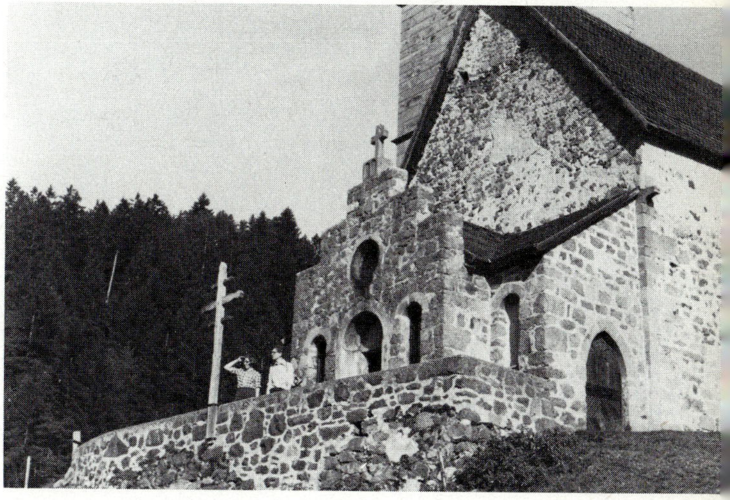

Scene P Short detailed shot: the cross on the spire.

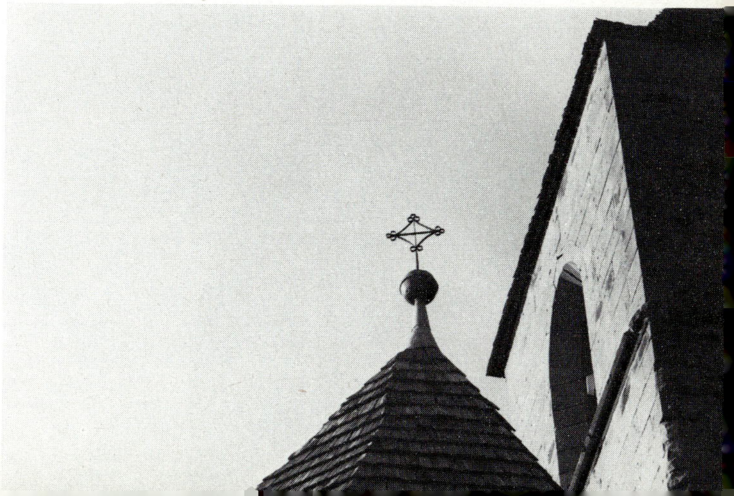

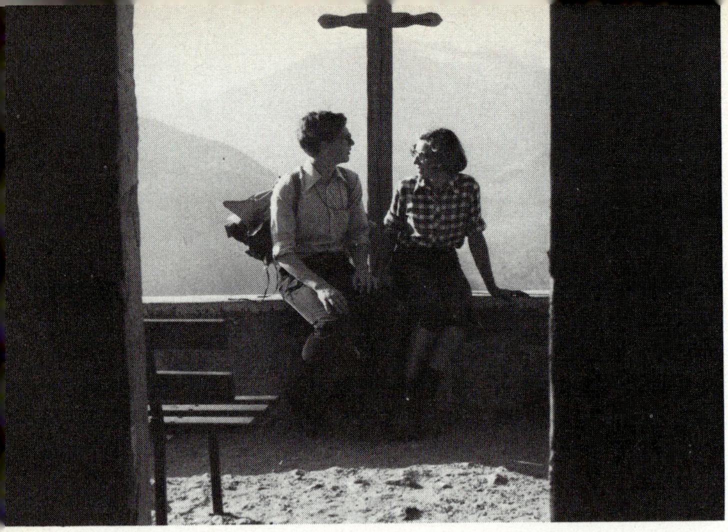

Scene Q Shot from the windows of the church of the hikers sitting on the wall.

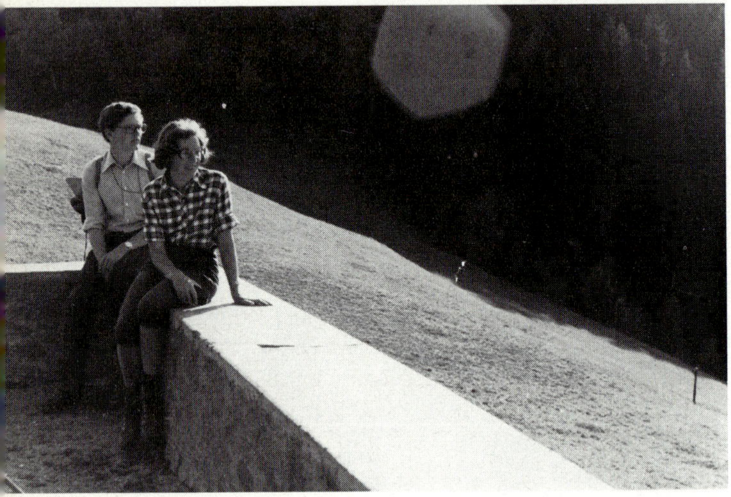

Scene R Change of direction to the side: a change of lighting in extreme backlight might result in light spots, but these can occasionally be very decorative. (They are caused by the refraction of light on the upper side of the inner lens and cannot be avoided. The more lenses the optical system possesses, the more frequently this will occur.)

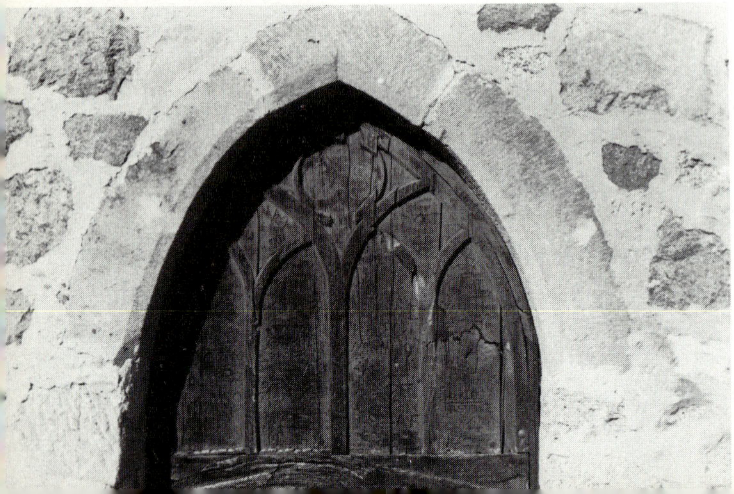

Scene S Insertion of a short shot showing detail.

Scene T Afterwards, a counter shot to R. A short scene may be blended in effectively between shot and counter shot.

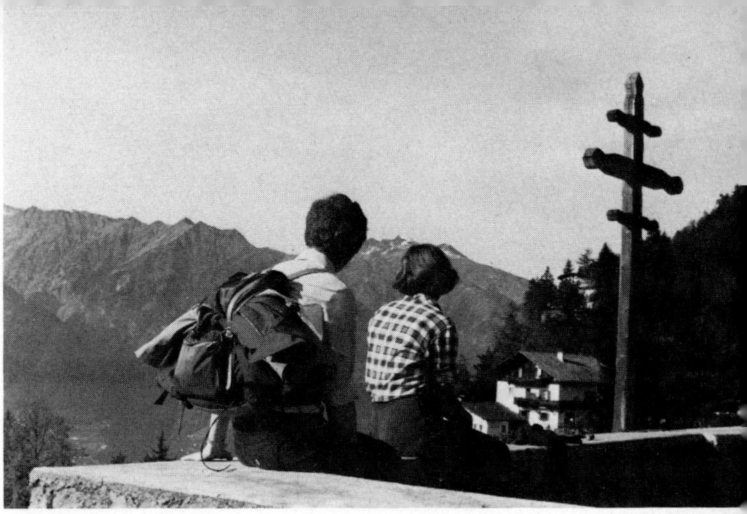

Scene U The two hikers depart, going left out of the picture. (The lighting contrast between scenes T and V is fairly considerable. An interesting effect can be achieved in this way.)

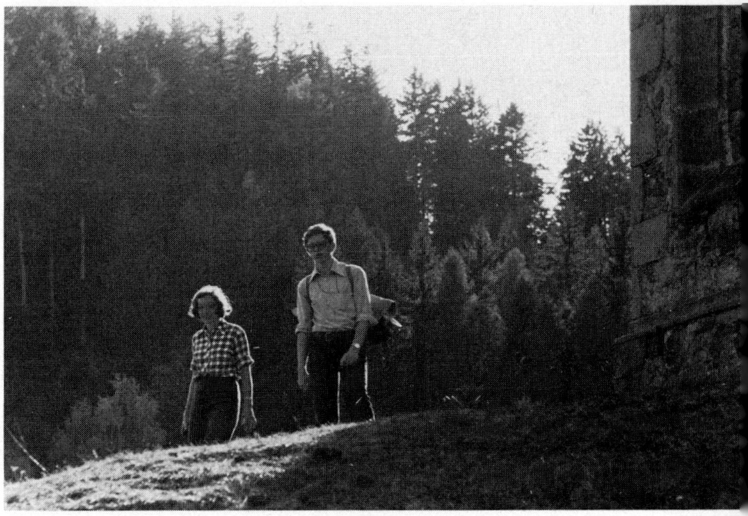

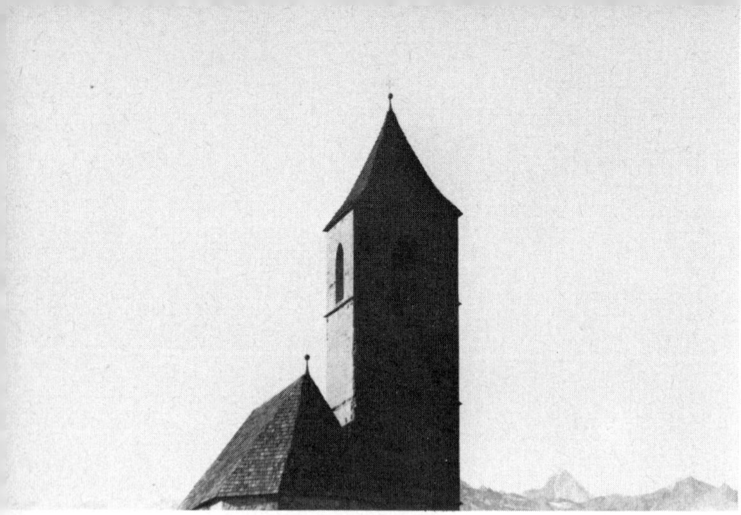

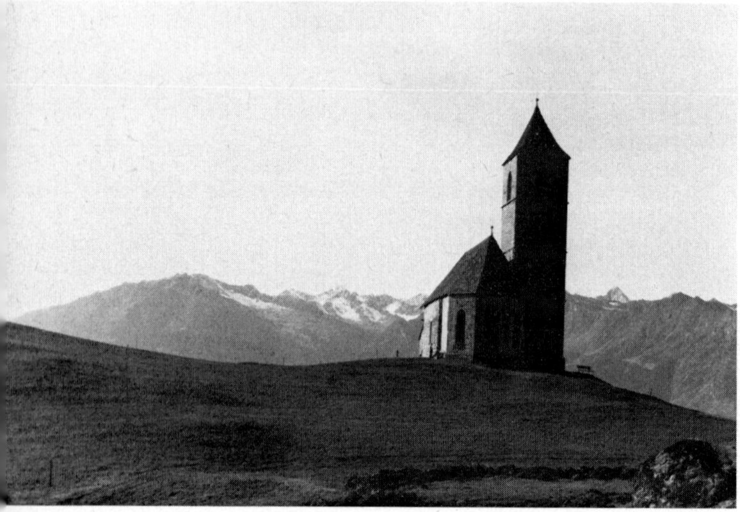

Scene V–W The final scenes bring the church back into the picture. Then the camera moves back slowly, until the entire landscape is included in the picture. After a few seconds, this is gradually faded out.

In a film of this nature, the scenes may last a relatively long time, since the theme is one of peace and contemplation, rather than presenting a hectic or hurried atmosphere. However, the scenes should not be too long, or the audience will suffer from boredom.

Obviously in filming such a theme it would be necessary to take more than twenty scenes, and later to sort out the most suitable for showing. A 15m. spool would certainly be sufficient however for a film of this type, even allowing for cutting.

Any holiday film can benefit from the occasional insertion of several such film episodes, each of varying content, as long as they do not detract from an impression of the film as a cohesive whole.

Theme for a length of film

While the last chapter discussed a sequence of scenes for a more or less improvised film, the following is to demonstrate how to create a plan for a length of film.

The exact length of a Super-8 film has been mentioned previously. It has a projecting time of about 200 seconds, or nearly 3½ minutes, which can be little, but can also be a very long time for a film. We consciously refer to 200 seconds, since all scene lengths are measured in seconds.

One can reckon on a length of about six seconds for a normal scene, which means you can take 30 scenes comfortably with a Super-8 film without getting into any difficulties. A time of 30 seconds will allow you to record quite a lot, not a whole holiday, but a Sunday walk for instance. Once you have attempted to fit a certain theme on to a length of film, it will soon become routine. For example, let us take the theme 'A Walk in the Woods'. From the 30 scenes three or four will be required for the introduction, and an equal number for the close, leaving free 24 scenes. Certainly this does not demand a script, but a draft or plan will serve to harmonise time and theme. At least some consideration of what the 24 scenes are to contain will clarify how long the film actually is. During a walk in the woods a few seconds can also be reserved for close-ups. The draft of a 15m. film might appear as follows:

Introduction:
Fade-in – A car enters the car park to the wood – People get out – Things are taken out of the car – A hand closes the door – Leaving from the car park.

Main Part
The family approaches and goes past the camera – The people are to some extent hidden by a branch in the foreground, as they move away from the camera – Blossom on a branch (close-up) – Shot of the wood – A woodland glade appears near the walkers – A child picks flowers – Close-up: some flowers – The child runs along behind his family, the flowers in his hand etc. – That is only eight scenes, out of a possible 24!

Ending:
Finally back to the car park – Packing the things away and getting into the car – The car moves in the direction of the camera – Fade-out.

A film plan for a 15m. film might look something like this. Naturally, the main section will be occupied by the family, and adjusted according to the season and surroundings, but much can be derived from our example for use in other situations. It is much better to make a purposely connected film than to take frequent shots, which will never fit together later.

The basic difference between the film and the still photograph has already been discussed. For instance, one could take two photographs every Sunday until the film is finished, but you should not attempt to take two film scenes every Sunday, as they could hardly be combined.

Making a draft for a 15m. film is actually the first step to making a script, and perhaps you will at some point decide to have an attempt at this. You then have a double pleasure: firstly, writing the script, and then making the film. It must be assumed that in the meantime you have become well acquainted with the techniques both of the camera and of filming. In addition, it is important to test out the limits of your possibilities. It would be pointless to include in a script things which only a professional could accomplish, particularly since the numerous techniques which are available to the amateur already afford him plenty of scope.

FILMING WITH A SCRIPT

Filming with a script is in itself more professional work, and anyone who has had the chance to witness work at a film studio will have gained an impression of this. Individual scenes are filmed which appear to the outsider to have no bearing on each other. However, due to the vast daily expense of professional filming, all the scenes with the same location are taken one after the other, irrespective of whether they follow each other in the film, or appear in varying positions.

You will without doubt have heard of the 'clapper-board'. This consists of two slats of wood, exhibiting the number of the scene to be filmed in accordance with the script, and simultaneously producing an acoustic signal for the sound accompaniment, if the sound is to be recorded as the film is taken. The clapper appears before every film scene, providing the 'cutter' with important information for the editing of the film. The procedure will not be quite as professional when the film amateur writes a script and then wants to make a film. Obviously we remain free to alter our work, should the occasion arise for taking better or different shots from those originally anticipated in the film script. Perhaps this also happens with the professionals occasionally.

Idea and construction

What should be the appearance of a film script devised by an amateur film-maker? There are several books containing patterns for scripts and film ideas, and these examples are suitable for learning construction methods, particularly of course if a few of the ideas can be realised.

The idea is the most important factor of all! It should be both attractive, and feasible with a few people and the smallest possible degree of technical sophistication. The idea must pose no insoluble problems for the amateur director.

Professional film-makers are blessed with almost limitless possibilities with regard both to studio construction and trick-film studios, and in choice of camera. While only a minor rôle is played by technical considerations in professional filming, amateur film-makers must view them as a deciding factor.

When a practicable idea has been found, the first thing to do is to discuss it with all the people involved in the film. Such discussion can inspire some valuable suggestions, since naturally everyone will view the project from a different standpoint. The various opinions will not only lead to some useful conclusions, but may indeed suggest a better form for the script.

Those concerning themselves with a scripted idea for the first time should aim above all to keep it short. Longer scripts can be written as it becomes more routine, but to begin with, one should be content with a 10 or 17 minute film. As a 3 minute Super-8 film allows about 30 scenes, 12 minutes would mean four films and about 120 scenes. For the beginner, this is a considerable amount.

The structure of the script is dependent on various factors, the most important being the film-maker himself. His attitude and way of seeing things will be imprinted on every film. Judging by experience, a lively, impetuous person favours fairly short scenes and frequent changes in the situation, a quieter, perhaps a rather old film-maker would definitely prefer longer settings and would not alter the taking standpoint so quickly. The temperament of every individual is in turn reflected in his filming – always providing that they have equal command of the technical elements.

Once the idea and construction are more or less established, the next point is for the script to identify its actors, the people who are to represent the various characters. Usually these are friends or members of the family, so there is no difficulty in suiting them to the right rôles, and planning their corresponding involvement in the script.

Further to this, the predominant questions are those concerning the content of the film, with reference to the theme of the film, the place of the action, your technical equipment, and last, but not least, the technical capabilities which you have in the meantime developed through handling the camera. Here it must again be stressed that a certain amount of experience is required before undertaking to film with a script, although you will increase your technical ability from film to film. Ultimately it is not a question of which camera is being used for the filming, but of who is using it. Even filming demands a certain amount of flair. It is not without reason that some film directors are world famous for their superb achievements, while many others remain more or less average. There is little significant difference in the technical provisions – the person is the deciding factor!

It might be beneficial to the construction of the script to note how a professional film is compiled. To this end, watch a film which you already know and by which you have been impressed. If you are already aware of what is going to happen, you are able to concentrate all the more on the composition of the film. Pay attention to the following: how did the director measure the scene length? Did he establish a general principle, or are they designed according to the content and hence very varying? Which setting did he use most frequently, and which less often? (Close-up, full length, medium close-up.) How does he handle shot and counter-shot?

Consider these questions carefully before watching the film, and then take particular note of the elements of composition. A successful director certainly knows how to make correct measurements, and from him the amateur can learn how to construct his film, and use this to develop his own ideas.

Finally, another tip for compiling a script: both you and the actors pursue occupations which only allow 'great' filmwork on holiday or at the weekend. Consequently your script should be devised in such a way as to accommodate as much filmwork as possible on one day. In addition, the external influences will vary on differing days. The film/montage is needlessly complicated when filming for the same sequence of scenes is undertaken on various days. Moreover, if all the filming is done on one day, there will be no problem with regard to clothes or weather.

The Script

The necessary prerequisites have been explained, and now the theory of the completed script must be put into practice. The following example is a script from which some friends and I have filmed. With the title and leader strip it is approximately 32m. long. The draft:

1 *The idea.*
A walk through the town. A foreign friend is shown round the town, his attention drawn to its most interesting features.
2 *The framework.*
The visitor is travelling by train and has a two-hour break in his journey before the next train departs. Beginning and end are at the station.
3 *The title.*
'Two hours to spare'
Not more than two films will be required, although a third might be kept in reserve. Two film lengths will give about 60 settings, so even if a scene has to be repeated here and there, you will still have a sufficient number of settings effectively remaining for filming.

The cover of the script contains instructions about which accessories the film requires, e.g. tripod, cable-release, remote release, etc., in order to avoid the possibility of anything being forgotten.

The list of utensils cannot be too extensive. You can also note here who is involved in the film, and, if necessary, the preferred colours of their clothing. Insofar as a number of scenes are to be filmed at the same location, there should also be instructions indicating which situation would be the most suitable for each shot, i.e. a sunny position, in the shade of the trees etc. On the other hand if, as in the following script, the site of the action changes from scene to scene, such directions will become obvious in the script.

Firstly, the pages of the script can be divided into 5 columns:
Column 1 = Number of the film scene
Column 2 = Form of content (picture)
Column 3 = Length of scene (time)
Column 4 = Setting (close-up = C, medium close-up = M, full-length = F)
Column 5 = Sound instructions
Write down the whole film sequence in the columns, as shown in the example. If the film is properly planned, there is little else which can go wrong.

Title: 'Two hours to spare'
Personae: Friend passing through on a journey (light travelling clothes, travelling-bag, pocket time-table, watch).
He (dressed in brown)
She (blue skirt, yellow blouse)
Camera accessories: Tripod and cable release
Close-up lens, lens hood, 2–3 films
Weather: sunny summer's day

No	Picture	Time in secs	Setting	Sound
1	Fade-in on the station forecourt.	8	F	street noises
2	Zoom: through the entrance.	6	F	street noises
3	Station clock: 15.00.	4	M	nothing
4	A couple walk towards the time-table board.	6	M	music, as far as possible without singing
5	A finger points to the arrival time.	5	C	
6	Platform sign showing time of arrival.	4	M	
7	'He' and 'she' loiter on the platform.	5	F	
8	A train arrives, going past them both.	5	M	blend in
9	The friend stands at the window and waves.	5	C	train noises
10	View along the train, all the doors opening.	6	M	
11	Fade-out.	1½	—	
	Fade-in.	1½	—	
11	The three meet up, laughing, on the station forecourt.	6	M	traffic noise
12	The friend takes a timetable from his pocket.	3	M	
13	Timetable. Departure time must be easily legible: 17.12.			
14	The three running towards a road.	3	M	
15	Red light.	1	C	
16	Amber light.	1	C	
17	Cars going by.	2	M	car horns
18	Green light.	1	C	
19	They cross the road, walking towards the camera and eventually past it.	6	M	light music
20	Guildhall market.	6	F	light music
21	Up the steps to the Guildhall.	4	M	blended in
22	View from there back over the church in the market place.	6	F	'This is the Guildhall and over there is the church'
23	A hand shades the eyes from the sun.	3	C	
24	The pigeons flutter round the fountain, the water splashes.	5	M	music again at full volume
25	They return and sit on the edge of the fountain.	6	M	
26	A hand plays in the water.	3	C	
27	An ice-cream vendor.	4	M	
28	They walk up to him and buy ice-creams.	6	M	light music

No	Picture	Time in secs	Setting	Sound
29	The friend licks his ice-cream.	3	C	
30	Fade-in.	6	F	
31	They go up the steps to the theatre's colonnade.	3	M	classical music
32	Feet on the steps.	4	C	
33	View through the pillars towards the colonnade.	5	F	
34	The spa hotel.			
35	Cashier's kiosk at the spa park.	4	M	fade out
36	The entrance fee is paid. A hand picks up the tickets and change.	3	C	
37	Bushes in bloom. The three – slightly out of focus – walk by behind the bushes.	6	M	light music
38	They stand by a pond with ducks on it.	5	M	
39	A duck comes right up close to them.	4	C	
40	Camera pans slowly from the pond up to the terrace of the spa hotel.	8	F	
41	A dance band is playing there.	6	M	light music
42	Musicians in close-up.	4	C	
43	Stroll through the park, up to a memorial.	6	M	
44	The three are seen approaching from the memorial. They stop in front of it.	5	M	

No	Picture	Time in secs	Setting	Sound
45	A hand strokes the head of the bronze figure.	4	C	
46	A look at the watch shows it is 16.50: another 20 minutes before the train departs (must be clearly visible).	3	C	
47	Moving away from the pond. The path is enlarged by means of a zoom effect from tele to wide angle.	6	F	
48	Street. Bus stop. Bus drives up – has 'station' on the front.	5	M	
49	The three get on.	5	M	street noises
50	Station square: the three get off the bus and go towards the station entrance.	8	F	
51	They disappear into the station (running past the camera).	6	M	
52	They look for the right platform. The friend waves from the departing train; the two on the platform wave as well.	6	M	train noises
53	The train disappears into the distance.	5	F	
54	Fade-out.	3		

All the scripted scenes together add up to less than 300 seconds. However, a safety margin has been included in the film's calculations since the setting of any of the scenes on the busy street could go awry. People hurrying past, a dense line of cars and other unaccountable factors may mean that one or another scene has to be filmed several times. This does not matter, since any uneveness has to be ironed out during editing in any case.

About 10 or 15 seconds must be added to the total for the title. There are many varying opinions about types of title, which will be discussed in the chapter 'Film Titles'. The manner in which the title 'Two hours to spare' should be produced will also be discussed there.

SCORING

The sound element of the film can also be compiled in various ways. In our example, only music and noises were used, but an explanatory text, or a conversation with question and answer could be equally effective: this is primarily a question of taste. The various possibilities of film technique are discussed in another chapter.

In the chosen example, obviously the type of music used is a matter of taste. One type could be used all the way through, rather than changing to classical music as in this case for the stroll to the theatre. It would be equally possible to associate one type of music with the station at the beginning and end of the film, and another contrasting type with the central part of the film. Moreover, our example allowed either for the music to be continued softly throughout the other noises, or to be faded out.

There are countless possibilities, and none is wrong. It is up to you to find the right way for your film.

The film 'Two hours to spare' shows that a film made according to a script does not demand a flair for acting on the part of those involved. They move as naturally as ever. Only here and there will you need to make a trial-run, in order to test whether time is adequate for the scene, or whether the picture corresponds to your expectations. However this is only a very gentle type of direction, and should not be allowed to affect the actors in any other way.

Amateur feature film

Anyone who has made a lot of films might one day come to try their hand at making a feature film. This will require a cast able to undertake a theatrical rôle; probably you will have a look around your circle of friends to find the most suitable person.

Often the search does not begin until the planning stages of the film are completed. It goes without saying that this will demand a script, which will naturally be far more comprehensive than the one for our short film. The various characters must be determined, and instructions regarding the action must be given in minute detail.

If the idea is to produce an amateur feature film, contact might also be made with an

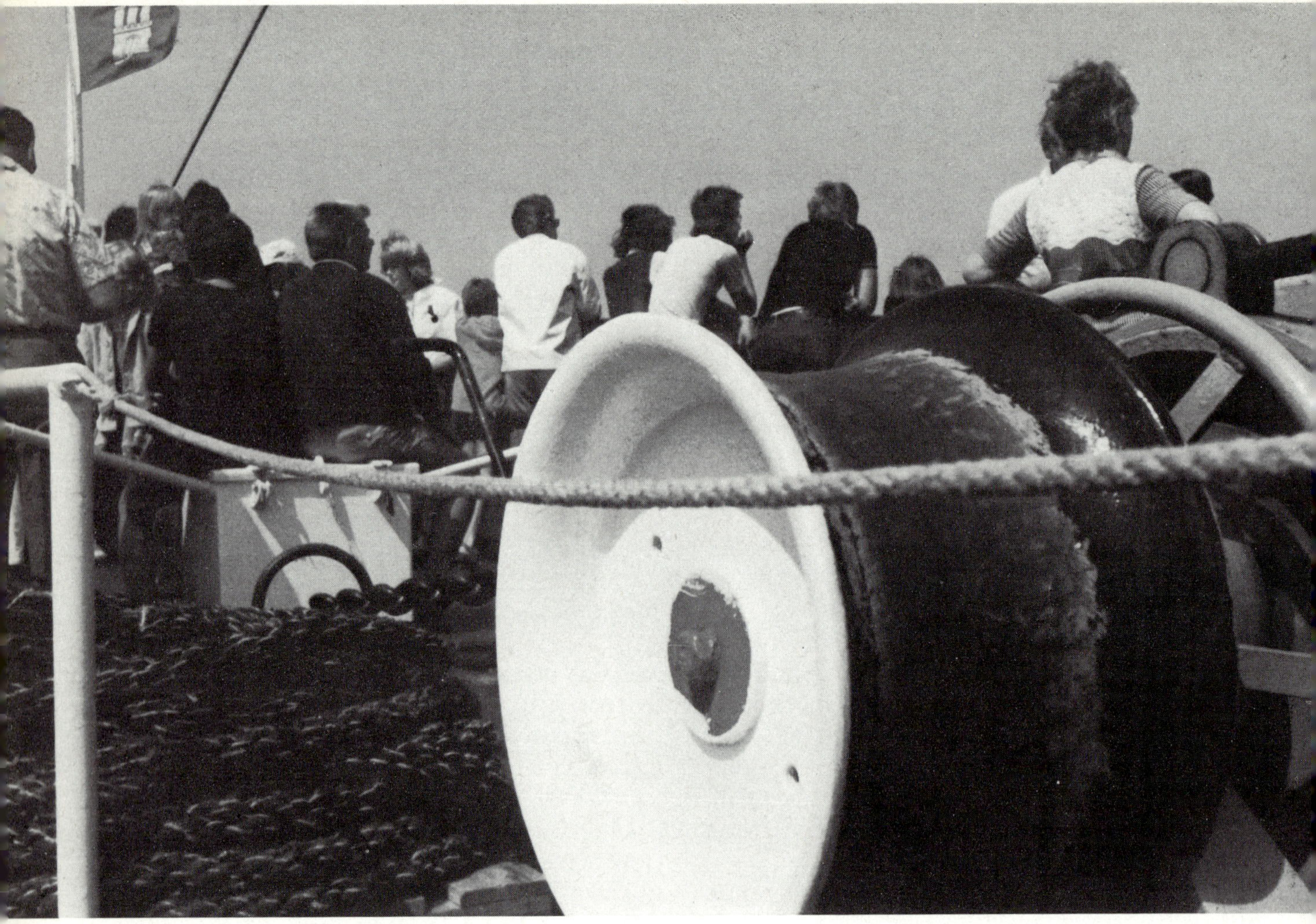

Worm's-eye view – from top to bottom. The foreground is emphasised. Such shots provide a great illusion of depth

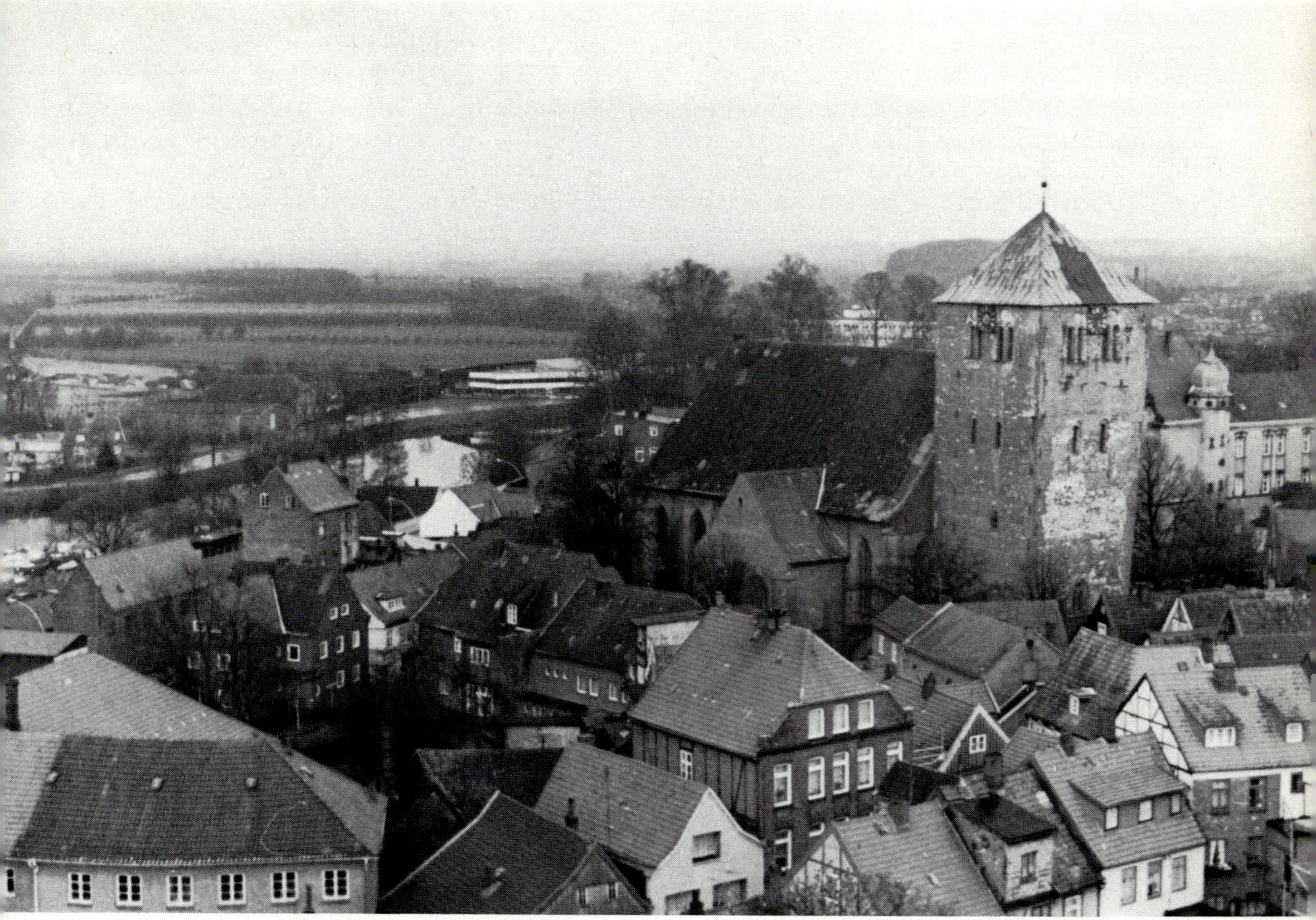

Bird's-eye view – from top to bottom. Here the overall view takes first place. The perspective serves as a clear introduction to where the action of the film takes place

amateur theatrical company. Such groups are nearly always enthusiastic about a private film undertaking, and above all, they will have already played a number of roles.

Often the amateur film team will decide that they want to film a crime story, particularly if there is as yet no script in existence. However, it is considerably more difficult to write a good script for an amateur crime film than it is for a light-hearted film. While it is in theory relatively uncomplicated to adopt the tricks and gags used in feature films, the actual technical creation of them is usually not nearly so easy. The danger lies in the fact that the script will be measured against the many crime stories seen on film and television. Most film amateurs necessarily have to proceed with fairly simple technical equipment, with which the problems of lighting, night-filming, and sound-recording can hardly be overcome. Moreover the precedents under consideration employ highly-regarded specialists for the various individual branches of filming – the amateur has to do it all himself.

Nevertheless, one need not abandon the idea of filming a crime story. I have, for example, filmed a crime story with a ciné-photography group at adult-education classes: the work was both successful and very enjoyable.

With the right partners, adequate time, perseverance, and above all a suitable script, even a crime story can be a success.

Finally, I should say that the only difference between the professional and the amateur film lies in their size: the scheme of composition is the same for both. Disregarding the cost, it should therefore be possible to realise the principles of the feature film with only amateur materials. There are indeed already a number of short films in which amateurs have shown themselves able to condense the theme with surprising success. As a rule, this demands harmonious group-work with enthusiastic theatre students or amateur actors, and often the cameraman is also the script-writer and director. It is not surprising that many take the first step to professional filming on the basis of this intensive schooling with the amateur film.

It is important that the script should be written in the language of the feature film, and should from the outset include a careful consideration of different camera settings and varying perspectives, which may combine to produce some enigmatic effects. All the effective techniques of scene transition should be employed: wipes, grease plates, fade-ins, fade-outs, and dissolves. While long scenes can produce an impression of epic dimensions, short scenes will lead to a dramatic climax, particularly by growing increasingly shorter.

If you have written the script yourself and are going to take the film, you will also be in charge of direction. This requires a certain amount of skill when working with a variety of people, all with a different conception of the script. The team spirit is important, as a good director can always take advantage of it in looking for the correct solution.

It is a different matter when the leader of the amateur dramatic group approaches you with a film suggestion and asks you to make the film. In this case it is important to clarify whether the script-writer is going to undertake the direction, or whether this should be in the hands of the cameraman, in other words, the amateur film-maker. The best solution is to ascertain, through lengthy discussion, who would be able to realise the idea most successfully.

When making a first feature film, one should on no account be sparing with the film. Every setting should be filmed often until you are quite satisfied that it is good. When the film is edited, you will discover that the various shots of the same setting are clearly distinguishable from each other; when the best have been chosen, the remainder can be cut out. You can reckon on a cutting ratio of 4:1. This means that 150m. of Super-8 film would be required for a film of 20 minutes running time.

Adequate acquaintance has already been made with the compilation of the script. However, with a feature film the director has an even more important task: he has to make a script plan, bringing together all the scenes in the script that are to be filmed at the same place. Obviously with a feature film the scenes are taken not in the order in which they appear in the script, but using the method that incurs the smallest possible cost. Consequently the director is responsible for stating in the script plan where and when each scene is to be filmed.

Documentary Films

We return again to the subject of film themes, this time in connection with documentary films. A small theme might be, for instance, a view of the town or a landscape, a castle and its grounds, describing a career, or a theme chosen from the fields of science, art, or technology.

In each case, the film deals with facts that are to be reported. All the facets of the theme must be explored before filming begins, so that the script includes carefully thought out directions concerning the action and sequence of the scenes.

Let us take for instance a view of the town, preferably your home town, as you will know it well. This is important, since with such a comprehensive theme it becomes necessary from the outset to confine yourself to one small section. It is of no particular significance whether the film theme is limited in respect of time or of subject matter. For a film about 'My home town' one might choose the following theme-lines:

1 'Buildings of long ago – town-planning today'
2 'Between 8 and 12 o'clock'
3 'Market Day'
4 'Sunday in the town'
5 'Industry in our town'
6 'Dusk'

This is enough to inspire some ideas; and one need not worry about filming a theme similar to one already filmed, since amateur films are generally made only for private presentation. Even professional films occasionally repeat a title and produce a new version of a film.

It is thus important to limit the theme to a segment of the whole. Taking the last example, 'Dusk', presumably various ideas will immediately occur to everybody, since a town on a summer's evening offers an inexhaustible supply of subject matter. Here I can only suggest some ideas which you could apply at will to any town or place.

The golden light of the late sun is always effective in such a film; moreover, in the evening the sun's rays cause long shadows, which should be included everywhere in the film.

The following example might inspire some ideas for subject matter:

The clock on the church tower shows slightly before 18.00. In the town it is time for finishing work. The working people are doing their shopping, but already the shops are closing. The vases are taken in from the front of the florist. Doors are closed. An innkeeper shakes out the table-cloths and folds them up, and puts the tables straight; he takes the menus inside with him. An apprentice pulls the grill down in front of the shop window and door before leaving the shop. Women with tired children make their way home, disappearing behind the front doors. A man home from work waters the flowers in his garden. People are sitting in the park and in the public gardens, enjoying the fine summer's evening. The café is very busy. Gradually it gets dark. The street lamps come on. Lights appear in the windows of the houses. Without doubt other things will occur to you, with special reference to your town. A film of this type could be filmed on various days, since the general action shots and the individual occurrences can be filmed independently of each other; it is of course crucial that the scenes should be suited to each other both in terms of theme and of content.

Documentaries concerning science, the arts, or technology are on the other hand more difficult to create, and require special advice and careful planning. As a rule, however, only amateurs with a particular interest and knowledge of a subject would concern themselves with filming of this type.

Other Themes

Occasionally ciné clubs will hold a film competition, for which a film on a certain topic has to be made. For instance, the requirement might be to make a film based on a certain piece of music. A record could serve for this, even though this might seem unusual. An attractive theme, and not so very difficult for anyone with sufficient time to investigate the possibilities.

The points already made with reference to film composition remain valid, except that in this case there is a definite stated time-length, and your task is to augment the music by fitting film scenes into this time-scheme.

The initial problem, then, is to find a topic to match the suggested music. Anyone wishing to undertake this task should be at least of average musical ability, but I would imagine that he would not be interested in the project if this were not the case.

Occasionally one will make certain associations or imagine certain pictures when listening to various pieces of music, and you must now try and fix such pictures in your mind. The main task is then to conceive a film on the basis of this, a pictorial representation of what you imagine when listening to the music. When this has been achieved, the next step follows: the pieces of music to be used for the individual scenes must be measured exactly in seconds, preferably with a stop watch. If you establish, for example, that a piece of music is 12 seconds long, then you will need 12 x 18 = 216 frames, i.e. a piece of music 12 seconds long will cover exactly 216 frames. The film editing must be correspondingly executed with the maximum exactitude, otherwise at the end of the music, picture and sound will not match each other. If there were just one frame too many in each of ten film cuts, this would result in a difference of more than half a second. While this may seem laughingly little, it would be clearly noticeable on a synchronised film.

Without doubt the theme 'make a film from a record' is one of the most difficult possible in the amateur film sector. It demands a great deal of fantasy and musicality, and above all a lot of time spent

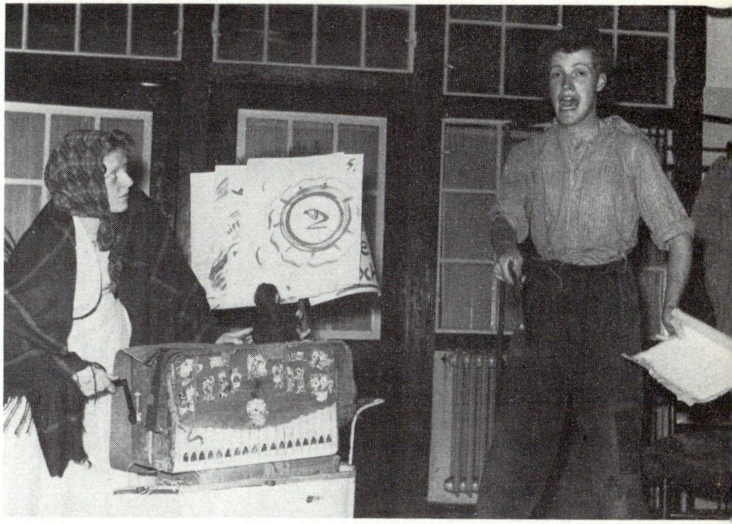

Plays – always popular

Outing to the airport:
Plenty of people mean plenty of life. The airport provides plenty for young and old alike, and for the camera

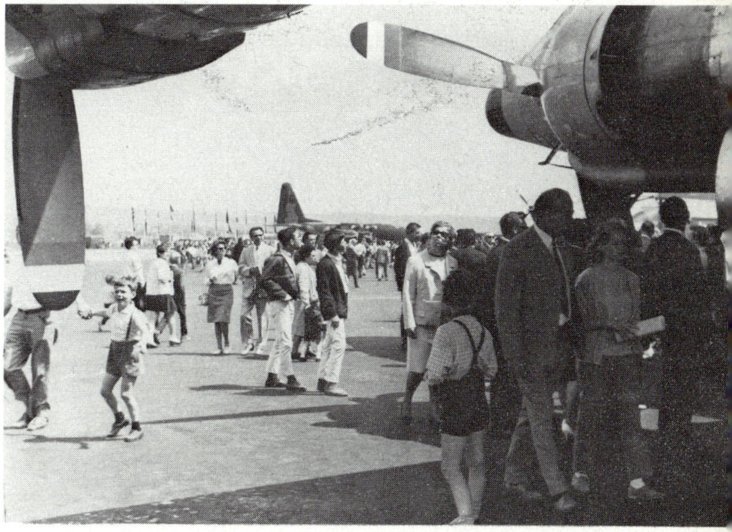

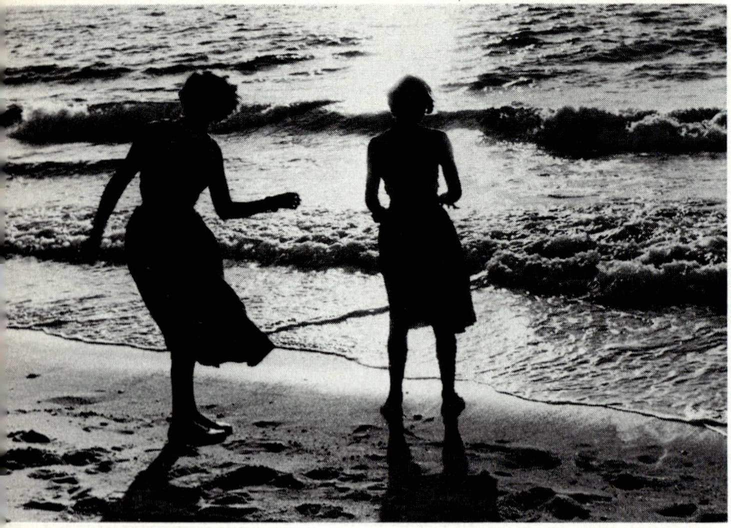

Girls by the sea with back-light – a popular film theme with many variations.

Holiday-film theme:
A man on the dunes – his long shadow adds interest

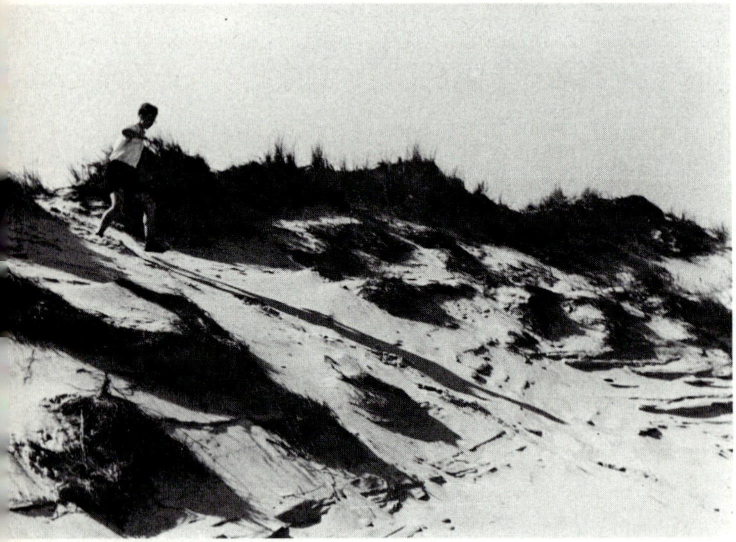

in editing and montage work.

To close this chapter, some further advice on developing filming ideas and gathering inspiration. There is a wide choice of topics, and from each with a certain amount of thought a film concept could emerge. Nor is it absolutely essential to write a script for every film. By far the majority of films exist without a script, often even without any preconceived ideas. Naturally, it is better to plan a film exactly from the wide range of topics available, or at least to make some notes about how it is to proceed; the 'red thread' makes filming easier.

The following is a list of possible topics, partly to augment and partly to summarise what has already been suggested.

1 *People as central figures.*
This includes all films of the children and the family, outings, etc. People and their surroundings. In its widest sense, the holiday is also implied in this. Individual themes will produce particular films, e.g. special birthdays, the first day of school, the garden party, Christmas, engagements, weddings, and much more.

2 *Hobbies*
Everyone has a hobby; ciné filmers often pursue another alnongside filming, and every hobby is suited to a film, e.g. stamp collection, the model railway, making Lego models, painting for pleasure, the joys and sufferings of the angler, etc.

Sunset: with which many holiday films close

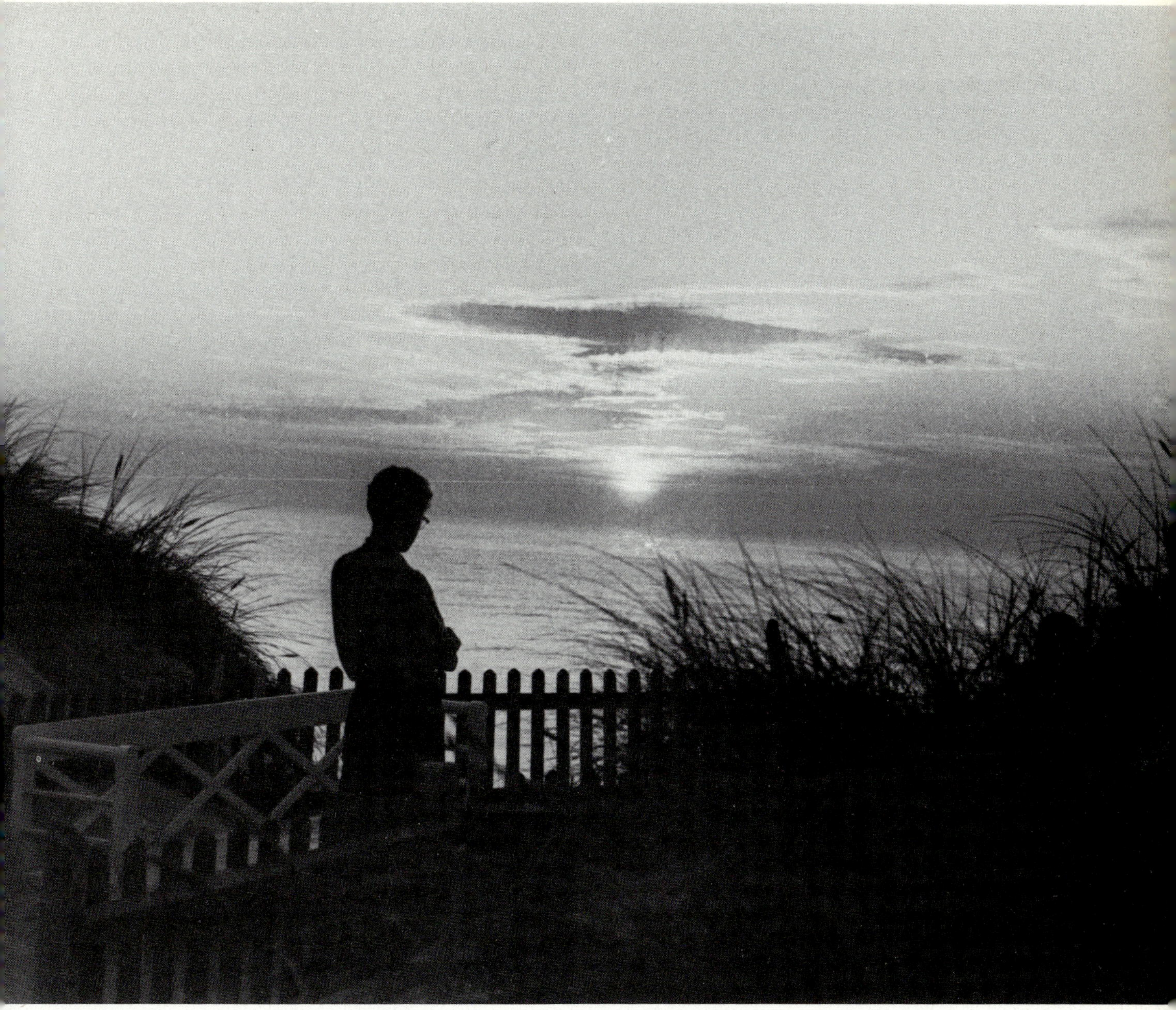

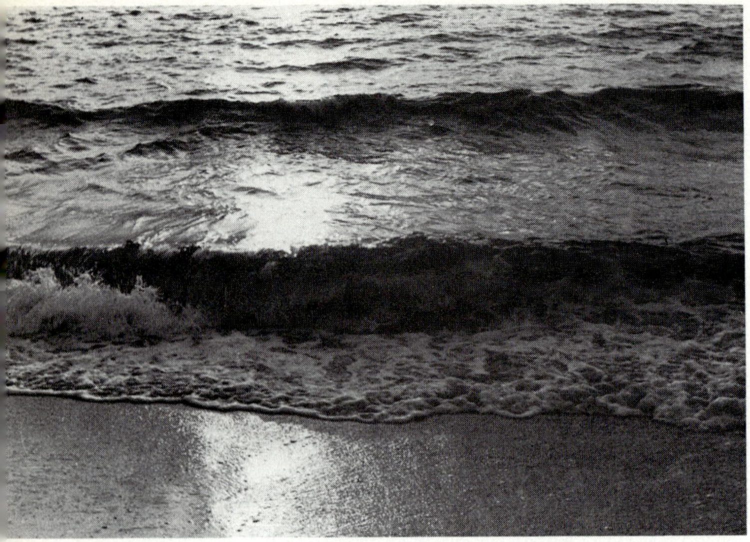

Under the heading 'sea', waves in the evening sun frequently appear

3 *Nature*
Our garden; winter guests at the bird table; the aquarium; insects; trees and bushes; flowers on the wayside; mountains and mountain walking; the hunt; rivers; lakes and the sea.

There are many other subjects within the world of nature which are suitable for filming.
Further topics might be:
4 *Animals, particularly pets.*
5 *Art and architecture.*
6 *Reportage, documentary films.*
7 *Sport.*
8 *Music, film.*
Everyone will pick out their own themes, according to their interests and their surroundings. Anyone who has gone through the whole process of devising and taking a film will notice that the next time everything seems much quicker and easier. If you are thorough to begin with, your ability to handle any theme can only increase.

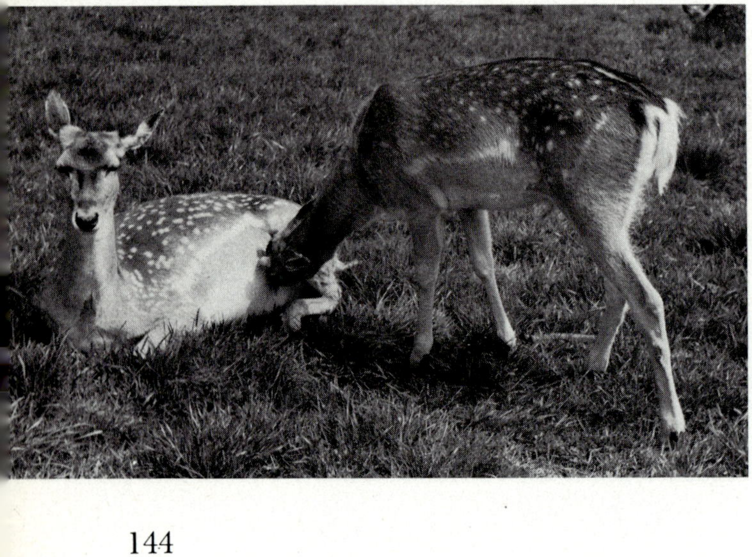

Animals are a popular film theme. Animals photographed in the wild or in the zoo usually demand the use of long focal lengths and, of course, a tripod

SPECIAL FILMING

The areas of filming which have not yet been discussed belong in the rather exceptional, special fields, and include techniques that, although nearly always realisable with the modern camera, are rarely, if ever, practised.

MACRO SHOTS

Only a few years ago, filming in the macro-range was more or less impossible for the amateur, but nowadays macro-shots can be taken with nearly all ciné cameras. As a rule, the modern camera is fitted with a reflex viewfinder, which means the subject is viewed through the lens and the focus can be set exactly. If a variable lens with a long focal length is used, often even the tele setting will be sufficient to produce a large image of small objects with a very short focal range. Should this result in the details of the small object being no longer in focus, a supplementary or close-up lens would come to the rescue. However, the best, because it is the least complicated, method of taking such shots, is by means of a macro-zoom-lens. And now that it is not only the high-class cameras that are fitted with them many amateur film-makers are discovering the remarkable charm of such shots.

What does a macro-shot actually mean? Macro stands for 'large', but implies that large images are produced of small objects. The macro camera can be used to blend very interesting close-up shots, e.g. flowers or butterflies, into any film. It is particularly attractive, however, to take a whole film on the macro setting: we might take the hobby theme 'Stamp collecting' as an example. The collector and the film amateur can produce an interesting documentary film with a macro-zoom. The postage stamps can be filmed as a whole, while details of graphically impressive examples are also possible.

Further examples are obvious. A keen gardener can begin a film about his plants with the smallest seedlings, ending with close-ups of the blooms. If your interest is insects, filming in macro range offers a number of possibilities. Previously,

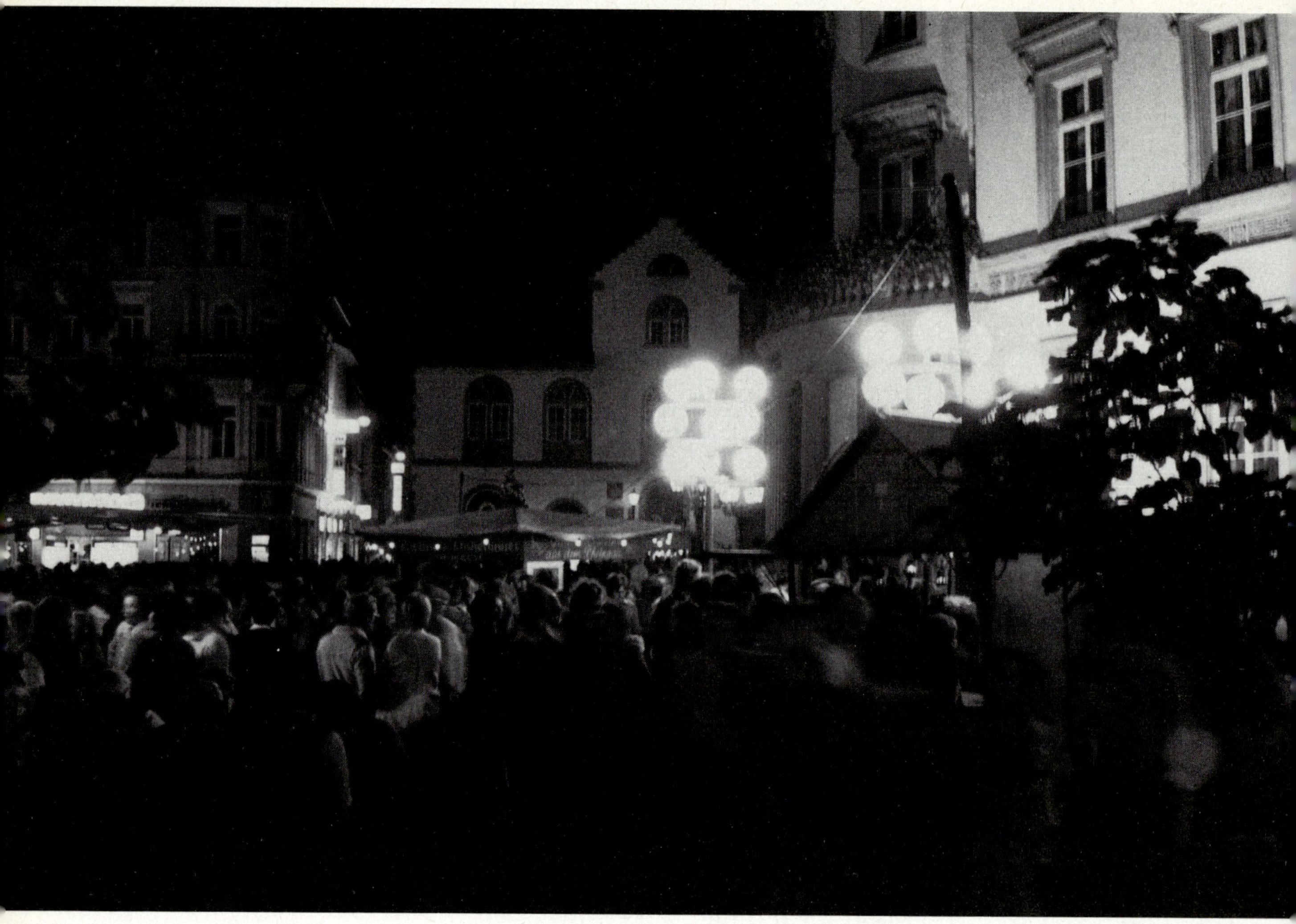

The greater shutter capacity of the XL-lens makes it nearly always possible to film, e.g. at festivals, fairs, in the evening, and at night.

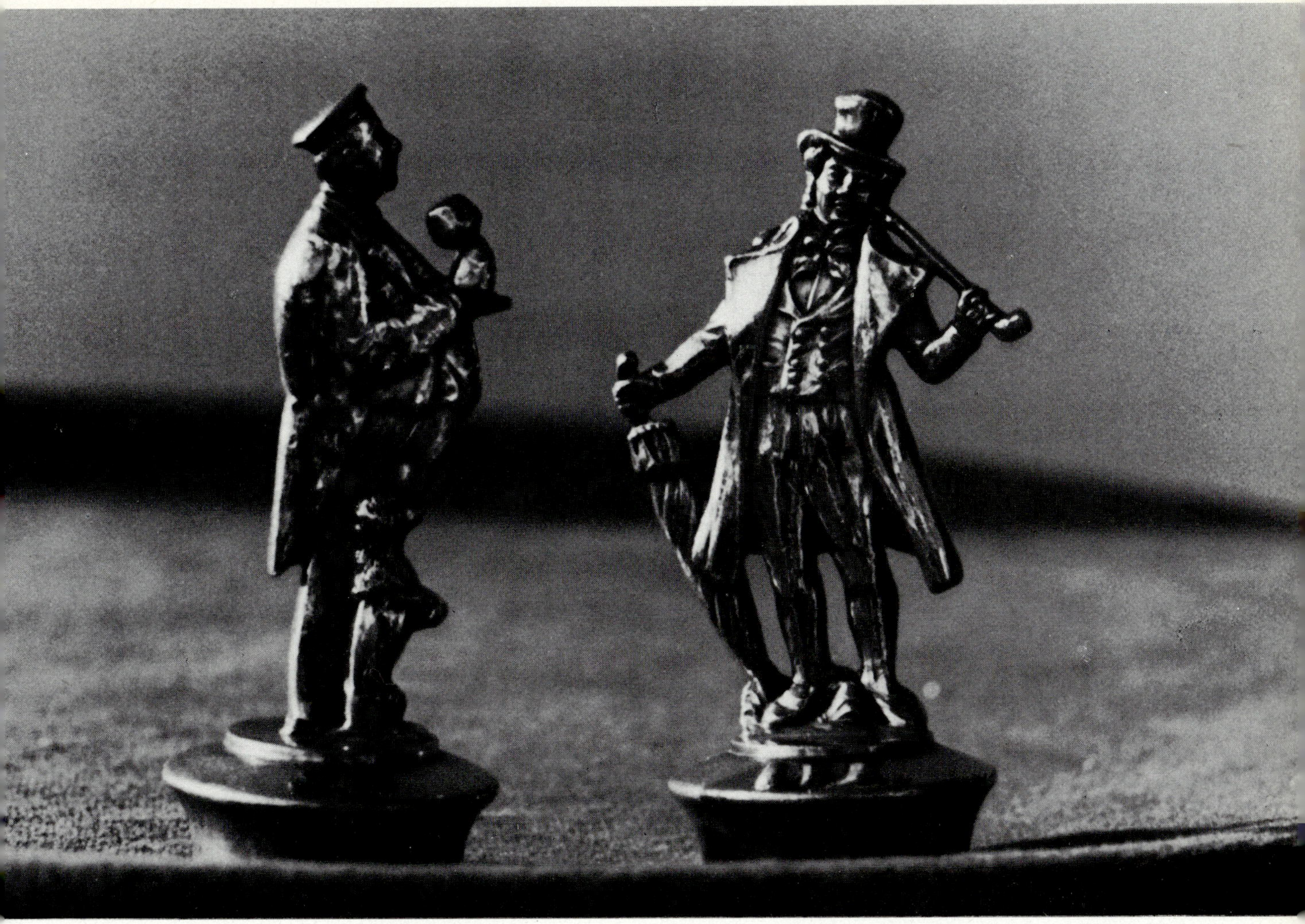

Macro-shots give large reproduction of small things. These two silver figures are not even 5cm. high, yet can completely fill the picture

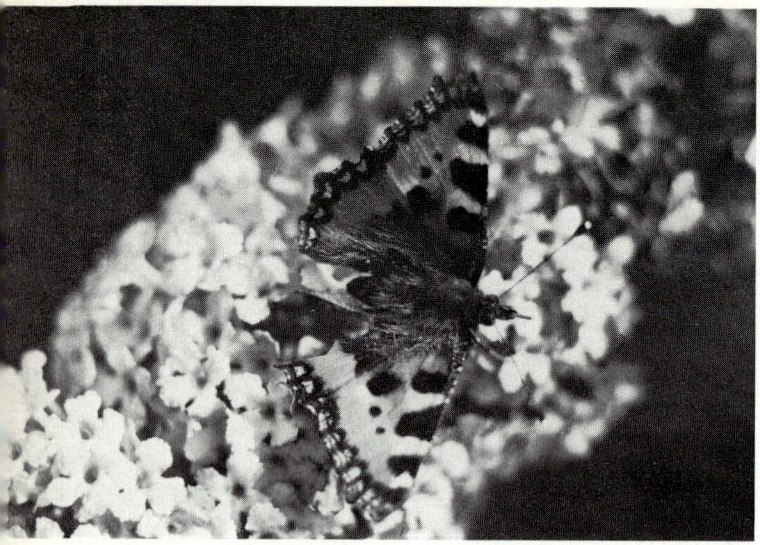

Close-up and macro-shots make an interesting change in any film

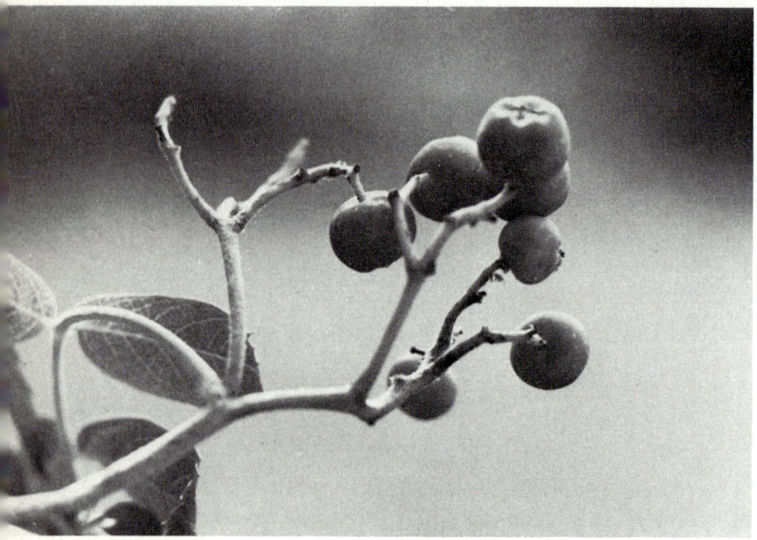

professional photographers had the definite advantage in this field, but with a macro-lens in the ciné camera, the amateur film-maker enjoys at least equal, if not better, opportunities.

During filming in the macro range, you will come across a problem which otherwise only rarely occurs: depth of field. In the close-up range depth of field is very small. Even with the wide-angle range, usually coupled with the macro-setting, depth of field must be measured to the millimetre; on a tele setting it is of course even smaller. This was no problem with the film practices previously discussed, on the contrary one has as a rule a particularly large depth of field, but with macro-shots it is quite a different matter. The nearer you approach the front lens, the smaller the depth of field will be.

Consequently the rules of composition can only be marginally applied to macro· filming and you must reckon that in the initial stages, the proportion of wastage will be considerably higher than in your other filming. Yet further difficulties will arise: a slight puff of wind might blow a flower out of the depth-of-field zone, and the slight movement of a butterfly or the minute alteration of the position of the camera could have the same effect.

To repeat, the focus can be adjusted, as with other shots, by using the reflected image in the viewfinder. Moreover, the light measurement remains unaltered for macro-shots, although difficulties arise through the film-maker being in such close proximity to the subject that he or the camera throws shadows on to it.

Is there any point in writing a script, for instance, about life in a beehive? Any element of direction is largely excluded. You are essentially dependent on chance.

It can be said with total conviction that macro filming opens up a completely new range of possibilities. As a rule, any film theme might include scenes taken with a macro-zoom. Being able to represent small objects in an extremely large form provides the amateur film with some alluring variants.

FILMING WITH FLASHLIGHT

Presumably flash-shots are thought of chiefly in connection with still photography. The use of flash equipment with a ciné camera is indeed rather unusual, and only meaningful in certain circumstances. It has already been discussed in relation to the timer, automatic prolonged-exposure control, and the single-frame device. For the aspiring film amateur, such a setting on the camera used in conjunction with flash light implies filming opportunities in areas as yet unknown.

The single-frame device can compress processes which occur over a very long time-span. In nature, such processes are not confined to the day-time, and consequently were practically impossible to film.

If the intention is to film a flower opening, light is only required during the taking of each single shot, but some blooms only open at night, and filming such a flower with natural lighting is not possible.

Only a few cameras possess a flash contact, which functions in the same way as on a still camera. The synchronisation cord from the flashlight is connected to the camera, thus producing a flash for each individual shot. When shots are being taken with flashlight, the camera is operated manually. Normally the stop calculator on the flashlight unit gives the required stop value according to the taking distance. The calculation of the guide number is, however, rather uncertain, since many ciné cameras are fitted with a rotary disk shutter in place of an iris shutter. The following formula applies for shots taken with flashlight. Guide number : Distance = Stop Value. If with the use of 15 DIN colour film the guide number is 24 and the distance 3m., the stop value is 24:3 = 8, which must be set manually on the camera. However, a test shot is to be recommended, due to the uncertainties which arise in the individual models. The value then arrived at need not be altered again during the entire filming time, since the flashlight operates at a constant level of brightness.

The light from flashlights has the same characteristics as daylight (colour temperature = 5600°K). If artificial-light colour film is used, a conversion filter must be used in the camera.

There is one factor to consider: only a limited number of flash-shots can be achieved with a battery loading, 40 to 60 shots, according to the flash equipment; but a normal-length film scene of 6 to 8 seconds will require 100 to 130 flashes. With batteries, therefore, the flash equipment could fail in the middle of filming, and all the preparations would be in vain. Since the flash equipment can only deliver an unlimited number of shots when mains operated, it must be connected to a wall socket via a mains cable.

For all film shots with flash light, it is important to use a stable tripod. As with all single shots, the camera and flash equipment must be so constructed that not the slightest displacement is possible from one shot to another.

UNDERWATER FILMING

Our main acquaintance with underwater filming is via cinema and television. It is evident in such films that specially designed equipment is essential for use in such an environment.

Any camera instruction leaflet will indicate that the equipment must be protected from salt-water; naturally this remains true for underwater filming, and to this end a camera housing is produced for some cameras. Camera housings are made of very strong material or a light plastic covering. The thin, lighter casings are sometimes fitted with gloves facing the inside, which allows the equipment to be operated from the outside. The most commonly used is a relatively simple type of rubber box, fitted with stabilisers, to hold the camera steady and prevent it being rolled. Almost any camera can be inserted into such casings. Correctly designed, above all with an efficient fastening, they guarantee the necessary protection, although only to a depth of about 10m. Most subjects for filming are to be found at a depth of 1–5m. The pressure is enormous at great depths, and only perfect equipment can be used for filming in such circumstances.

At great depths a special metal housing is required, which is in each case only suitable for use with one certain type of camera. Here, all the setting adjustments are repeated on the exterior. A casing of this sort is not only heavier, but also more expensive, often in fact even more costly than the camera itself. However, it offers protection at any depth that a sports diver might reach. Under water the weight of the casing is insignificant, since it is relative to the buoyancy of the water. The deeper you dive, the less the effect of the net weight of the equipment.

Difficulties of nature arise when you dive to a depth of several metres. The light calculation is quite different under water, and everything seems nearer: not only the eye, but also the camera is deceived. Moreover, not only is the light rapidly diminished, it also changes its colour to a blue-green shade.

While such colouring is absolutely natural in deep water, it means that the light is too weak for filming. Certainly film lamps do exist for underwater filming, as seen in

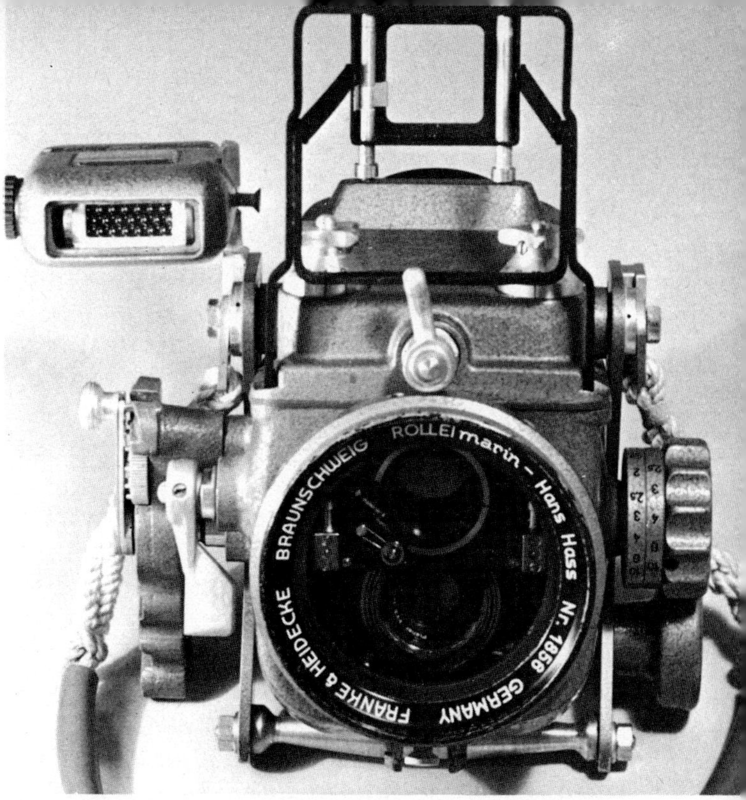

Rolleimarin underwater-camera housing for binocular Rolleiflex 3.5 f with exposure meter attached (Sixtomat in Lugyphoto casing)

Cousteau's films, but generally the expense is too great. Films which serve the purpose of scientific research naturally demand the best equipment, which the amateur will not possess, and the latter is here more or less at the limit of his possibilities. This is not to say that amateur film-makers, who are at the same time perfect sports divers, cannot combine the two hobbies. All the necessary equipment is available on the market. Should the intention be to augment the film's effect with underwater scenes, here are a few tips.

It is best to film at speed 24, which will compensate for the movement of the water and produce smoother filming.

Underwater shots should not be too short, as longer is required to observe everything when the film is projected than for land shots.

The wide-angle setting of the variable-focus lens is correct for filming other swimmers or large objects, while fish can be filmed on a normal setting. If a precise distance setting is desired for taking close-ups, it is possible to make a measuring stick, e.g. from steel wire. In this way starfish etc. can be filmed full-size.

Underwater films are most effective when they are mysteriously dark. However, the silent world must not lack contrast on film, and back-lighted shots are a particularly good way of providing this underwater. This can be practised with the aid of the floating particles always apparent in the water, which shine in back-lighting. The exposure meter is, however, easily deceived by this. This means that either the camera setting must be corrected manually, or the film speed must be adjusted to 2 or 3 DIN higher than that of the inserted film. Then the water appears darker and deeper, while the subject appears more luminous.

Underwater, the taking distance should be at maximum a third of the range of sight, the limit usually being about 2m. distance, and the water must be extremely clear, even if clear visibility does exist to up to 6m. below the surface. Incidentally, the film-maker, as well as the camera, will require a viewing mask.

First attempts at underwater filming should be as uncomplicated as possible: star fish, sea urchins,and other small animals that do not bolt away are particularly suitable objects. One needs to be a skilful slow swimmer to film fish at a closer proximity – the best way is to approach from the front or from the side.

Occasionally live fish are filmed which live not in open waters, but in an aquarium, and such films can be deceptively similar to the real thing. A couple of scenes of aquarium fish might be added subsequently to a film of a holiday by the sea – an addition which could not fail to be effective.

There is no great problem involved in filming in an aquarium. The camera is mounted on a tripod and the lens directed exactly at the aquarium or a section of it. A pane of glass inserted into the aquarium will prevent the fish from swimming out of the focused area, since the area they can move in can be temporarily confined to keep them within focus.

If the aquarium is placed on a windowsill, there is sufficient light for the shots. Even here the light-green shading will appear, because, you are filming through the water.

It is rather more difficult when the available light is not adequate. In this case the film lamps must be arranged to shine light down into the open aquarium from above, as this will avoid reflections on the glass panes. Such lighting should however be used with due care, since the warmth emitted by the halogen lamp will soon warm the water, which will not suit the fish. The lamp should therefore only be switched on for the length of time required for each scene.

WIDE-SCREEN FILMING

Cinemascope is the name given to a special wide-screen and stereophonic process, a name with which amateurs are also acquainted. Film for cinemascope is taken with a wide-angle lens, and projected by means of a compensating lens on to a curved screen of 2½ times the usual width.

In the time of Double-8, accessories existed for certain cameras so that such an effect could also be achieved with 8mm. film. This optical accessory compressed the picture laterally as it was taken (the size of the picture on the film was not altered), and a second accessory (sometimes one and the same) was positioned in front of the lens during projection, in order to rectify the picture once more. The ratio of the sides when projected was 1:2, or usually about 3:4, and had an effect similar to that of cinemascope in the cinema.

In the course of the conversion from Double-8 to Super-8 cameras wide-screen filming has almost disappeared, and indeed the 8mm. size has become excessively expensive. In professional filming, a 70mm. size is used for the cinemascope process, and it is an experiment which the ciné-filmer

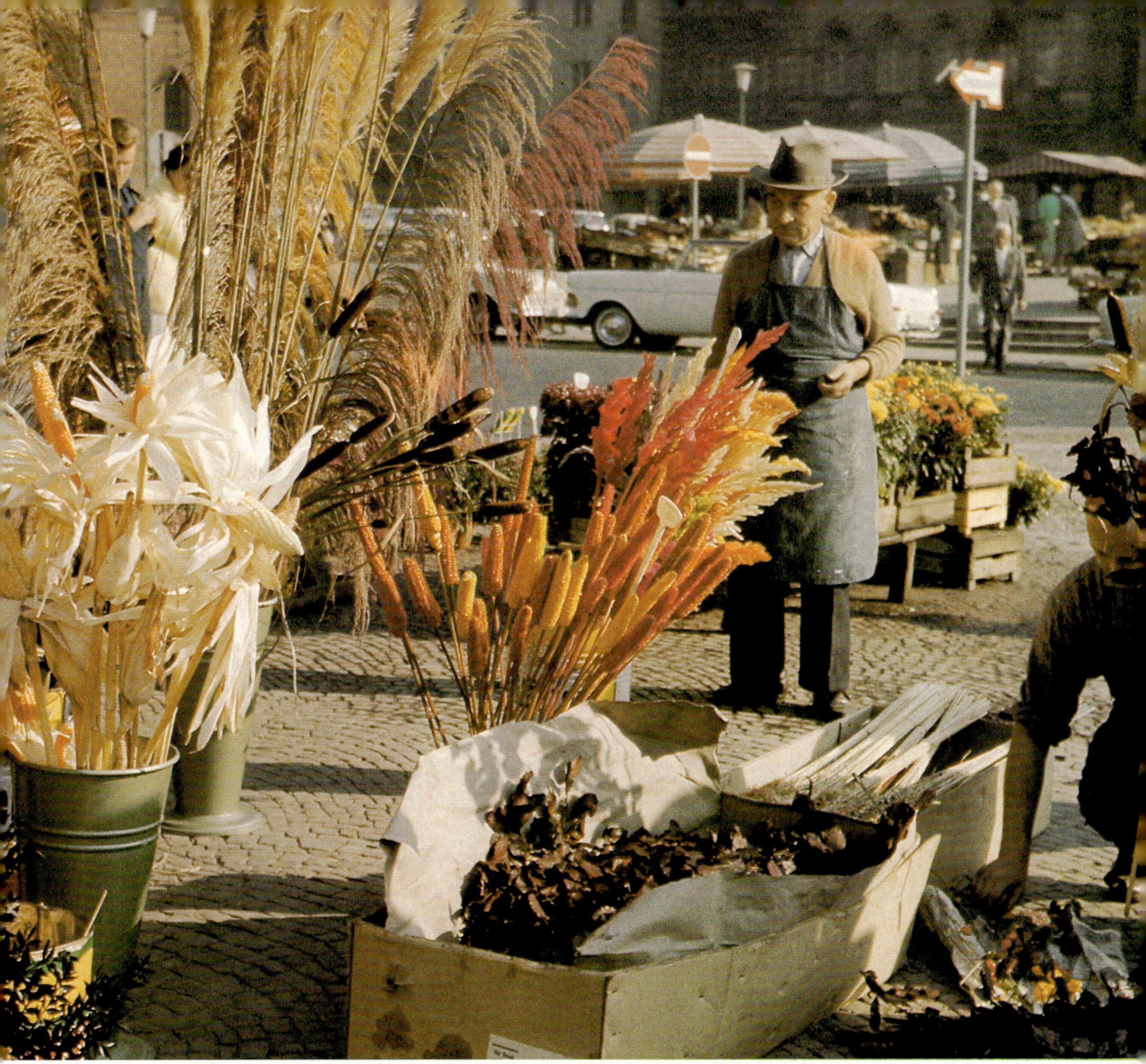

Plate 13: At the market, the dried-flower stall provides an almost exotic atmosphere contrasting with the bustle of the city

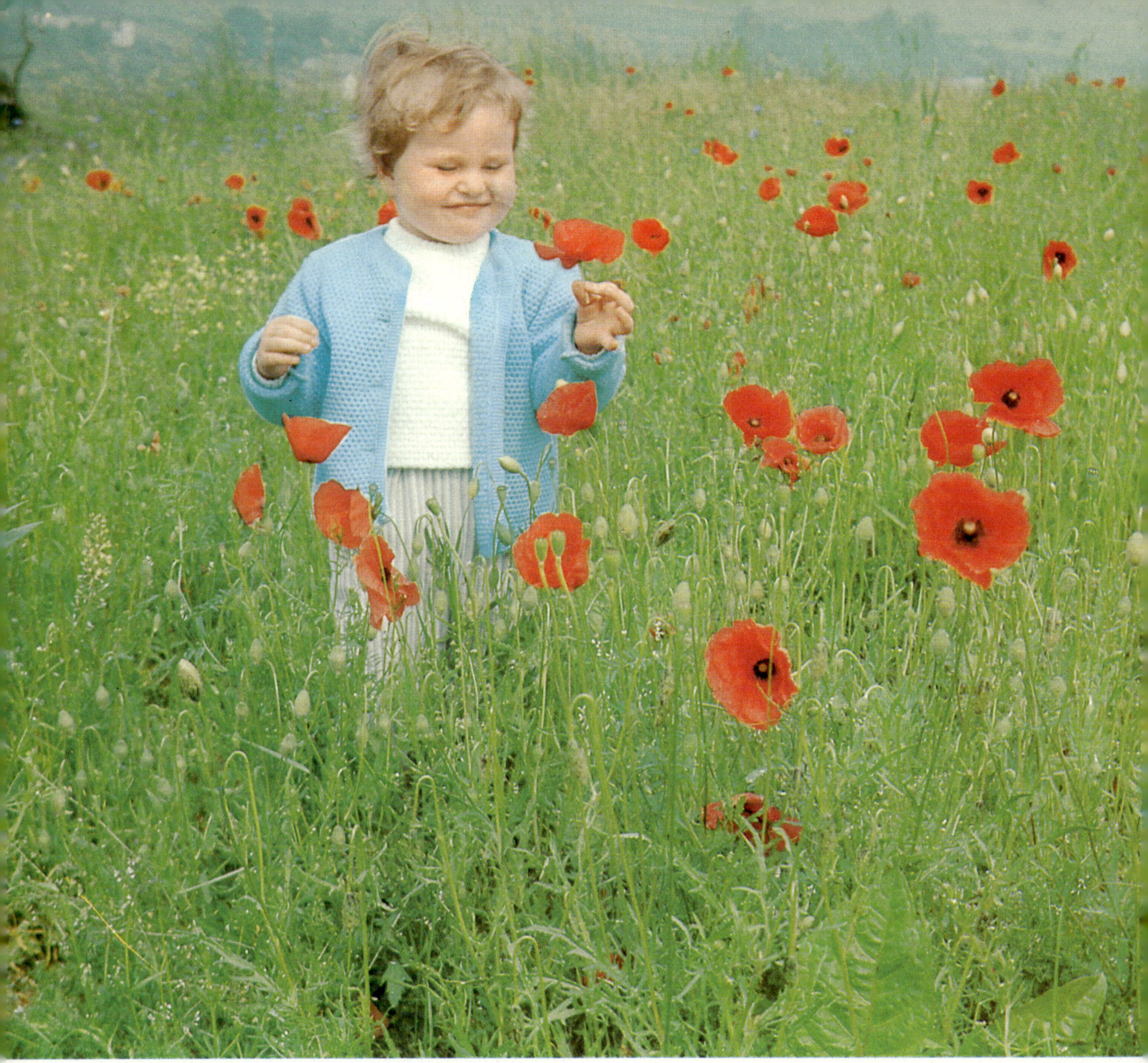

Plate 14: The striking foreground 'makes' the shot. An impressive effect is caused by moving in on the child with a variable lens

would do better to forego.

TRICK FILM

Trick shots have already been discussed both in connection with the single-frame setting and with trick lenses.

The trick film occupies a quite special position, since it is dependent on things which the normal film does not recognise, apart from film shots taken on the slow-motion or time-lapse setting, which only implies a film trick. This is not what is meant by the trick film.

Usually by trick film, cartoon film is understood, and it is often forgotten that other types of filming are also included within this category. The cartoon is without doubt the most well known and widespread of all methods of trick filming, particularly on account of the masterpieces produced by Walt Disney.

Only a few people are able to make cartoon films, since they demand not only considerable talent in the form of graphic ability, but also a great deal of time. Each individual phase of movement, though barely distinguishable from the next in the film, is produced from numerous drawings. This process can certainly be simplified with the use of a constant background and components which do not move. However, only those who consider themselves to be suitably artistically gifted should attempt to make cartoon films. In a similar way, there are quite definite means of bringing 'dead' objects to life in a trick film, and consequently it is possible to make trick films with marionettes, soft toys, and things that can be bent. Each phase of movement is recorded, the smaller the alteration in the movement made from one single shot to the next, the more flowing the action will appear when the film is presented.

One or two single frame shots can be taken after each phase, which depends both on how much the object is to be moved from shot to shot, and how fast the action is to appear when projected. In every case it is desirable to take a small test-shot, which will provide a conclusive illustration of this. For example: a doll is to raise her right arm, which demands about 1–1½ seconds = 18–27 single shots. Eighteen settings mean either the movement is divided into nine phases and two single shots are taken per setting, or one decides on eighteen phases and captures each in one single shot.

With any trick filming it is extremely important that nothing is allowed to move during the scene, other than that which is supposed to appear to have moved. Backgrounds and above all the camera must not be altered even a millimetre, otherwise the total effect is endangered and much time wasted.

As already mentioned, there is one area in amateur filming where trick shots are frequently used, namely for the title shots. The possibilities here are almost limitless. Above all, it is an area in which even those with relatively little experience of ciné filming may concern themselves. More will be said about these possibilities in the chapter on film titles.

EDUCATIONAL AND COMMERCIAL FILMS

Films that exist for a specific purpose always occupy a certain special position: this includes all types of instructional films, training and further-education films, and commercial filming.

The film resources are chosen from a repertoire of possibilities to fulfil the intended aim as well as possible. Commercial films in particular, especially those for television commercials, are produced by experts and with every technical refinement. Careful observation of these often very short film spots will prove clearly how perfectly they are filmed. In such a film everything must be right, beginning with the models, and including colours and lighting to the last detail. Everyone can learn an enormous amount from these films that is applicable to his own amateur film work.

A commercial film is obviously made to advertise a certain product, and the more subtly the audience is presented with the product, the better the film. Not until one actually tries to make such a powerful assertion on film in about 15 seconds, which is often accomplished in a commercial, can one realise how extremely difficult it is.

In filming for educational purposes, the emphasis is on portraying the examples clearly, and comprehensibly, and this clarity, rather than brevity, is the determining factor. In order to make a good instructional film the entire range of composition possibilities must be employed.

Teaching films frequently consist of a mixture of real film scenes and trick shots. Many things can be clarified by once showing relevant objects, and then producing a simplified sketch of the same process, concentrating on the important points. If for instance a finishing process in an industrial works is to be shown, filming will no doubt begin in the assembly shop with the machines or conveyor belts. Finally the most important details can be represented as an animated cartoon, in order to clarify a process that might otherwise be difficult to understand. In such cases, trick film is a useful aid.

It is hard to imagine an instructional film without the addition of acoustic information and commerical films without sound would be equally inconceivable. Each technical process is embellished by verbal explanation. We will return to the possibilities of film sound in the chapter on film sound techniques.

Amateur film-makers are unlikely to be entrusted with the task of producing an educational or commercial film, since the technical requirements would as a rule transcend the means available to the amateur, and hence there are film companies who devote themselves exclusively to such work. The members of such firms, however, often arrived at their careers via amateur filming.

Yet even in this area it is quite within the range of possibility for a film amateur to combine his hobby and his career, indeed the career may become more enjoyable if coupled with the hobby. Occasionally the hobby is suitable for assisting professional affairs in a unique way.

Using ciné film for professional purposes is certainly not new, although still unknown to many. A picture says more than a thousand words, so the saying goes. How much more then can be conveyed in a small film.

Many a possibility can be developed on this basis. One can for instance help a friend who requires such a film, but has neither the equipment nor the expertise with which to make it. A film of this type can be a commercially effective medium, a fact that the experienced amateur film-maker is able to exploit!

TECHNICAL FAULTS

Before such important sections as film titles, film editing, and film sound recordings are considered, we might discuss the technical faults that repeatedly occur; the following is a compilation of the most common mistakes.

Film partially or completely black
There are two fundamental causes for the entire length of film being black, in other words, unexposed. This is either the fault of the cassette jamming and this remaining unnoticed, or of a defect in the shutter mechanism.

Many cameras have a film-transport control light, indicating the correct running of the film and allowing this to be checked. If the fault cannot be traced, it is essential to consult a photographic dealer.

If the film is partially black in places, this is usually due to some disorder in the camera's functioning.

Film transparent
In this case it is as a rule the automatic exposure meter that is not working properly, which means that the aperture remains open at its greatest value (1.8), and nearly always results in total over-exposure. If this happens, the battery for the automatic exposure control should be checked in the first instance. Often this will reveal the source of the fault, since the battery normally has a life of only 12 to 15 months.

White patches during scene change
Such patches usually occur if the shutter remains open at the end of the scene and the next frame is exposed. When projected the bright frame appears as a flash on the screen, and consequently such patches should be cut out during editing. Generally such an exposure should not occur during a pause in filming, and if it does appear on a film occasionally it has usually resulted by accident. Should it occur frequently or indeed at every scene change, the camera

should be returned to the manufacturer for an adjustment of the rotary-disk shutter. An expert adjustment will eliminate the defect – on no account should this adjustment be attempted by an amateur.

Bright pictures at the beginning of a new scene

This occurs extremely seldom and always in the same circumstances: the first scene is filmed in relatively dark surroundings, which entails the aperture being almost fully open for the shot. The following scene is taken in very bright surroundings, which requires only a small aperture if the shot is to be correctly exposed. The automatic exposure control in this case requires a certain amount of time to change from a very wide to a very small aperture, and this is effected during the scene transition, as the three or four bright pictures prove.

When you have come to realise that the camera requires some time to change between extreme aperture values, you can make use of the release button in such a situation, which will ensure that the automatic exposure control has functioned effectively before the film is released. Otherwise one can allow the aperture to alter itself and then operate the release half a second later. In both cases any bright pictures at the beginning of scene, after the change from dark to light, can be avoided.

Yellow or bright stripes at the edge of the picture

This fault occurs only with 2 x 8 film, and then because the film is wound too loosely on the spool when it is inserted or wound on. This results in the edge of the film being exposed, thus causing the stripes. This fault does not appear in Super-8 cameras.

One-sided or partial lack of definition

If the side or a part of the film is not in focus, this is nearly always due to a previous accident with the camera. Even if there is nothing to see on the camera's exterior, the optical shaft might be displaced by such an occurrence, which would result in all the pictures being out of focus. Occasionally this fault is apparent in the viewfinder. Remedy: the camera must be sent back to the manufacturer immediately and adjusted. Do not attempt to do it yourself.

In order to ascertain that the fault is not in fact located in the projector, the film in question should first of all be screened on another projector. If it then appears faultless, it is the actual projector that requires repair.

Viewfinder image in focus – picture not in focus

In this case the viewing lens on the camera is not adjusted to your own eye! Refer to the chapter on variable-focus lenses to discover how this is accomplished.

Film scene partially out of focus
If some shots within the film are not in focus, the distance has not been set correctly. When a variable focal length (zoom lens) is used, the object in the tele range of the lens moves out of the depth of field. The method used to remedy lack of definition is described in the section concerning the variable-focus lens.

Picture trembles when projected
This can be caused in various ways. Usually a trembling shot is caused as a result of excessive fast movement of the camera, and occurs particularly often when a pan shot is filmed too quickly. The fault may also lie, however, in the incorrect adjustment of the camera's claw feed system, or in the projector. In this case, which seldom arises, the equipment in question should be given to an expert to adjust.

A further reason for trembling shots is the use of a tele focal length on the camera without a tripod. It is seldom possible to maintain a stationary position with ranges over about 30mm. focal length. If the film horizon trembles, it is nearly always the natural result of filming without a tripod.

Film is predominantly blue
This occurs when film is taken in daylight but on an artificial light setting, or with 2 x 8 film, if artificial-light film is used in daylight.

Film is predominantly red
This is the converse fault: in this case, the camera has been set to daylight, while in fact artificial lighting has been used, or a daylight film (2 x 8) has been present in the camera and artificial-light filming has been undertaken.

Film is constantly too bright or too dark
If the battery is functioning adequately, this problem is usually due to a fault in the automatic exposure mechanism. If the same fault appears repeatedly, the camera should be overhauled. Besides this, the following possibilities should be checked:

1 You have used an Ektachrome 160 film in a fairly old Super-8 camera, overlooking the fact that the automatic device on the camera is only suited to a normal film speed of 15 DIN. The camera's instruction booklet will provide directions with reference to this.

2 The automatic exposure control has at some point been switched off, and you have subsequently omitted to switch it on again. Since the aperture cannot then alter, a great deal of film could possibly be incorrectly exposed.

A habit should be made of switching the automatic mechanism back on immediately afterwards, when the aperture has been operated manually for a specific purpose.

Picture has dark corners
This occurs only very seldom with a ciné camera. It may arise if a tele lens hood (from still photographic equipment) is used in the

wide-angle range of the camera, since the viewing angle of the lens is then greater than the opening of the lens hood, which necessarily results in the corners not receiving any light.

Scratches through the film

There are several explanations for a scratch that runs through the whole film from top to bottom. Rarely would such a scratch occur as a film is being shot; is might be that the film has been changed on the beach, and sand has been blown into the camera. If an abrasive grain of sand is caught at the film gate of the camera, such a scratch might appear. The best method of guarding against this is by blowing into the camera each time the film is changed thereby preventing dust or similar matter from being trapped in the film gate.

Sometimes, although luckily this is rare, these scratches occur in the film viewer or the film projector, if the equipment is not regularly cleaned. Anywhere that comes into contact with the film must be kept scrupulously clean, since there is a great risk here of the film being damaged.

Worm's-eye view (J. Schubert)

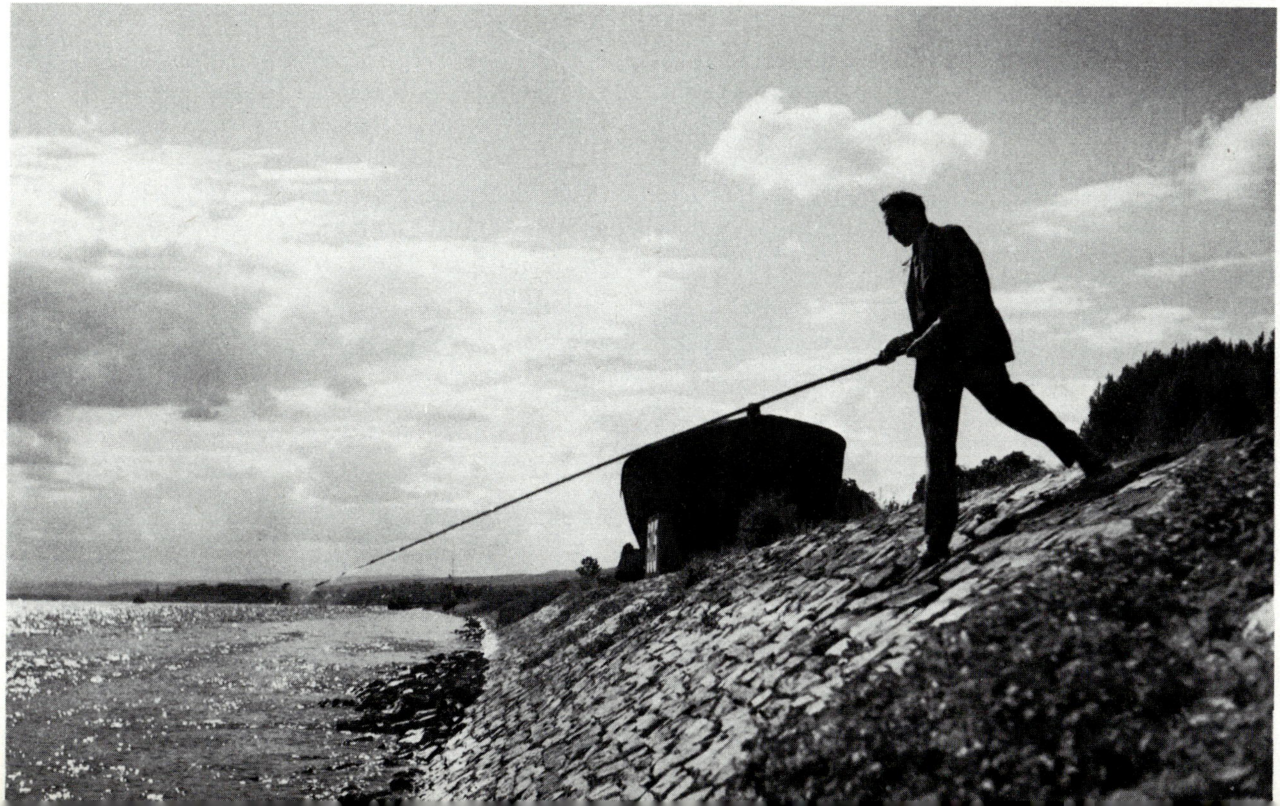

FILM TITLES

A title belongs to a film as a cover belongs to a book. Never would a book be offered without a cover, but unfortunately most amateur films are presented without a title. This is a pity, for whoever saw a film in the cinema without a title? An amateur film requires neither a detailed nor an original title, but a title should be chosen from the range of possibilities.

What should a title include, and what purposes does it serve anyway? It should both give the film a name, and say enough to make the audience eager to see more. The shorter the title is, the more effective.

Many amateur film makers have quite varying methods of creating titles, but the title itself remains basically uncomplicated.

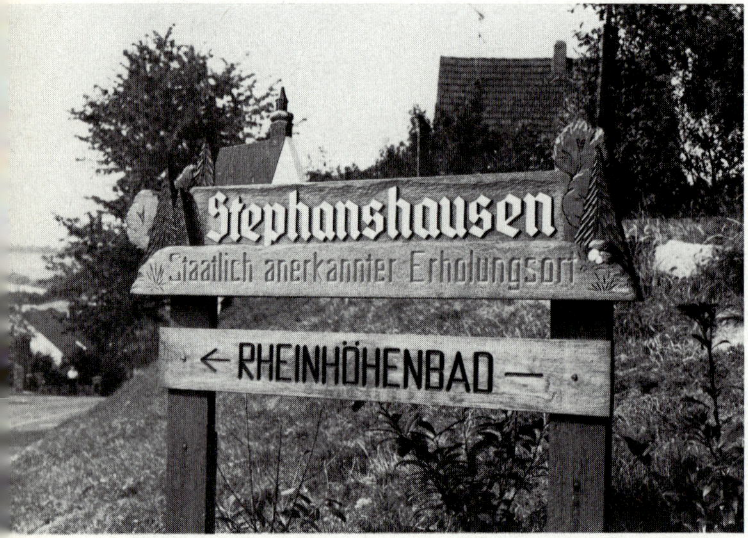

CHOOSING THE TITLE

One should if possible try to find natural titles, although perhaps the word 'natural' does not quite reach the heart of the matter. It implies titles that appear particularly pertinent to the film, which can be shot without any alteration or addition to the surroundings.

Frequently a sign showing the name of a place can be chosen as a title for a holiday film. Indeed in many towns the place name is attractively carved, which has a very

A natural title, on offer all over the place

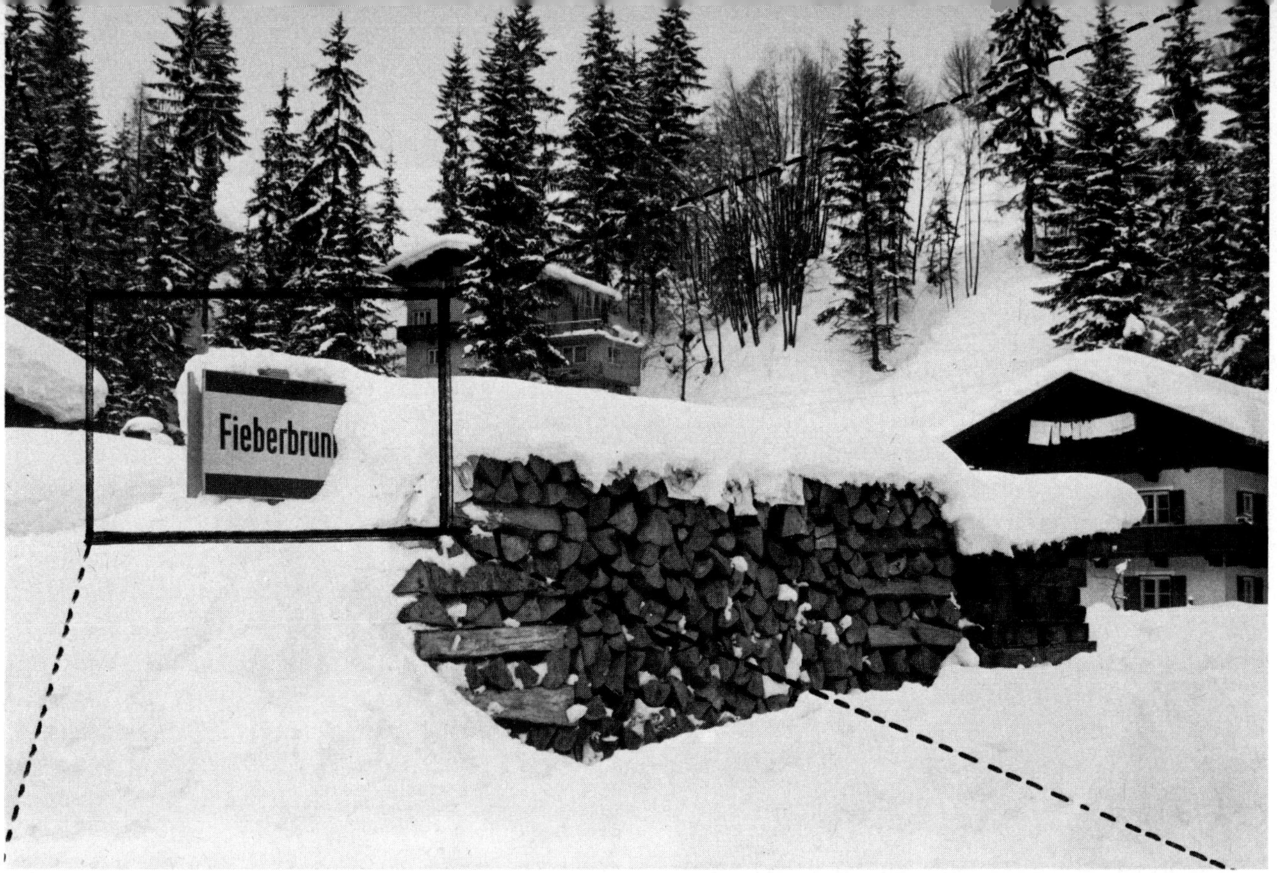

This natural title is produced by a travelling shot, and a tripod, of course:
1. Shot of the winter landscape (full length)
2. Travelling shots along the lines shown as allowed by the camera
3. Close-up of the sign as title.

decorative effect in the film. A hunt round the holiday resort will no doubt reveal a sign, showing what is necessary for the title. Nothing further is then required, except to focus the camera and take a picture of the subject. That is all. Such a title, combined with trees or branches moving in the wind, will provide impressive movement right at the beginning of the film.

A film can benefit greatly in this simple way with a 'natural' title. In place of the sign, there are numerous other objects that would be equally suitable: a time-table board, a station sign, posters, newspapers, etc. The possibilities are limitless.

Movement in the title: often buses bear the name of a town on the front as an indication of their destination, and this can be filmed to provide a living title. The camera remains still and continues filming as the bus departs.

A similar method is possible with ships or trains, with or without additional treatment, nor need it be a place-name that is filmed for the title. A visit to the zoo might begin with the information concerning prices displayed at the entrance or with a sign on a bus going in that direction. A sign-post pointing to the zoo would also be a suitable subject. Equally a carnival might be introduced in the film by means of a placard, Pictures of this type – signs, placards, invitations, etc. – which are usually very colourful and decorative, provide excellent opportunities for making titles, without requiring accessories or the need to draw a model. Natural titles are, in a broad sense, those that can be filmed without technical aids, without for instance the title lettering (yet to be described) but which nevertheless contains a very personal element.

For a winter holiday film, titles can be made by writing in the undisturbed snow, perhaps 'Good skiing' or 'Sun and Snow'. If the area chosen is lit diagonally by the sun, the resulting contrast between the shadows of the snow crystals and the written text will enliven the picture. A pair of sunglasses or the point of a ski might be included in the picture to further enhance the white of the snow.

An effective transition to the first scene can be achieved by the sight of a skier moving in on the text, the camera being directed meanwhile at the skier and following his tracks in the snow. The next scene then demands a counter-shot, in which the skier travels toward the camera. The result will be not only an almost perfect snow title, but also an ideal picture transition.

A similar impression can be created in a beach holiday film, where the title can be drawn in the sand. Mussels and seaweed can be collected and included in the title text in order to add colour, or the title might even be created out of small mussels.

The transition to the film can be accomplished by a method similar to that of the skier in winter: a child in bare feet tramples over the mussel title, and then filming of the child continues, which will no doubt entail a readjustment of the focus.

There are many circumstances that will allow the creation of titles in a similar or almost the same manner. A little thought will constantly uncover new ways of producing titles of the type filmed without technical accessories, and yet rarely failing to be effective.

TITLE LETTERING

In order to augment the choice provided by natural titling, the next step, which follows on logically from the first, is to procure a set of title letters. The set normally consists of 120 letters, numbers, and symbols, from which words, sentences, or names with numbers can be made.

The 120 pieces are so compiled, that the most frequently recurring letters are available in an appropriate quantity, which means that no difficulties will arise with the usual texts. Should there still not be enough letters, several words or sentences may simply be combined, according to one's personal taste and requirements – even in different colours.

How is the lettering used? That is very easy, but firstly the different types of lettering must be described.

Magnetic lettering

The neatest method entails the use of magnetic lettering, which adheres everywhere to metal surfaces. The basic equipment includes a metal board about 30cm. by 40cm. in size. As this is usually matt black, it will bring the white or coloured lettering into relief. If a black background is not wanted, the colour can be varied: sometimes coloured sheets of paper for changing the background colour are included in the pack, otherwise they can be acquired afterwards. Moreover, a photograph, a prospectus, or a magazine could be laid between the title board and the lettering – there are really no limits to what can be devised. Magnetic letters can of course be affixed to any metal surface, e.g. on a car door, a letter box, a garden fence, in short anywhere where there is metal. These few examples are sufficient to prove that the possibilities here are almost unlimited: everywhere is a title background, and everywhere titles can be filmed!

Adhesive Lettering

Another type of title lettering consists of self-adhesive pieces. A sticky backing allows the letters to be fixed to any surface, and then removed and used again.

Titling with adhesive letters can serve in certain circumstances where the use of magnetic lettering would be inconceivable. Since no title board is required, the letters can be packed in a small box, and consequently they are no problem to carry round on a journey, which means that the title can be filmed in the place where the action occurs. This is very much suited to the requirements of many ciné-filmers, since they usually have plenty of time on holiday and can complete all the film work adequately.

Magnetic letters on a balcony rail. A direct transition to the first scene is achieved by means of a fade-in on the balcony

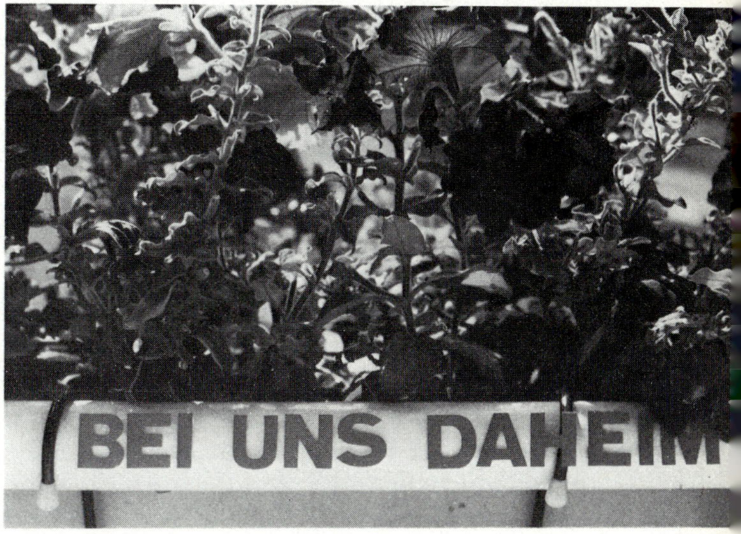

What method is used to create title shots using adhesive lettering? Again suggestions exist in abundance. A few are alluded to here.

The letters can be affixed to smooth surfaces, for instance window panes. The point raised with reference to lettering and picture backgrounds is considerably simplified here: the whole title can be shot in the original. However, one must not forget to take a tripod on holiday. The following example will illustrate what is meant by this. As the film title, let us choose 'A holiday at the sea-side'.

You are staying in a guest-house by the sea. The text is stuck to the window pane, which should of course be clean, and the film is taken through the window facing towards the sea. Then the window is opened, filming continues, and the sea appears without the text in front of it. Possibly the focus will need to be adjusted between filming the text at close proximity and the sea further away, although in some circumstances this might be solved automatically in the ciné camera by the large depth of field. The example shows how a film can be begun with a title, and then followed by an immediate transition into the first scene.

These letters can be used in a similar way for filming a title on the car: the text is affixed to the side of the vehicle. Begin on a wide-angle setting at a taking distance that allows the whole car to be presented in the picture. Now move in with a zoom lens, until the entire picture area is taken up with the title. After the normal length of time for reading the text, the car is driven off and the first filmscene reveals a view of the countryside. This type of film title can be created without difficulty anywhere and anytime.

It hardly requires saying that adhesive titles may be affixed to any wall, on the railing of a bridge, or on anything which appears suitable for use in making an interesting title. However for many ciné-filmers the greatest advantage lies in the fact that the film can be completed while still on holiday. Without a doubt the same applies to you as to many others: anything that is not finished immediately remains a considerable time in its half-completed state.

Finally another tip: avoid sticking the adhesive letters to paper. Often paper will remain on the sticky surface when the letters are removed, which will lessen their adhesive effect. On smooth surfaces such as tiles, glass panes, varnished wood, etc., the adhesive letters can be used more or less without limitation. Should the adhesive properties still, however, fade, a glue in a liquid form exists for applying to the lettering, which when dry leaves the letters as good as new.

Other lettering

A third type of lettering consists of cardboard, cork, or a similar material of varying strength. These letters can only be placed on a small base, which must be level in order to avoid the letters sliding. This is rather impractical, and this lettering is used relatively little.

Equally little used are the title boards designed with grooves to hold the letters in position, with the additional aid of hooks or points on the underside of the letters. Boards similar in style but of larger size are often employed in offices as notice boards.

Thus all types of lettering can be arranged for the title in any way that occurs to you, and once you begin to make titles, you will constantly be inspired with new ideas. Some ciné-filmers only make films so they can produce new titles; sometimes an interesting title is already completed before the film has even been seriously planned!

TITLE SHOTS WITH CLOSE-UP LENSES

Anyone who has already considered the matter of the close-up shot will by now possess a close-up lens, which makes it possible to use even small objects as a title, e.g. an entrance ticket, a prospectus, a post-card, a menu, or even a bill. Such things are not particularly related to any one film theme, but with a certain skill they can, as a title, be fully integrated in the film, which would be difficult to accomplish without the aid of a close-up lens. It would be barely possible to take a full-size shot of an entrance ticket or train ticket with a standard lens.

The bi-fo lens has already been mentioned in the section on close-up lenses: its main area of use is with the title shot. The lens has two sections, allowing the production of images in two differently focused areas. The smaller portion portrays the foreground at a distance of about 25cm. while the larger part does not alter the remaining area of the picture.

For instance: compose a small text and place at a distance of about 25cm. in front of the front lens of the camera, which is then set to accommodate the usual subject in the normal way. For this purpose the title text must be small and short, since a distance of 25cm. does not allow a large picture area.

A title shot with a bi-fo lens can be very effective, if the text is stuck on to a pane of glass, and the necessary distance is observed. The sharply focused text will then appear in front of an equally clearly defined landscape. If a sheet of perspex is included in your luggage, title shots may be filmed at any time on the holiday, using the title lettering already discussed.

WORK ON THE TITLE TEXT

Although much has already been said about the ways title and lettering can be used, the subject is by no means exhausted.

The following is to explain how varied the texts may be and how easily they can be constructed, as well as providing some details about certain tricks that can be employed to achieve quite magical title effects.

Firstly, however, a few words about the method itself; it is clear that title lettering will be used, not so clear, however, are the numerous ways in which they can be used.

Arrangement

Whichever sort of lettering is used, the position of the camera in relation to the titling surface is important, and is above all dependent on the smallest possible distance setting that the camera allows. A magnetic board may be hung on the wall and the camera positioned in front of it at the correct distance – on a tripod, of course.

With non-magnetic lettering, which must be laid flat, the camera must be positioned vertically so that the letters are not displaced.

Judging from experience, a simple and practical method is to place the title lettering on the floor, so that nothing can slide. Moreover, in this way it is possible to forego the magnetic board when using magnetic lettering, should another base prove to be more attractive and suitable.

Laying out the title text demands scrupulous exactitude. The letters must be balanced, and arranged in an even and tidy manner. It is not particularly important that the text is positioned in the middle, but the letters should appear to be formed on an invisible line, generally running parallel to the edge of the picture. If the letters tilt or are not evenly arranged, it produces an annoying effect on the screen. Finally, the title is an invitation to the film.

However, there is an exception to every rule! Sometimes a title is deliberately constructed to suggest a state of confusion. For a title such as 'Carnival magic' it would probably seem absurd to be pedantic about the exact arrangement of the letters. This is however an exception, though the title remains a question of personal taste.

Background

Title backgrounds play an important rôle. Title lettering comes in many colours, backgrounds in every colour, and a psychological study of colours is not necessary for one to know that they are of great significance. Consequently the colour of the title background should not be unrelated to the content of the film. For example, a light-green background would be suitable for a title like 'A walk in the springtime', while 'The autumn' would be on rust-red, 'Christmas' on dark green, 'A holday in the snow' on white or blue. Taking this into consideration, the right colour can be used for the title in all circumstances. Thoughtlessness about the appropriate colour can lead to an embarrassing mistake; an extreme example might be placing the title 'Our silver-wedding anniversary' on a gold background, or vice versa.

There are countless different methods for the composition of titles. If a photograph or a calendar picture of the landscape filmed is used as a background, the effect can be remarkably attractive, in as far as the title, by virtue of the picture, bears a direct relationship to the film, particularly if the first film scene is able to portray the same view as the picture used for the title background. This is easily arranged by taking a colour photograph of the subject at the same time as you film the first scene, which can then be used subsequently as a title background. Equally successful would be finding a post-card that corresponded to the scene to be filmed. The taking position of the photographer can be established from the post-card, and the film also taken from this point.

This method may still be used, even if the title picture and the opening scene do not exactly coincide. A skillful ordering of the letters can be used to cover up any small variations in the picture, so that the two more or less correspond to each other.

Can you draw? Then there is nothing more satisfactory than designing the title yourself and using one of your own pictures as a background. It is even possible to dispense with construction and draw everything yourself. Anyone possessing this talent, can give his titles an individual flair that no other method allows.

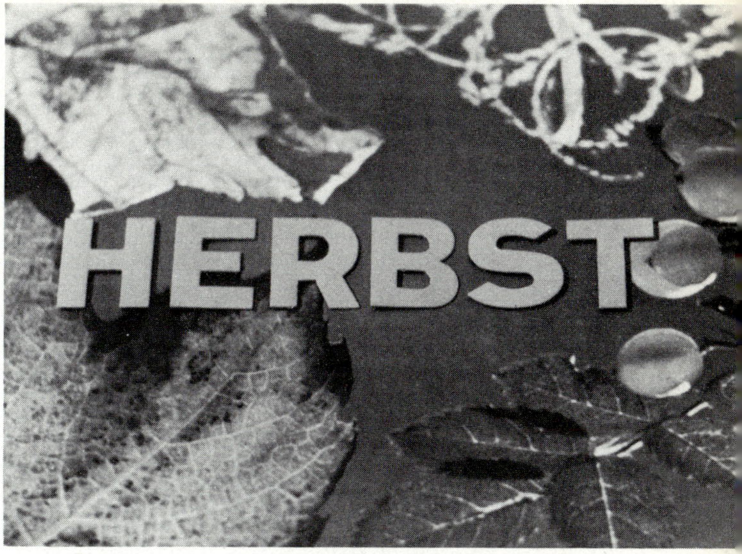

Title letters on the page of a calendar

TITLE TEXTS

The title text is of great importance, and should be short, and to the point. It must remain on the screen long enough for the audience to be able to read and digest it. Preferably let the text remain rather longer than you consider necessary, allowing for the fact that it is unknown to anyone else. *You* have taken the film and conceived the title, and so do not need to read it to know what it says. A good method for measuring the time required for the title is to read the title out loud clearly and slowly, and then add two or three seconds, depending on the length of the text. If the title is combined with a fade-in, fade-out, or dissolve, only the time when the picture is still should be counted. You may depend upon this as a general rule of thumb.

A combination of different styles of writing, or the same lettering displayed in various colours, will add interest to the title text. If the title consists of a whole sentence, the most important word in it can be emphasised in this way; it is also a useful way of distinguishing between main and subsidiary titles.

If the main title is to be followed immediately by a second subsidiary title, television films can again be used for inspiration. Should a picture serve for the background, this should not be be changed. An attractive effect is produced if the picture remains, while the overlaying text is altered. If care is taken to ensure that neither the picture nor the camera is moved, it is even possible to blend the text from one shot into another, which gives the film an almost professional quality.

It has already been suggested that the title should say something about the film, without promising too much or awakening false hopes. 'Holiday 1976' is for instance a very general title, fixing only the time, without making any comment about the content of the film. Many titles are this simple, but as a result, rather uninspiring; the announcement should be rather more precise and original. Even titles such as 'Good climbing', 'By the seaside' or 'A holiday in the country' suggest a more exact definition of the film's action, although still being very factual, and they can be made more effective by the addition of a sub-heading. The title 'By the seaside' might be perhaps amplified by 'Where the north wind blows ...' and could be combined with music.

If the intention is to film two texts one after the other, the best means of combination is a dissolve. Let us take as an example the title 'Good climbing'. 'Good climbing' is the main title, 'A climbing tour in the Southern Tyrol' is the sub-heading. By combining the two texts with a dissolve you can produce a very impressive title. Moreover not only are short texts easier to film, but a relatively long text is made easier to read if it appears on the screen as two short texts.

Subtitles are also frequently used, if the film is not to be supplied with a soundtrack. The texts are blended in at various points in the film giving necessary information. While there is no formal rule that the information must be provided exclusively in the form of a text, some method of supplying it must be devised if the film is to be easy to understand.

If we consider a travel film, in which the location is frequently changed, an explanatory text will be required each time to elucidate the scene transition. In some circumstances a sign-post might be sufficient, but would seem rather uninspired if used repeatedly. In this case the map trick-title would be preferable, to which we will return in the next section.

Subtitles are then chiefly necessary if the film is planned from the outset as a silent film. In this case the title is attributed with a far greater informative value. If the film is to be supplied with a sound recording a less illuminating title can be used, particularly if the film is to be accompanied by a spoken text.

For example: 'Good climbing' as the title picture. The title remains long enough for it to be absorbed (about three seconds) then the spoken text adds, 'A report from a climbing tour in the Sella'. The end of the spoken text must coincide with a slow dissolve into the first scene. A title prepared in this way demands little information in the text, since

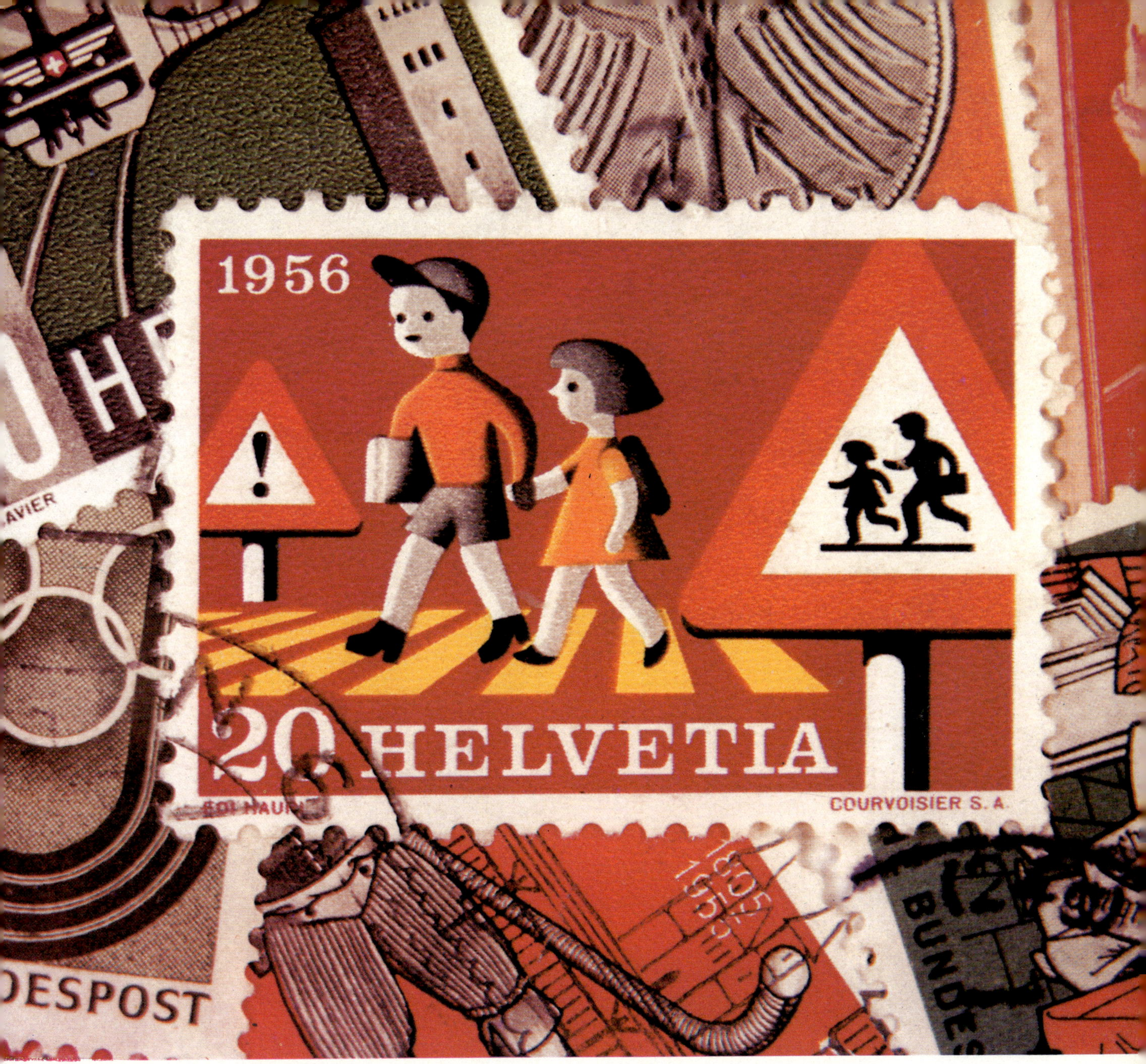

Plate 15: A stamp collector can also use his collection when filming

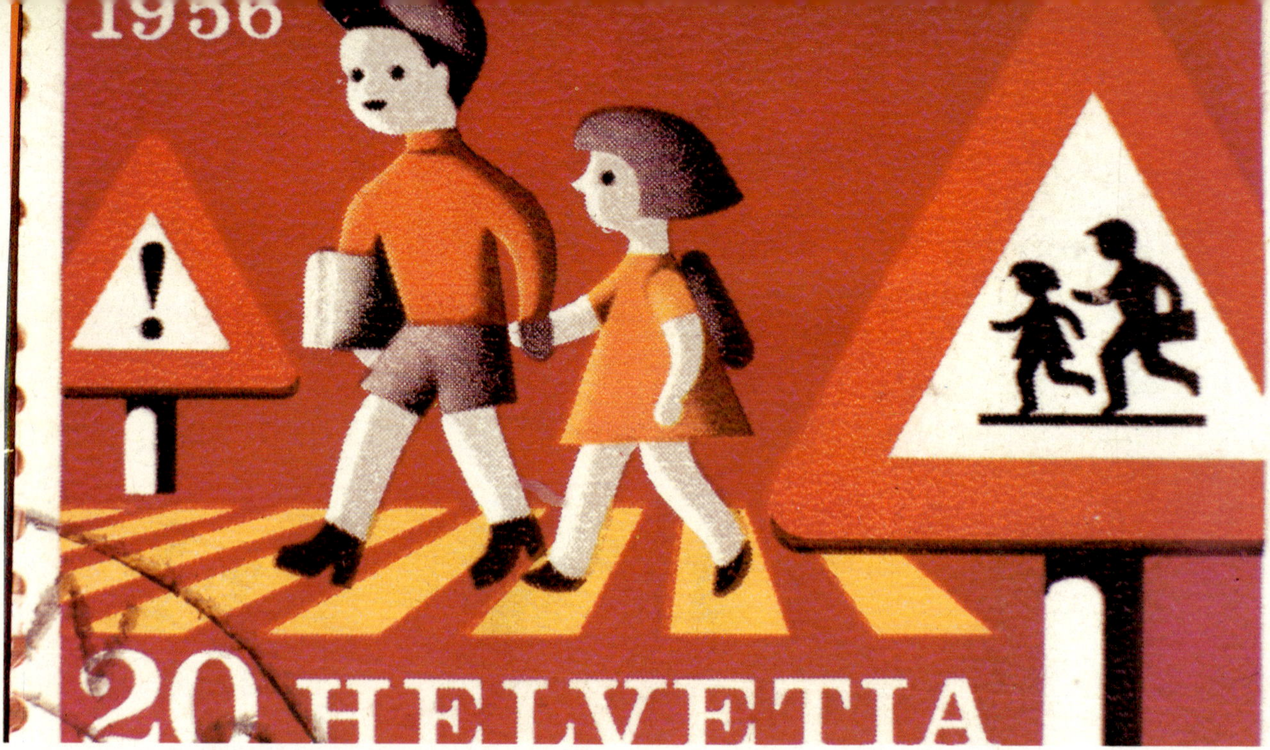

Plate 16: These shots emphasise the outstanding features of the stamps. Other hobbies can also be shown on film

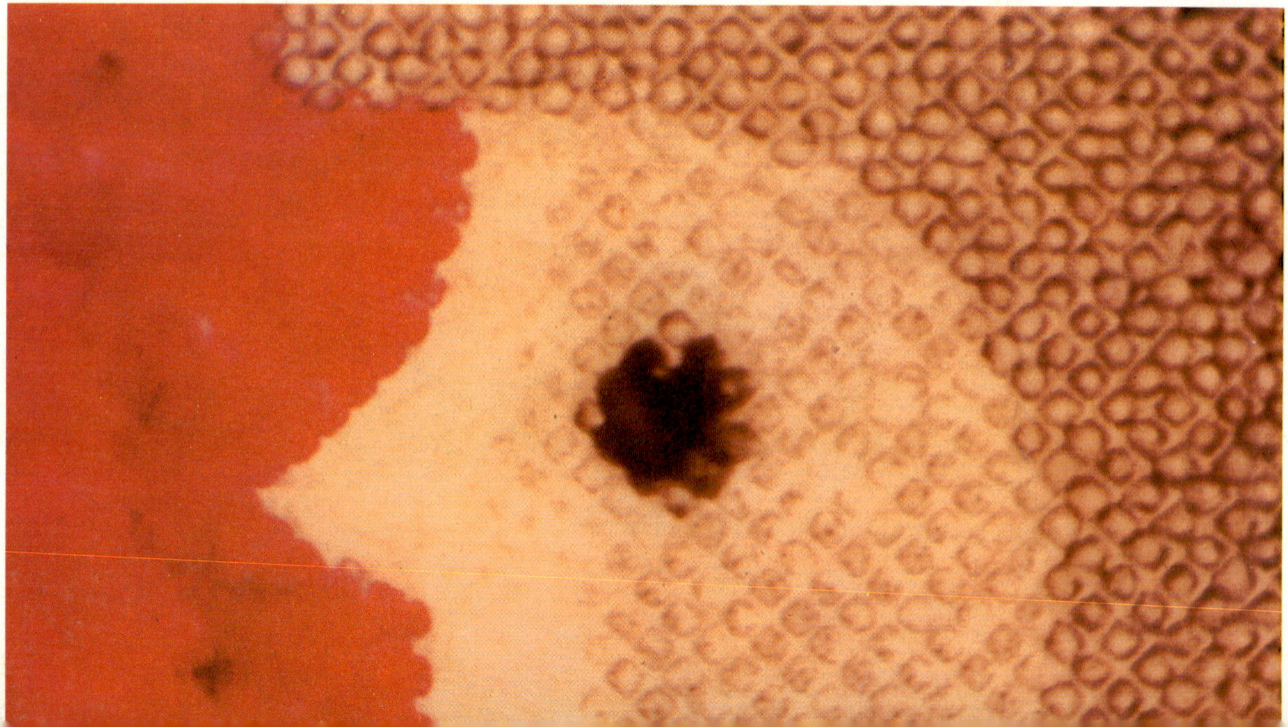

this is added acoustically.

Divided opinion exists concerning the 'End' title. Many amateurs regularly use it at the end of a film, presumably because it is a technique used in professional filming, but it does not do more than stress that the film is at an end, which is obvious in any case. In my opinion it is a relic from the past history of filming, and one that can be readily omitted.

It is no less effective if the last scene, obviously a successful closing scene, is slowly faded out. Often the effect of the word 'End' is far too harsh, but again, the decision is a matter of personal taste. However, we will return to this topic in the next section, where it is discussed in terms of trick titles.

Repeatedly the film title is combined with the name of the author, which usually demands a second text blended into or over the first. Our example would then appear as follows:

1 'Good climbing'
2 'Experiences in the Sella'
3 'by and with ...'

Whether one's name is blended into the title or not is as much a question of taste as the use of the word 'End'. If the author is a member of a film club and his films are occasionally shown to a wider audience, there is indeed a point in blending in the name. On the other hand, films screened only in private company rarely require a name on the title. In professional filming, the matter is of course quite different, since the film is normally shown to people unknown to the author. The often lengthy introduction is usually the only opportunity the professional film-maker has to make himself known to the public.

Finally to repeat: every film-maker is alone responsible for the form of his film texts. However, a good rule is: choose short title texts, which contain the optimum amount of information!

TRICK TITLES

A short association with the filming of title shots brings with it an awareness of the constant stream of new possibilities which this style of film work suggests. There is hardly another area within the field of ciné-filming which allows one's fantasy as much freedom it enjoys here.

This applies in particular to trick titles. A single-frame setting, available on almost all modern ciné cameras, is essential for the creation of trick titles. It has already been discussed in the chapter concerning film equipment. The single-frame setting is the device on the ciné camera used to expose single shots, and its method of use has also been discussed in relation to camera techniques.

Without doubt the creation of the title shot is for many ciné film-makers the only occasion when they use this setting and it is indeed in this area that the single-frame setting can be most useful.

Amateur film-makers rarely take trick shots in the normal course of filming, although most serious ciné film-makers will make an attempt at some point. Once tried it is more or less certain that most people continue to use this method of taking title shots. The repertoire of possibilities is inexhaustible.

Titles made with lettering

The requirements for faultless trick-title shots are firstly that the camera possesses a single-frame device, and in addition that there is a halogen lamp available, and secondly that a steady tripod and long release cable are employed. That the camera must not be displaced even half a millimetre when taking single-frame shots cannot be sufficiently emphasised.

For trick titles which demand easy handling of the letters, the magnetic or layout letters are the most suitable, while conversely adhesive letters are not very useful. Trick titles on the screen seem to bear a magical flavour: the letters appear and disappear as if guided by a ghostly hand, they dance about on the screen, arrange themselves in order, mix themselves up again, and so on.

However the secret is easily unveiled and it is not difficult to create this film-magic for oneself – with trick filming.

The simplest trick title is without doubt the word 'End'. As with other titles, the effect created on the screen is of one letter in the text appearing after another, so that the title is actually composed in front of the audience. This is always fascinating for anyone unacquainted with the method.

The practical requirements are as follows:

Lay out a smooth base on the floor (a piece of red or other coloured card is sufficient). Secure the camera on a tripod perpendicular to the card; the edging of the card must extend outside the limits of the picture area. Make a trial run by placing the letters where the title is going to be, and note their positioning exactly. Using a halogen lamp the letters can be illuminated in such a way as to produce shadows. We will return to this topic in the section on lighting for title shots.

The shot begins with the empty base, which is filmed for about two seconds. Then the camera is set to single-frame and letter after letter is placed in position. The first letter is contained in four or five exposures, the subsequent ones each in three until the word 'End' is complete. Filming then continues for another two seconds.

If the title contains more letters the process is rather more difficult. Let us take the example 'Our summer holiday'. In this case it is particularly important to lay the letters on the base at the outset and to note the arrangement. Otherwise the viewfinder will show that there is no remaining space, while there are still three letters missing. Now prepare the camera for filming, and begin by filming the title base for about 1½ seconds. Then set the camera to single-frame, lay an O, being the first letter, on the board and expose four single shots. Continue in the same manner letter for letter until the title is complete. Finally the whole text is filmed for three seconds, since, as already stated, a trick

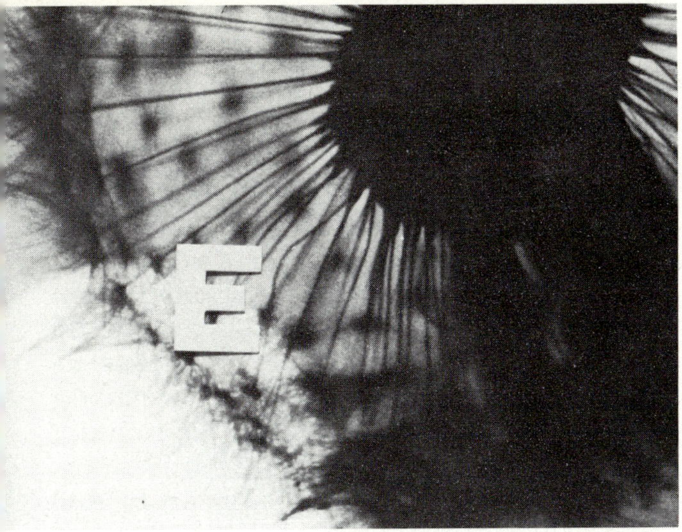

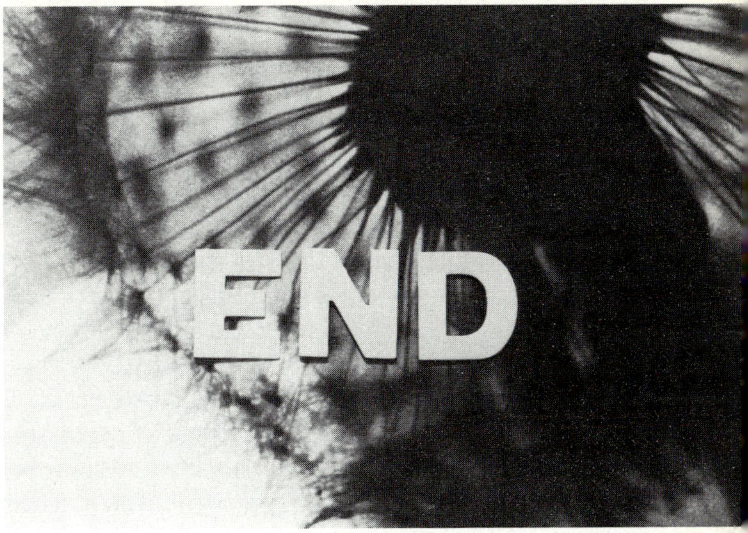

The four phases of a trick title of four letters

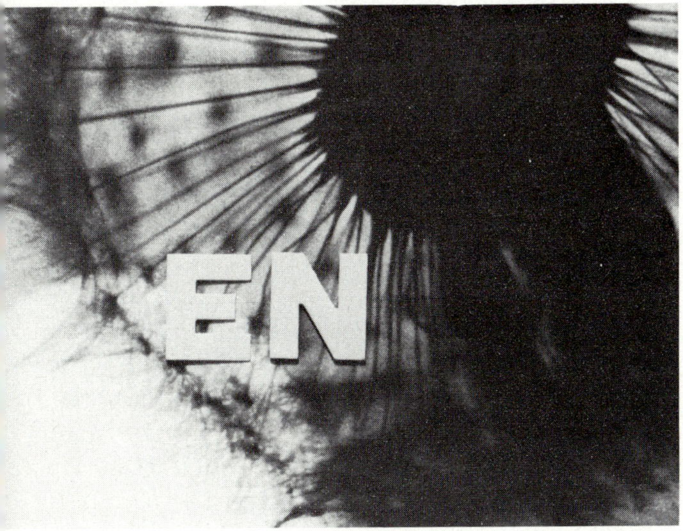

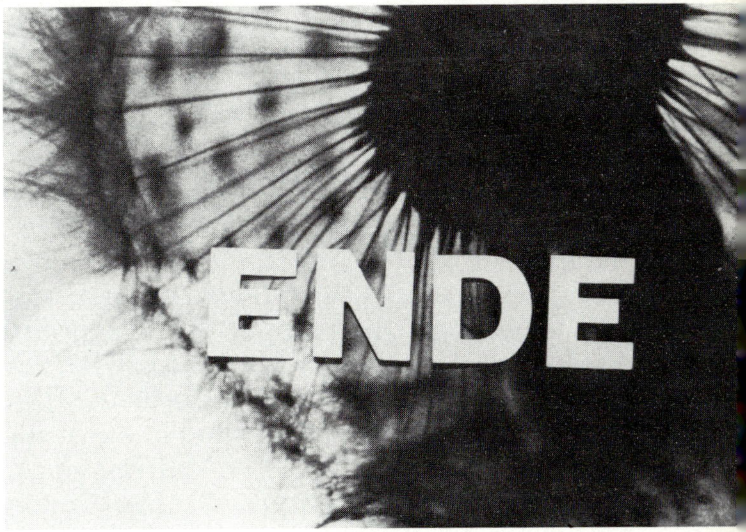

title is more difficult to read all the time movement is involved.

There is no absolute time-span for a trick shot. Our example consists of 16 letters, at four exposures per letter, which experience has proved to be a reasonable number; this means for the total procedure: 16 x 4 single shots at 1½ seconds at the beginning + 3 seconds at the close: with a frame speed of 18 frames per second this equals 27 (= 1½ sec.) + 64 (= 16 x 4) + 54 (= 3 sec.) = 145 single-frame exposures, which ultimately represents a total screening time of about eight seconds. If this seems too short, five exposures can be made per letter, if on the other hand this amount of time is too long, only three need be made. Everyone can use his own discretion.

However, a title length of eight seconds is normally exactly right. An opening title might begin with a fade-in, which has a gentle and thus impressive effect on the film. In this case the picture on the screen only slowly becomes apparent.

Different again is the handling of even longer title texts. Long titles can be very effective in a silent film. Let us take for example the title 'Anyone who has been a traveller has a story to tell'. This consists of 41 letters and one sign. A text this long, filmed in single shots, would take too long to construct. 42 x 4 = 168 shots, plus the film prior to this and at least another five seconds for the completed title. The resulting screen time of about 20 seconds is however too excessive for a title. It would be no less effective if the text were to appear word for word rather than letter for letter. Four single shots are exposed per word, so that the time needed for the display of the title remains quite normal.

Sometimes a word sequence and a letter sequence are combined to give particular emphasis to one section of the title: for instance, in the example 'Grandma and Grandad celebrating their golden-wedding anniversary', the first part of the text appears word for word, while 'golden-wedding anniversary', without doubt the dominating expression, appears letter by letter. Moreover, if the last section appears in gold lettering, contrasting to another colour for the first part, the important phrase is doubly stressed.

As already stated, the background of every title is of great significance. Our 'traveller's' title might for instance include a map of the particular area as a background, the film title of a golden-wedding might include an invitation card, or the menu of a restaurant. Backgrounds of this type give the title a very personal flavour. The examples are sufficient to at least indicate the manifold possibilities.

Another type of film title is one created with 'dancing' letters, and although this uses the same lettering as previously the method demands rather more time and patience, and it is recommended that its application should be limited to use with short titles.

While the technical construction does not vary, the screened effect is totally different: the magical effect is far greater, since the letters do not suddenly appear in their place, but rather wander about the screen until they find their goal, as if remote-controlled. The way in which the title text is finally formed is extraordinarly impressive.

Trick titles of this type are created in the following way. As with any title, the text must be tried out on the board and the arrangement noted. To avoid uncertainty, indicating marks can be made at the edge of the board, outside the area visible in the viewfinder, so that the position of each letter can be relocated with speed and accuracy.

The next step is the initial filming of the empty title board, after which the first letter is moved slowly into the angle of aperture from the side. As soon as the camera's viewfinder reveals that the letter is in the picture, let it remain there for the first shot. Then it is moved again slightly, the next shot is taken, and so on, until the letter reaches its destined place. The smaller the movement between each single shot, the more easily the letter moves towards its place in the film. If the movements are too large the letter will appear to jump.

It is additionally interesting if the second letter originates from a different position from the first, and in this way the direction of each letter can be varied.

It is evident that this is only suitable for a short title, since one must reckon on twenty shots for the movement of each letter, which means 100 to 120 single-frame settings for a word consisting of 5 or 6 letters. This makes a title of this sort rather long.

Another new variant of the trick shot is achieved by the simultaneous wandering of several letters from various directions searching for their place in the title. The process demands particular concentration, since mistakes can very easily occur. All the letters which are to appear to move must be slightly repositioned after every two camera shots. Moreover, they must only be moved a little, until they finally become a word. Whether the letters dance in in turn, or the word is started from the end or the middle does not alter the method in any way.

An additional trick can be included by constructing the word wrongly, so if the word 'holiday' is to be portrayed, the letters appear but form the word 'yolidah'. After this has remained for two seconds the 'y' and the 'h' change places, one reaching its destination, from above, the other from below, so suddenly the correct word appears on the screen. Naturally the trick should only be used if the content is suited to it. A lively episode might well be begun with a 'crazy' title in this way, perhaps a film of a carnival or something similar.

The form in which longer title texts should be filmed has already been discussed; they should appear in syllables or in words, or indeed occasionally as a concept ('Golden wedding' for example). In the following we can extend the possibilities to include yet a further variant. If the text is too long for individually moving letters, the method in the following example may be implemented: Lay out the text

Between spring
and summer

in two rows and note the arrangement of the individual letters. The plan is to make the two rows of the text appear line by line. First, the top row appears, from the right, the 'B', then the 'e' etc., consecutively, but with the correct interval between the letters (so that on the screen the rows of text appear to glide into the picture area). The effect is heightened if the letters run at a constant, even rate. Finally the second line can appear from the same direction; equally, both lines can approach their goal simultaneously, the one from the right the other from the left. The choice embraces a number of variants.

One can work miracles with the single-frame setting. Attempt new tricks with title letters and trick settings constantly, and it will not only quickly become routine, but also generate new inspiration.

Map titles

The map trick title is created without lettering and is particularly suitable for intermediate titles with a travel film, appearing wherever a new destination is reached. No other method can portray this change as graphically; at the same time it acquaints one with the area traversed. Besides the map, a number of coloured points, preferably red, as available in the title lettering set, are required.

A simple example for the map title: let us take the day's journey from London to York. Following the last scenes showing shots of London, the scene is faded out and the map appears. A 'snake' consisting of red points moves slowly from London to York and remains there, with the name filmed as large as possible, followed by a slow fade-in to the first scene of York.

How is this red snake guided from London to York? Naturally with the aid of the camera's single-frame setting. This is not difficult: when the camera has been mounted on a tripod, the map and accessories have been made ready, the map must be so positioned in the viewfinder that the points London and York fit into the field of vision, if possible not too near the edge, and are clearly legible. The first red point is now positioned in the area of London, and the map filmed for about two or three seconds. Whether or not this entails a fade-in is not crucial. Finally the second point is laid next to the first, four single frames are exposed, then the next and so on until about six points of the snake have been filmed. Whether you use more or less than six points depends entirely on your own judgement.

When the first section has been filmed in this way, the first point is removed and placed at the front and another four frames are exposed. The process continues in this manner: each time the last point is positioned in front of the others, which remain unmoved, so that the movement of the 'snake' appears very smooth, and the largest portion of the snake does not move.

On arrival at its destination the snake correspondingly decreases in size until one point remains, laying on the name 'York'. Then the first scenes of the town follow, with or without a fade-out.

This type of subtitle is useful for films in which the surroundings frequently change, and the basic principle can be easily adapted to suit any given situation. A toy car or a model train in place of the points from the lettering box might prove more suitable if the journey is taken by car or train. The object is then allowed to move or fly across the map using small movements and single shots. The mode of creation is in principle the same, but the title immediately shows which means of transport was used for the journey.

Title blending

Blending the title into the running film is a very professional method, and is a possibility that has been more frequently exploited since ciné cameras have been fitted with a macro-setting. It is not possible to blend in the title without a macro-setting, and it requires additional accessories besides.

A mount exists for some camera models, which includes a disk to be fastened in front of the lens; the letters, which must as a rule be smaller than those normally used, can be affixed to the disk. Using this equipment the title and the movement can be filmed simultaneously.

In this instance the section of the picture behind the title will probably appear out of focus, since the depth of field according to the close-up setting will not be adequate for the entire picture, but since the interest is concentrated on the title, the lack of definition is barely noticeable.

Conversely it is possible to focus on the background at the expense of the title. The deficient focusing of the title can be transformed into a new trick, but this demands the use of a tripod. The title can almost be made to disappear by shifting the focused plane, while the background appears clear and in focus. The title on the glass disk is filmed on the close-up setting, then the distance is slowly altered from the macro setting to the distance of the main subject. The title lettering in the close-up range becomes less and less well defined, until it blurrs almost into invisibility, while the background is increasingly focused and the effect is almost of a dissolve. Endless experiments can be made involving this shifting of focus during title shots, especially in the macro-setting. Another example: the effect of a two-lined title on two different surfaces can be very interesting if the focus is shifted from one (foreground) to the other (background). However, in order for this to proceed harmoniously, title lettering in various sizes must be employed, so that the texts, filmed at varying distances, appear to be more or less the same size on the screen. The smaller letters are placed on the glass disk for the close-up setting, the ones on a title board at a corresponding distance. Here again the work must of course include the use of a firm three-legged tripod, since the position of the camera is liable to be altered minimally even when the distance is adjusted.

Although the procedure for a title shot has been described before, it is briefly re-examined for the purpose of this example. The first title text, on the glass disk, might read for instance:

'By car' (smaller lettering)

the second, placed at a greater distance on the board, states

'Right across France' (larger lettering).

Naturally the first title is filmed purely as a text, without a coloured background. As it becomes undefined the focus is shifted to the second title, under which a map of France might be laid or the French national colours or anything else: fantasy knows no bounds.

This change from one plane to another can be repeated several times, as the text demands, although the title should not become too long. It can however tolerate up to three or four settings.

If the camera is fitted with an automatic dissolve mechanism, this can be used to create title shots of a very elegant nature. Certain advice concerning the construction of the text is required, in order to be able to exploit this technique to the full. The text may consist of one or more lines, but those which are to be connected by means of a dissolve should be of the same sentence constituency, in other words, the lines of the text should be positioned in the same place within the image field. Hence when the film is projected one line runs into another – an effect which cannot be produced if the lines of the text are placed in varying positions.

Planning the filming is of prime importance, before the first scene can be dissolved in with the title. In this case unwanted dissolve should not be simply cut out (as with fading-in or fading-out) since the remaining scene will frequently be too short.

Trick lenses – title shots

The three-sided prism has been previously introduced in another section in connection with trick lenses. This prism, with its three parallel running fields, can be used for the creation of interesting titles. Texts containing only one line or word are the best suited to this.

The prism is so positioned that the divisions lie absolutely horizontal (parallel to the side of the picture), so that the text can be seen three times. It has already been stated that the prism can be turned in its mounting. When the (three fold) title has been filmed for about two seconds or is of the right length, turn the prism slowly until the text appears vertically, and halt the camera again. When the next text is exactly in position, return the prism to a horizontal setting, where it again remains stationary for the required length of time.

When screened, this results in the following effect: the text, displayed in triplicate,

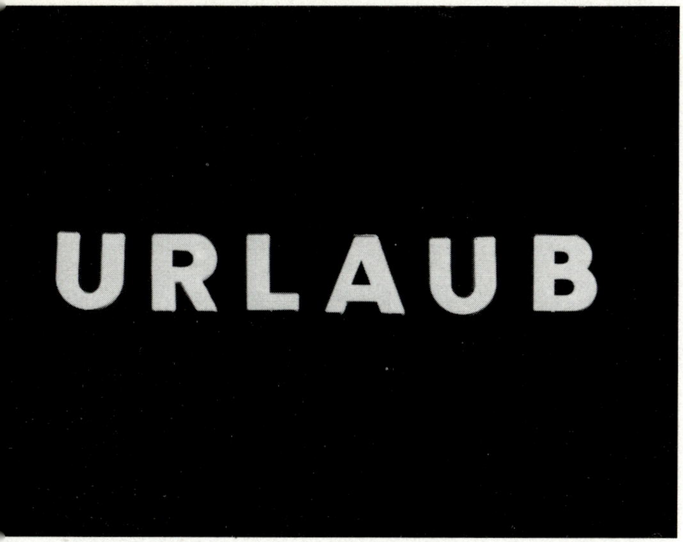

Title out of normally-set lettering

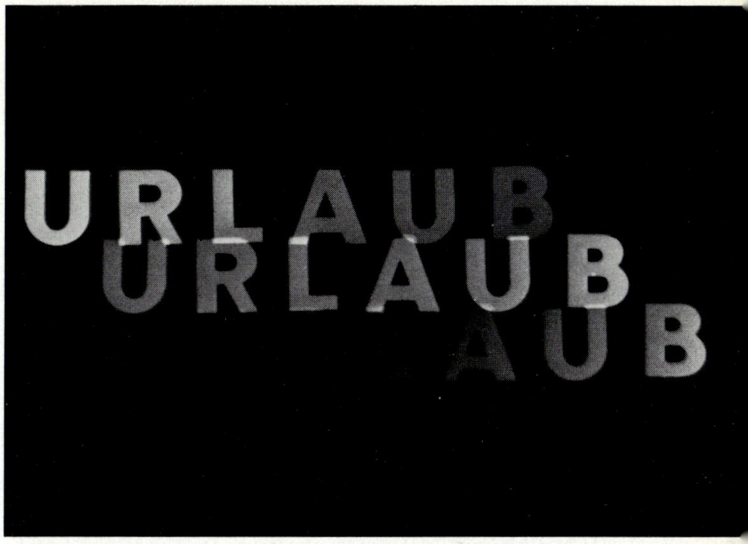

Shot taken with a 4-way parallel prism

Title shots with trick lenses:

Shot taken with 3-way parallel prism

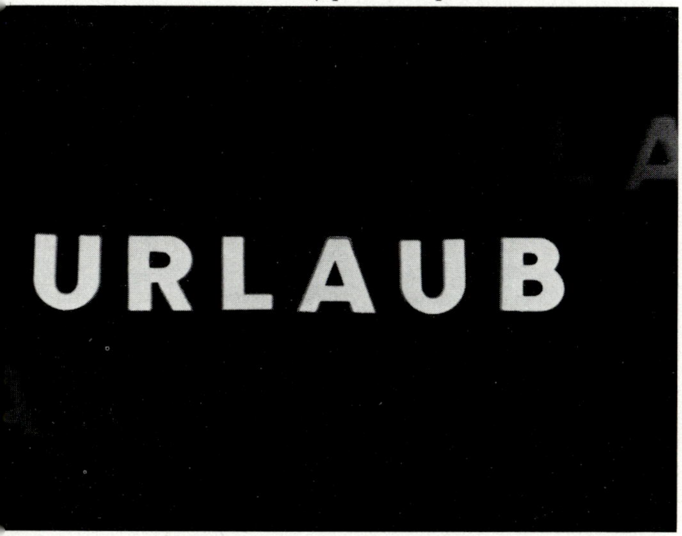

Shot taken with 3-way sector prism

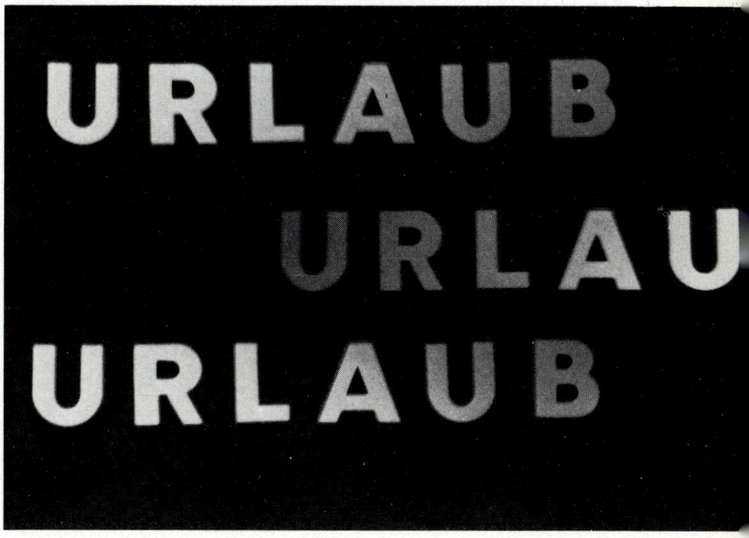

appears on the screen and is then turned throughout 90° in this setting, when a new text appears, which is then turned back throughout 90°.

Title shots provide interesting scope for trick lenses, which are indeed otherwise of very little use. Other trick lenses can of course be used in connection with title shots, although the three-faceted prism in its delineated form is the one most suited to the purpose.

Nearly all methods of filming titles allude to the use of title lettering. Only those people with some graphic ability can manage without. For trick titles, however, title lettering remains a basic elementary accessory.

TITLERS

Preliminary note: since modern ciné cameras are equipped with an excellent reflex viewfinder, the era of the titler is almost past. In the time of Double-8 cameras hardly any models possessed a reflex setting, and the ciné-filmer who wanted to produce something special in this field was nearly always forced to use a titler. However, in early days the leading camera manufacturers used also to market titles to correspond to their equipment – which is nowadays no longer the case.

If no exact viewfinder control existed (the faults caused due to discrepancies in parallax are well known), the amateur film-maker had to work with a fixed focusing control and a specially developed close-up lens in order to be able to produce full-focused images of the title and the titling surface. In modern Super-8 cameras this requirement is satisfied without accessories by means of the reflex setting in the viewfinder.

Blending titles into completed film

However, in certain areas the titler still maintains its significance, even now. There is for instance no possibility of blending a text on to an already completed film with the use of such equipment.

One type of apparatus, unique of its kind, the 'cinegraphica' can achieve not only this, but also much more that many an amateur has long desired. Surprisingly, although this equipment is by no means new now, it is relatively little known.

The apparatus functions as follows: small adhesive letters are stuck on to a title board, and the film is projected into the machine from the other side. Then both picture and text are filmed together by the ciné camera via a transparent mirror. A close-up lens, which forms an integral part of the cinegraphica, ensures that the focus on this plane is always constant, and that film can be taken with any camera. The titling surface, which is black based, can be lighted with the aid of a small opening on the exterior of the box-shaped equipment. The process is clarified by means of a diagram.

Other techniques
The cinegraphica can also be used to take a transparency as film, if instead of the film a transparency is projected, and it can be used to copy a well-loved 2 x 8 film on the Super-8. To this end a 2 x 8 film is projected into the cinegraphica and filmed with a Super-8 camera. In this case the opening for the title remains shut. Further to this it is possible to make duplicates of your own films, particularly useful if a holiday is taken with friends or relations for instance, but only one film exists of it, or if a 'golden-wedding' film is to be presented to several people.

Professional methods
Titlers can achieve a greater amount, or improve on the quality of, the titling. The following modes of titling are best known via the cinema and television, and a titling studio, as in every film studio, includes titlers of this type among its equipment. A titler will allow the following possibilities:

Travelling titles
A travelling title, sometimes endlessly long, will nearly always appear at the end of a television programme, in other words, the names of all those involved rise over the picture surface at a constant rate from below to above and then disappear.

The names or perhaps an introductory text at the beginning of a film are either stuck or typed on to a roll of paper, which is then slowly unrolled in the machine in front of the running camera, always from bottom to

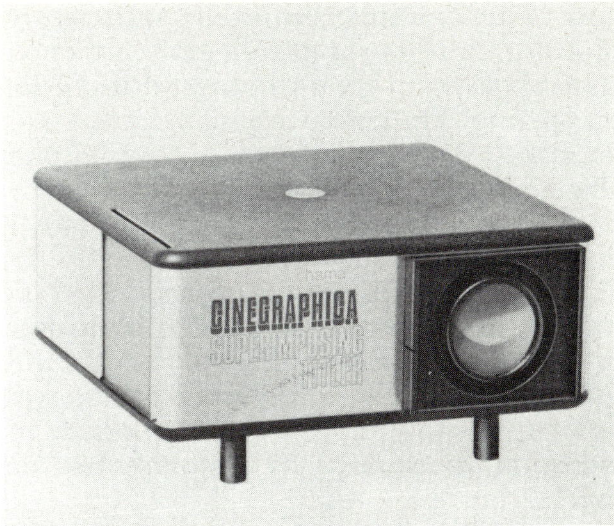

'Cinegraphic' title. Not only is it suitable for many types of trick titles, but can also produce duplicates of the film

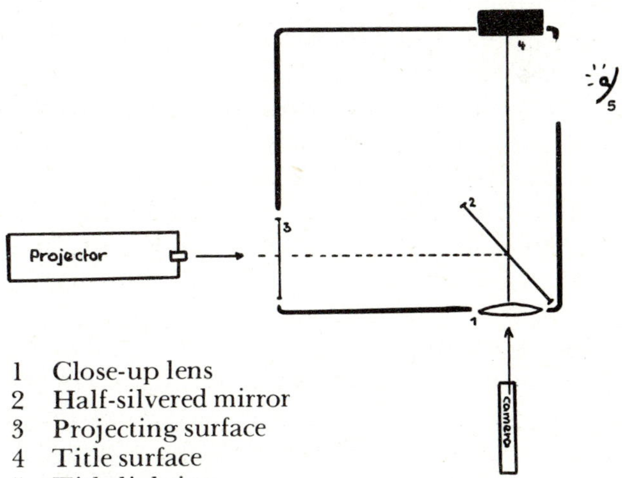

1 Close-up lens
2 Half-silvered mirror
3 Projecting surface
4 Title surface
5 Title lighting

top. The movement must be sufficiently slow for the text to be easily legible; if the text ascends too quickly it can cause difficulties in reading. The tempo at which the text is to be rolled depends ultimately on trial and error. The trial should be undertaken by someone who is reading the perhaps rather long text for the first time.

A travelling title may also be written on transparent material, if the text is to run over a coloured background or a background photograph. Titlers possess two rollers over which the roll of text is transported: in addition it usually has a holder for the background pictures.

Running titles

The difference between these and travelling titles exists only in relation to the direction of movement pursued by the written roll; the text runs from right to left across the picture and must only consist of one line. This method of titling is often demonstrated in professional filming.

Only one line can ever be read at a time, and only then if the text emerges from the right and departs from the picture to the left. Its technical composition is barely distinguishable from that of the travelling title.

Flip-over titles

The text is placed on a transparent or coloured titling board, and once it has stood long enough the board is flipped forward, which means that the board must be fixed at the bottom edge of the picture, never the top, in a way that allows a rotating movement. Professional films have also acquainted us with this method: the text flips forward and out of the way, and the next one appears on the screen.

Flip-over titles are also easily connected with the first scene, if a pane of glass is used and the opening scene is already apparent as the last text plate is flipped over. If the shifting of focus from one filming surface to the other is also combined, the total result is a very versatile method of filming. The flip-title can be fairly imitated without a titler, especially by using the example previously described, in which the title text was affixed to a window-pane. By opening the window the subject is then revealed as a continuation of the film.

It is also possible to simulate the running title, in this case by filming a sheet of paper, on which the letters appear as they are being typed. Arrange the camera in such a way that only the paper on which the typed text appears is visible on the film, and the resulting impression is almost equivalent to that of the running title. A title constructed with this rather technical appearance will be particularly suitable for certain film themes.

Swivelling titles

The swivelling title is similar to the flip-over title insofar as the titling surface is rotated in both cases, but with the former, the pivot is at the side of the board, and in the middle. The text can be rotated horizontally or vertically on to the next title.

The background surface on each side should preferably be black or all one colour, so that the two texts can be joined to each other seamlessly. The text is divided between the two sides and both can be prepared in advance. Once the first title text has been filmed, the board is slowly rotated on to the next, the process being repeated as often as necessary. This is yet another method of titling frequently employed in professional filming.

If you have no titler at your disposal, nearly all these methods can be improvised; it is simply necessary to ensure that the positioning of the letters is not altered as the board is swivelled or flipped-over. Magnetic lettering is less suitable for this purpose than adhesive lettering. Glass or synthetic materials are more suitable for this type of work.

Titles on two planes

Film titles on two levels have already been discussed. Obviously this possibility also exists in conjunction with the titler, above all to associate the text with small objects.

A 'revolving stage' as an accessory to the titler provides a platform for small figures, a vase, a candle, or similar objects which allow for yet further variants in titling.

The title text can for instance be stuck to a pane of glass in front of the revolving stage, so that objects positioned behind are filmed at the same time as the titles. An example of this might be a film about playing chess : 'The regal game'. The title appears on a sheet of glass, and behind it, the king revolves on the stage; an ideal title for a chess film.

There are many other examples which can be realised in a similar way. In each the text remains stationary and easily legible, while an object related to the film is depicted in the title. A particularly striking effect is achieved by virtue of its rotating motion.

There are countless forms of title to be created with a titler, and new combinations and variants are ever current. All in all, the titler is a real gift to ciné-film makers.

LIGHTING FOR TITLE-SHOTS

In principle title shots can be created under any sort of lighting, and inasfar as the title is filmed together with the scene, this will naturally occur in daylight.

However, most titles are trick titles, and these, plus titles made on a titler, are created at home. Usually only the evening remains free for this, necessitating the use of artificial lighting, in which case a film lamp, which is generally available, becomes the light source. If the work includes a titling board, a small photographic tripod may be used, as it is a great asset if the lamp can be moved freely around the room on it, leaving both hands free for releasing the camera and arranging the letters, particularly in trick titles. Moreover, it is extremely tedious to have to hold a hot lamp repeatedly in the hand.

It is important to remember to set the camera to artificial lighting before the title filming begins. If this is omitted, a considerable amount of time is wasted, particularly in the case of trick shots.

The camera's aperture is opened fairly wide for taking title shots with a halogen lamp, which is related to the fact that in the main, light-coloured letters are used on a dark background, which naturally absorbs a lot of light. A metre's distance generally implies an aperture value of 4 to 5.6, but this does not signify anything, since no depth of field is needed: the board has absolutely no depth.

Contrast effects

If certain reasons exist for not making a trick title, light can be used to add movement to the title, as we have already discussed briefly at the beginning of the chapter. Most letters do not lie on the titling board like paper, but are indeed 2–3 mm. thick, and this depth is very important for contrasting lighting. Consequently, when purchasing the letters it is important to consider whether they might perhaps be too flat.

To test this factor, the title should be arranged and the film lamp positioned quite level. In this way each shadow throws a longer or shorter shadow on the board, producing a more formative effect in the title. By moving the lamp the shadows can move even during filming, perhaps beginning with a curve from right to left and then moving back during the next title. Despite its simplicity, the method means that the dead letters can be brought to life, even without the use of a trick setting.

Coloured light

Coloured lighting – two or three changing colours – add variety to the script. However, the same effect is achieved by placing a filter in front of the lamp or the camera lens.

Although colours add life they should be used sparingly. For instance, take a trick film using filters in the three colours red, yellow, and blue, changing the colour filter after every third or fourth setting for one letter. As a result not only does the letter change its colour, but the whole titling process flickers with colours.

As with much else this is of course a matter of taste, but nevertheless provides another variant of coloured-light effects.

Coloured lighting can be used for film titles when the background of the text is itself not coloured. If a colour photograph or a coloured film scene is used as background for the title shot, the application of a filter will naturally completely alter the original colours. This effect is hardly ever desired, except perhaps when the aim is to produce an unreal impression corresponding to the theme of the film.

Light reflections

Finally, I would like to point out something which is often not noticed until the film is projected: if the title lettering is placed on a shiny background (panes of glass, synthetic materials, foil etc.) this may result in the lamp causing reflections, which produce ugly marks on the film, although this can be avoided if the lighting is correctly adjusted.

If the lamp is positioned on the side of the camera, the light will fall obliquely on to the titling surface, and hence the reflection will also only be visible from the side (angle of incidence = angle of reflection, a basic law of physics). Moreover an oblique positioning of the lamp means that no shadows from the tripod legs will cross the titling surface. These mistakes can of course be observed in the viewfinder . . . but often no notice is taken of them.

A related occurrence, although one which happens inadvertently, concerns different shadows. These may appear when trick title shots are filmed which require the letters to be moved after every single shot. As a rule a long cable release is employed, but the hand used to move the letters might in some circumstances throw shadows when the film is released which are still within the scope of the camera. Should this occur frequently, it might mean that the title cannot be used. Therefore it is important to ensure that the titling board is quite free for the shot before every release. Even I have made this mistake.

TITLE LEADERS

Many television programmes possess title leaders. The same introduction heads the same programme, both with regard to the picture and acoustics. Large film companies use a title leader as a trademark, for instance the roaring lion of Metro-Goldwyn-Mayer. Sometimes the same sign will be used for decades.

A film leader need not, however, be the exclusive privilege of television or professional films. Every anateur can also produce a sign, which might be symbolic, or might be related to the name or the house of the film-maker. Possibilities exist in profusion!

For example, a friend of mine used one of his son's toy knights for his film heading. He filmed the knight frame by frame on an entire length of film, and cut off a few frames for each film as required. At some point he will have to film another 15m. of the knight.

To some extent the inspiration for a heading depends on chance: some people never find one, others never want one. Amongst all the pros and cons to be considered, these film leaders certainly have one positive advantage. Often the opening scene of a film is not satisfactory, since the focus has to be set or adjusted as the first scene is being projected; if this process is completed during the leader, the correct focus is established by the time the actual film begins. Naturally a favourite extra piece of film can also be used for this, but the leader provides a more attractive effect.

Anyone who is artistically gifted can also produce his distinguishing title graphically.

Finally a word of advice in this connection. Many amateur film-makers are in the habit of filming a 'leader' at the beginning of every Super-8 cassette, but for quite a different purpose. It is merely for use in the developing laboratories and bears the words 'This film belongs to . . .' (plus name and address). Should the film reach the developers in a damaged packing, or the sender has written illegibly, the owner is still assured of his film being returned to him.

It is a fact that every year thousands of ciné films and transparencies are returned to the owner from the developing laboratory only with great difficulty, if at all. A sender's title on every film will guard against such loss.

'TWO HOURS TO SPARE'

When the scripting of this film was discussed it was stated that we would return to the composition of the title, which logically belongs in this chapter. In accordance with the main possibilities available within the framework of title techniques, there are of course a number of ways in which this particular title can be created.

The following illustrates several examples, which can be applied to any other film theme.

We are already aware of the title 'Two hours to spare'. The simplest method is to lay the text on a neutral titling board and film it for about five seconds in the usual way, which is quite sufficient for good reproduction. This can be supplemented with the use of a fade-in and fade-out, which is possible on most cameras.

Immediate reference can be made to the content of the film, by suiting the title background to the theme. The letters may for instance be placed on a station timetable or an open railway guide. In our example this would provide an immediate connection with the first scene at the station, and an additional emphasis on the factors of arrival and departure.

The title must not necessarily appear prior to the first film scene. Since the timetable does not emerge until scene 5, there would be nothing unusual in mounting the title between the fifth and sixth scene. One should remain free of the idea that the title belongs unquestionably to the beginning: many feature films prove the converse.

Another method of title composition would incorporate the station clock, which appears in scene 5. The clock is filmed in close up for the title, and after a few seconds, adhesive lettering appears on the clock face forming the title. Obviously the clock can only be filmed if it is hung or stands in the street. By using the trick methods previously discussed an object which is significant in the film can be included in the title picture without difficutly.

If the camera possesses a dissolve mechanism, this will facilitate yet further interesting titles: the first scene, of the couple strolling across the station forecourt, is faded out as the text is faded in, and finally the picture is dissolved back to the zoom scene, the completed dissolve process lasting about three seconds. Since the title is very short, it is sufficient for it to remain stationary for only about two seconds between the dissolves.

This results in an impression that the text is blended into both the scenes following on from each other. A blended title of this nature obviously requires exact preparations, including the planning of film direction, but the result will make the effort worthwhile. It is easy to discover other titles that might allow a blend-in or a dissolve, and this example is solely to offer inspiration.

Anyone interested in graphics could combine the title lettering with a drawing, perhaps on the lines of the following suggestion: the words 'to spare' are drawn or painted very large on a piece of drawing card. Then the words 'Two hours' can be placed in a different position, perhaps laid across the other words. In order to do this the colours must be atuned to each other, perhaps the background 'to spare' in a strong colour such as red or blue, and the lettering in white. The way in which the title is produced, is not as decisive. The letters might appear together or one after the other as in a trick shot. Consider the effect that you are aiming to achieve.

A slight modification of the title is of course also conceivable, as might occur if the name of a magazine or newspaper is to be incorporated into the text. In our example it would be possible to use the newspaper *The Times*, in which case the title of the film would be altered to run 'The Time = 2 hours', whereby the name of the newspaper is used for the first part of the text and lettering is employed for the remainder: '2 hours'. If the paper is bought at a newspaper stand and you explain your idea briefly to the salesman, he will certainly have no objection to you including the newspaper stand in the title picture.

Alterations in the title occur spontaneously as a fresh idea springs to mind, and frequently the suggestion is so good that it should be realised immediately if possible, without being restricted by the script.

Ready-made Titles

This theme can be brought to a close with a tip for those who for various reasons cannot or do not wish to make their own film titles. Even this does not mean that the film is denied a title, since there are various firms which produce ready-made titles, which need only be to be stuck on to the beginning of the film.

It goes without saying that ready-made titles are void of any individual flavour. They are produced to cover a wide number of frequently occurring situations, yet the choice is so large that it is possible to find a title text to suit more or less every film.

Some firms will also take orders for film titles with a text compiled in accordance with your wishes. This means you at least receive the optimum text, although little can be done to influence the composition of the background, or the use of tricks etc. A ready-made title is still better than no title at all.

In my opinion there are hardly any valid reasons sufficient to justify the omission of a title. As the years go by your films will increase in value, both for you and your family, and this worth is further augmented by the use of attractive and original titles.

Shot from bird's-eye wiew (J. Schubert)

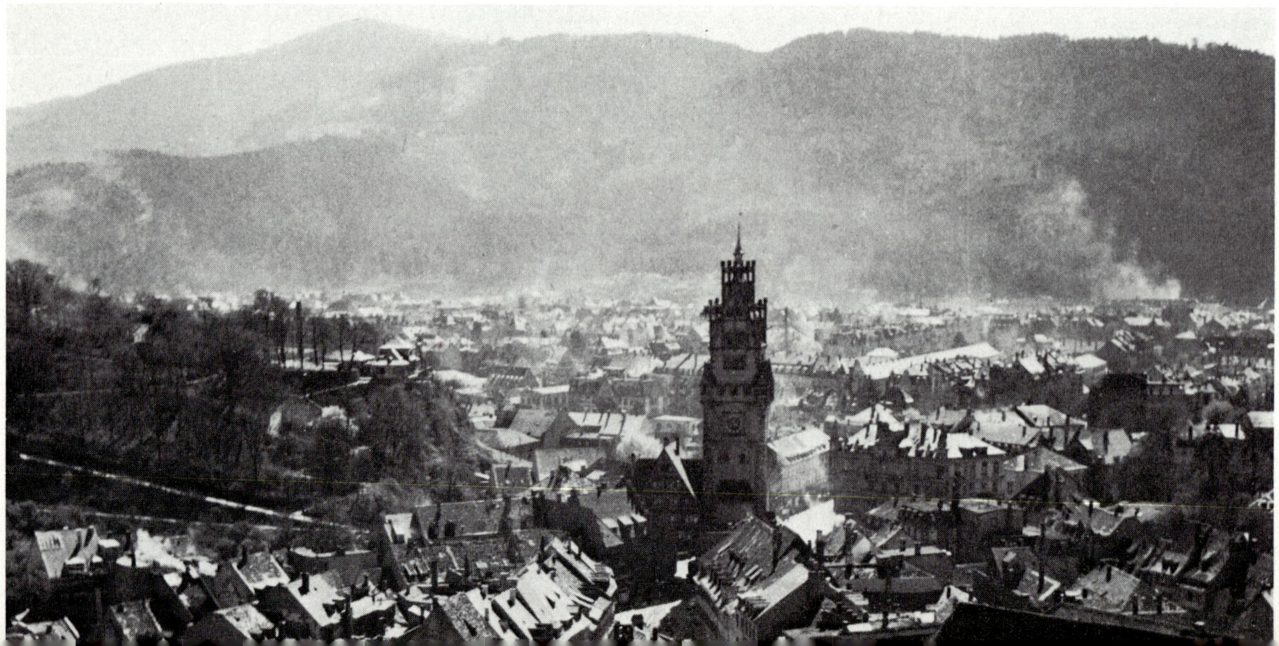

FILM EDITING AND MONTAGE

THE MEANING OF FILM EDITING

Some film-makers question the meaning of film-editing; they would rather have a film as it stands on its 15m. spool, or film the shots in the sequence in which they are to be projected. Most film-makers are not, however, content with this. Anyone who regularly attempts to produce films with a story-line, and who additionally films titles will know that film montage is an essential requirement. No film even in the realm of professional filming, emerges from the camera in such a perfect state that editing may be omitted. There are even 120m. films with more than 200 joins!

With this a part of the question is already answered. Editing the film will iron out any unevenness which necessarily occurs during filming. Moreover, it can be used to heighten or extend the interest of the film, depending on whether the scenes remain at their original length or are shortened. Above all, however, the scenes must be in order, since it is rarely possible to film frames according to the sequence dictated by the plans or script.

For these reasons no amateur film-maker who maintains certain standards of quality can manage without film-editing. At the same time this indicates how multifaceted the hobby is, since in professional circles this work would be accomplished by a 'cutter', a highly-paid specialist who forms the connecting link between the film being taken and the end product. The amateur filmer must prove himself a 'Jack of all trades' and carry out this work alone. A number of tools are required if the work is to be executed correctly and as perfectly as possible. Obviously all the equipment used, plus the necessary materials, must satisfy certain requirements.

The tools and materials required for film-editing constitute the following: a film viewer – a splicer – a single-frame counting mechanism – film-sorting equipment – film cleaner – a small pair of scissors of good quality – soft brushes – thin white cotton gloves – film cement – empty film-spools of adequate size.

THE FILM VIEWER

The film viewer is a logical and necessary requirement for use with the splicer. However, anyone who counts himself amongst those film-makers who do not rearrange or correct their filming will hardly require a film viewer. The film is appraised critically in the viewer scene for scene before editing is begun. The equipment may be halted at any time, so if there is any doubt each frame can be looked at individually. Consequently the screened picture must be clear, bright, and well focused, and no less important is that moving the film does not cause any scratches. In addition, the equipment must be fitted with a marker rod. We will return to this point.

The function of the viewfinder is to allow the film to be observed. Anyone who has tried to find a scene on a Super-8 film without a technical aid will know that this is almost impossible, since the picture is so small that it can hardly be recognised.

In the film viewer the picture is projected over a mirror in a normal picture size of about 7 x 10 to 10 x 15cm. This size is quite sufficient for the film-maker to be able to judge the picture with regard to definition, colour, etc. Finally, however, the viewer should not usurp the projector: it is a technical aid for use in processing films, and since one would normally be alone when viewing the pictures in it, the size of the picture is not of any great significance.

However, the first requirement is a well-defined picture. Before purchasing such a piece of equipment, it is important to test whether it will answer all the necessary requirements.

As already suggested, this applies in particular to the way in which the film is guided. You should pay attention to this, since it is your responsibility to see that the films are treated carefully. Neither the film trap nor the transport mechanism should cause any scratching on the film, even if it is moved back and forth several times in the viewer. The best machines are those in which the film is guided at the sides and the central area of the film is not touched at all. Moreover, there must be cog wheels to guarantee even viewing.

Some film viewers are equipped with halogen lamps, but while more light obviously produces a better picture, this is not a major factor. In contrast, the already mentioned marking rod is of greater importance, and should be an integral part of every film viewer. When functioning, this makes a small notch on the edge of the film. If you wish to make a cut in the frame visible on the focusing screen, the position can be noted exactly with the aid of the marker, and the mark can be found easily later, even though it is very small. It is deliberately kept small so that the film is not damaged, should you decide in due course not to make the cut after all.

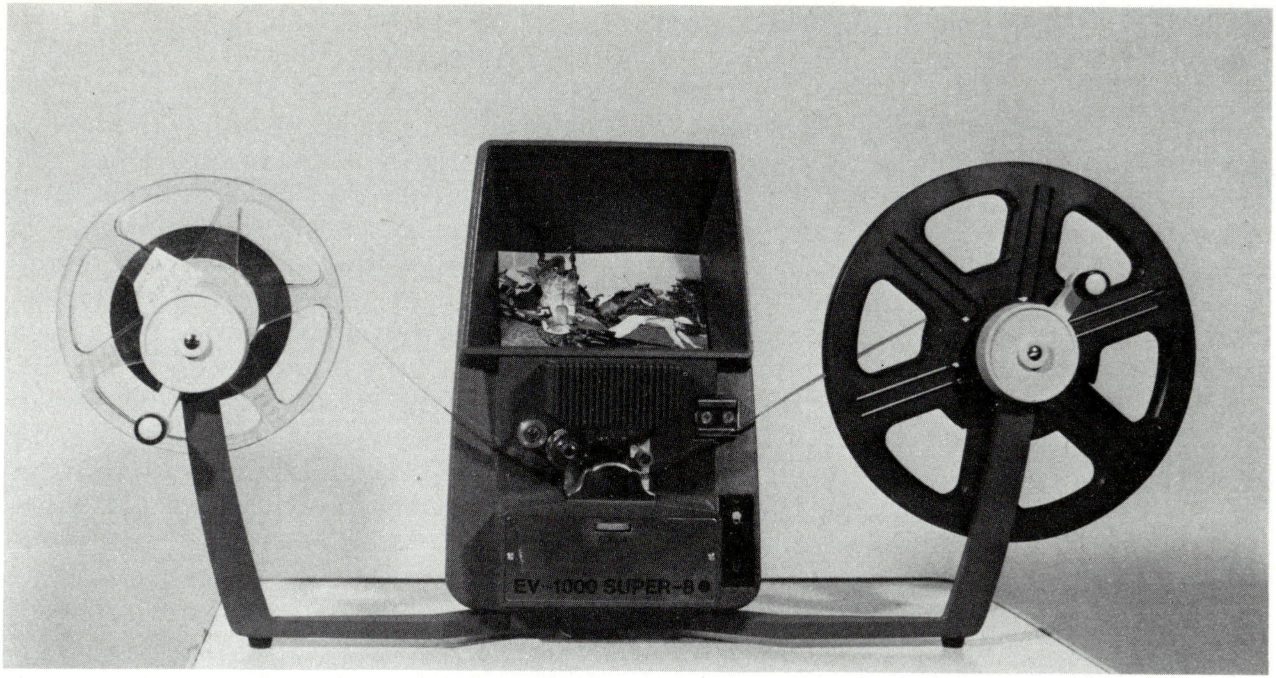

Film Viewer

Most film viewers are operated manually, which is to say that the film is transported by means of hand-driven cranks. The advantage of this is that you can determine exactly at which speed the film is to run. It can be transported fast, or one frame at a time: there are no restrictions. Only in a few models is transportation powered by an electric motor, as in a projector. While this will indeed result in a far more even viewing, manual functioning is nevertheless to be preferred. The picture can be stopped or wound back immediately, while a motor must first be stopped and then reset. It is quicker to find a picture manually.

Film viewers are as a rule equipped to take 120m. film spools, which is certainly the most popular size, since most projectors cannot transport larger spools either. Should one wish to join greater lengths of film on to one spool, however, a 120m. spool should be used initially and then later several rolls can be joined together and rewound to form the desired length. If one frequently or always works with larger-sized spools, it is of course easier to purchase a viewer that can accommodate these larger spools (180m. or 240m.).

Nearly all modern film viewers are produced for the usual Super-8 size. Some models can also be used for 2 x 8 films, and this is the so-called dual equipment. There is no longer any equipment of this type on the market made exclusively for Double-8 film. Anyone who is still working with Double-8 films will supposedly change to Super-8 in the near, or not so near, future, and would hence purchase a viewer that will take both formats. However, on an adjustable viewer one should ascertain that the transport system for both types of films incorporates separate sprockets rather than rollers, for two reasons:

1 A sprocket holds the film exactly in its perforations, guaranteeing an exact conveyance of the film;
2 With a roller mechanism the film is conveyed along its entire surface, which can result in damage. This is not generally possible using sprockets, since only the edge of the film is touched. Test the equipment very carefully before you make a decision.

The important function played by the film viewer with regard to film editing will become clearer in the section on the technique of film montage. Finally, it is important to mention an additional piece of equipment, which can be used in conjunction with the film viewer:

THE SINGLE-FRAME COUNTING MECHANISM

Relatively few amateur film-makers have to prepare film to a predetermined length, but for those who do, the single-frame counting mechanism is of the utmost importance. In some viewers it is inserted, in any case there is some method of connecting it to the viewer. As a result, each frame is counted as the film is conveyed through the viewer.

A counting mechanism becomes necessary when exact timing is all important, perhaps to connect a piece of music to a film. For example: a scene of the correct size is to be fitted to a piece of music only 2.5 seconds exactly. In this case the frame counter must count 2.5 x 18 = 45 frames before the cutting point is reached.

The usual holiday and family films are not dependent on such exactness. Usually a simple method is sufficient to offer a rough estimate of the length of the scene. This simply entails preparing a strip of card which shows with the aid of a scale the lengths implied by 1 to 5 or 10 seconds. This can occasionally be of help in shortening long scenes by the right amount.

On a Super-8 film, 18 frames are only 8cm. long, although generally estimated to be longer. It is also seldom realised that a film scene ½m. long is projected in 6 seconds. Once these values have been appreciated, it is possible to see the proportions involved in editing in a different light.

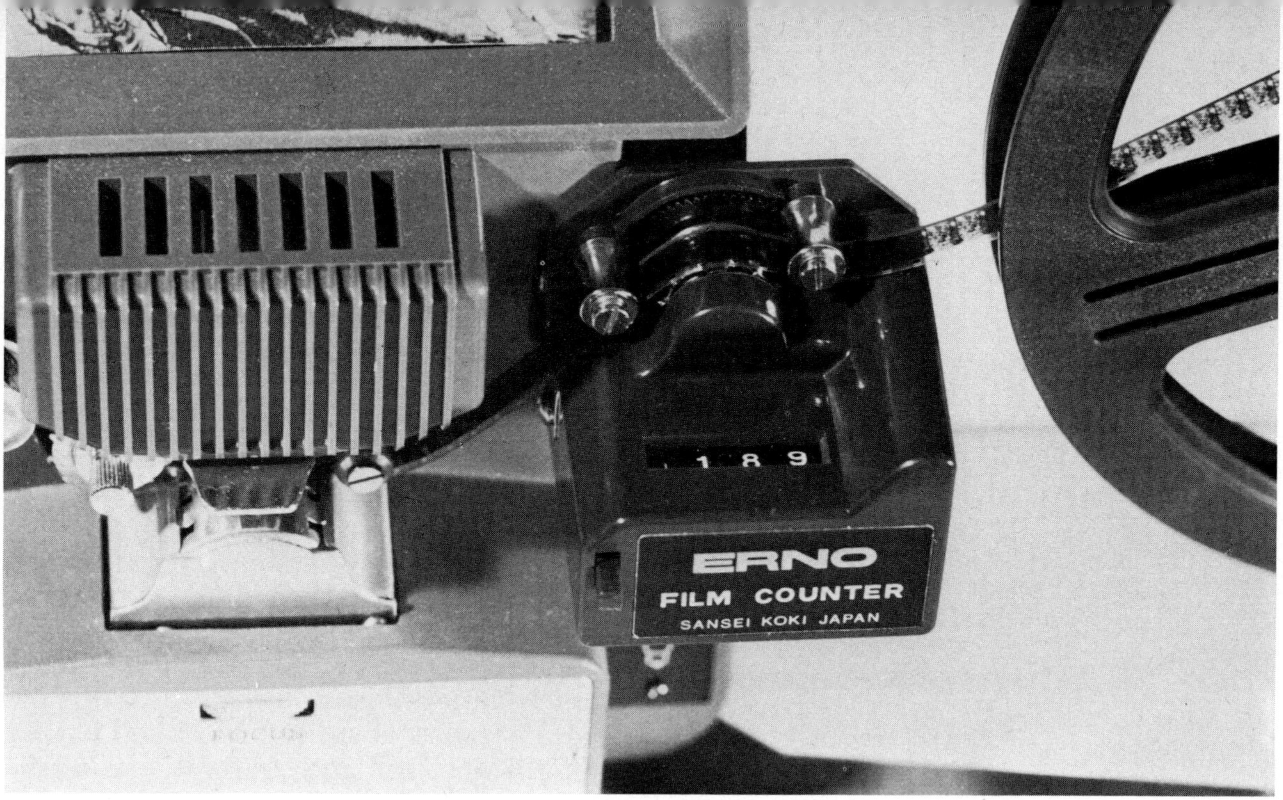

Single-frame counting mechanism, very important for precise filming editing

The next piece of necessary equipment to be considered must be the splicer.

THE SPLICER

Even those who only wish to join up the films in sequence will require a splicer. It is a precision instrument, for joining a film is a matter demanding absolute exactness. The space on the film from one perforation hole to another must be exactly correct to within 1/100mm. If the adjustment is wrongly made, it will cause trouble when the film is projected: the film begins to flutter or to tear. Moreover, the splice must be so small that it does not intervene in the projection, in other words, it must pass the film gate of the projector invisibly, nor must it be thicker than the rest of the film or the film will get caught in the film-gate.

Unfortunately splicers do exist which do not satisfy these requirements, and consequently you should always test a splicer, before deciding on any one model. There are various models and systems, all serving the

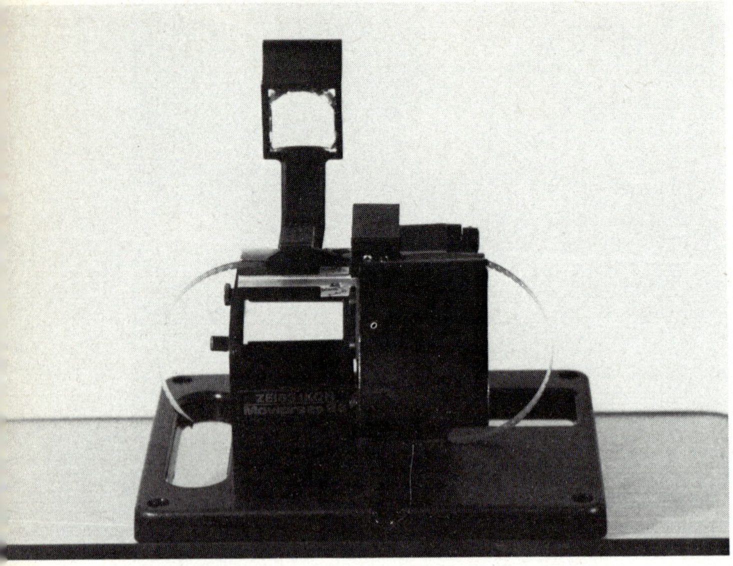

Film plane

same purpose, but functioning very differently.

Naturally the splicer has seen many developments, which are closely related to the history of the ciné camera, film sizes, etc. The first ciné films had a length of 13m., 16m., or 17m.

The first splicers existed for 16mm. film; those used today are still to some extent similar to these. When Double-8 film appeared a short time later, this was soon followed by the production of the first splicers corresponding to the new film. In the meantime there were combined splicers, comparable to the dual equipment of the film viewer. However, the combination was always based on two formats, which either matched each other or bore the same perforations. There is for instance an excellent splicer for use with both Super-8 and Double-8 films.

The cutting and joining processes have also developed and considerably altered with the course of time. In the beginning the equipment was not as precise as it is today, since it was all more simply constructed. Slight irregularities were not as significant as they are in the modern, highly developed Double-8 projectors and the new even more modern Super-8 equipment. Naturally, the manufacturers of splicers have had to take this into account, and constantly refine the equipment.

Some of the first splicers for 16mm. films still exist today. At that time the two ends of the films to be connected were simply cut straight and stuck over each other with the correct distance between the perforation holes. Where the pieces overlapped the film was about 3mm. thick, which meant that at every splice the film was necessarily twice as thick as the normal strip. This could not only lead to disturbances in the projector, but also the focus was shifted at this point and the film pressure mechanism emitted a clearly audible crackling.

Simple Wedge Splicer

In order to compensate for this deficiency a simple wedge splicer was developed, which, like the other splicers discussed here, uses film cement. In this instance the emulsion coating is scraped off one half of the film, as with any splicer, but in addition the film base is trimmed in a tapering, wedge-shaped fashion, so that the other half of the film lies diagonally to the trimmed edge. This results in a considerable weakening of the edge of the splice, but it is still adequate. However, if this method is used the splice might jump in the projector. Before we discuss more modern equipment, a word should be said about the emulsion coating mentioned here.

It is commonly known that various bases are used for the film: polyester, triacetate, or acetate. We will return to this subject at the end of the chapter. For the moment we will concentrate only on acetate films, since polyester film cannot be fixed with film cement.

It is important that the emulsion-coated side of an acetate film is scraped carefully, and the dust this causes removed with a small brush before the film cement is applied.

Film cement is a fluid film adhesive which is produced by various manufacturers, although the only important distinction between the different products is in their name. Once the ends of the film have been approximately prepared, a thin layer of film cement is applied, which takes about 8-10 seconds to dissolve into the film base. The splice is then pressed together in the splicer using the device designed for this purpose and held firmly for about another 15 - 20 seconds. Although the splice will be welded firmly in about half a minute, the film should now be wound round a spool and left for 20 minutes before it is projected.

Double-Wedge Splicer

The double-wedge splicer is rather more advanced than the simple wedge splicer. Both ends of the film are trimmed into a wedge shape (double wedge) so the edges will match each other; theoretically no unevenness will exist - theoretically, because the double-wedge splicer must be adjusted exactly to within 1/100mm. if it is to work precisely.

The trimming process varies little from that of the conventional splicer: a small file is used to ensure that the emulsion coating is separated from the film base. In a wedge splice (there are hardly any others now) a diagonally positioned scraping tool is used to scrape away the emulsion coating from the base. Ideally, once the splice has been joined it should be no thicker than the normal film strip.

In a number of models this scraping process is designed for manual operation, and this is by far the most common method. After some practice it is possible to achieve very good splices using this method. Since the file is operated manually, more or less even pressure can be applied. Consequently it may happen that in one place more pressure is applied and the film is scraped

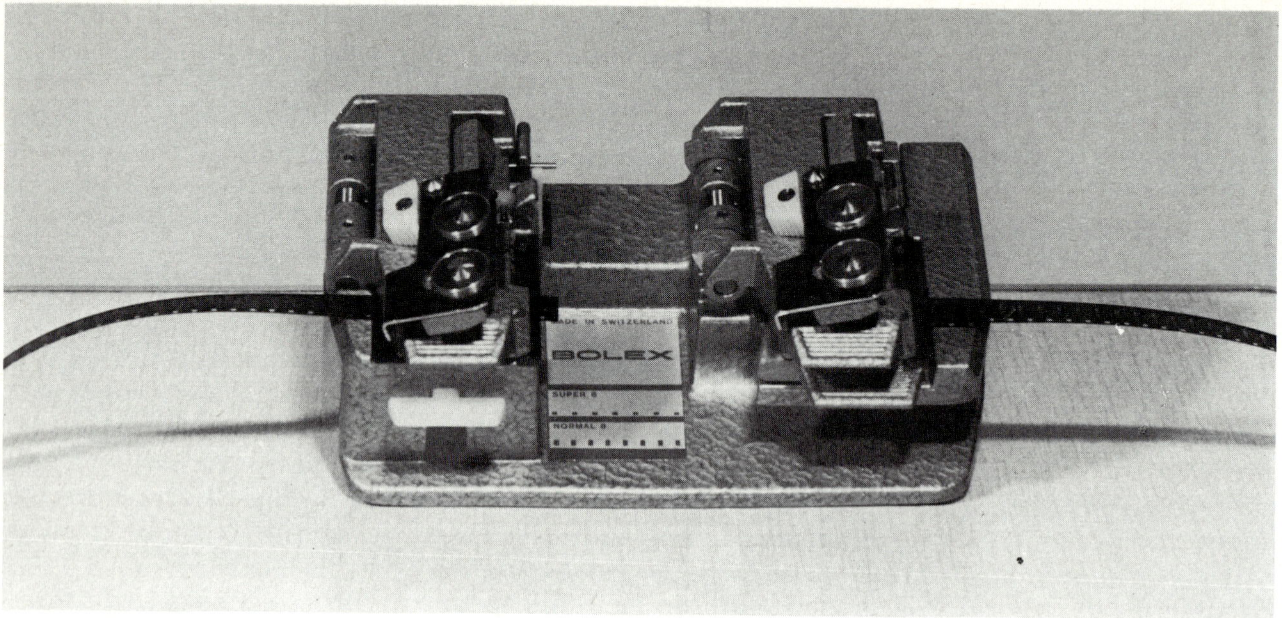

Double-wedge splicer

thinner, in others less pressure results in a splice which is thicker than it should be. A certain amount of practice will help to eliminate the occurence of this problem.

More even splices are produced by a splicer that possesses one or two scraper blades that are electrically powered by a battery motor. These scrapers are so adjusted that film is scraped exactly as far as is necessary; from then on the motor runs idle, which means that the film edge is no longer being altered. The various pieces of equipment of this type ensure that the splices are without doubt even, assuming the equipment is correctly adjusted.

Scraping produces dust! It has already been suggested that the dust must be removed with a brush before the film cement can be applied. However, the subject of dust alludes to a large problem, which occurs in every splicer during the scraping process. It is a common fact that dust is a special enemy of the film, and must therefore be constantly removed with the aid of a brush, and an anti-static cloth, both from the film and from the equipment itself.

If you fight shy of this dust, there is another solution: the most advanced pieces of equipment do not produce dust. A film plane is used to remove the shavings from the film, and both the film ends are prepared without any dust gathering. With this equipment, more than with any other splicer, the adjustments must be absolutely exact: the work can only be accomplished faultlessly if all the measurements are set correctly. While this sort of equipment enjoys a favourable reception in professional circles, it is relatively little used amongst amateur film-makers.

Chemo-Splicer

The 'chemo-splicer' holds an exceptional position among the other splicers, since in this equipment the two film ends are welded together chemically, whereby they meet each other rather than overlap. Instead of being cut and trimmed in the normal way, the film is divided along a serrated line, which means

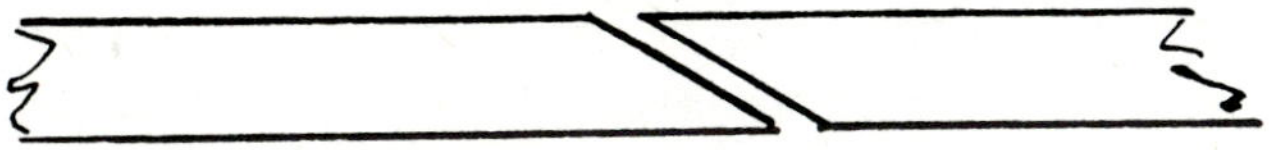

Diagram of a film splice (cross-section)
Above: double-wedge splicer: both sides are trimmed
Below: single-wedge splicer - only one side is trimmed

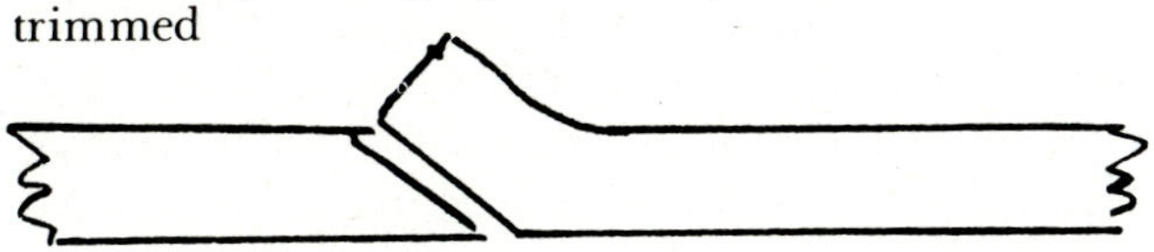

that the cut edge is five times longer than usual. The two serrated lines complement each other exactly and are joined by a chemical product specially developed for this purpose.

The fact that any thickening of the film is impossible makes this splicer unique. However, there is one disadvantage for hurried or anxious film-makers; each splice requires at least two minutes drying time!

Joining Polyester Films

It has already been suggested at the beginning of this chapter that in many aspects acetate films and polyester films are completely different, and this refers above all to joining the film, since polyester films demand an entirely different process. All the

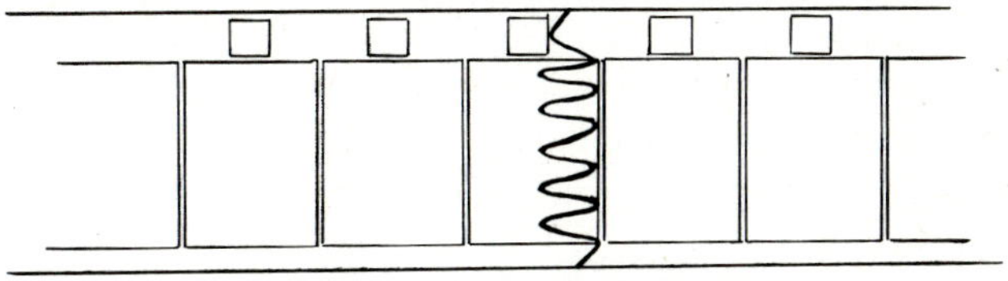

Cutting edge of a chemo-splicer

splicers already mentioned are only suitable for acetate films, but there are a few models which will take other films.

Should the film industry ever be converted to polyester films, wedge splicers, film planes, and chemo-splicers, plus the adhesive they employ, would be obsolete. Certainly the optimist believes that in this event the industry would be in a position to produce an appropriate adhesive. However, up until now there is little to indicate that such a change to polyester film is to be expected in the foreseeable future. There are some splicers on the market for joining polyester film.

Dry Splicers
All the newly developed models work with a binding agent which is placed around the film. The first phase of work consists of the film being trimmed in the splicer and the trimmed ends being precisely matched up to each other. In the next phase the adhesive foil is laid on to the splice and joined to the film. The principle is very simple.

There are naturally already several models, functioning to more or less the same standards. Some are automatic, others attempt to keep the manual operation as minimal as possible. While the simplest models demand that the film is cut and turned over for sticking, in the more advanced equipment everything is completed in one automatic process.

The type of binding agent used will also vary from model to model. Some machines use small tags, others a roll of adhesive tape, depending on their construction. If the splicers are correctly adjusted (exactly the same applies as for wedge splicers) the splices themselves should be barely discernable.

One great advantage of all splicers developed according to the dry-adhesive method is that they can be used for both polyester and acetate film. Hence a dry splicer is a true 'universal' splicer, functioning independently of the film base, although only for Super-8 films. It is important for those working with soundtrack films that such films can also be joined in the dry splicer. The binding agent leaves free at the edge a portion equivalent to the width of the sound track. Whether the soundtrack has already been added, or this is to be completed later is of no significance; the track will not be affected by the binding

Automatic dry splicer

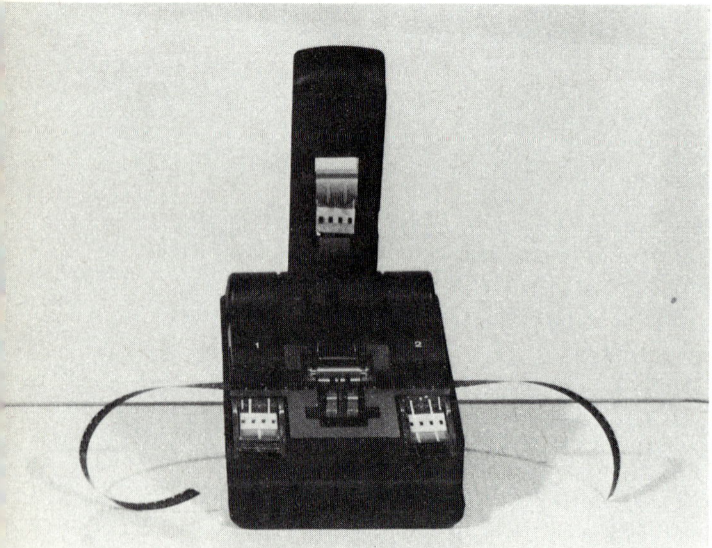

agent. The only exception to this is the stereo sound film. Anyone whose intention it is to produce films with a double-sided soundtrack and to use a dry splicer for editing, must make allowance for the fact that the compensating track, in other words the narrower of the two, will be covered up.

Additionally it must be said that everyone who pursues ciné filming as a serious hobby will sooner or later be presented with the problem of splicers. There are various factors which govern the choice of the model, not least of all the price. It is worth saying in this connection that the top-quality wet splicers are generally more expensive than the best dry splicers.

However the choice is made, it is above all important to check carefully and thoroughly that the splicer functions with the optimum amount of precision: the adjustment must be as fine as possible. Morever, the manual manipulation needed should not be too great.

OTHER ACCESSORIES

Without doubt the most important tools required for film editing are the film viewer and the splicer, but over and above these there are several other things which can make film processing considerably easier.

Although the advice given in specialist shops is generally very good, the following paragraphs add a few comments based on practical experience.

The most important in this connection is an arrangement which allows the editing and montage work to be orderd and reviewed. The nature of this will depend on how you work and how you want to review your films. Rarely are all the necessary pieces of filming collected together on the same 15m. film; they frequently appear on varying rolls, which means that the work includes gathering up the individual parts and cutting them out. When the work is unplanned, the various parts are strewn over tables and chairs and the floor. Obviously there are various ways of achieving one goal, namely order. However, in order to work with the optimum amount of precision, a piece of equipment designed for this purpose is necessary:

The Film-Sorter

The film-sorter, which is combined with a display viewer, is an invaluable aid. Some magnetic clamps, numbered in sequence, are mounted on to one side and under each clamp sits a scene. In addition the light box makes it possible to check with a magnifying glass that one has in fact sorted out the right scenes. The work is considerably simplified by the existence of a scale on the front edge of the equipment, indicating frame quantities and their value in seconds with regard to Super-8 film.

Not so sophisticated is the film-sorting equipment one can construct for oneself, without a light however. This has been tried out many times and is simple to make. It consists of a board which fits the working area,and on to which a row of plastic washing-pegs are glued. The pegs are numbered in order and have the same function as the magnetic clamps on the sorting desk.

Obviously the suggestion can be modified. Instead of a board, you might smooth down a slat of wood, hang it on the wall, and stick a row of headless pins into it. Then the scenes can be hung up carefully by a perforation hole. In my opinion, however, the washing pegs provide a more suitable method.

Both methods facilitate an ordering and appraisal of the film as it is edited and mounted. Their size depends on how much film you intend to work on at once. Normally 15 to 20 clamps would be sufficient.

An arrangement of this sort is particularly worthwhile if you do not possess a work room where work can be broken off at any time and everything can be left as it is. Most amateur film-makers are required to undertake their work in the living-room, and usually there is only time for this in the evenings. On the other hand it is hardly possible to complete all the work for a holiday film, for instance, in one session, and consequently you must have some aid which enables you to put away the half-finished work in an orderly manner so you can continue it later. It is impossible to guarantee that odd film strips which are left lying around will not be scratched; moreover it would entail too much work to sort them out again.

The above comments make it quite clear that no film-maker editing his own films can manage for long without some system of ordering the film. Both methods described will serve the same purpose.

For those only now beginning with editing work, there is a simple way in which they can help themselves at the outset. Save all the little 15m. spools which you received from the developing laboratory with your film. When you have about fifteen spools, perhaps friends will be able to contribute, these can be put to good use, insofar as the spools can be numbered and used to make a small archive. Each scene is wound on a different spool until the work reaches completion.

Naturally you will need to note immediately on a sheet of paper or an exercise book, which scene or sequence of scenes is played on to which spool during work. After every splice, one of the little spools is vacated, leaving room for a new scene.

The Film Spools

It has already been said that a film which is returned from the developing laboratory is wound on a 15m. spool. Since several of these 15m. films will generally be edited and mounted together, the film must be wound each time onto a larger spool. You must first of all be clear about the number of films to be processed and have ready spools of the appropriate size. Film spools are made in a vast range of sizes, the most popular being those designed for 60m., 90m., and 120m. film lengths, which means that four, six, or eight films, each of 15m., will fit on these spools respectively. Obviously there is no point in being determined to fit 95m. of film on to a 90m. spool. When the film is screened, one would simply get annoyed because the spool would be too full and the film would slide off the spool as it was being threaded. It is better to have a 120m. spool, with 20m. spare.

Some amateurs initially overlook the fact that at least two spools of the desired size are needed for cutting and joining the film. The film scenes are wound on to the first spool once they have been joined in the right sequence, and when the work is complete the film must be made ready for screening, in other words wound back on to the other equally large spool, otherwise projection would begin at the end and the picture would be upside-down.

Despite the availability of sorting equipment, one might want to preserve the film in sections on little spools during processing, since this has proved to be an easier way of obtaining an overall view of the film. It becomes obvious in practice that one can never possess too many film spools. One should have at least two empty spools of each required size available.

Brush and Gloves

In the discussion concerning the damaging effects of dust during film preparation it has already been suggested that a soft brush is essential for work with the splicer. Once the film has been scraped in the splicer the ends must be cleaned with a brush and thus freed from any remaining particles of dust. The film will only stick to and dry permanently on a clean film surface. In addition, the brush should also be cleaned occasionally.

Many film-makers always handle their film wearing a pair of thin white cotton gloves, which ensures that no finger prints reach the surface of the film. This extreme cleanliness during film processing is by no means exaggerated, but some people, such as myself, prefer direct contact with the object, which is partially denied when gloves are used. Those who can work with gloves certainly employ the cleanest method, but even without gloves cleanliness in film-editing is of prime importance.

Film Cleaner

It goes without saying that once the splicing work is complete the film must be thoroughly cleaned, since the dust produced by scraping or by the film cement is conveyed over the entire film. In order to avoid any risk of these particles of dust damaging the film during projection, they must be thoroughly removed beforehand.

Some film viewers are equipped with a built-in film cleaner, which fulfils this function to perfection. It consists of two felt-covered drums through which the film is moved as it is wound back. The two drums are impregnated with a fluid which serves a double purpose: firstly it cleans the film and secondly it acts as an anti-static agent, which means that any traces of electricity are removed and fresh dust cannot gather.

The effect lasts a fairly long time, but this care should be repeated about once a year. We will return to this in connection with the after-treatment of finished films.

If the viewer does not possess any cleaning equipment this could be inserted subsequently in the form of an accessory produced for that particular model. Should you, however, be one of the film-makers who do not edit their films, and so do not possess a viewer at all, the cleaning process can of course be undertaken in a different manner and with simple means: a soft cloth soaked in a cleaning agent. The use of an anti-static cloth is preferable and the effect is the same.

The following applies whether a cloth or the felt drums are used: the film must only be allowed to get damp, since it must be completely dry again by the time it reaches the wind-on spool (about 20cm.). Otherwise the film will stick together on the spool, and thus the exact opposite effect is achieved to that intended.

FINAL OBSERVATIONS ON THE THEME OF FILM EDITING

Before turning to the subject of film montage, in other words the combination of several 15m. films, there is room for a few final and fundamental observations concerning film-editing. I assume that after some practice the actual physical process of film-cutting will not present any problems.

With an increasing command of the cutting and joining techniques, you will grow to realise the fact which is emphasised in this chapter: the end result is determined far less by the physical handling of the film than by the personal style of the film-maker. Naturally, the first requirement is that the cutting and splicing work is effected without fault, but this alone is not enough.

During editing you determine not only what is to be seen, but also the whole tone of the film. The film presents your interpretation of a certain subject, and this influences the viewer to the extent that he is affected by the presentation. Viewed in this way, editing the film is equally as important as taking it.

The 'cutter' can present a theme in two entirely different ways. He can tighten it up, heightening the excitement; equally he can produce a film of epic dimensions. Naturally this requires rather more than a basic knowledge of how to cut and join film. Some film-makers whose actual achievements in filming are of no more than average standard, are able to hide any weaknesses by

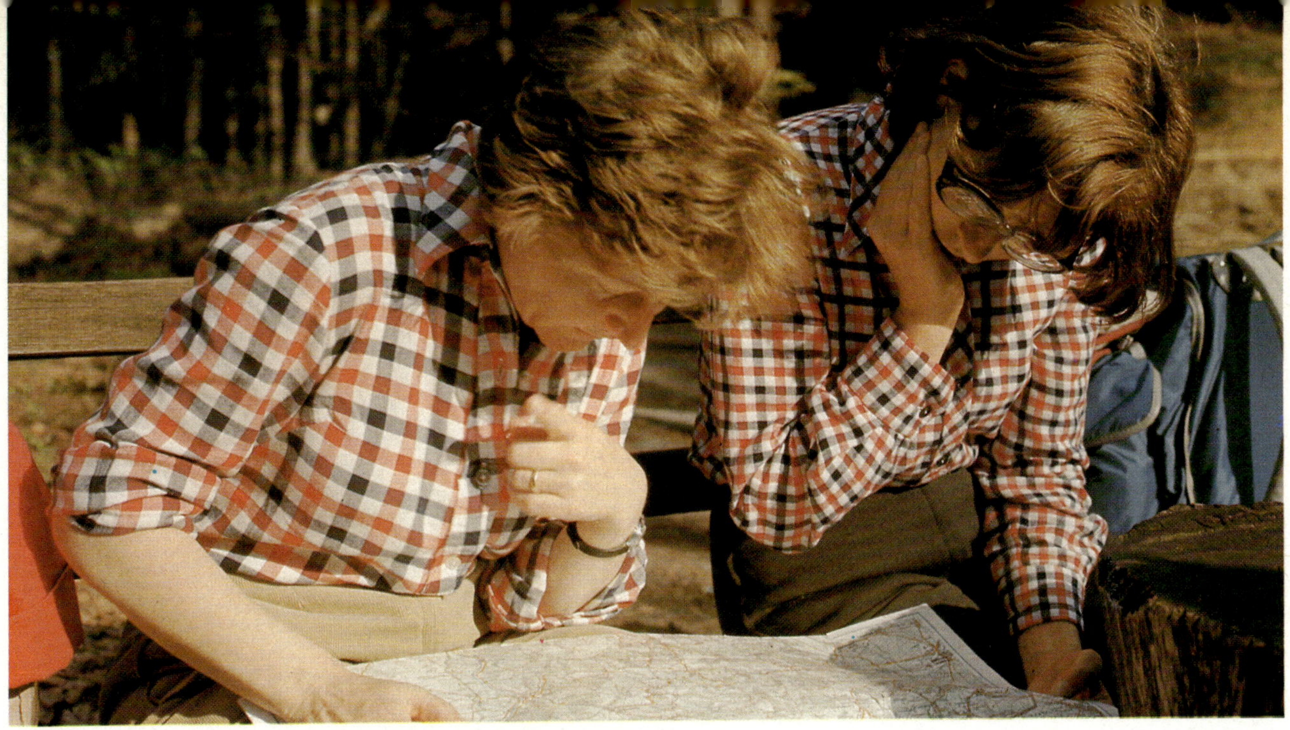

Plate 17: A look at the map is a part of the hike. The next shot moves in on the map. The scene must emphasise the rest at the top of the mountain after a strenuous climb

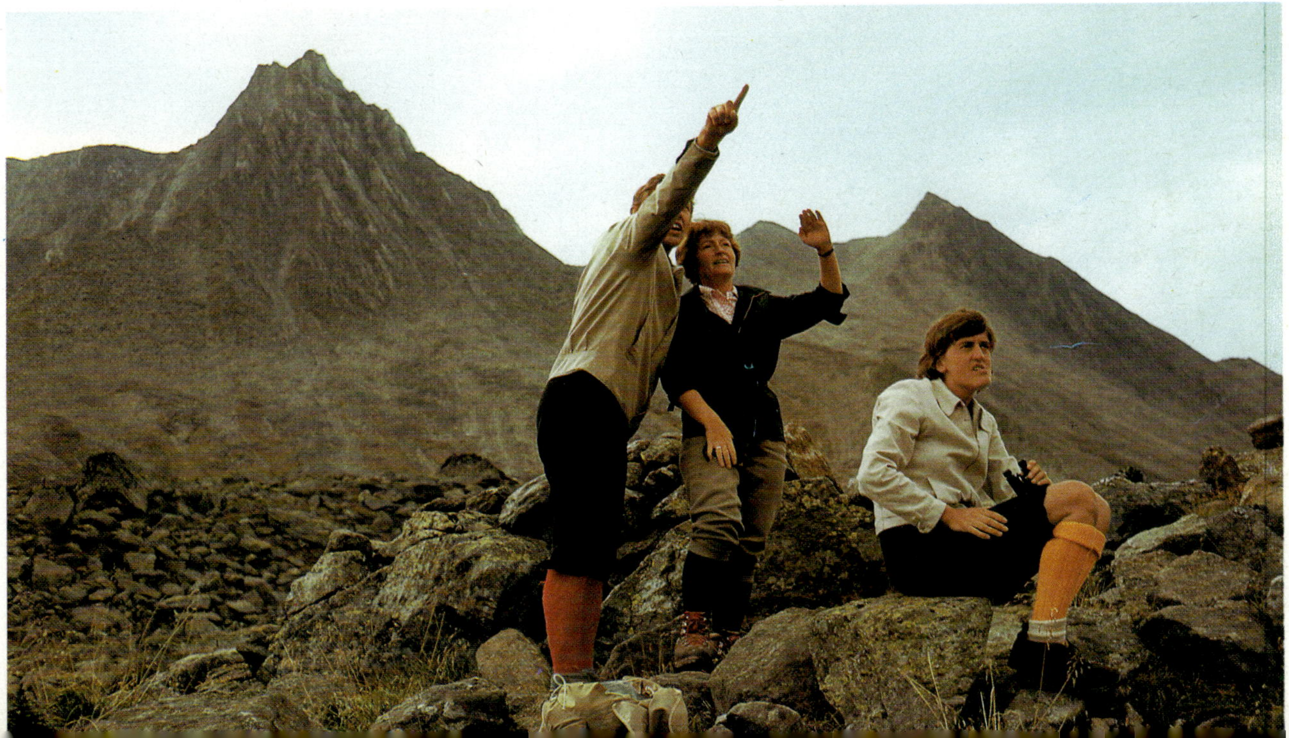

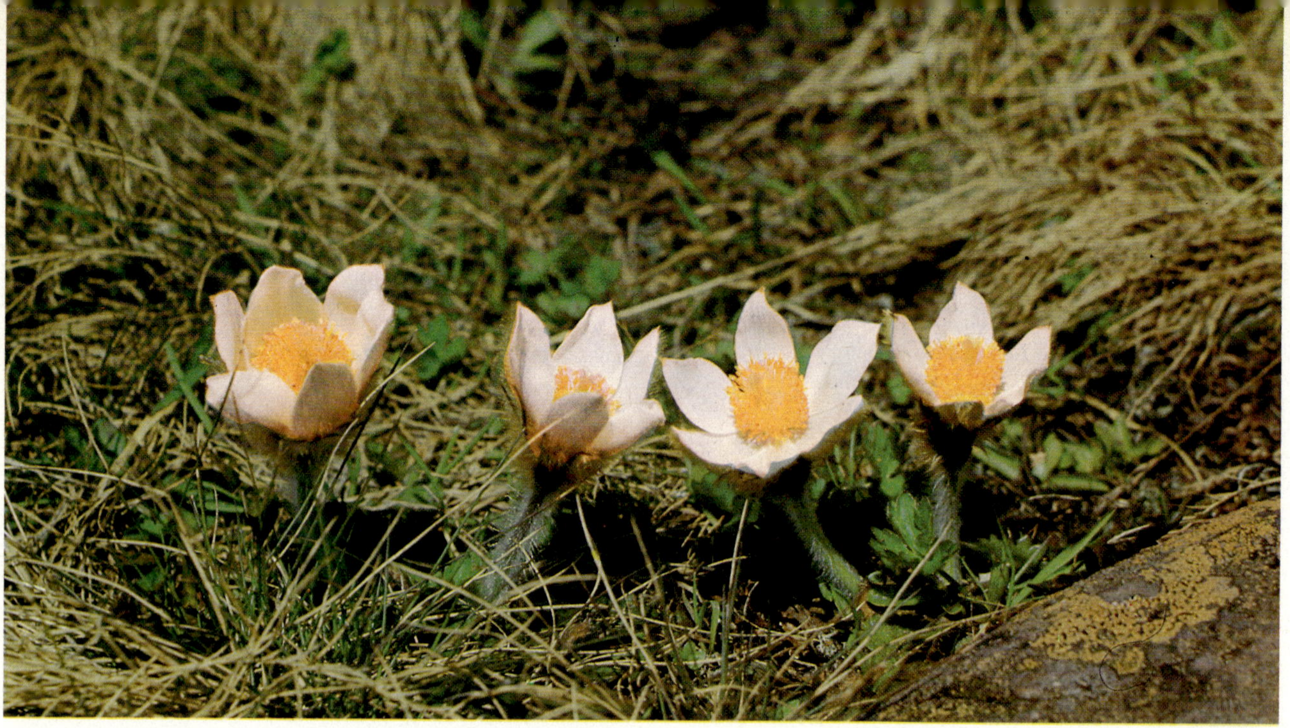

Plate 18: Close-ups of the flowers should not be omitted from a film concerning a particular area of the countryside. Insects can only be filmed in the macro-range.

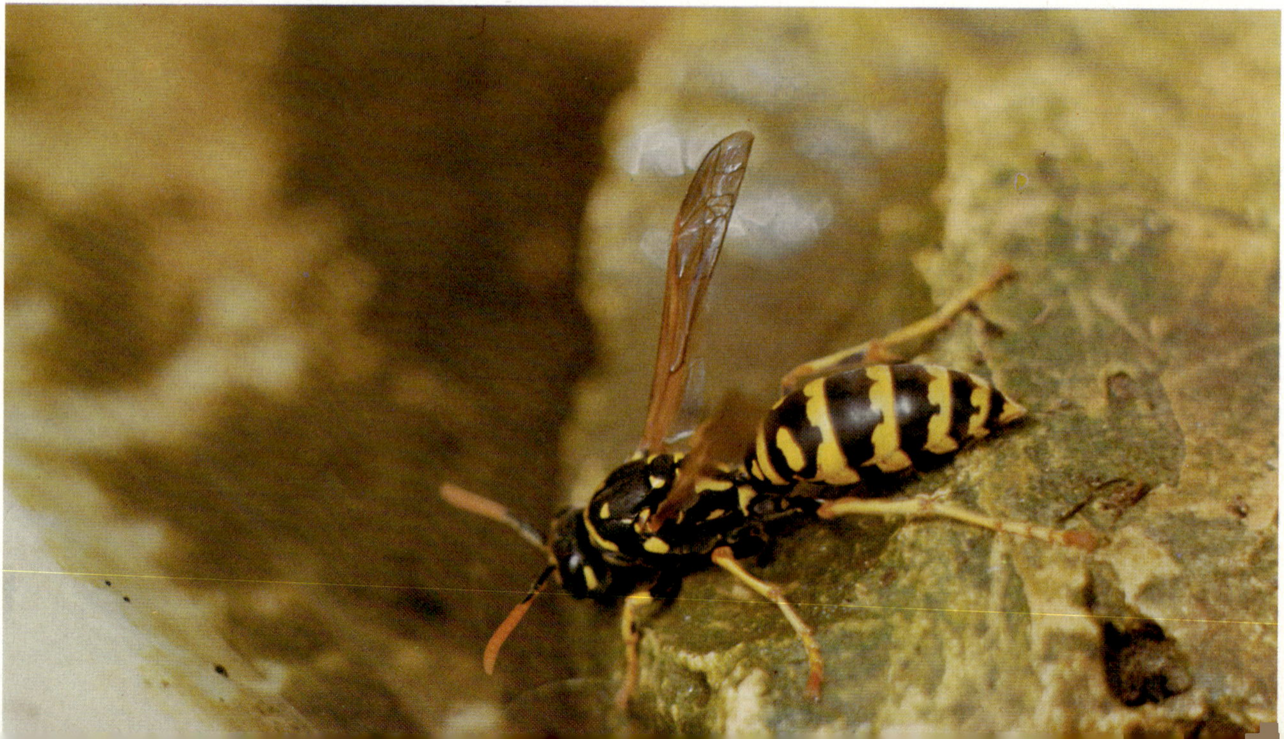

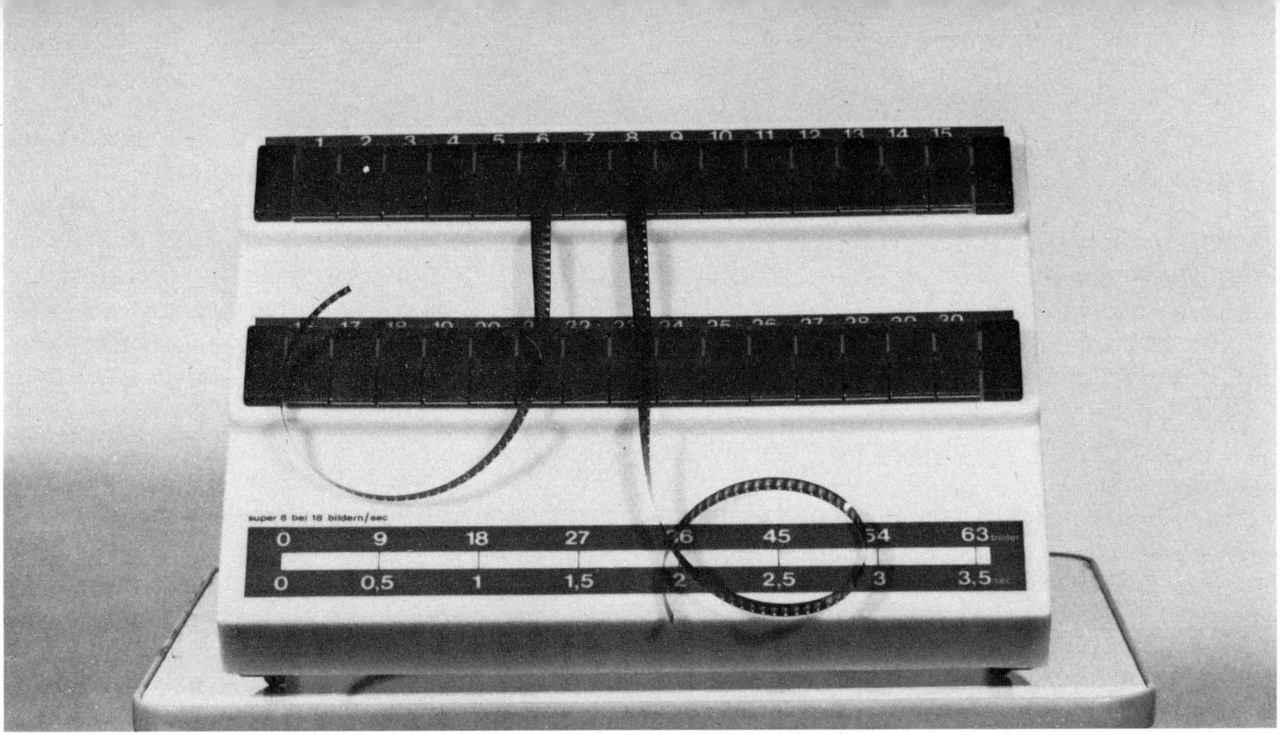

Film-sorting equipment
Sorting bench with light box, to which the film scenes adhere magnetically.

virtue of their talent for brilliant editing. Unfortunately it can also happen that a superbly shot film is subsequently cut to pieces.

Thus a true command of film-editing includes a certain amount of talent, but this aside, there are many things to be learned or imitated which are discovered by careful observation wherever the opportunity allows.

As the cutter you enjoy total freedom concerning your films: there is no one to say that one way is right and everything else wrong. Your decision depends on how *you* want the film to be. I can only hope to inspire some ideas and offer some examples about how this might be done, which is not to say that every example could not have been dealt with in a different manner.

With increasing experience it becomes clear that every situation has its own rules, yet different people will react to it in varying ways. If this were not the case, presumably everything would be equally monotonous, and every holiday film would ultimately bear the same appearance.

The first task in editing must be: make more of the film! For this, simply joining the individual films together in chronological order is not sufficient. If it were only a matter of chronology we need not spare a thought concerning montage and the dramatic theory of films. The only essential requirement would be a splicer.

These thoughts concerning film-editing bring us nearer to the question of how the professional film manages to produce a sensation of mounting tension and sustain a certain impression throughout the course of a scene. By making an exact analysis of such films in terms of the individual parts in them, you will come closer to understanding the basis of such effects; your films will benefit.

EDITING PLAN AND FILM MONTAGE

Now that the essential equipment has been described, its use discussed, and the technique of cutting and splicing has been explained, we can concentrate in the following on film montage itself. As already stated, this will vary with the individual, but no film-maker can do without an editing plan.

The film work begins from the moment at which the film is returned from the developing laboratory, and you immediately make a brief viewing of it in your projector or film viewer. Every film must be viewed critically and exactly. After the first showing make a brief note on the wrapper indicating the content of the film, if necessary, furnish it with a number, generally according to filming sequence. This rough marking of the film is completed during the second and third showings. If there is no script or at least a well-thought-out concept of the film, this should now be devised.

The next step is then to use the notes in considering how the film or films are to be edited. By projecting the film you will have already discovered which scenes are unusable and not to be taken into consideration during planning. If there is a possibility of additional scenes being filmed at a later date, this must also be included in the plan.

When choosing your film scenes you should proceed with a large element of self-criticism. It is better to not even think of using only partially successful scenes, as you will live to regret it every time the film is screened. It is preferable to produce a shorter film, using only the faultless shots.

Editing Plan

An editing plan is not of course as extensive as a script, but is used to establish the choice of scenes and the sequence in which they are to be arranged. Excellent ideas for titles will often emerge in the course of the work, or one might realise that available material could be used in a much better way than was

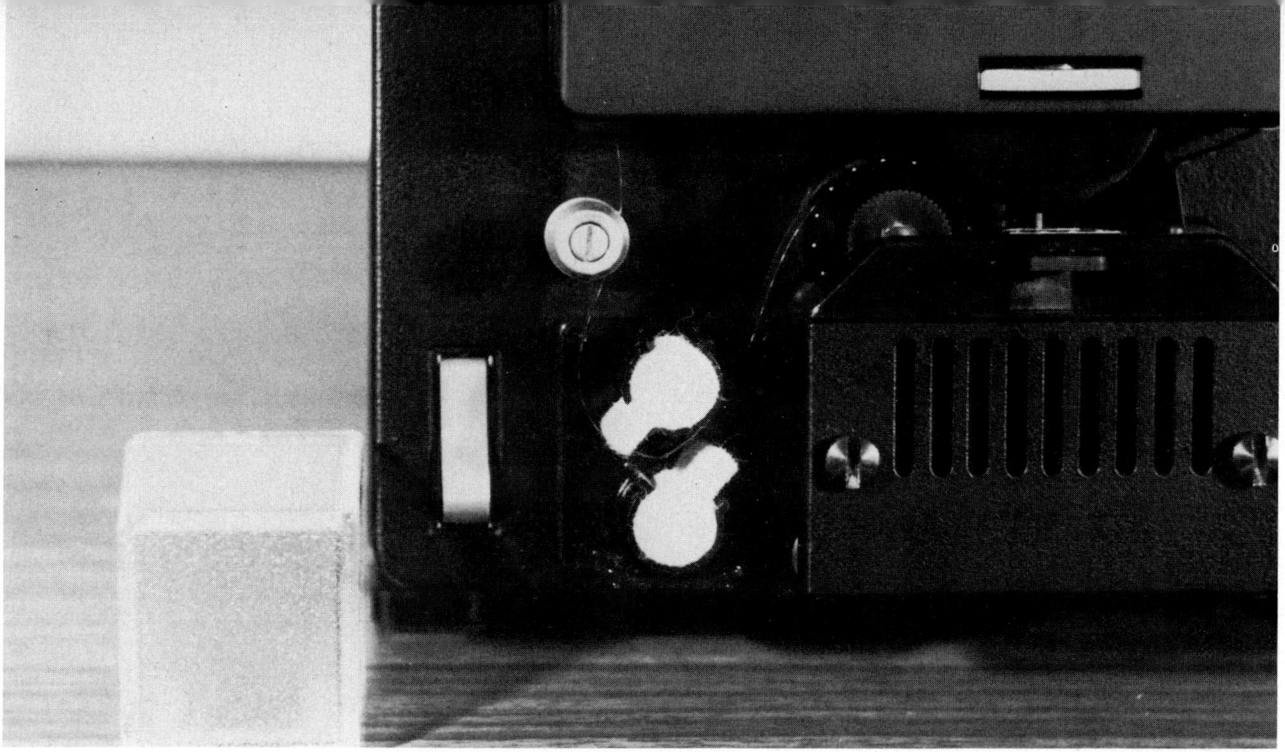

Component of the film viewer

Film cleaner
(additionally built-in accessory)

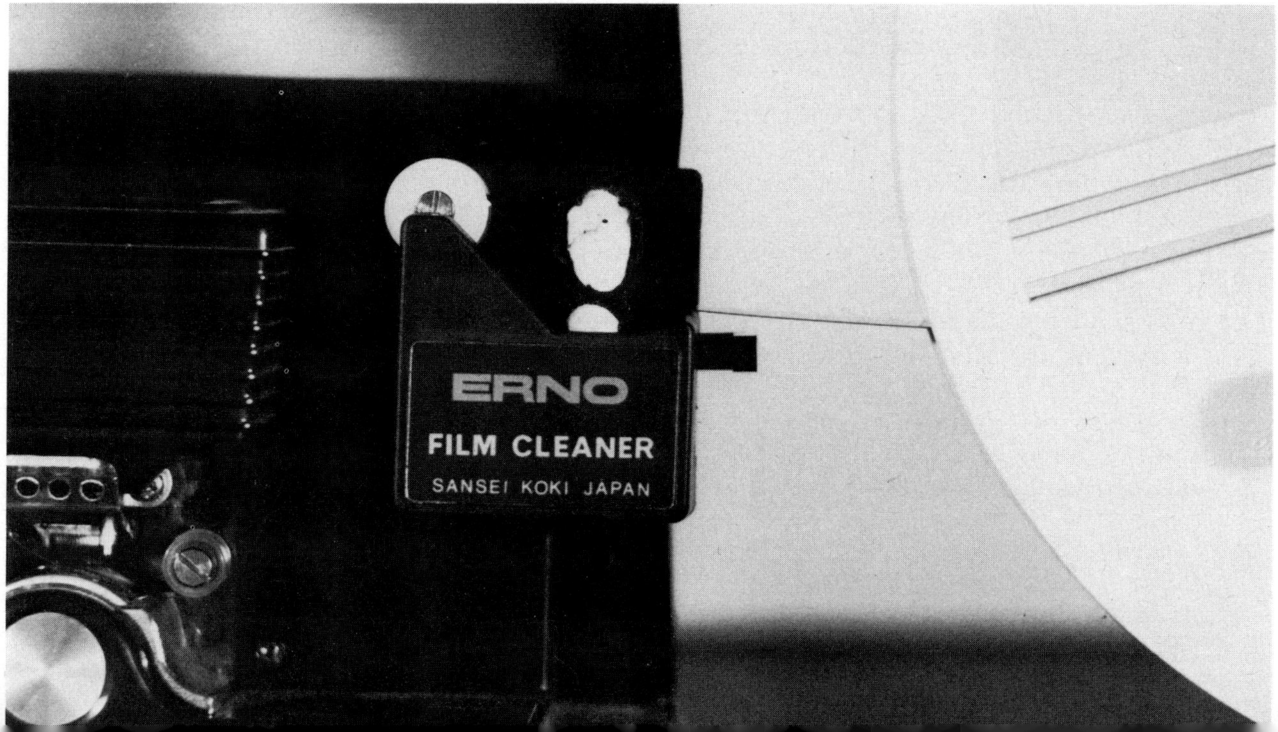

originally planned. What does this matter? The main point in the film is its final form, and no one will be interested afterwards about how this was achieved.

The film shots must be sorted out so that an exact plan for their compilation can be established. The points where an explanatory sub-title becomes necessary are marked, equally one indicates where a hard transition must be tempered down.

The next important step is for the editing plan to establish a logical and correct running order for the entire content of the film. At the moment we are not concerned with scene length. This will normally bring to light the fact that many of the scenes which are to be screened one after the other are presently to be found in quite different places on the film. There will certainly also be scenes for which it initially seems impossible to find a place in the plan. These scenes should be preserved, since a quite new attitude might be developed during the course of work.

This then is the first step to editing the film. Sometimes it is also the most time-consuming, but successful film-editing is largely dependent on a plan such as this.

The Rough Cut

The next step is to make a rough cut on the film, which means that the film scenes are compiled in the planned sequence. A film sorting bench, as described earlier, is an invaluable asset at this stage. The rough cut ensues in accordance with the editing plan: the plan establishes the sequence and the shots are actually sorted out.

The rough cut also demands a considerable amount of time, since the scenes have to be located in the various parts of the film and then joined together, but this is chiefly dependent on your filming technique. If the scenes are filmed with due consideration, the present work is made easier.

Once the rough cut is complete and the entire film has been structured in accordance with the editing plan or film concept, it is for the first time wound on to a large spool. Then the film is screened, preferably on a projector, enabling you to make a critical appraisal of your work.

Once screened on a large projection surface some scenes will without doubt reveal some deficiencies. If you decide on one, note the place! In addition, the juxtaposition of the scenes will not always be to your satisfaction, in which case, write it down and make an alteration! A projection of the film after the rough will certainly demonstrate at least one failing, namely in the length of the scenes. To the extent that the scenes are too long they can of course be shortened. Excessively short scenes rarely appear, but if a scene is judged to be too short it must either be cut out altogether, or used in another connection by adding it to another suitable scene.

Length of Scenes

At this point we must turn briefly to the points already made regarding scene length while on the subject of cutting film, and to the subject of 'dramatic theory' in film editing. The lengths of the scenes echo your personal style equally as much as their sequence, and this is a factor you may choose to exploit to a greater or lesser extent. There are however some elementary points to be stressed, since many film amateurs unconsciously make errors which ultimately result in their film being described as boring. Thus it is important when editing the film to reflect on whether your intention is to stress a tense moment or emphasise the serenity of the film, depending on its topic. The right cutting and correct scene length has a significant influence in determining whether your film is going to be interesting and worthwhile.

It is useful to make comparisons with the films shown on television. A film portraying a landscape will use long, epic scenes with the addition of appropriate music. Conversely the scenes of a crime story will be shorter, becoming increasingly brief as a dramatic climax is reached, and will be emphasised by hectic music.

This can only be achieved by means of appropriate editing. Usually one feels inhibited about cutting the scenes too short, but if the excitement demands this, one might for instance make nine short scenes out of three long ones. The scenes are cut to a third of their original length and then pieced together in an alternative order. If the effect of the sequence is to heighten the tension, it is hardly noticeable that the same scene appears three times. The end justifies the means!

Any suggestion of an exact length has been consciously avoided in the previous sections, simply for the reason that one cannot be established. Any length might be right or wrong depending on its context and the style of the whole film. For instance: you film a picture of the countryside, life on the water. The film depicts a portion of the bank with the reeds swaying gently to and fro in the wind. The water is slightly ruffled. Scenes of this type convey a sense of tranquility and do not include any dramatic happenings. The mood is further emphasised by the sun playing on the water. Suddenly there is life in the scene: a frog appears, jumps into the water and causes ripples which gradually disappear again. Both scenes must be shorter in order to emphasise the life element. Then the film continues at its calm pace until the next change. This example helps to clarify the task of film editing: all the scenes with a water theme are collected together in order to create the scene sequence, and it is still possible to introduce excitement into the film despite an overriding air of stillness.

Treatment of Shot, Counter-Shot

The theme 'shot, counter-shot' has already been discussed in detail in connection with filming techniques. The length of the scenes filmed should always be very generous, and not until it is edited does 'shot, counter-shot' obtain its ultimate composition.

The initial requirement is to make a critical appraisal of the two inter-related scenes in the viewer, in order to determine exactly the right cutting point. Once the first scene has been considered, there can only possibly be one point at which the second scene can be cut. This is very important, since the two scenes might otherwise overlap. In other words, no part of the scene must be shown twice, but equally, there must not be any gap. The action of the first scene (shot) must end exactly where the second scene (counter-shot) begins.

As already suggested, the film must be taken in generous proportions. Let us return to our example of the family filmed walking through a gateway into a park. Firstly, you film the shot, in which the family walks into the park, distancing themselves from the camera, then having overtaken the family you follow with the counter-shot, which entails filming the family coming into the park and towards the camera. Once screened it becomes obvious that a fairly large part of the way is seen twice in the film, and it is exactly this which you have to edit out. Precision work of this nature, which requires absolute exactness, is barely possible without the use of a film-viewer. However, even actually filming the 'shot, counter-shot' phenomenon demands precise handling.

Increasing experience will enable one to consider various factors during the actual filming which simplify the subsequent work of film-editing. One can for instance ensure that the people walk through the gateway in the same order in both scenes, or that a door is not opened with the left hand in the shot, the right-hand in the counter-shot. While these are trivialities, a consideration of these obvious if subordinate points will not only aid the work of film montage, but also distinguish a properly edited film from one which is simply joined together.

Superfluous Scenes

The very first screening of your film after the rough cut will pose the question: does it contain superfluous scenes, which only add unnecessary length, and would it not be better to omit certain scenes either partially or completely?

You should take advantage of being able to exclude certain shots to the extent that this can help to tighten up the film. Experience has proved however that it is sometimes difficult to part with a technically perfect but nevertheless superfluous shot. Despite this it still remains advisable, since compact action provides the film with an essential element of excitement. The following example is used to demonstrate this.

1 Scene: Standing on the platform.
2 Scene: The train arrives.
3 Scene: Picking up the cases and approaching the door of the train compartment.

4 Scene: A hand opens the compartment door.
5 Scene: Getting in the train.
6 Scene: A window is opened in the train.
7 Scene: Waving from the window.

This is a normal film sequence, but it could be considerably compressed, since scenes 3 and 5 are superfluous, and in addition a direct change from a full-length to a close-up shot can be very impressive. Such is the case with scene 5: if someone looks out of the train window, it is obvious that he must previously have got onto the train. Too many foregone conclusions make the film boring, and it is exactly that which you want to avoid.

Compiling Rough Cuts
It is advisable to note down as many of the deficiencies as possible when the rough cut is screened, which allows for subsequent modification of the mistakes. The process can be repeated as often as necessary, and with every new rough cut you will again find something that could be improved. It may happen that the original concept is totally rejected in favour of a new idea that has suddenly occurred to you by virtue of your close involvement with the film material available. There is no reason not to follow up a fresh idea. It might even occur that some discussion results in a completely finished film being re-edited.

Anyone who is frequently involved with processing films will be aware of such experiences. If the new idea really is better, there is no point in stubbornly adhering to the initial concept.

A suggestion: it is worth making contact with friends or colleagues also interested in ciné photography – nor is this as difficult as you might think. Have a communal presentation of the totally uncut films and then discuss the way in which they might best be revised. Other people will frequently judge your films completely differently and sometimes the problems can be solved by discussion. Experience has proved that this is often a way of achieving the optimum in film composition.

The Provisional Final Form
It is as a rule difficult to predict when the final form of the film is actually complete, and it is clear that there are varying paths leading to this goal. One important point can be made on the grounds of experience: if the film is to be revised after the rough cut, it should be left alone for a week in the meantime. Working on the film without any breaks can result in you becoming 'blind' to faults. On the other hand the space of a few days allows an objective judgement of what is yet to be altered.

Every amateur film-maker occasionally finds a point where he wishes he had made a fade-in or fade-out, since the scenes do not transfer harmoniously one to the other. Even those who always film more fade-ins and fade-outs than they need, on principle, will sometimes realise that one is lacking at an

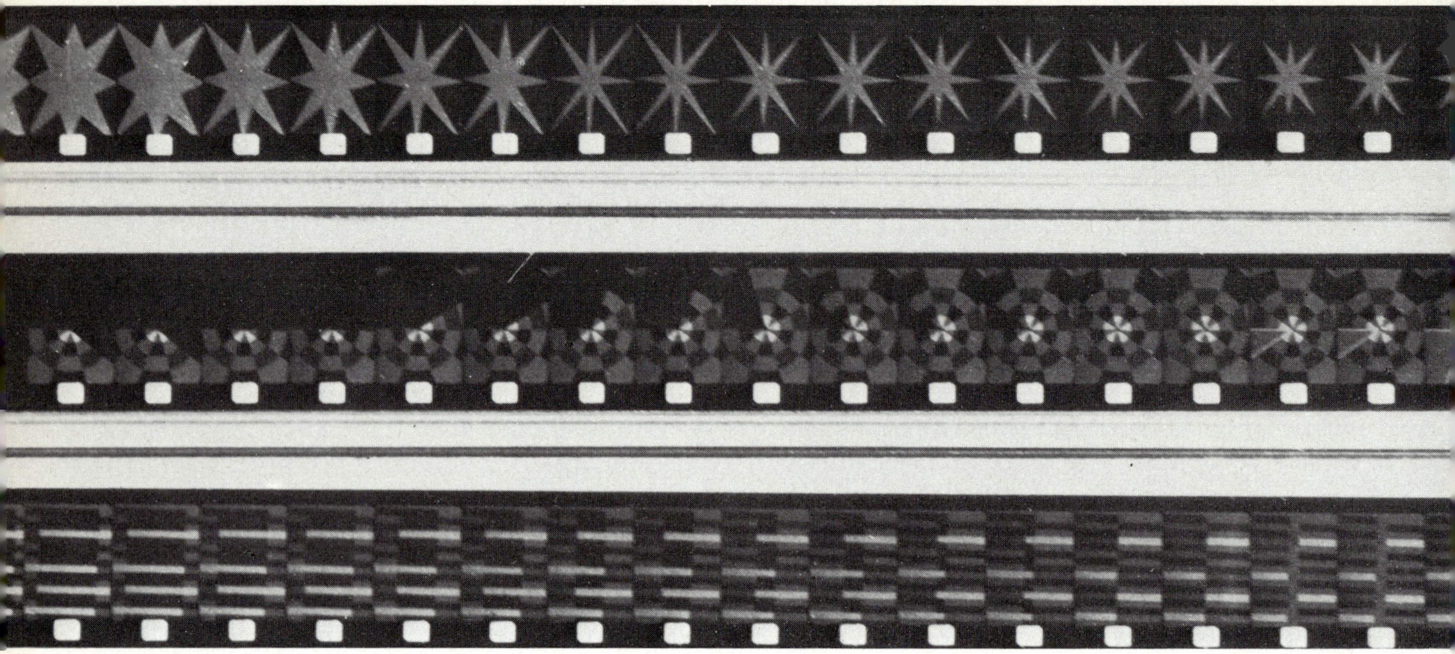

Trick inserts
They are sold in assorted packs, and stuck between two film scenes when a dissolve is lacking

important point. Since this happens to every film-maker the accessory industry decided to make a virtue of necessity, insofar as they produced a 'pseudo-fade-out'. This consists of a grey wedge, which is used to darken the picture area, producing the effect of a fade-out. This can be used in emergencies as a substitute for a genuine fade-out.

Another interesting combination of two scenes is achieved with the aid of a ready-made 'trick', which is joined in between two scenes in order to create a trick transition there. The ornamental trick motifs – circles, stars, lines, etc. – will blurr, gradually leading to the next scene. It is worth considering the effect created by these trick inserts. They are sold in packs containing a variety of motifs.

Leader and Ending

The beginning and ending of the film is obviously also to be included in the montage work. The first scene begins as a rule with a fade-in, where it is of no consequence whether this reveals a title or leads directly to a picture. It is a good idea to add a piece of black leader in front of the fade-in for the sake of the effect when projected. It is more attractive than when the fade-in appears on a white screen. Moreover, the black leader serves an additional purpose, insofar as it can be used to provide a musical introduction, if the film bears a sound track, which means that the music can already be heard before the first scene begins.

The same applies for the end of the film: a black strip is added after the final fade-out which considerably intensifies the effect of the fade-out, and means that the return to bright lighting is not so abrupt. The light in the room can be switched on while the black filmstrip is still running.

It is commonly known that all Kodak films are returned from the developers with a white leader, which is eminently suitable for the first piece of the film. Since it is thicker and hence firmer than normal film it is much better for threading into the projector: the normal thin film sometimes gets stuck in the automatic threading mechanism.

Besides this however the white leader has yet another very useful characteristic: it can be inscribed with a felt-tip pen, which means it is possible to make a note of the title of each film. In addition, it is easy to establish whether the film has wound on to the spool backwards, since the white leader must obviously be at the front, and whether the right film is placed in the right cassette. Any remarks concerning the film must in any case be noted on the cassette, which brings us to the next topic.

Labelling the Film

What are the necessary notes to be made on the cassette of a finished film? These depend chiefly on the method employed in the film archive, but they should be as detailed as possible. The following example has proved very valuable in practice:

1 Title:
2 Filmed by:
3 Film Location:
4 Film type and length (running time):
5 Whether or not sound is included.

The notes make it possible to compile a programme of films at any time, but, in other ways as well, ordering and reviewing the film archive can only be advantageous.

Care of Films and Equipment

The importance of proper cleaning and care of the ciné film has already been described in detail in the section concerning cleaning of the film during splicing, and it is obvious that this care must be extended to all equipment and accessories. As has been stressed, the greatest problem here is dust, which naturally gathers on the film during the joining process, and is unavoidable.

It has already been stated that some film viewers are equipped with cleaning apparatus, which is without doubt a very convenient way of cleaning and preparing the film; there is, however, one difficulty associated with this: it is essential that the small felt drums impregnated with the cleaner are additionally cleaned from time to time. A hard brush (e.g. a tooth brush) should be used to remove the dust from the felt, and at the same time to tease the felt so that the rubbing surface remains smooth. Obviously there is a limit to the extent to which this process can be repeated, and it is becomes necessary to renew the felt drum after a certain time, depending on the use of the equipment. If this point is ignored, the felt grows hard and may cause total or partial scratching of the film. It is essential to check this regularly in order to protect the valuable film!

All completed films must be cleaned from time to time, apart from during montage work. A clean cloth which does not fluff serves the same purpose as a cleaner, as long as the pressure applied to the film is not too great. Moreover, the cleaning surface of the cloth must be changed often, since there is otherwise the danger of scratches being produced by the dust on the cloth. Some film-makers use the previously mentioned anti-static cloth, similarly used for records, for cleaning their films. Again there is a risk of fine scratches being caused if the rubbing surface is not often changed: but most anti-static cloths lose their effect once washed.

Maximum care in protecting the films against dust is equally necessary during storage. As a result modern film spools are already delivered in tightly closed boxes or cassettes, which can be put to further use in an archive. The boxes are designed to prevent any further formation of dust.

It is wise to clean each film after three or four screenings, since the warmth produced in the projector always encourages dust to gather on the film.

Every ciné-filmer is aware that his films will age with time. The ageing process manifests itself through the film base (acetate or polyester backing) drying out, and the film becoming brittle. This has been far more the case in the past than it is with modern films, but even our films will age after a certain time. The process can be delayed by means of a film 'keep-fresh bag', a small tin-foil pack which is pierced in the film-spool cassette. The small holes allow a chemical reagent to escape from the bag, which ensures the long-lasting resiliency of the film. After two or three years the bag will lose its effect and must be replaced.

It is neither usual nor advisable to store films in light places. In the past it was thought that they would fade if they were left in daylight for too long. Although there is no actual proof of this today, it is always a good policy to be careful. In any case, the film cassettes are normally made of a non-transparent material which hinders the light, and hardly any film-maker would store his spools on an open shelf. The best method is to keep the films in their cassettes in a closed cupboard.

SOUND FILM OR SILENT FILM

Anyone who considers that he does not need to add sound to his films usually bases his decision either on ignorance of the technical possibilities or on a desire for convenience.

Those who can still remember the first cinema films will be aware that it was only due to a lack of technical provision that the films remained silent and in those days a pianist would be employed to relieve the situation by playing a musical accompaniment to suit the action of the film. With the arrival of sound film, the pianist bowed out – only a few enthusiasts wanted the continuation of silent films, but they were cast aside by technical advances.

Nevertheless, good feature films from the time of the 'flicks' still retain their attraction, though some have been supplemented by sound in the meantime. Others exist in archives and are screened only occasionally for a special purpose.

Either on the grounds of convenience or ignorance, amateurs do not for the most part exploit the sound potential to its fullest extent, if at all. Let us first consider the argument of convenience. The reason mostly offered is lack of interest or lack of time, yet one makes time during leisure hours for so many more or less important things that it does not appear to be a valid reason. If one has the time to take a film with all due consideration, to cut it and supply it with titles, one has already donated far more time than is essential for the sound composition. There are moreover hobbies which lay a far greater claim on one's time. If one can justify the time spent on editing and montage, in order to create a good film, then the business is only half completed if the sound is not also added.

On the other hand the more serious fact to have to consider is that many amateur film-makers do not add sound to their films out of ignorance – ignorance of the technical possibilities. In an extreme case, they may not even know that the amateur is able to produce a sound accompaniment. Some think that it is not possible with the equipment available, and many are above all unclear about the cost entailed by sound composition. It is not nearly as expensive as is generally supposed.

The main aim here is to indicate which methods exist, and as a result it will become clear that with most equipment sound filming is not beset by problems. The films can be taken on any camera, as long as the sound is added to the film afterwards, which is our prime interest at present. Later we will discuss the most modern achievements in the field of sound film.

Child and animal – interesting to film on sound film

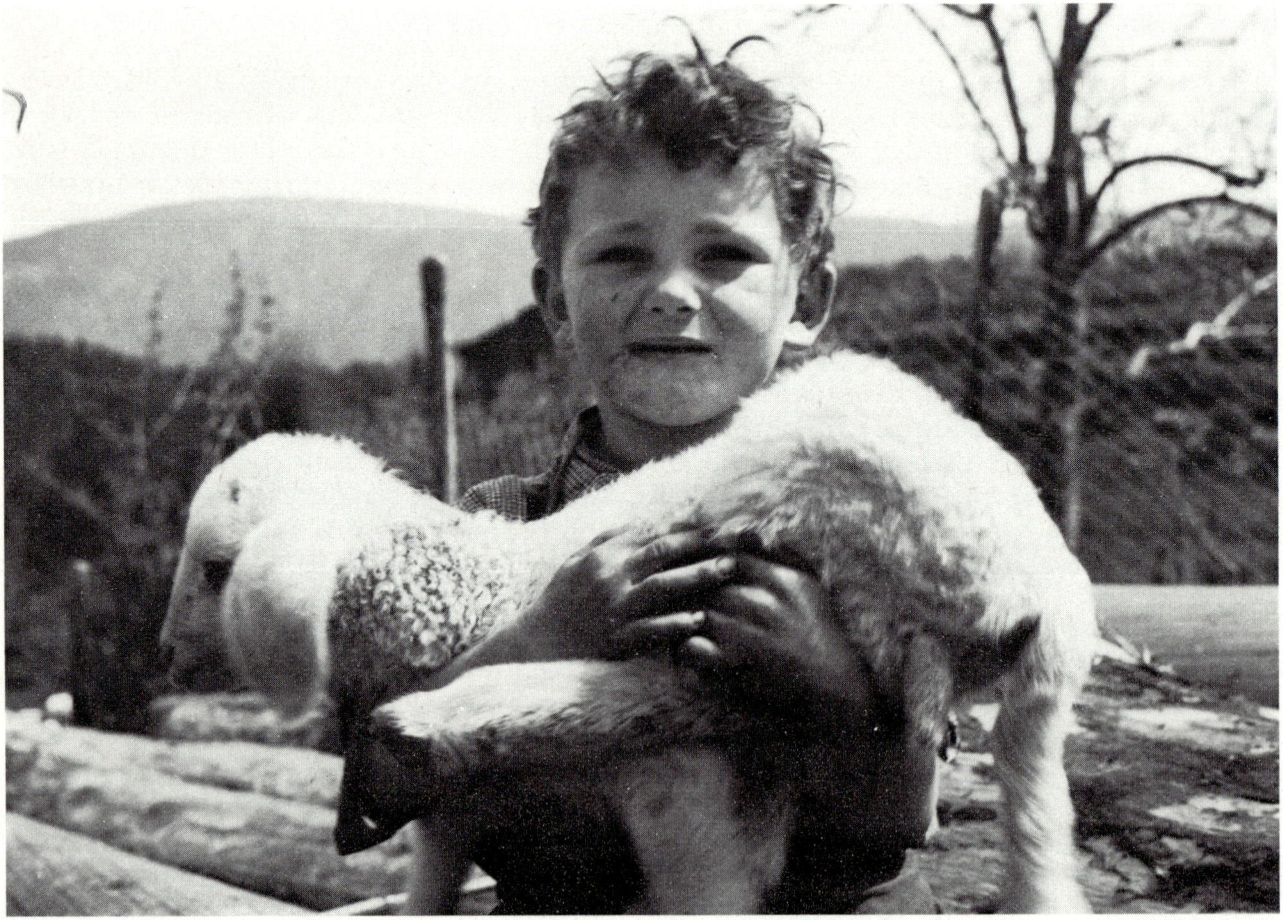

FILM SCORING: TECHNICAL POSSIBILITIES

Film scoring and projection are closely connected, but we will return to the latter in more detail in the chapter on film presentation. At this point it should be said in passing that this factor must be borne in mind when a projector is purchased.

Anyone who still continues to project his films silently can use any projector suitable for the purpose, but if the intention is to score the film according to the so-called two-track system, one must begin by purchasing a projector with a built-in sound coupler. Some models can however be adapted if necessary. Finally, there are magnetic-strip projectors, in which the films are scored and presented by the one-track system, For Double-8 and Super-8 film-makers there are also dual-sized projectors.

We begin our discussion of the technical possibilities with the simplest method, closing the chapter with an examination of the most modern achievement, the sound-recording camera.

PICTURE AND SOUND PROJECTOR AND MUSICAL EQUIPMENT

The simplest method is without doubt to find a piece of music which is suitable for use with the finished film and then to play it on a tape-recorder or record-player as the film is projected, which is more or less equivalent to the presence of a pianist in the time of the silent films. Occasionally film and music will be slightly out of step with one another, but this is not of crucial importance.

This method of co-ordinating picture and sound is practised relatively frequently, since most amateur film-makers film predominantly on holiday, at festivities or comparable happenings, where it is hardly ever possible to record the sound simultaneously, and it must instead be added to the edited version of the film.

In practice this will take the following form: let us take as an example a film which you have taken in the mountains. The selection on offer from the record companies will certainly include suitable alpine music, or a better method would be to record some music which complements the particular film. Running the film and music together is a simple way of enhancing the film's effect.

COUPLING PICTURE AND SOUND (SYNCHRONISER)

The situation changes as soon as an explanatory text is to be included in with music. The text is generally designed to correspond to a certain film scene and must be spoken at the same point each time. Technically this is no problem, but it requires a piece of equipment which couples the projector with the tape recorder or cassette recorder, so that the machines function in sychronisation, which means that they run at equivalent speeds. There are various ways in which this can be achieved.

As an example we again choose the tape-recorder, which has already proved its value in the first method. In addition, it is necessary to obtain a coupling attachment. The sound coupler connects the projector and the tape recorder and ensures that both run in total uniformity, so that no displacement between picture and sound is allowed to occur. Thus the process has a distinct advantage over the first method described, where a 120m. film would show a discrepancy between picture and sound, inevitably caused by variations in the mains electricity supply. A sound coupler (synchroniser) on the other hand will guarantee an invariable (synchronised) process.

This method, by which pictures and sound are delivered by two different pieces of equipment, is the previously mentioned two-track system, so called since one track is used for the picture (film) and one for the sound (sound-track). This two-track system has many advantages. It can include any available tape-recorder or cassette recorder, which many people possess anyway, and does not require any special equipment for exclusive use with film. Above all with this process you achieve a quality of sound which corresponds to your tape-recorder, bought to satisfy your sound requirements. A lover of classical music, or anyone who desires optimal musical reproduction, need not renounce a sound accompaniment because it is not in accordance with his ideals.

Every tape-recorder with horizontally positioned spools is suitable for film sound recordings, and nearly every projector can be connected to synchronising equipment if furnished with the appropriate plug. The projector must however usually be sent to the manufacturer for this. The cost of these additional fittings should be carefully considered beforehand, since, often, the value of the projector does not justify them. If one seriously intends to work with the two-track system, one should instead reflect on purchasing a brand new projector with built-in sound coupler.

In the days of Double-8 film, which has in the meantime been almost completely superceded by Super-8 film, there existed a whole range of equipment which seemed in part to be quite fantastic. Many projector manufacturers developed their own systems, fundamentally based on adapted tape-recorders. Today only the standardised systems exist.

One system remains to be mentioned, and in this the projector and the cassette recorder are combined to form one unit. Sound cassette and film move through the same driving shaft, so any discrepancy between picture and sound is impossible. The one factor to note is that both the film and the audio cassette must have a start mark, which occupies the same position when the recording is made and when it is reproduced. This system is very useful for those who habitually record music and sounds on a cassette recorder, or who record the sound backing during filming itself.

One disadvantage of the conventional two track system is the inconvenience associated with film projection. The projector, tape recorder, and synchroniser demand a great deal of space and must be well arranged, easy to operate, and not liable to fall over. This can be rather troublesome, particularly if the films are not to be screened at home. In practice, the same equipment must be used for both the initial recording and its reproduction, which means that you are required to take all your equipment with you.

Magnetic Recording with Projector

We now come to a system which is being increasingly employed for ciné film: the magnetic sound system. With this process a magnetic-strip 0.8mm-wide sound track is welded on to the completed film, and the sound for the film is recorded on this track. One of the invaluable advantages of this is that it only requires one piece of equipment, since the sound is both recorded and reproduced in the projector as the film is presented. The sound is recorded either via the tape recorder, which serves as the carrier of various musical recordings, or else it is recorded over the microphone belonging to the magnetic sound projector. The distance from the film gate to the sound head is equivalent to 18 frames.

This is an internationally standardised system, which means that all sound films made with a magnetic sound projector can be screened on any projector designed for this process the world over.

Obviously the sound on a magnetic strip can be erased and re-recorded as often as necessary, as with a tape recorder. Thus a film which already includes sound can be rescored without difficulty, if the first composition is not adequate and better form must be found. Experience shows that every ciné-filmer becomes more critical and fastidious as time goes by.

Over the years, the sound heads on the magnetic sound system have been developed almost to perfection. The frequency range is also improved, that is to say, increased, from year to year, and further developments will without doubt produce even better results. Meanwhile, the sound quality of this system is so good that all sound information is superbly recorded on the film. The narrow sound-track, 0.8mm. wide, has a frequency range of 40–10,000 Hertz.

The process of sound recording is considerably simplified in some of the high-class sound projectors: they include a frame counter which facilitates the speedy location of any particular shot. Anyone who possesses such a counter on his projector can add a sound insertion at any chosen point on the film with very little trouble.

Stereo sound is a fairly recent innovation; in order to be able to exploit the potential of the stereophonic effect one requires a special magnetic sound projector, since the sound track is double sided; thus the projector itself requires two recording and two reproduction heads. The reproduction is of course transmitted by two loudspeakers. Indeed any stereo unit can actually be included in the film presentation, if a connecting cable leads from the projector to the amplifier.

There would seem to be a trend towards the increasing use of this new system, and hence a few words about it. Both the stereo projector and the magnetic sound projector can be viewed as the equipment of the future. It is important to stress that not all two-track projectors necessarily include stereo reproduction.

In a two-track projector one sound-track is used for speech and one for music, and then both tracks are combined, when produced. This has the great advantage of allowing the film-maker to record the sound on one track after the other, and enabling him to erase one track without affecting the other. If the spoken track reveals a slip of the tongue, the matter can be corrected without the music on the other track being disturbed. This example demonstrates the great benefit of such a system. Of lesser importance is the potential to make stereo recordings, which is certainly effective but nevertheless entails considerable technical difficulties.

The two-track system has yet another implication; if the film is taken with a sound recording camera, i.e. with life-sound (we will return to this subject), the second sound track can be used to record music. Moreover slight inconsistencies in the original sound can be skilfully concealed or made inaudible without affecting the life-sound, which only exists on one track. This is a new and very enticing way of combining the two new systems: the life-sound (sound camera) and the two-track sound projector.

The two-track magnetic sound system is relatively new, so the choice of models is not yet large. Moreover, it is naturally more costly than the magnetic sound process, but presumably this will alter as its use becomes more widespread.

Finally it is important to mention a sound reproduction process which is combined with some magnetic sound projectors:

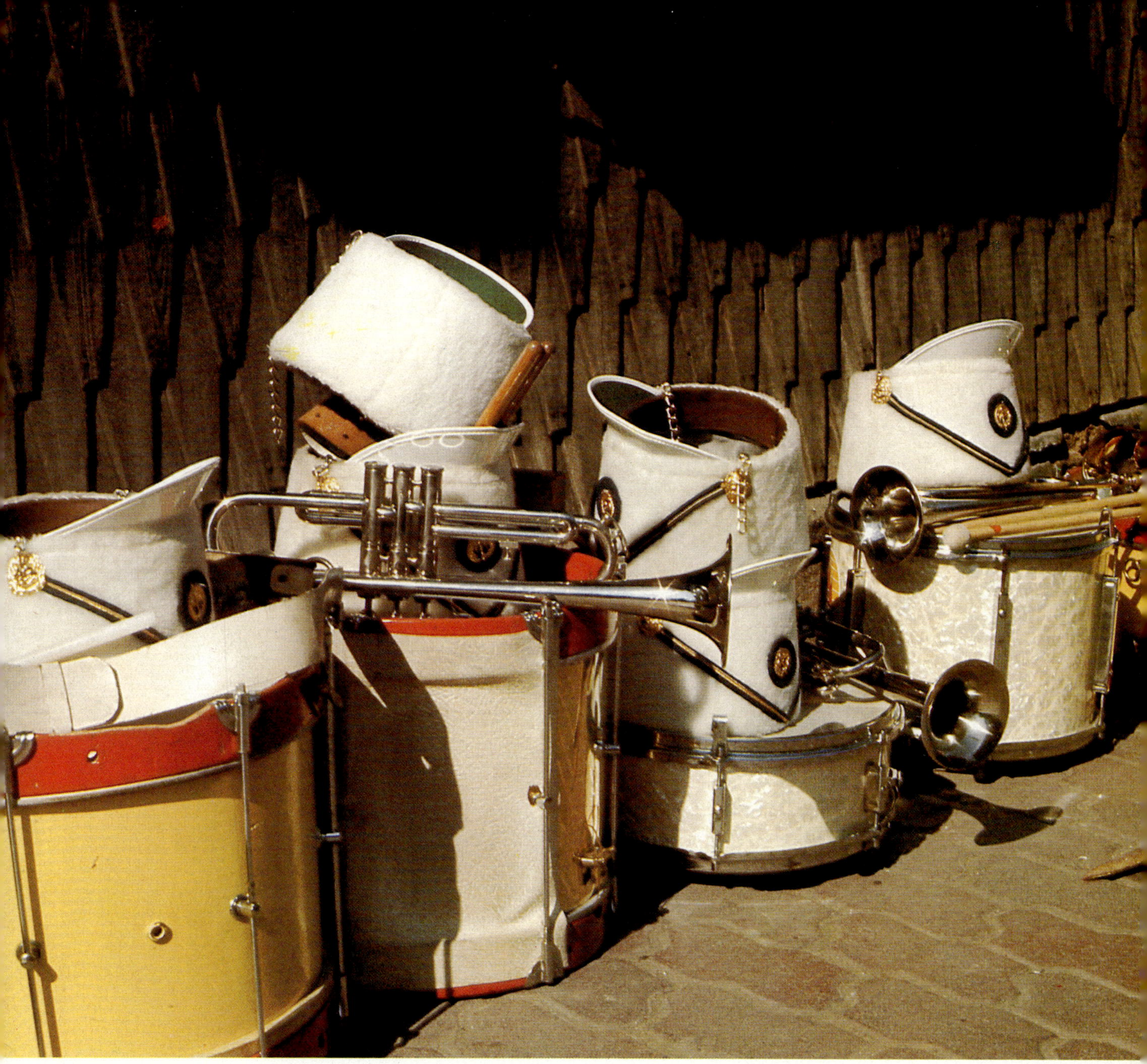

Plate 19: A film of a band concert, plus sound, might be brought to a conclusion with a shot of this type

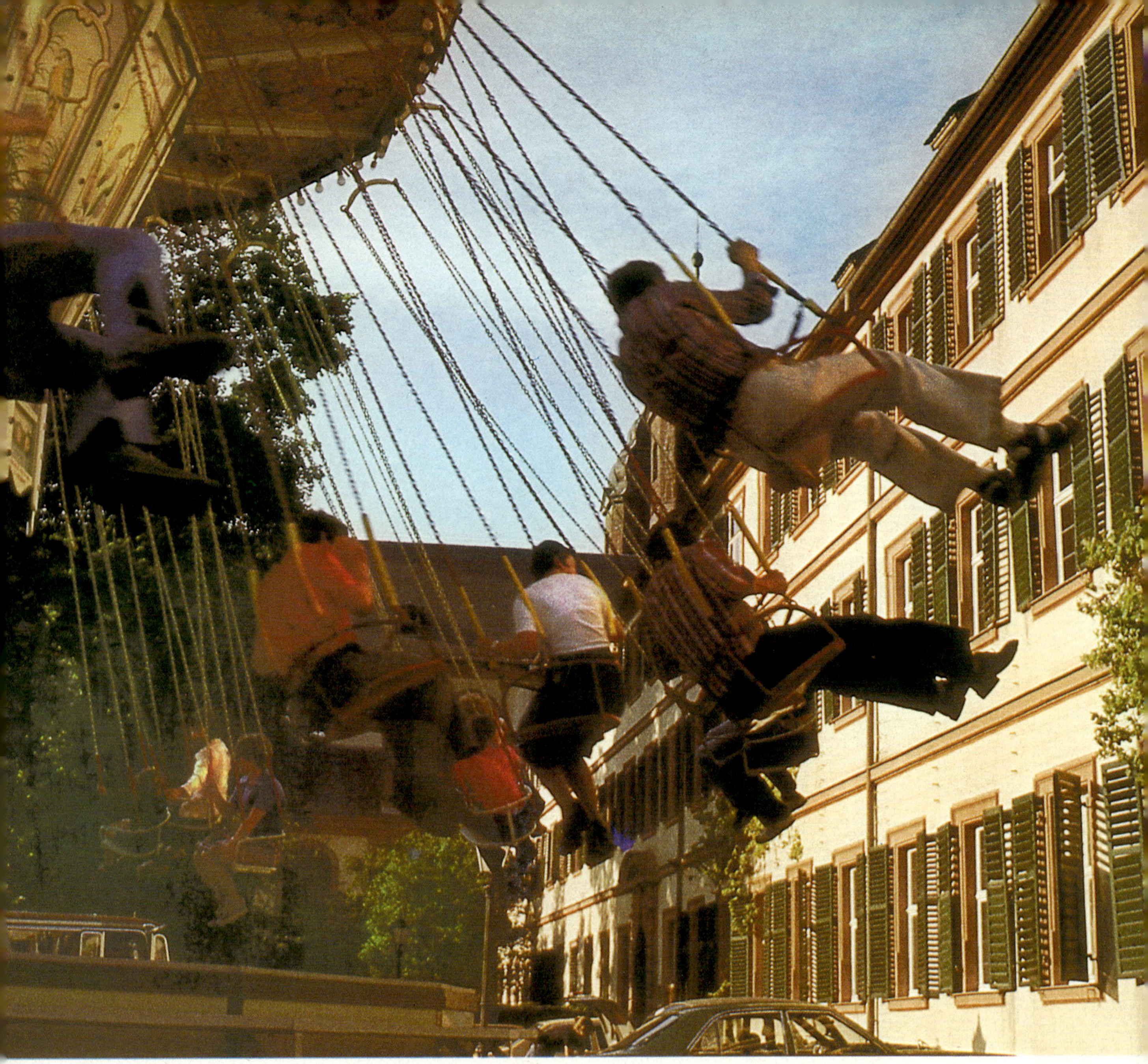

Plate 20: Film taken at the fairground is full of surprises. Since this includes a rapid change of scene, the sound accompaniment should be recorded separately

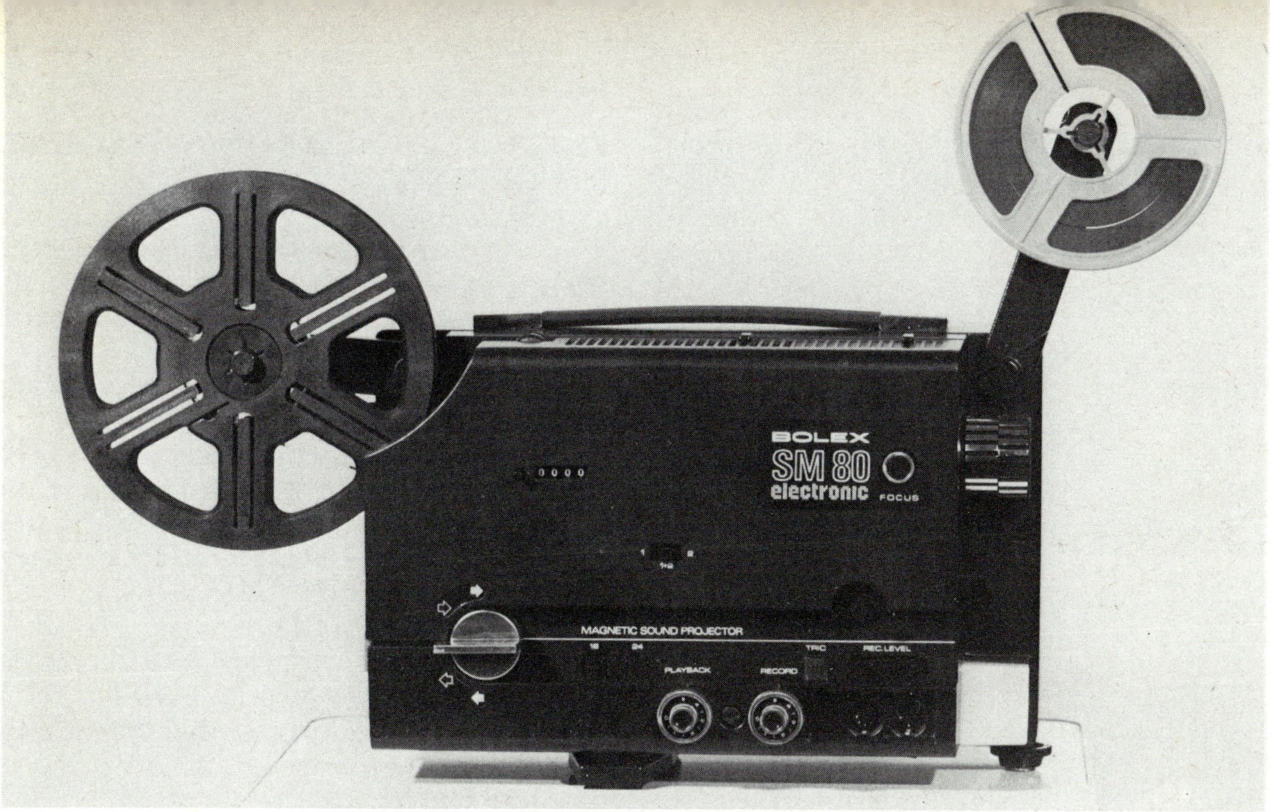

Modern magnetic sound projector

Controls for sound recording and reproduction

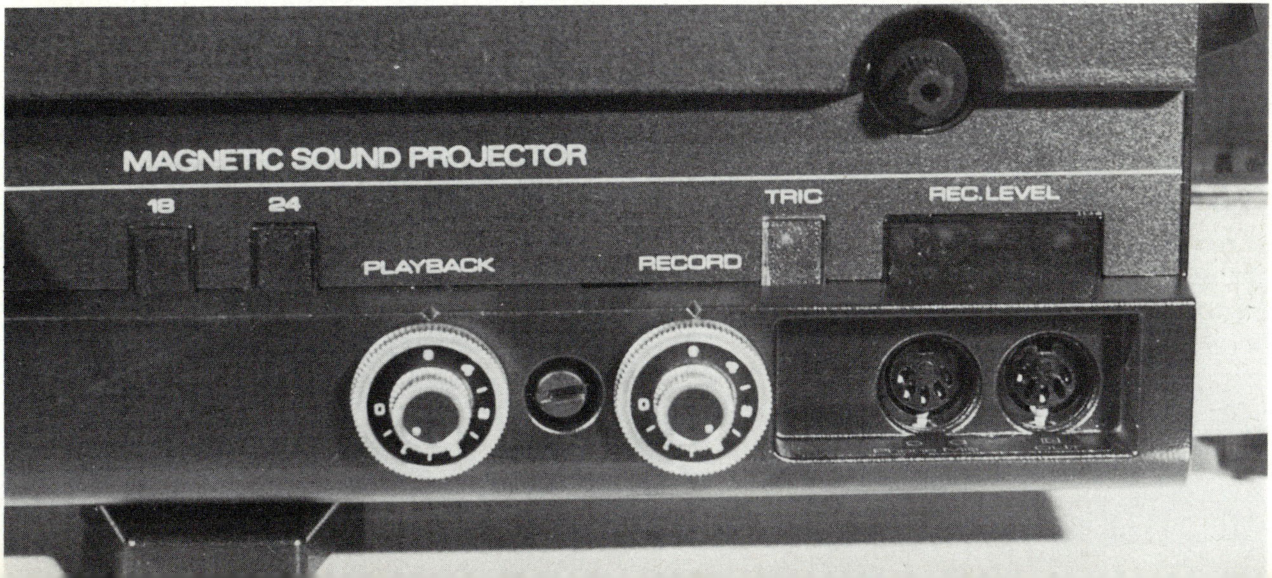

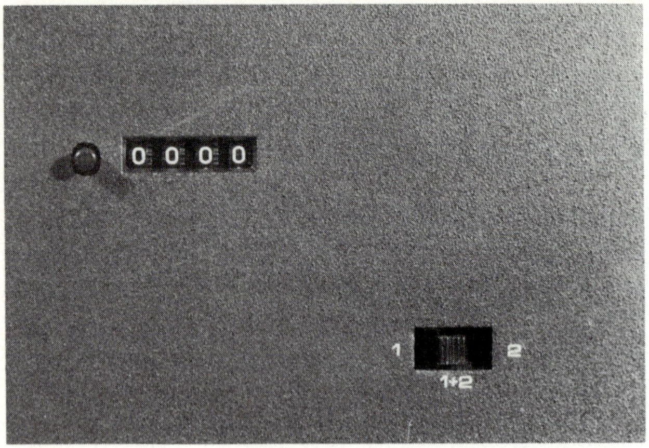

Frame-counter on a sound projector

optical sound. The sound is beamed through the sound track by an exciter lamp and thus the recorded sound is reproduced on a negative film. Optical sound cannot be altered or erased, nor is this necessary with finished feature films.

Optical sound is only of peripheral interest to the sound-film amateur, since he is not personally able to score his ciné film by this process. In the future this would probably become possible with optical sound films when the aim is to procure the occasional film of this type to screen alongside one's own. There are currently hardly any on the market, but again this is determined by public demand.

PICTURE-SYNCHRONISED SOUND RECORDING

The developments in this area of ciné photography are by no means at a standstill. Constant progress is made, particularly with reference to the sound film.

Ciné Camera Recorder

For some time now ciné cameras have been produced that allow the simultaneous recording of the picture and the sound which goes with it. A special cable, which connects the camera with the cassette recorder, is essential for this.

By virtue of this electrical connection the recorder is switched on automatically at the same time as the camera, so that the sound is recorded as the camera films, resulting in absolute synchronisation.

In practice however this process is not totally without its problems. The aid of an assistant acquainted with the subject must be enlisted if the process is to function faultlessly. If the sound is to be correctly recorded over a microphone simultaneously with the film, both taking directions must exactly coincide. The film-maker is hardly able to accomplish this without help, since the direction of the lens is constantly changing and the microphone must follow this movement continuously.

Both pieces of equipment – recorder and camera – are provided with markings. Naturally both tape and film must again start at the same start marks when the film is screened, otherwise the sound will not coincide with the picture. We will return to this in another context.

Sound-Recording Camera

For about two years now sound-film cameras have existed in which the sound can be recorded on sound-film cassettes. This requires a Super-8 film which is already provided with a sound track. The basic equipment of the sound-film camera naturally includes a contact point for the microphone. A recording sound head inside the camera will immediately record the sound during filming.

The sound is of course in no way affected when the film is developed, so one will finally possess a film with synchronised sound, which can be reproduced on any magnetic projector.

The sound film cassette is larger than the conventional Super-8 magazine and can only be used in a sound-film camera; there are many indicators to suggest that this is the sound system of the future. All the well-known manufacturers produce cameras based on this concept and as far as possible these reflect the latest developments made in the very new area of sound-filming.

Thus anyone filming with a sound film camera will generally require an assistant, unless he is working with a boom microphone. The method of operation is barely distinguishable from that of the silent ciné camera, the only new feature being the simultaneous sound recording.

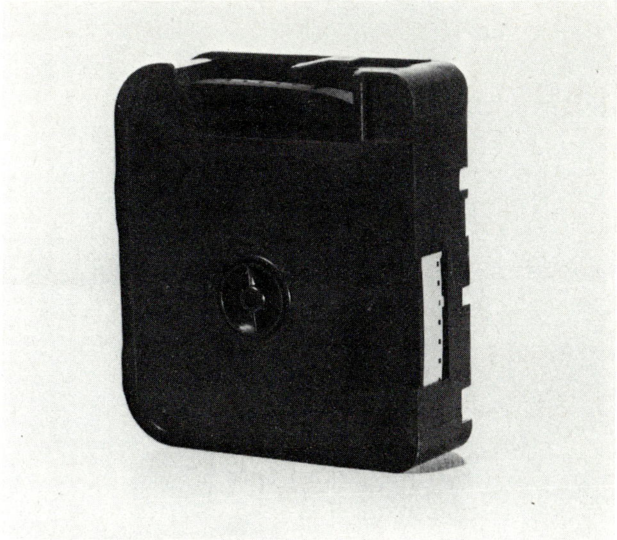

Sound-film cassette
The film gate for the film shot is at the side, the opening for the sound recording at the top

In order to accomplish acoustic recordings of optimum quality, it is desirable to bring the microphone into the closest possible proximity with the subject recorded. There are two reasons which demand that this point is observed: firstly, the smaller the distance between the sound source and the microphone the better the quality of the sound, and secondly, it avoids the risk of the operating noises of the camera also being recorded.

Naturally, one must ensure that the assistant does not impinge on the camera's field of view, otherwise the most excellent example of synchronisation is rendered useless. Particular care is needed in this

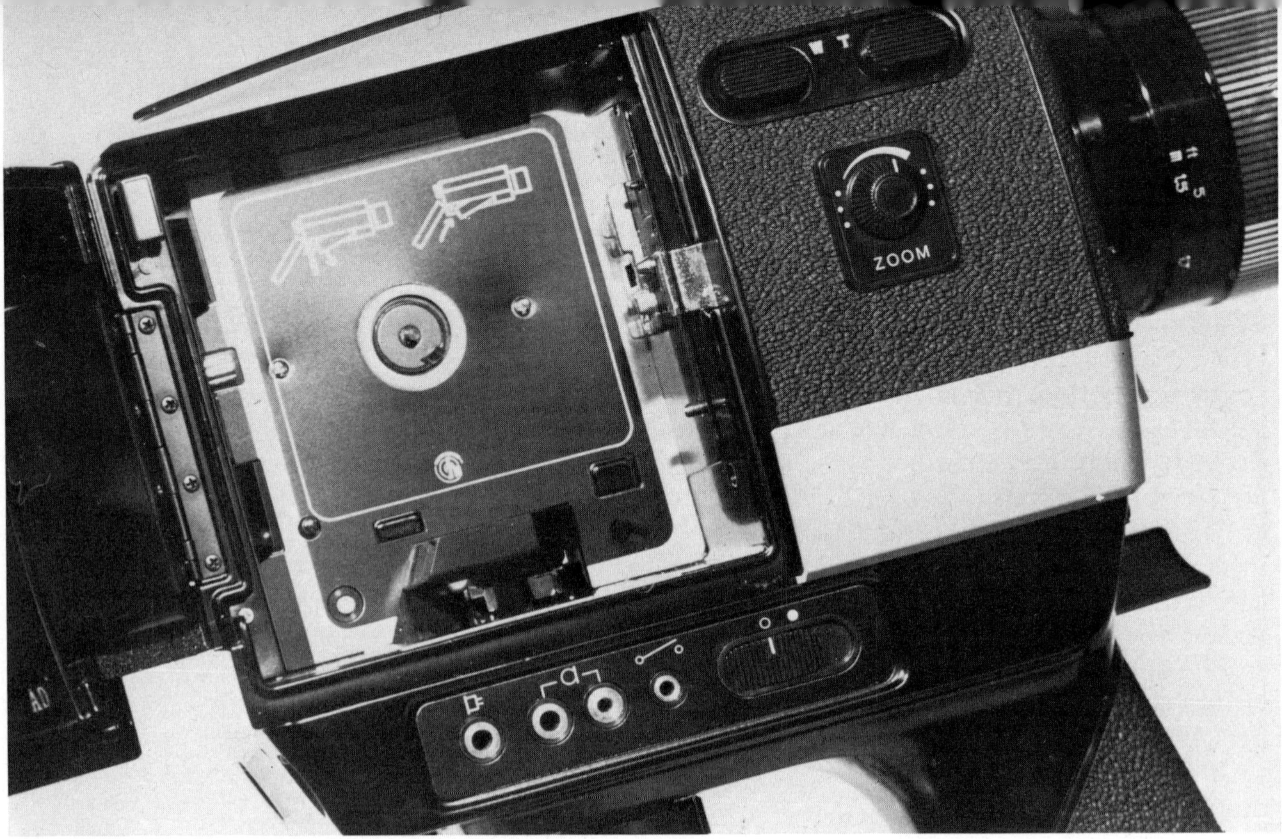

Super-8 sound-recording camera. Open without a film. The sound head is visible on the bottom edge of the camera

respect for shots taken with a zoom lens or a wide-angle. When using a sound-film camera one must concentrate both on the picture and on the sound.

Immediate control of the sound is made possible with the aid of earphones, which will establish the exact impression created by the sound recording as it is made. The earphones form a part of the basic equipment of many cameras, but if not they can be purchased as an accessory.

Those who want to remain as independent as possible and to make sound films unassisted can in certain circumstances use the already mentioned boom microphone. It can be screwed on to the upper side of many sound-film cameras and is positioned on a telescopic rod at a height of about 60 – 80cm. in front of the lens. The microphone is fixed rigidly and is thus always facing the recording direction, so that only the sound which is associated with the picture is

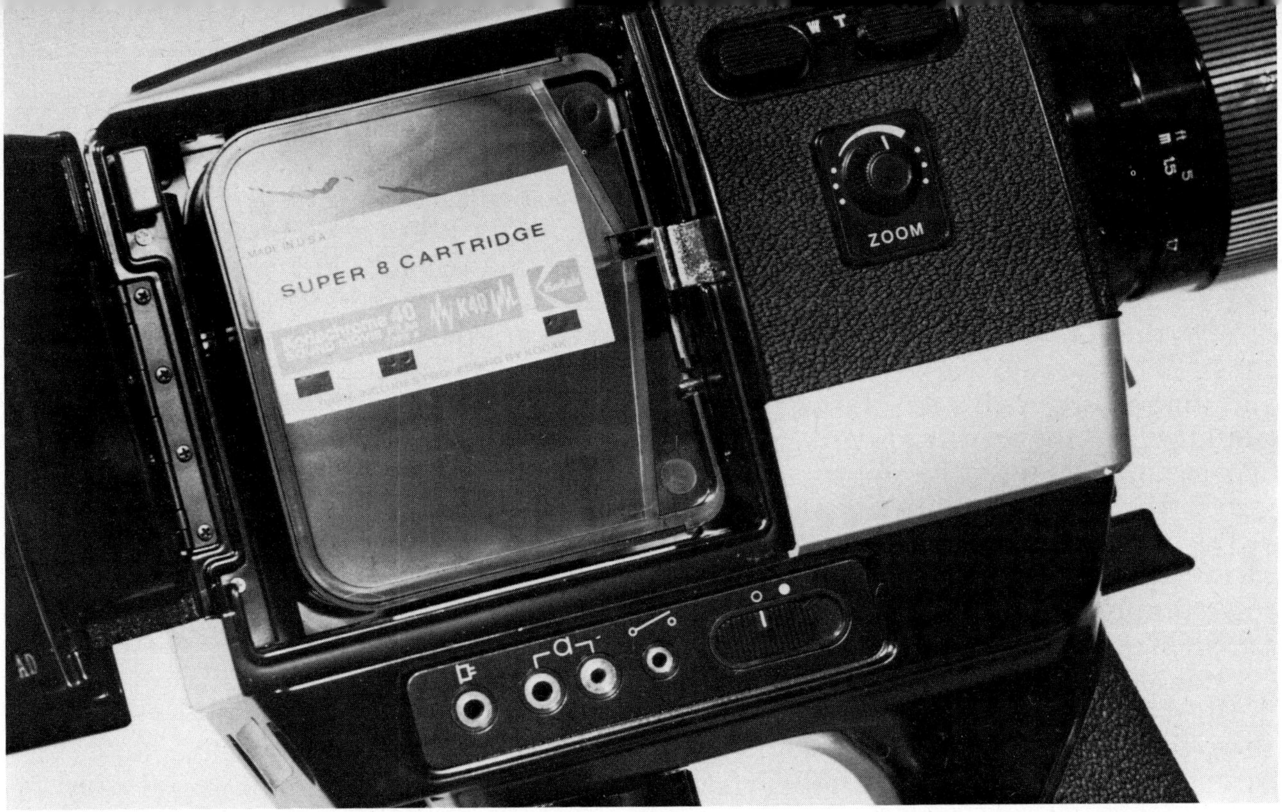

With cassette inserted

recorded. Its distance from the camera can be altered, depending on the length of the telescopic rod, in order to prevent the camera's own noises being recorded.

The telescopic microphone is a very practical aid for filming in the close-up range, e.g. children playing. The microphone provided with the ciné camera is a directional microphone, which means it only records sounds in front of it, and the recording will not include any slight noises infiltrating from the side, as long as they are not too loud.

Some microphones can be employed with a remote release. The camera is placed on a tripod and then the film-maker can move with the microphone up to the object being filmed activating both picture and acoustics simultaneously by means of the remote-control switch. However, in some circumstances the cameraman may be able to run back to the camera to take the film himself. The effective radius must be established correctly beforehand.

Musical Accompaniment

The potential of the sound-film camera is not yet exhausted. With some cameras, as long as they provide access for a rerecording cable, it is possible to record the music simultaneously with the film, so that is produced by the tape-recorder as a direct accompaniment to it. This presents us with a very attractive, but rather problematic, opportunity. In my opinion it is more satisfactory (and above all more convenient) to accomplish this by means of a magnetic-sound projector.

Should the sound recording bear any faults it is of course possible to erase it and then supply the sound track with other sounds or music. Obvious mistakes can be repaired by this method, smaller inconsistencies should be tolerated.

It is certainly not easy to edit a sound-bearing film. If the film was planned in the abstract, and has been shot faultlessly, editing may not even be absolutely essential, hence film montage will also become unnecessary, since the life-sound is matched to the chronological order. If this process is employed, the sound, conversation, or whatever is used to provide acoustic information, can be altered without it being chopped up, and consequently editing a sound film should be largely unnecessary.

However, it is possible to make small corrections. Picture and sound, both in the camera and in the picture, lie 18 frames apart, which normally represents one second of running time. Thus the occasional discrepancy between sound and picture lasts only one second, after which correct synchronisation is re-established. If the irregularity is disturbing, this second can be concealed subsequently by means of a musical addition. Further to this the whole film might for instance be embellished with music, as long as the music remains as a quiet background. Then in places which require correction, the life sound can be blended out, and exchanged totally for the music.

Anyone who has experience of working with a sound camera will be aware that one does not need life sound for the entire film. The film still maintains an impression of a 100 per cent synchronised recording if the life sound is only occasionally included.

Life-sound films should as a rule be produced in accordance with a script. In this case the film scenes must be filmed in the correct sequence, as represented in the script, so that the possible error margins are kept as small as possible and hardly any correction is required.

It is relatively easy to make a sound film without a spoken text, but, conversely, making a feature film with life sound can prove difficult. The problems lie not in the filming of the shots, but in the fact that lip synchronisation must be maintained. Lay actors are naturally not used to repeating the text absolutely correctly without any slips, and a subsequent correction of the life sound is important in order to preserve lip synchronisation. For this reason it is generally preferable to add the sound after the film has been made; even professionals adopt this method.

We must return once more to the two-track projector since it has been developed along with the life-sound system. It provides the ideal method of eliminating or minimising the errors contained in life sound.

The camera uses only one sound track for the recording, so that the second remains free for additional recordings. As already described, this allows the recording of, for instance, music on the second track, which is soft enough not to influence the original sound on the first track. Only where some correction is required is life sound muted by the dominance of the recording on the second track. Irrespective of any other potential variable, it is extremely important that each track can be revised and erased independently of the other.

If you are about to purchase a ciné camera you should investigate this new system thoroughly. Without doubt it opens up opportunities almost unknown until now, but one should be aware that some of the techniques associated with conventional ciné filming are not practicable with life-sound filming. One cannot for instance

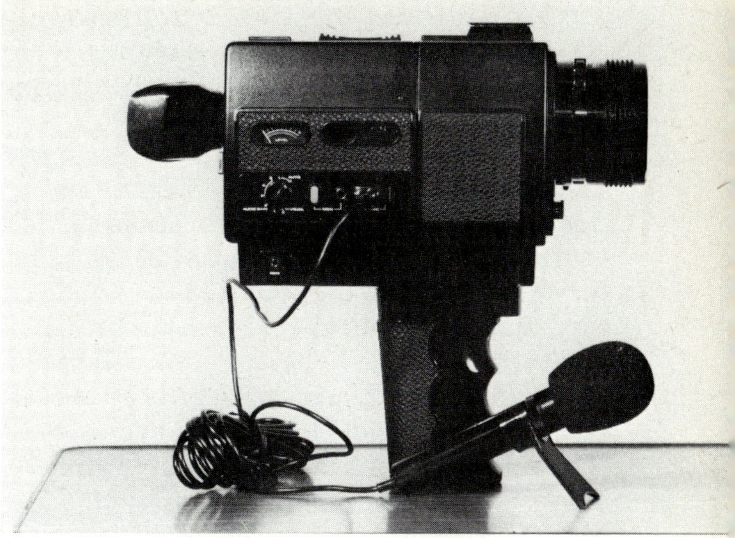

Sound-recording camera with microphone attached

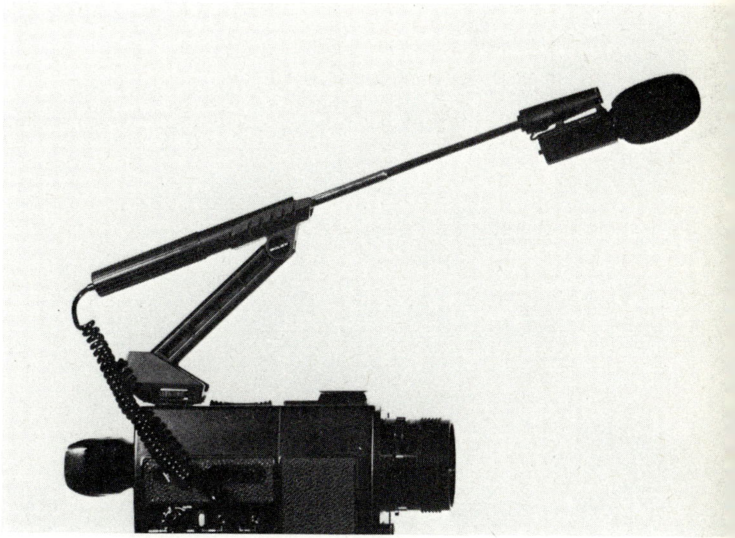

Boom microphone in position. The telescopic support can be extended about 1m. A rigid connection between the camera and the microphone guarantees that the recording direction remains the same

produce dissolves together with life sound, equally it is not possible technically to combine life sound and trick settings, nor would there be any point.

It finally remains to say that one can use the usual Super-8 film, i.e. without sound track, in a sound-film camera, and then add sound to it in the conventional manner. Anyone who uses the sound-film camera in this way, producing picture-synchronised films on certain occasions and otherwise exploiting the many possibilities which subsequent sound recording implies, will certainly come to value the system highly. There are certain circumstances in which the noise of the surroundings is not disturbing, when one wants to capture the original sound of a particular event. Films of dance performances and fairs for instance succeed by virtue of their originality, if when the film is edited a life-sound section (in a part of the film which is to remain unaltered) is combined with carefully mounted film which has been post-recorded.

The various models of sound-film camera are no different in principle. All employ the same type of film, and it is only the handling of it which may vary here and there, as in all other cameras. The handling of each individual camera is described in detail in its instruction booklet.

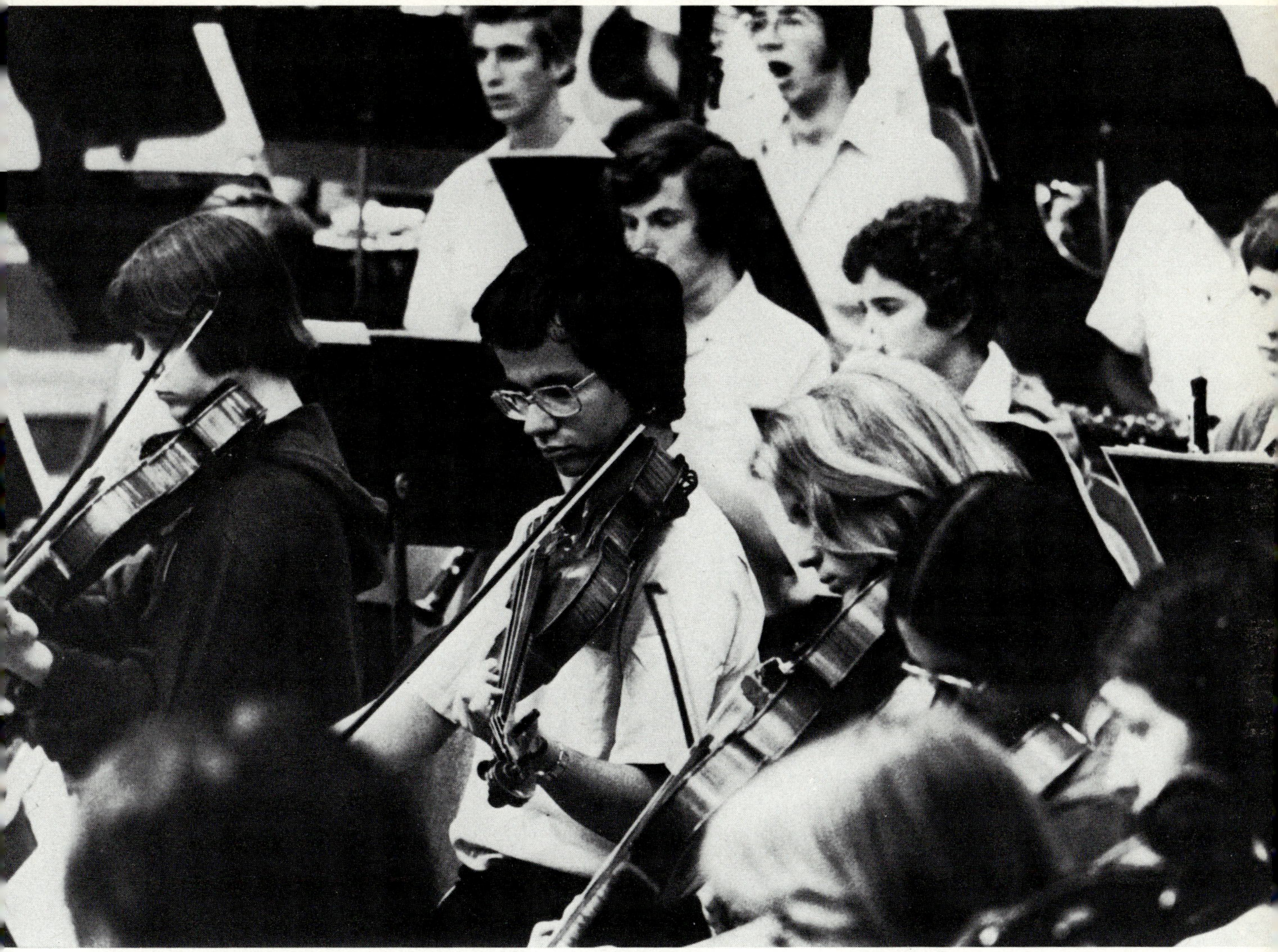

Music film scenes are best taken with a sound camera

THE PRACTICE OF FILM SCORING

Professional film-makers work on a film according to a script which establishes exactly every detail of the film, including all the sound recordings, but although this is without doubt the superior method, it is generally too troublesome for the ciné filmer. Most amateur films cannot be devised totally in advance, at least with regard to sound recordings, particularly since they are very much dependent on chance.

Despite this restriction, however, adding sound to a film would be inconceivable without a certain amount of planning. It is less problematic to create one continuous sound recording than it is to complement the various parts when a life sound or some acoustic rendering is involved.

Anyone who attempts to score his film without a plan will soon realise that a minimum amount of preparation is essential. It is not usually sufficient simply to add some apparently suitable music from a record or tape. The following example might serve as a guide to how to plan sound recordings.

PREPARING A SOUND RECORDING

Time Plan

Title: *Holiday in the mountains*

Scene Number	Picture	Time in secs	Setting	Sound
1	Leader, black, no picture.	5	—	Alpine music
2	Title: fade-in. 'Holiday in the Mountains'.	5	Close-up	
3	Dissolve to 1st scene: rushing of mountain stream in the morning sun.	8	medium close-up	Life sound or blend in: noise of the water

Scene Number	Picture	Time in secs	Setting	Sound
4	Camera passes slowly to a village at the end of a stream.	5	full length	Music
	Remains stationary.	6		
5	Tracking shot to the church spire.	4	medium close-up	Life sound: or blend in church bells
6	Entrance to the church with people approaching it.	6	close-up	

Each scene is outlined in a scheme of this type, the exact time playing an important rôle.

All the technical work, such as splicing, montage, and title creation, must already be completed before the sound work can begin. The processes have already been discussed in detail in previous sections, particularly in the chapter 'Filming with a script', which must again be referred to in relation to the following paragraphs.

Combining Text and Music

If the film has been taken without the use of a script, the first step is to make an exact measurement of the entire running time, in order to determine how much time is available in all for the music and/or spoken text. Hardly ever, even if there is a second track for the music, will one continuous piece of music be suitable for the entire film. Consequently, the next step is to arrange which scenes or parts of the film are to be connected with which music. It is often not at all easy to find the right pieces of music.

The next step which the preparations demand, is that all the music which is to be used in the film should be on hand. If music is to be taken from records, it is advisable to record it initially on to a tape or cassette. This makes the work easier, since some insertions will need to be tested several times. It is easy to locate the sound insertions on the tape, whereas on a record this cannot be done precisely, or only with difficulty, and might moreover damage the record.

The next step is to co-ordinate the music with the sounds in the film. Either these were recorded with life sound or they must be selected from a sound-effects collection. When everything has been sorted out, all the sounds including the music must be combined on one tape. As a rule one requires more music than sound effects, since there is only occasionally any point in including original sounds in the film, assuming the film has not been made with a sound-film camera.

The next step concerns the spoken text, and usually involves the most problems, beginning with the voice, which does not sound well over the microphone. Not every voice, however appealing, is suitable for work with a microphone, and in addition, fautless pronunciation is an important requirement.

The text must be established in advance. Only a few people feel capable of giving a good commentary or perhaps even improvising. Generally a good method is to write out the text and then to say it oneself, in order to make it agree with the length of the film. If your own voice is not suitable, the text can be read on to a tape or cassette so that the whole film text is conserved at once. The sound track can then be used later whenever required – the commentator is only needed once. Moreover, the recording cannot be affected by any background noises if everything has been said clearly on to a tape.

The initial preparations obviously include the checking of all equipment: the sound heads in the projector must be cleaned, the tape recorder must be in working order, the re-recording cable must fit and function, otherwise one might have a few unpleasant surprises.

Stripping Equipment

In most cases a sound strip is used. This means that a sound track has to be added to the film, which one can either do for oneself or have done by a manufacturer. A special machine is required, produced exclusively for adding the strip to the film. There are various models but they all work on the same principle, which basically entails sticking a 0.8mm.-wide sound track on to the edge of the film with a special adhesive. Some models have a built-in motor, others can be used in conjunction with a projector, and anyone wanting to add sound to a lot of film should consider acquiring such equipment. A do-it-yourself soundtrack costs only half as much as one would have to pay to have it done, nor is the process likely to present any difficulties.

Summary

We can summarise briefly which preparations are necessary before the addition of sound can begin:

1 Make a time plan for the sound recording.

2 Measure the length of the film; determine which portions require sounds or music.

3 Select music and sounds and record on to a tape.

4 Determine the text and speak it on to a tape.

5 Check functioning of all equipment.

6 Add sound-track to film.

LIP-SYNCHRONISED RECORDING

The possibility of making so-called lip-synchronised recordings has already been discussed with reference to the sound-film camera. Lip-synchronised filming has become almost a catchword in advertising, and not only in connection with the sound-film camera.

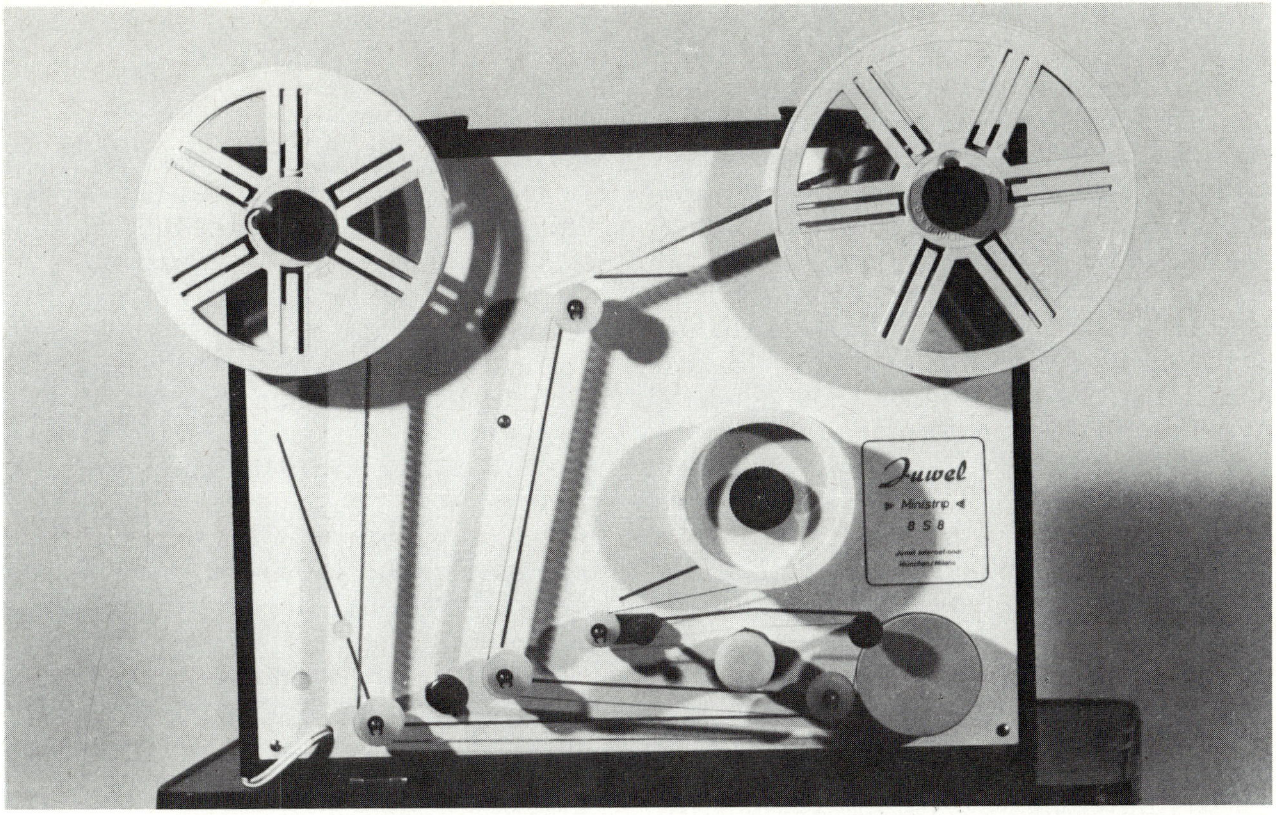

Juwel stripping equipment for adding sound track to a ciné film

Lip synchronisation means, as the words themselves suggest, that the sound and lip movements are synchronised exactly, in other words, they coincide. This can be achieved on film in two ways: either text and picture are recorded together by means of a sound-film camera, or the text is spoken, but the film taken silently, in which case the text must be transferred subsequently from the tape to the sound track and at the same time synchronised with the lip movements. That this implies a great deal of difficulty can be deduced occasionally from synchronised television or cinema films, and these are the concern of professionals! Anyone who desires a sound-film camera should consider that in the amateur film it is in fact very seldom that lip-synchronised film shots are produced.

Effects which are very similar to those in a lip-synchronised film can also be created without a sound-film camera. Texts and sounds can be recorded at the same time as filming takes place (with or without a connection from the camera to the tape), and then blended into the film, irrespective of which sound process is chosen. Life-sound scenes of this type will enliven the film remarkably. Moreover the occasional insertion of synchronised sounds will give the film an almost lip-synchronised effect.

Although lip-synchronised films are very pleasing both to look at and to listen to, one must be quite clear that they can only be created with great difficulty without a sound-film camera and even then there are problems with production. We will return to this subject later.

Anyone who is especially interested in this topic should compare the different equipment with which it is possible to achieve faultless lip-synchronised filming, and should study the generally very detailed instruction leaflets.

PRACTICAL ASPECTS OF FILM SCORING

There are various methods of scoring magnetic sound film, as already outlined in the previous chapter, the most widely used method being to add the sound on a sound strip. This system is used by nearly everybody who records sound, and hence it explains why nearly all sound projectors are designed for the reproduction of these magnetic sound films.

Scoring with a Magnetic Sound Strip

We can thus presume that any film-maker concerned with sound for the first time will work with this process, although this shall not prevent us from mentioning other methods.

Scoring magnetic sound film requires a film which bears a sound track, and a sound projector in which it is possible to undertake sound recording on this track and afterwards reproduce it.

The more frequently one scores film, the more one's skill and speed increases, but one's expectations of the recordings grow in the same proportions. Consequently it is very helpful if the sound on the film can be erased again. With the first attempts one is simply happy to be able to couple both sound and music, but later everything must be correct.

The simplest method, as we suggested, is to supply the soundtrack with music appropriate to the film from a record or cassette. For this purpose it is usual to connect the tape recorder to the sound projector by means of a re-recording cable, for which there is a sound socket on the projector, and the recording level is set, as on any recorder, either manually or automatically.

When a new section of film begins, the music should also change. It is rarely suitable to continue one complete musical work throughout the whole film.

Using a Microphone

The second possibility we described has many a friend, and entails providing the film with both sound and speech, all in one stage of work. This can be easily accomplished by using a microphone, as long as care is taken to ensure that any other noise in the house is largely prevented.

The process is very simple: the music for the film is compiled on the tape as usual. During projection, the projector is set to microphone recording, so that the music is transferred from the tape to the sound track via the microphone, which is placed in front of the tape-recorder's loudspeaker. One should establish in advance the distance at which recording is most successful. The text must of course exist in written form.

When a spoken text is to be added to the film, the microphone is taken away from the loudspeaker and the commentary spoken into it with the music still playing; since the microphone must necessarily be removed from the loudspeaker for the commentary, the music continues, softly audible in the background, returning in full volume at the end of the text, when the microphone is again directed at the loudspeaker. With this simple method one can achieve a blended effect, as produced by working with a mixer unit. When everything is completed, the impression given is quite 'professional'.

It is evident that the method contains a number of possible sources of error, which can only be avoided by taking great pains and applying one's concentration. Background noises in the room or the house, the incorrect positioning of the microphone, mistakes of pronunciation, or the operating noises of the projector and tape recorder are some of the reasons for this process being only occasionally used. These sources of mistakes can however be eliminated, if the process is modified to some extent. It means only a little extra work.

Superimposed Sound

Firstly, the music is recorded onto the film, not of course over the microphone, but directly from the tape recorder to the projector, via a re-recording cable. In this way no distortion of the sound in the microphone can occur, one need not worry about keeping a constant distance between the microphone and the loudspeaker, and any possible background noises are insignificant. A better musical recording could not exist.

The second and third stages involve superimposing the sound effects and the spoken text on to the music. For this the film is wound back, in order to proceed with the second step, the recording of the sound effects which have been prepared in advance on a tape.

Every sound projector possesses a trick dial, with which the already recorded sound can be erased partially or completely if the

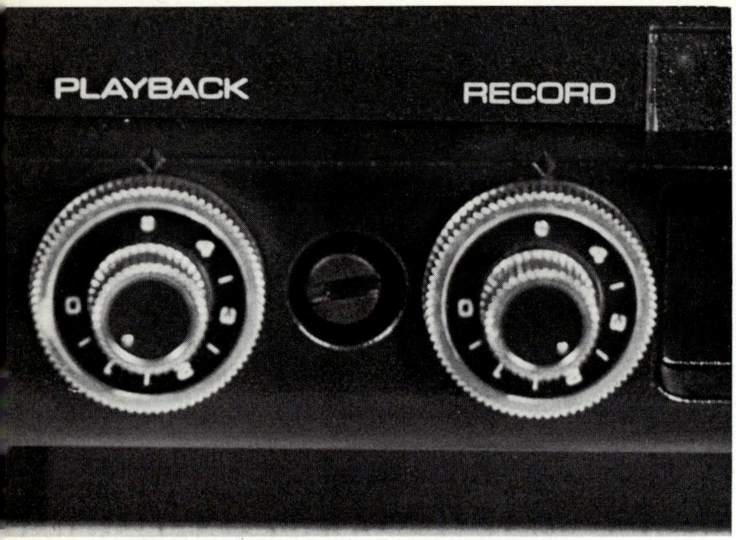

Playback and record dials on a sound projector

second recording is to superimpose the first. The trick dial is provided with a scale on which to set the extent to which the first recording, in our case the music, is to be muted as the sound effects are recorded on the film. The musical recording of the first stage is totally maintained, and is returned to normal volume as soon as the track dial is again set to nil. The music fades into the background each time a new sound is blended in, and is again audible at full volume immediately afterwards. Experiments will demonstrate how far back the trick dial needs to be turned. Whether the music should be completely faded out for some sound effects is a matter of personal taste.

The third stage proceeds in the same manner, so that finally the text is recorded. Two points are important:

1 One can superimpose up to three recordings. If a fourth were added, the first would no longer be audible.

2 The most important sound recording must always be left to last, since the last recording is the one best heard, and this is nearly always the spoken word. Thus superimposed sound recordings must proceed in the following sequence:

Musical recording
Sound-effects recording
Speech recording

Finally, a few general guidelines for your first attempts at this method, though these are not to dissuade you from experimenting for yourself.

With some sound effects it is essential for the music to be faded out and to return afterwards. This is dependent on the type of sound effect. Sounds such as cars and traffic are difficult to combine with music, while on the other hand sounds from nature, for instance bird-song, splashing water, etc., almost demand a musical background, which in addition will nearly always complement a spoken commentary.

There is also the possibility of correcting a recording made by this method, which can be accomplished subsequently on one track. Should you decide when you listen to the recording that it would be better to eliminate the music, the recording (assuming that it exists on tape) can be re-made in the same place, by setting the trick dial to erase the original recording totally. Thus the first unsatisfactory recording is erased, and exchanged for a new recording without any acoustic background.

The Mixer Unit

Some film-makers value sound superimposition very highly, but do not favour the three-stage method. In this case the mixer unit provides the ideal solution.

With a mixer unit one can undertake several recordings simultaneously, since it is equipped with separate sockets for various sound equipment (record player, tape recorder etc.). Music, speech, and all other sound effects can be mixed as desired in one phase by means of the recording regulator at each access point. The sound can be heard on head-phones as it is recorded, and can thus be regulated.

This is certainly an elegant method, but you will hardly be able to manage without an assistant when you have to operate several pieces of equipment at once. The ultimate effect is no different to that achieved with the trick dial in several stages, but some people consider that using a mixer unit requires less time.

Stereo Sound Recording

There are always some ciné filmers who remain convinced that the sound track of a ciné film is too small to give good musical reproduction. This is true, insofar as a good tape recorder will have a higher frequency range, but it is important to remember that in the film the most significant feature is the picture, and the sound, whether music or text, is only there to intensify the film's effect. Thus in the context of the film the music is never an end in itself, as might perhaps apply to a stereo record. The quality of sound required for the film is usually achieved on a good strip projector. Anyone who wishes to hear a perfect rendering of a concert will certainly not turn to a film for for it.

However, it is possible to add sound to a film the quality of which will conform to quite high expectations. This is achieved by the use of a stereo tape recorder: the necessary equipment for such combinations is easily obtainable. The tape recorder is usually connected to the projector electrically, rarely mechanically. There are various ways of doing this, but in principle they are barely distinguishable.

With this system it is important that both the film and the tape have a visible start mark, which must be positioned in the same place when the sound is recorded and at every presentation thereafter. To this end the tape is furnished with a coloured adhesive marking, and on the film the transition of the leader into the film or title is usually recognised for this purpose. The most exact method is to mark a small area on the side of one of the frames contained in the black leader, and to locate the exact point in the film gate of the projector. If the position of both start marks is correct, the same provisions are made for each performance.

In principle this system facilitates the same variants as the one-track technique. Music can be played on to the tape, and then a commentary added to the tape as the film is projected. Some modern tape recorders possess a trick dial, with which one is able to achieve the same effects as described for the magnetic sound projector. If there is no dial, one can also make use of the mixer unit here.

If a four-track tape recorder is used, one is able to record each track independently of the others, as applied to the two-track magnetic sound film, both tracks being reproduced in parallel, providing that the tape recorder is technically equipped to accommodate this. In this case one track can be used for the music, the second track for all the other sound recordings, and each track can be erased exclusively of the other.

Write-on Tape

Write-on tape provides the best two-track method of recording sound, and has the important additional advantage of only requiring the film to be projected once for the recording process, as subsequent sound recordings can be made without the film.

In practice the process is as follows: firstly the write-on tape and the film are marked with the necessary start marks in the usual way. An important requirement is that all the musical insertions, sounds, and texts have been determined on paper, so that each point of insertion is immediately recognisable when the film runs. Hold the microphone in your hand as the film and tape are played together, and each time a sound is inserted or changed, either knock lightly on the microphone or say a number or some other signal into it, indicating the position of the sound insertion. This is continued throughout the whole film. At the end, the film has been transferred completely on the tape, insofar as each insertion can be recognised by the signal on the tape, independent of film projection. It is significant that this process entails the use of a write-on tape, which is a tape with a matt backing, which can be written on in pencil.

The second playing of the tape ensues without the film. Now at every audible indication of a sound insertion, the tape can be supplied with a visible marking, for instance, all musical insertions might be represented with a figure, while all spoken ones are represented by a letter. With the aid of the now visible insertion marks on the back of the tape, the individual sections of sound can be recorded, without the film having to be projected again. Not until the tape has been completely arranged, a job which might extend over a few days without causing any difficulties, is it again played together with the film. The start marks ensure exact co-ordination. This is without doubt a method which spares the film as much as possible.

Film Scoring with an Impulse Device

We return briefly to the picture synchronised recording and the much over-used term 'lip-synchronisation'. The sections of sound to be recorded by this method can be played on any tape and sound track, if the camera and cassette recorder are connected by means of an impulse cable. Film recordings which include synchronised sections are always effective: an occasional appropriately blended-in scene will be sufficient. If the sounds are synchronised in a number of places in this manner, the overall impression is one of a perfect sound accompaniment.

The recording can be made either with a spool tape recorder or with a cassette recorder. In both cases the coupling is by means of a small electrical impulse device, which does not vary in principle. However in order to exploit the cassette system to the full, one should use a sound projector which includes the recorder as an integral part of the equipment, as has already been mentioned in another context. If the start marks are correctly positioned no discrepancy is possible, since picture and sound have one and the same source of power.

Recording with a cassette in this way has some distinct advantages: one can prepare varying cassettes for the same film, offering groups of varying interests a film with one of a selection of different recordings. This would seem particularly interesting for giving showings in different languages, which could be used to eliminate many a problem in school and training situations. The tempting factor is here that a double recording can be made with very little trouble, and the price of a cassette is surprisingly small.

We have already mentioned two-track recording in connection with the write-on tape. The projector and tape recorder are made to run parallel to each other by means of a control impulse on the tape. This requires an impulse control, which might be added to almost any projector as an additional installation after purchase. This method is known as a unified system, since the actual model of the projector and tape-recorder are unimportant.

Using this unified system, impulses are received by the impulse control from the tape recorder, and then transmitted to the projector, which guarantees absolute co-ordination. A new impulse is constantly transmitted after every fourth frame. The impulses are applied to the tape (outside the audible track on the tape) before the recording is begun. However, this means that the tape can only be used in one direction.

Fisrtly, the tape recorder is connected to the impulse control (without projector), which ensures that the impulses are produced at absolutely constant intervals when the tape is running. The tape is now supplied with perforations similar to those on the film, but in this case invisible. When the start marks on both film and tape are in position, recording continues as with any other two-track system, except that the unified process here guarantees that the two pieces of equipment run in absolute parallel.

A four-track tape recorder is again the best

equipment for this system, since it allows separate recordings to be made on both tracks. If a stereo recording were to be made with the unified system, this would indeed be the crowning of the sound system. It would however require the use of two-track stereo equipment since the impulses would otherwise be audible.

Life-Sound Recording

We must briefly return to 'life sound' in connection with this sound system. As already described, the sound may be recorded as the film is taken by the use of a special connecting cable from the camera to the recorder. Again in this case the impulses on the tape are regulated to ensure the parallel functioning of camera and recorder. The impulses can be transmitted to another tape via the impulse control by means of a special cable, which obviously sounds easier than it actually is.

'Life sound', however, inasfar as it is not directly recorded in the camera, offers not only some excellent opportunities but also entails a number of problems, which to some extent can only be overcome with the appropriate technical equipment. One is here very much on the borders of professional filming, where the film and sound work is carried out by highly qualified specialists with excellent technical resources; the requirements here are completely different.

The End of the Film

Normally one will arrange for both the film and music to end simultaneously, irrespective of the sound system used. One does not require a stop watch in order to achieve this perfectly, since it can be achieved by employing a small trick, which I have recently learned myself.

The film is marked, with a coloured sticker, at the point at which the last piece of film is to begin. The tape is positioned in the tape recorder at the sound head, but so that it runs in the wrong direction. Then camera and tape are started together. As soon as the end of the film is reached, the tape is stopped and turned over again, so that the desired piece of music is now positioned to run in the right direction. Then the film is wound back to the point marked. The film now begins with the start of the musical recording, and thus the last note of the music is heard exactly as the film ends. This is an easy but nevertheless effective method.

Finally a small tip:
a whole collection of aids which facilitate sound recordings have been discussed in detail: the mixer unit, tape recorder, connecting cable, and much more, and in the course of working with sound film you will accumulate many recording leads, impulse leads, etc. The various leads are all of similar appearance, although their functions are entirely different. Experience has shown the wisdom of labelling the leads, so that their use is clearly indicated. Usually use of the wrong cable can be very annoying, but apart

from this some sort of organisation can save a lot of time.

Superior camera with nearly all technical refinements

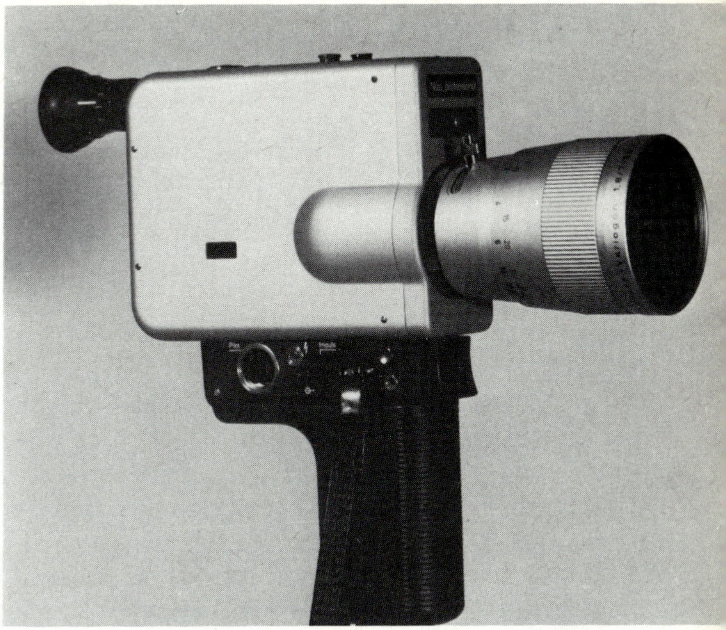

Sockets for two-track sound recording; left, pilot sound socket; right, impulse socket for connection with a cassette recorder

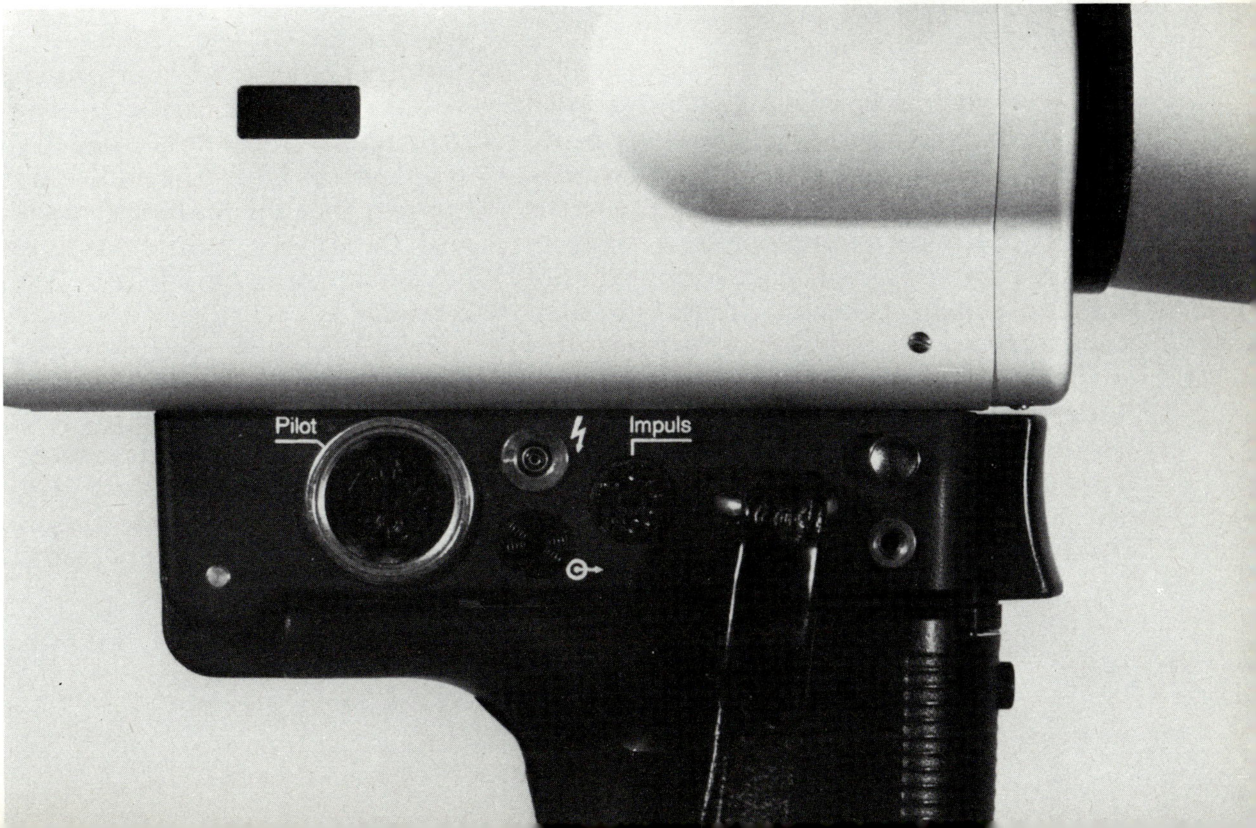

THE SOUND LIBRARY

In the last chapter, the various methods used for making film sound recordings were described in detail, and, with regard to this, a sound library can be very useful. For this one needs portable, battery-operated equipment, a tape or cassette recorder, which is independent of the sound system and can be used without being coupled with the camera.

In this way many sounds can be recorded and collected together to form a sound library. They can then be blended into a particular film at any time according to the known methods: church bells, a rushing stream, cow bells, and other sounds do not demand synchronisation, indeed it often proves advantageous if they are not recorded at the same time as the film. Any ciné-filmer with experience of sound work will assemble a sound library as a matter of course. Judging from experience, adding the sound to a film afterwards always demands the use of sound effects, which is difficult to achieve without a sound library.

MUSIC LIBRARY

To find the suitable music for a film is frequently no problem at all, but it can also be very difficult sometimes, since it has to match the film thematically, without however forcing the film itself into the background. Careful consideration must be given to the choice, which will of course be heavily influenced by personal taste.

There is one fundamental rule to remember: choose music which you like, but avoid songs and 'hits', since it might well happen that the audience suddenly join in with the singing. While this might of course be very amusing, it is definitely not the effect intended.

Most film music is chosen from the range of good light music. However, you might at some point make a film for which classical music is to be used, for instance a film on an art theme, or concerning a visit to a castle, stately home etc., where the music might originate from the same period as the subject of the film.

The best suggestions are in fact those offered by professional films. Often one receives the impression that the music has been written especially for the film, even if one recognises it as a certain work of a well-known composer.

An equally masterful effect can be achieved for the amateur film in the course of time, above all with the aid of a music library, which has proved itself in many cases to be a real treasure-trove. This can be illustrated by taking a travel film as an example.

Any film of a journey to foreign parts is naturally best accompanied by folk music of the country in question. Since one does not want to use the same music for the entire length of film, a certain amount of selection is necessitated. Perhaps it was possible to record some of the music on the journey itself, but this alone is rarely enough.

In circumstances such as these the music can be collected systematically, by recording all the apparently suitable pieces of music from radio programmes and amassing them in the library. Occasionally one also records a piece of music by chance, which later proves itself to be right for a film. On one journey in Spain we were haunted by a certain piece of music, which came from every bar, out of many windows, and from countless transistor radios, so naturally I recorded it and used it in our travel film. Nowadays it is a tune which is hardly ever heard, but it is stored in our sound library!

Since one will on the whole know the music in one's own library, it is often possible to make a connection between the music available and that required for a film. Everything becomes easier as time goes by. At first one records music more or less indiscriminately, pieces which can perhaps only be used once in a film, but since the tape can be re-recorded if necessary, one can afford to be generous. It is indeed in this way that one builds up a versatile collection.

You will very soon come to realise that it is extremely difficult to manage without a library of film music, or rather, of music suitable for use in a film. One also develops the ability to distinguish intuitively between music which might be suitable for using on a film, and that which is less likely to be of use.

With time either these pieces can be collected on tape, or the appropriate records can be purchased, and with a good range of music from which to draw providing the sound for your film can be a very enjoyable task. Moreover, work can progress far more rapidly by this method.

Anyone who is able to play their own music and produce film music of their own creation will naturally find this a great asset. It is hardly possible to give the sound accompaniment of the film a more individual flavour. Music played at home can be recorded on tape and used on a suitable occasion in conjunction with a film. It is only very rarely likely that one is able to compose one's own music, and even then it would be very difficult to compose all the music for a film. A very attractive method is to compile a pot-pourri of folk songs, hiking songs, and similar melodies interspersed with improvised music.

Many of the programmes on radio and television have a constant introductory tune, a signature tune. Many amateur film-makers also use a signature tune for their films. This combines well with the film title, and must of course be readily available in the music library.

SOUND-EFFECTS COLLECTION

When a film is scored, an acoustic accompaniment will become necessary at certain points, which cannot be achieved by a text or music, and hence one requires suitable sound effects.

The simplest method is of course to obtain a ready-made collection of sound effects. These sound-effect records or tapes, specially produced for the accompaniment of films or slides, contain everything which might be included as standard sound effects, and these are clearly arranged and described. Thus, for instance, sounds of the swirling of the sea, traffic noise, ship's sirens etc., can be re-recorded without difficulty onto a film sound track. Whether the sea sounds were recorded on the North Sea or the Mediterranean is unimportant – and the same applies for many things. Consequently these 'sound collections' are no bad solution.

Those who prefer to record their own sounds, would do well to produce several collections and to label them exactly. Recording sounds outdoors with a tape recorder or cassette is often fairly tedious. Certainly one procures the original sound for the film, but unfortunately it is not always of the best technical quality. When recording, it is advisable to allow for fairly extensive editing, by recording generously and then selecting the best parts. The availability of adequate sound effects to choose from is important.

For those who cannot carry a tape recorder with them, but also reject the use of ready-made sound effects, any of the sounds required for the film can be produced by yet another method. Besides being able to achieve much with the aid of a variety of running speeds on the tape recorder, one can produce many sounds by very simple means.

A few examples of this, applicable to many films:

Rain:
A cup of dried peas rolled about on a sieve. The microphone is held underneath and very close to the sieve.

Fire:
Cellophane paper screwed up directly in front of the microphone. If match boxes are crumpled up, the fire crackles even more.

Wind:
A silk scarf is drawn across a table top under the microphone. The faster the movement the greater the strength of the wind.

Surge of the waves:
The water at the edge of the bath is splashed by making gentle movements, without splashing the microphone.
Thunder:
Thin sheet metal is shaken at some distance in front of the microphone (theatre thunder).
Skiing:
A ruler is pulled across a carpet or blanket. The intensity of the sound is altered by varying the distance from the microphone.
Pistol shot:
A slat of wood is used flat to hit a table top; the microphone is positioned as close as possible.
Footsteps:
Synthetic foil is pressed in a 'step rhythm' close in front of the microphone.
Walking in the snow:
Small bags filled with starch are squeezed in front of the microphone in the rhythm of steps.
Steamer toot:
A wide bottle is filled with water and blown into near the microphone. The more water the bottle contains, the higher the pitch.
Clock:
Clock sounds of varying pitch can be made by knocking on a wine glass with a small piece of wood.
Waterfall:
Blowing into the microphone with more or less force.

A child drinking from a bottle - noises necessarily ensue! (J.Schubert)

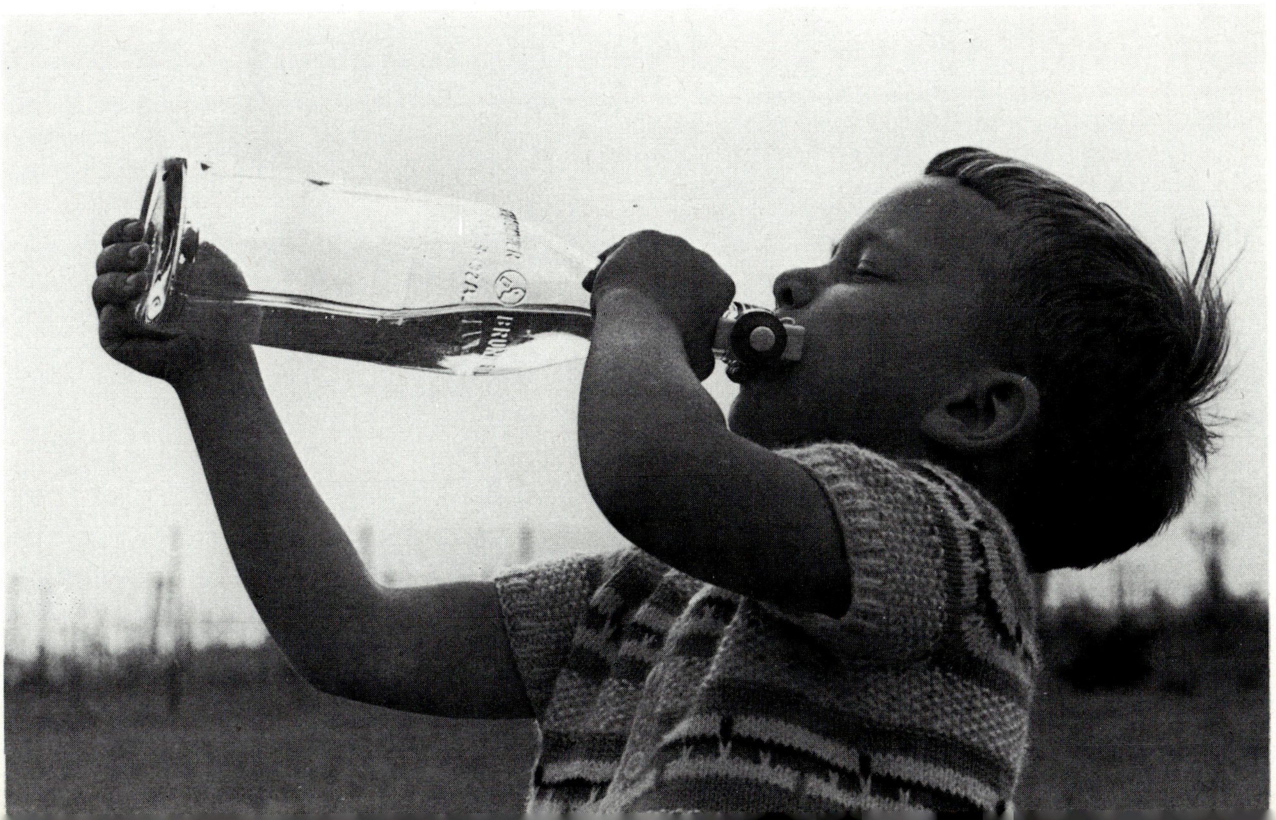

Other examples can be produced with the aid of a tape recorder. Many features can be altered by adjusting the speed of the tape. If the speed is halved, the tape recording will be an octave lower. Hence it is possible for example to transform the ringing of a cow bell into the booming of a huge church bell, or to turn a normal piano chord into rolling thunder. The imagination knows no limits.

FILM PRESENTATION

The presentation of the film is the climax of the work of the amateur ciné-film maker as well as the professional, since this is the culmination of all the work that has been so far discussed.

All the preparation carried out in connection with the film would be completely senseless if its aim were not to be able to present as attractive a film as possible.

Hence the presentation of the film, although it requires the least amount of time, is the whole essence of filming; similarly in still photography, it is not the taking of the photograph, but the completed photograph album that is of the most importance.

But to consider presentation itself, and with it the projector. While the range of choice nowhere approaches that of the camera, there are still a number of factors to be checked carefully when buying a projector. It is of course of no significance whatsoever by whom the camera and projector are manufactured. All Super-8 films are the same and can be presented on any projector. Nor do any difficulties concerning fitting and adjustment arise if the camera and projector are produced by different manufacturers. Conversely, however, Super-8 films and Double-8 films do require different presentation equipment. Projectors showing exclusively Double-8 films are no longer made, since Double-8 films are hardly ever used nowadays. However, there are some two-way projectors. On the other hand a normal Super-8 projector can be used for Single-8 film, since the only difference between this and Super-8 film lies in the magazine; the film itself is of the same type.

Deciding on a projector includes making a choice between films which are presented silently and those presented with sound, since two different systems exist: silent projectors and sound projectors. This need not necessarily influence the performance of the projector.

The exterior appearance of the projector can vary considerably. An aesthetically pleasing casing, built around a piece of

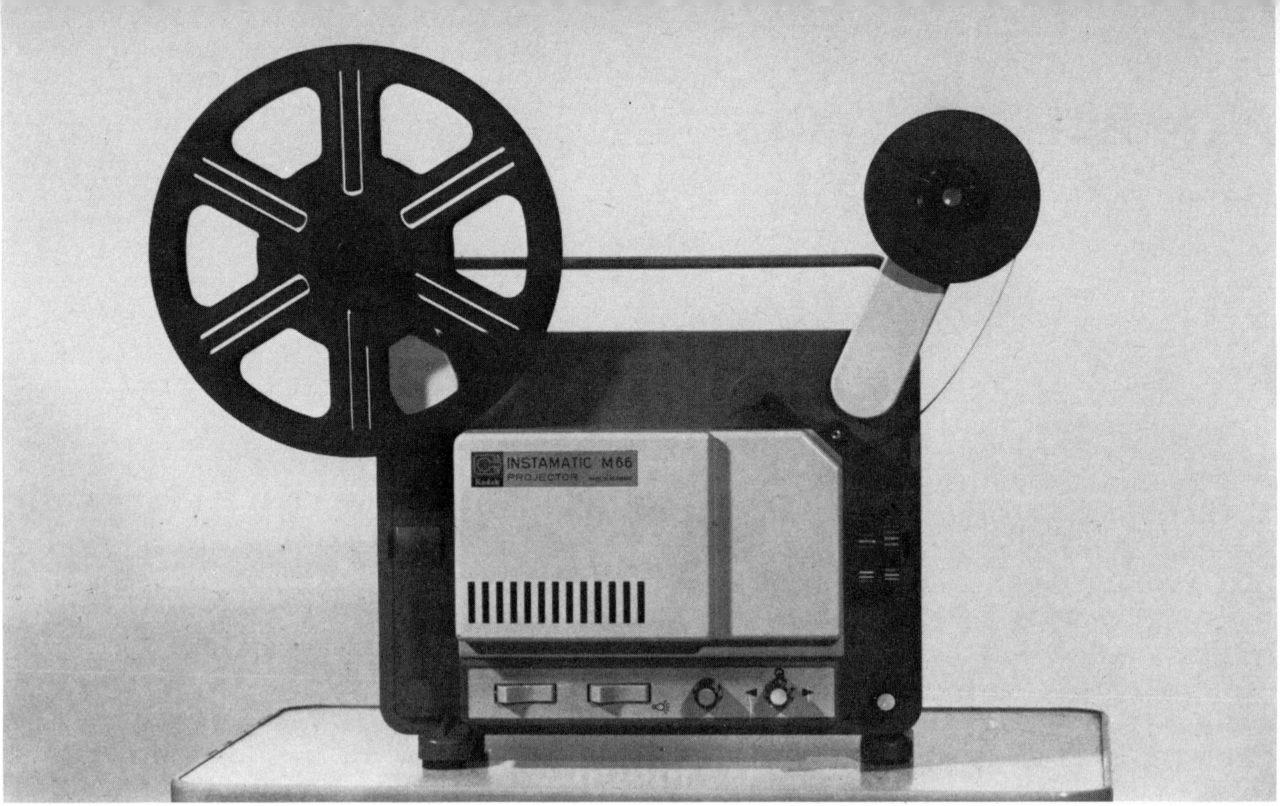

Simple silent-film projector with automatic threading and 120m. film spool

equipment which answers all the requirements, is the perfect solution, but otherwise the exterior of the projector has no significance. The joy of possessing an attractive piece of equipment can only be derived if it functions faultlessly.

THE SILENT-FILM PROJECTOR

The simplest projectors are silent projectors with the barest minimum of fittings.

The most important function of a projector is the transport of the film, since this determines how often the film can be presented faultlessly. These simple projectors are sometimes fitted with rubber cylinders to transport the film. The cylinders are normally conical, which means that the film is only guided at the edge, the middle remains untouched. In some models, however, contact is made between the cylinder and the entire width of the film, which necessarily causes the gradual appearance of running marks on the film. Usually after ten presentations the film is full of running stripes, which cannot be removed. Hence a film which has taken great pains to produce is rendered at least partially worthless.

Projectors in the standard range are better equipped. The film is transported mechanically and more reliably, since the perforation of the film is guided over sprockets. Thus the film is transported at the edge only, and since moved by two rollers, this is done evenly. Hence when purchasing a projector particular attention should be paid to the method of film transportation, since this has a considerable bearing on the quality of the projection.

Projection Lamp

Modern silent- and sound-film projectors are fitted with halogen lamps, which provide considerably more light than the lamps previously in use. The ideal light form would be a dot-shaped light source, preferably inserted into the optical system. Halogen lamps come closest to this ideal. They have considerably smaller filaments than other projection lamps.

Modern projection lamps burn with a low voltage of 12 or 24 volts or 24 volts, and some with 8 volts, all of which require smaller filaments than lamps for 110 or 240V. mains voltage. However low voltage supplies demand a transformer which reduces the usual mains voltage of 240 volts to the operating voltage of the lamp used. These transformers are built into low-voltage projectors.

The most popular types are halogen lamps with the following voltages:

8 volt - 75 watt
12 volt - 100 watt
24 volt - 150 watt

These lamps are produced in two styles: the older lamp has a valve base and is about the size of a flash lamp. It can only be used if the projector has a permanently fixed concave mirror, which totally projects the light for the projection on to the film gate. The second type of lamp is of more modern construction, and is itself fitted with a projection mirror. This has the advantage that when the lamp is changed, a new mirror is immediately available. Certainly these lamps are rather more expensive on account of the concave mirror, but mirror and lamp are fundamentally at the correct distance

Halogen lamp

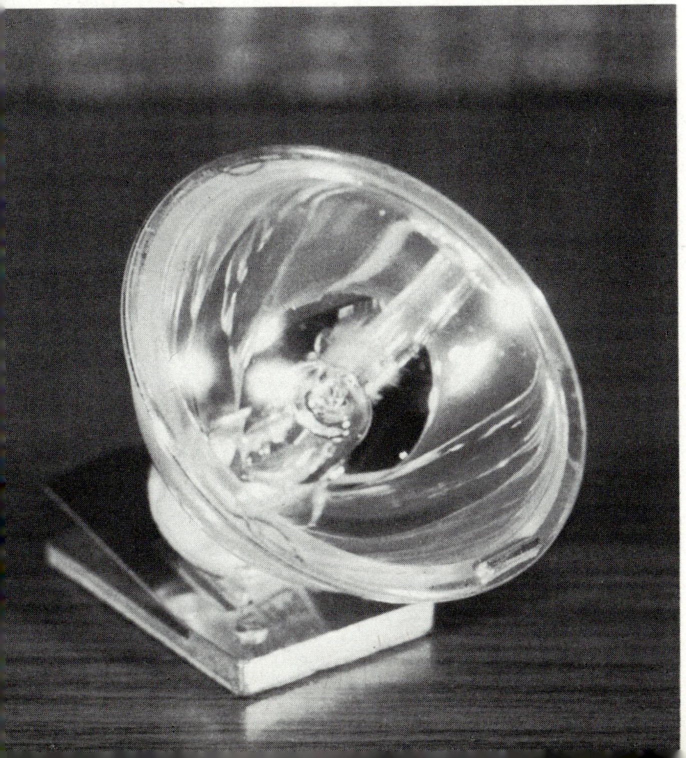

from each other, so the question of lamp centring becomes a thing of the past. While this type of lamp becomes equally as hot as any other, since it is directed at the lens, the outer-case of the projector will only be warm, whereas previously much of the equipment became extremely hot. On the other hand, the light and the halogen lamp will be equally hot; their burners require an operative temperature of 300°C.

Fan

The heat means that the film projector must possess a fan, in order to protect the film and the film gate. The effect must be powerful enough to ensure that all parts of the projector, with which the film has direct contact, are adequately cool, but on the other hand it must not be so loud that the fan noises disturb the performance, particularly since a second motor to transport the film is also in operation. This second motor and the fan must together be as quiet as possible. This is a point to check before purchase, by paying close attention to the noise level. Should there be a choice between a number of otherwise equivalent projectors, preference should be given to the quietest.

Film Transport and Operation

Mention has already been made of the second motor necessary for film transport, which also powers the claw which passes the film in front of the film gate of the projector. The claw has a very important function.

In principle, the film is transported in the same way as in the camera. A rotary-disk shutter rotates behind the film gate, between the lamp and the film, as in the camera. While the dark sector covers the film gate, the claw brings the next frame into position in front of the film gate. The frame is projected in the light sector, and this as in filming, occurs 18 times per second. Smooth presentation of the film depends on the exact adjustment of the claw and the rotary-disk shutter.

A speed of 18 f.p.s. is the standard setting for film presentation, identical with the ciné-camera speed. If the projector were to run rather slower than the camera during filming, the result when projected would be a slow-motion effect.

However some projectors possess a setting which allows the film to be presented at various speeds for specific purposes. A slow-motion or time-lapse effect can be produced by altering the running time when the film is projected, even if this was not originally intended during filming. The film might be presented at three frames per second: if it was taken at eighteen frames per second, this means it is presented at a sixth of the original speed.

Such effects can be useful if certain sequences of movement are to be reduced to their individual parts, for instance in sport. This has been discussed in detail in the section on image frequency. An automatic finishing process in manufacturing can also be further clarified in the projector, if a slow-motion setting could not be used for filming, or indeed the necessity for one did not reveal itself until later.

However, only a few projectors are fitted with an adjustable projection speed, and as a rule the setting is only very rarely used. On the other hand nearly all equipment can be used at 24 f.p.s., for use with purchased ready-processed film. Filming in professional circles is almost exclusively executed at 24 frames per second, and hence such films must also be presented at this frequency.

With regard to running speed, there is one common mistake; if a speed other than the normal speed of 18 f.p.s. is used on the camera to achieve a specific effect, the projector must still of course be set on 18, since the desired effect would not otherwise be apparent. For instance, if a time-lapse sequence is taken at nine frames per second, and when reproduced the projector was set to 9 for this scene, the time-lapse effect would be neutralised. The corresponding setting of camera and projector, though fundamentally correct, must be reversed in a special case of this type.

Single-Frame Presentation

Some projectors are designed to facilitate single-frame presentation. If one assumes that the film should capture life and movement, a single-frame setting is in itself not 'film-like', it resembles a presentation of slides. However, there are cases in which an individual frame should be retained on the screen for a longer time, which this setting allows.

However, with regard to a single-frame presentation, it must be remembered that it is not good for the film to remain at the film gate for a protracted length of time, on account of the heat in the projector, since this reaches a considerable temperature in spite of the cooling system. The film becomes very hot at one point, dries out, and might easily tear later at that point. Consequently a single frame should not be presented too often at the same point in the film. Since the cooling of the equipment is often dependent on the running speed of the projector, the fan turns faster at a higher speed, and will be least effective when the film is stationary.

There is yet another argument against repeated observation of single frames: nearly all film frames are individually unfocused. The exposure times corresponding to the individual speeds have been discussed in detail elsewhere. Hence single-frame presentations of a ciné film and the projection of transparencies cannot be compared with each other.

The Lens

The lens is an important component of the projector, though in some equipment it is often found to be of rather poor quality. In this case distortion occurs, which means that the sides of the picture are distorted, the corners are dark, and partially unfocused. Consequently it is of the utmost importance to compare the optical systems of the different models before making a purchase.

Modern projectors are fitted with a variable-focus lens, which is not of course adjustable to the same extent as the zoom lens in a camera. In a projector they can be adjusted within a range of focal length of about 12 to 30 millimetres, but often the limits are even narrower. The 'normal' focal length during projection is about 15 millimetres, similar to that of the camera. This is sufficient, since the projection lens must only be adjusted until the projected picture acquires the desired size on the screen.

Obviously the quality of the projection lens has a determining effect on the presentation of the film. To buy a high-class camera but a cheap projector would be a false economy. A good ciné camera deserves an equally good projector.

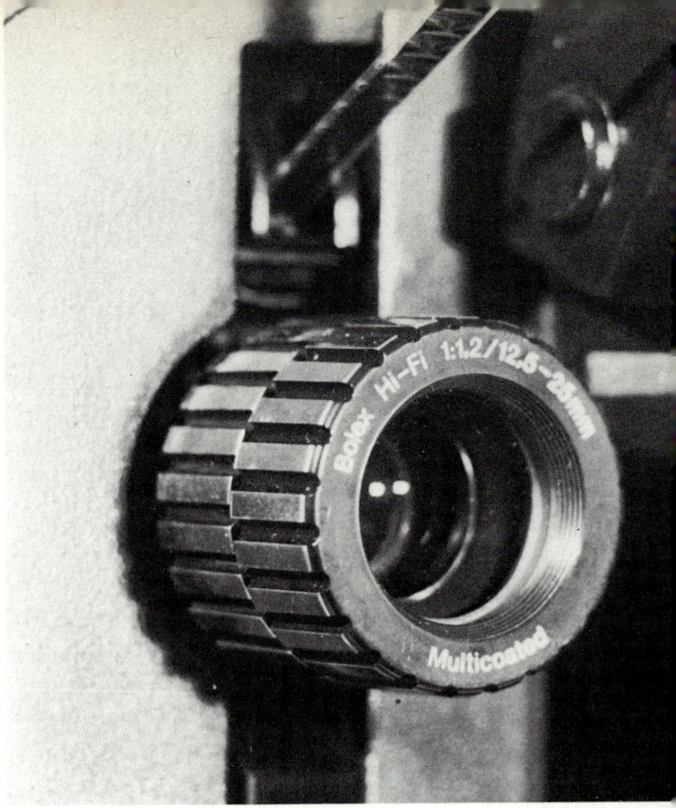

Variable-focus lens of a film projector

Automatic Threading

In previous years there were hardly any ciné projectors with automatic threading, and even if it were present, it frequently failed to function. Today very few manufacturers produce equipment that does not possess this automatic device, which has become an integral part of even the simplest film projectors. The film is secured into the inlet opening and runs through the projector automatically. If a take-up spool is used, the film even threads itself automatically onto the spool. This automatic spool process is included as part of the basic equipment of most projectors.

Size of Spools

Finally a word on the size of the spools accommodated by the film projector. The maximum most equipment can take is a 120m. spool, so one spool can contain eight 15m. films. Experience suggests that this size provides the right length of film, namely about half an hour. If considerably longer films have been compiled, they will of course require a projector which can take larger spools, but even in this case, a break after 25 minutes is to be recommended.

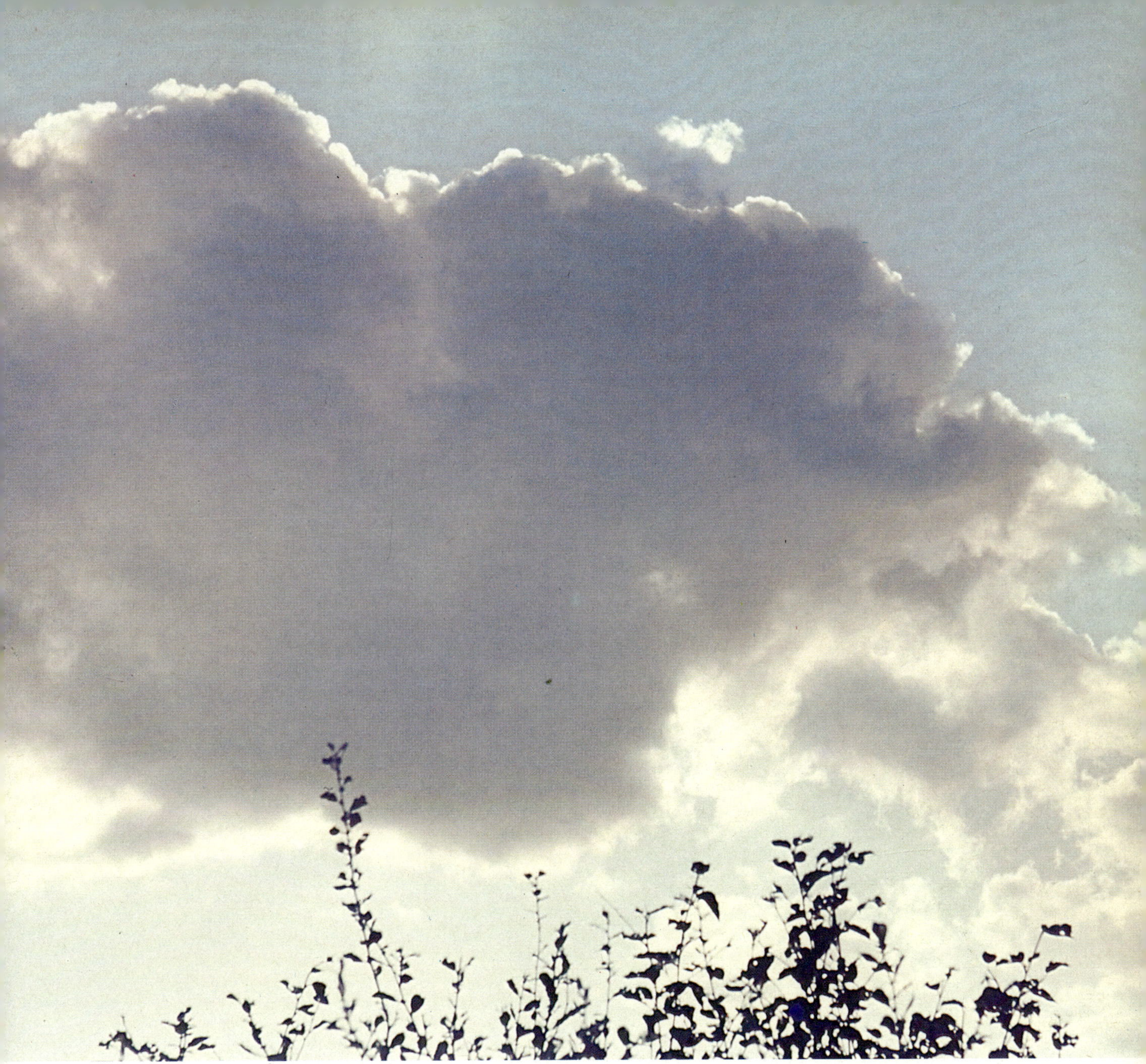

Plate 21: Cloud formations such as these are eminently suitable for a film with an extreme time-lapse setting. The clouds then move across the screen very quickly.

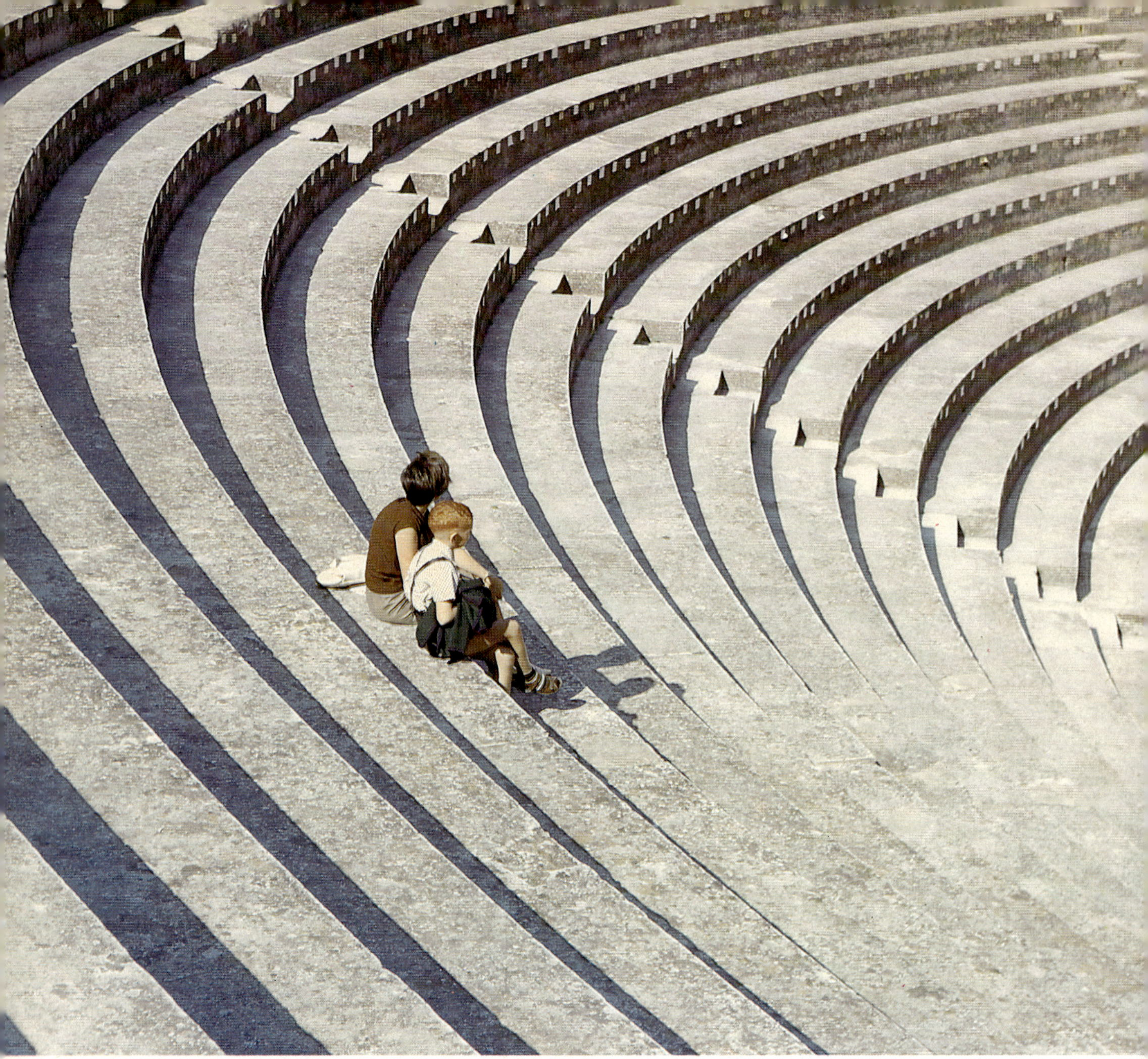

Plate 22: In a film, the landscape and the people must combine to form one unit. In this scene the couple were filmed descending the steps of the amphitheatre

Most projectors are designed for spools of this size, a few for shorter, and some for longer films. This is a point to consider when buying.

EQUIPMENT FOR SILENT OR SOUND FILM

Some silent-film projectors can be transformed into sound-film projectors by virtue of an accessory, namely,those projectors which can be operated in conjunction with a cassette recorder via a connecting cable, so that tape and film are run simultaneously. In this system it is important that the corresponding running of film and sound is ensured.

Such equipment can be distinguished from silent projectors only insofar as they possess the potential to be connected with various types of sound equipment. All the other functions remain unaltered.

In the chapter on sound film it has already been stated that normally any projector can be adapted for two-way scoring. A few other models, those referred to here, are designed for this from the outset. In practice, however, it seems that very little use is made of this dual usage. Usually such equipment is only bought in order to be able to keep that option open; later one frequently decides nevertheless to buy another projector with an integral sound system.

THE SOUND-FILM PROJECTOR

This category includes all equipment which contains an integral sound system. Some reference to the points already mentioned in relation to film scoring cannot be avoided here.

In recent years, sound-projectors have appeared on the market in confusing quantity, and it is easy to be rather bewildered by the enormous choice available. On the other hand, this abundance indicates a distinct tendency towards the use of sound film. Obviously a silent film can also be presented on these projectors.

Much of the description referring to the silent-film projector can of course be equally applied to the sound-film projector. However, since the fittings are necessarily more expensive, their prices are always higher than those of silent-film equipment, to some extent quite considerably so.

With sound-film projectors it becomes even more important for the operating noises to be very slight; the sound track must be audible above the projection noises! Equally, more critical than in the silent projector is the constant running speed of the film. Without sound it would be barely noticeable whether a film is presented at 18 or 19 frames per second. The movement itself is even faster, and small variations are not apparent. However, if the film is scored, such changes become perceptible acoustically. The ear reacts more sensitively than the eye,

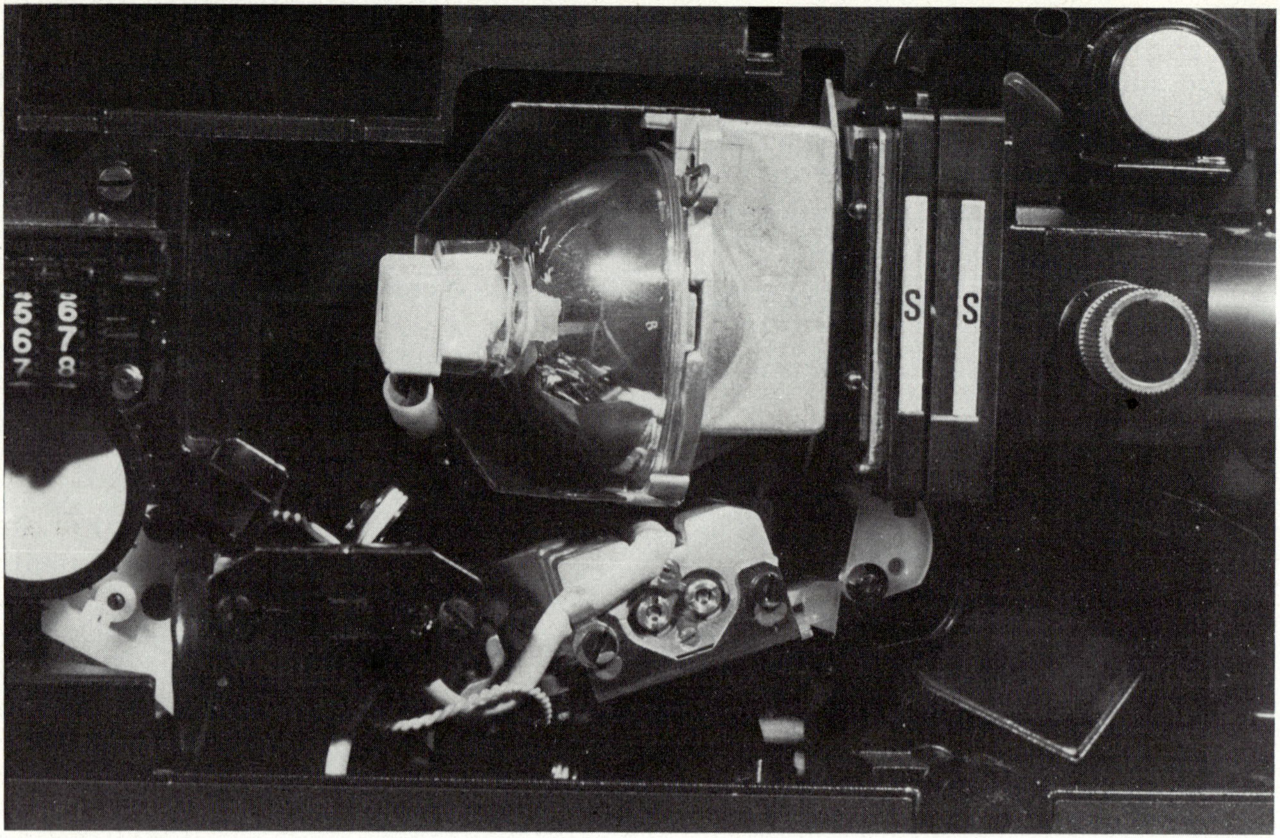

Sound projector open. The halogen mirror lamp is in the centre, beneath it are the sound heads

and hence great importance is attached to synchronisation.

All sound-film projectors are larger than silent-film equipment, since the sound elements require additional space.

Since the films become somewhat thicker when a soundtrack is added, obviously less sound film will fit on a spool than silent film. Consequently much sound-film equipment is designed to accommodate larger film spools. A 120m. sound-film requires the same spool as approximately 140m. of silent film; the next usual spool size is for 180m. It does not matter that sound films tend to be longer, since the optical effect is combined with an acoustic one, and this is far less tiring for the audience.

The different sound systems have been discussed in detail elsewhere: projectors with built-in cassette recorders, magnetic sound projectors, and stereo sound projectors with double-sided sound track. They can be distinguished only by their sound elements, otherwise their functions correspond to those of the silent-film equipment.

Every projector must be mastered thoroughly before the first performance is given. Sometimes faults occur while the projector is in operation, and to this end all the necessary handling must also be practised in darkness.

Finally a word concerning the changing of lamps. Obviously a projection lamp will not last for ever. One can reckon on an average life expectancy of 25 to 40 hours, though this can differ greatly in differing lamps. As a rule only a rough estimate, if any at all, can be made of how many hours a lamp has burned, and consequently one can rarely anticipate when it will fail: it should be a matter of course to have a spare lamp permanently in the house. Naturally, one must also be able to replace the lamp, and this must be practised several times. This is not a great difficulty with any equipment, but one does need to practise it in advance. The same also applies to a silent-film projector.

PROJECTION ACCESSORIES

The accessories in this field are limited, but they are generally necessary.

Projector Case

The projector is larger than the camera, and this necessarily creates a problem – where to put the equipment when it is not in use. The best solution is a carrying and storage case, which not only looks tidy, but also has enough space for all the necessary accessories, that usually form the basic equipment: spare lamp, spool, mains cable, sound connecting cable etc. Each component has its own allotted place in the case.

Projection Table

A projection stand is indispensable if there is no table available to hold all the equipment. A projection stand can be folded up like a ladder and requires hardly any space, a factor which is often very important. Above all, however, a projection stand guarantees a stable base for the projector and has, additionally, an extra surface on which one can place a spool, a spare lamp, and other accessories. Light and easily transported, the projection stand can be set up anywhere without difficulty.

There are also small projection stands that can be placed on a table so that the projector is at the right height.

For film makers who possess a tripod, there is also a projection platform which fits

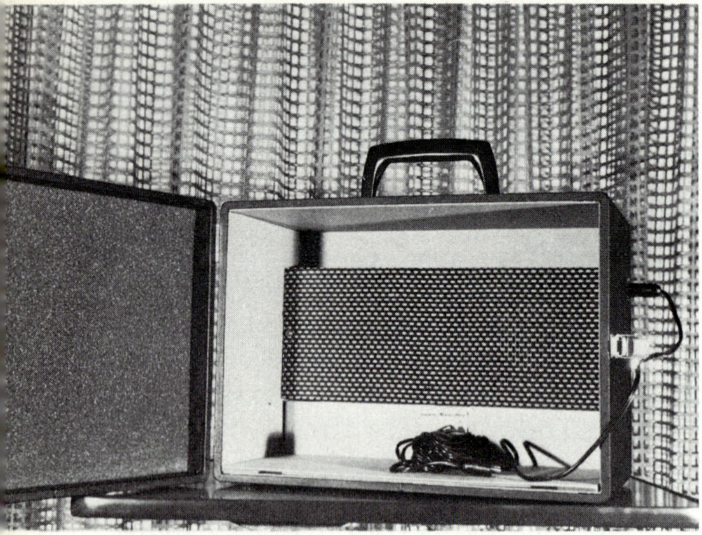

Sound case open

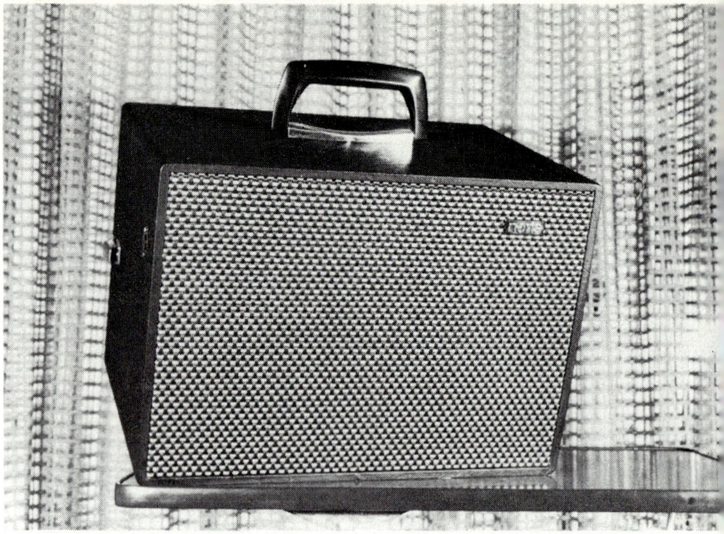

Sound case closed

onto a tripod. These wooden or plastic platforms have enough space to accommodate the projector. They are screwed onto the tripod (which is of course only advisable with an absolutely firm tripod, preferably one with a central support). A projector, particularly a sound projector, is quite heavy. Though the projection platform might appear to be a convenient solution, it is not always totally foolproof.

THE PROJECTION SCREEN

Projectors would be pointless and film presentation impossible without a projection screen. It is well known that there are numerous ways of projecting a film. Many surfaces could be used for projection, but usually provide only a makeshift solution. What characteristics must a projection screen possess in order to provide the best possible quality of film projection?

Firstly the setting in which the performance is to take place is important. If one merely wants to test a film at home, a white wall or door will suffice, but otherwise better projection and above all a larger picture is essential. The correct size can be achieved with a hung-up sheet or white tablecloth, but they cannot usually be stretched so taut that all the folds are eliminated, yet a projection surface free of

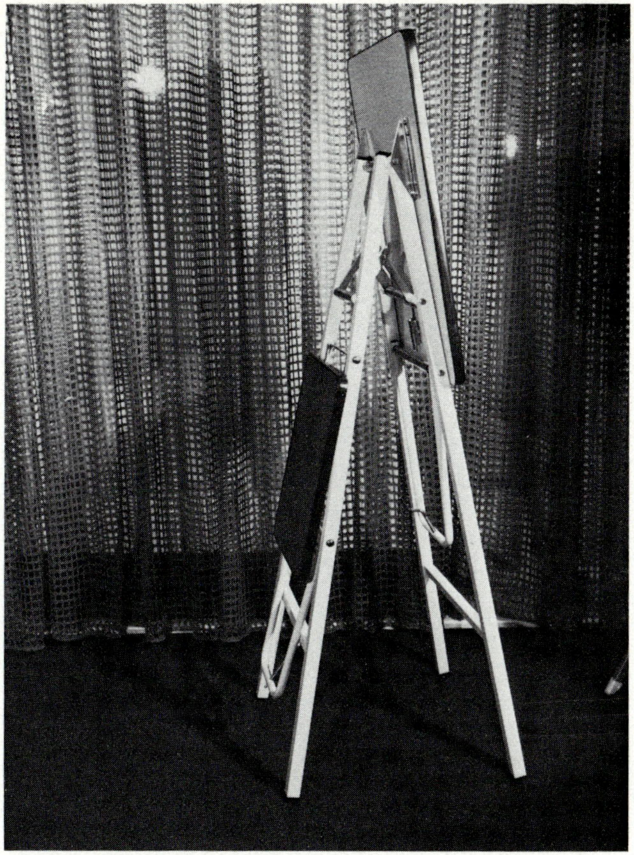

Projection table folded up

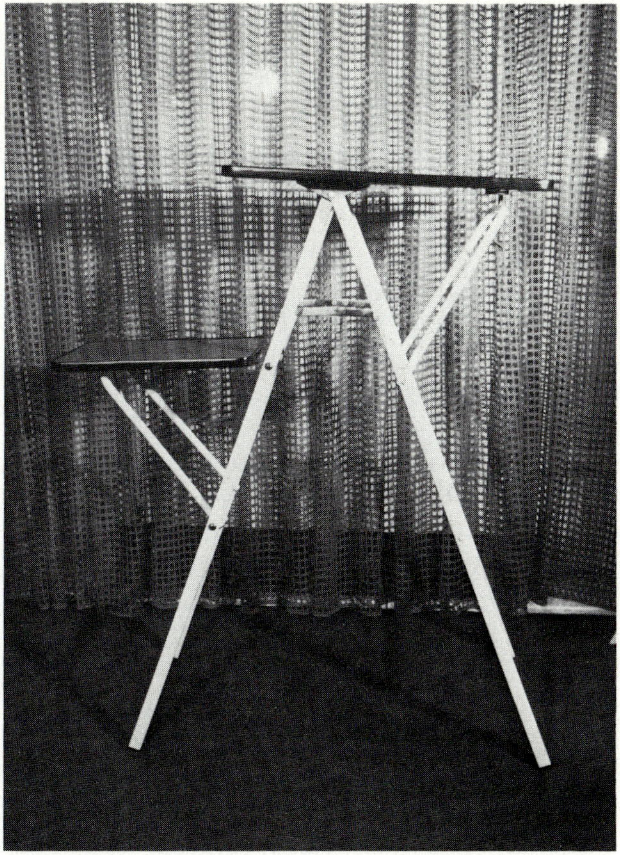

Projection table open

folds is absolutely essential. Folds in the surface result in lack of definition, and shadows and stripes in the picture.

Anyone who believes that he can save on the expense of buying a screen is usually cured of the belief once he has seen a projection on a really good screen. In any case one often has quite false notions of the cost of such a screen: it is in fact the cheapest of all the equipment mentioned up until now, and to be mean about its purchase would be almost grotesque!

There are three different types of screen: the normal white screen, the crystal-beaded screen, and the daylight screen. The size and mechanical construction of the frame have nothing to do with the three types.

Normal Screen
A normal screen consists of a thick material, the surface of which is snow white. This smooth surface guarantees an optimally focused picture. The structure of the screen is levelled by the special treatment of the surface.

Crystal-Beaded Screen
The most widely used type of screen is certainly the crystal-beaded screen. The surface is sprayed with small crystal beads. In a good-quality screen these are so small that they can barely be recognised as little beads with the naked eye.

In contrast to the normal screen, this screen has the advantage of a brighter projection since the crystal beads have a greater power of reflection, although this does imply one limitation: the crystal screen has a very sharp reflection angle, so that only those sitting in an almost straight line in front of the screen can see an altogether brighter picture. Anyone sitting at the side sees a darker picture, sometimes even darker than on a normal screen.

A crystal-beaded screen is very suitable for presentations made in a long, narrow room, but if a number of people are dispersed around the room, perhaps sitting around a table, the normal reflecting screen is to be preferred, since then everybody can see an equally bright picture.

There are also other reasons which can make a white reflecting screen preferable to a crystal-beaded screen. It is certainly true to say that the picture on the former screen is better defined, since the structure of the crystal beads without doubt disrupt, the focus. Opinion is divided as to whether the brightness or a better-defined picture is the most important factor of projection. Most people give priority to greater brightness since they believe that a picture cannot be produced brightly enough. Thus there are two opposed views, both of which have something on their side. Everyone makes their own decision depending on which factor they value most.

Daylight Screen
A third type of screen is the so-called daylight screen. This is a projection screen with a silver-coloured surface, often of synthetic material, which can be used in semi-dark rooms without further darkening.

This is the most modern of the range of projection screens, and is used especially where rooms cannot be darkened at all, or only imperfectly. This is for instance an advantage should one want to show films or transparencies on a light summer's evening, but there is only an undarkened room available.

Other Types
Besides these three types of screen there are several others, though they are only seldom used.

A plastic screen made of synthetic material is good value for money. It usually has a linen surface, but by no means has the luminosity of a genuine linen screen.

Stand up or Hang?

Whether the screen is stood up or hung depends very much on conditions. Some screens can be hung up regardless of the type of projection surface, and these resemble the big maps found in schools. This type of screen has the advantage that it requires hardly any space when it is rolled up, but has the disadvantage that it requires a wall hook or similar, which cannot be inserted into every wall. Moreover this type of screen must be left to hang for a few minutes before projection commences, so that the folds produced by rolling it up are given time to disappear.

A greater part of the available range of screens is occupied by those that can be stood up. Usually these are combined with a metal tripod with a spanning device, so that the folds caused by rolling it up are immediately smoothed out. This type of screen is also practical since its height can be altered within a considerable range. The best position for the screen is centrally in front of the projector. If the projector has to be tilted because of the height, this necessarily results in a distortion of the projected picture, in other words the sides of the picture no longer seem parallel to each other and the picture tapers towards the top or bottom. The screen and projector can only be in line with each other if the heights of both coincide, which is absolutely essential for a straight picture with right-angled corners. Consequently the possible height adjustment of a screen is an important factor, and makes handling very easy.

Permanent Installation

Anyone possessing a projection room can have a screen permanently installed. This is without doubt the best method, but also the most expensive. There are various installation alternatives, allowing for the selection of one suited to the room used. For instance, a screen stretched on a sturdy wooden frame with adequately long screws can be fixed to any wall. This is the best type of screen because no folds are allowed to form. Since the screen is permanently left hanging, it will of course gather dust. Some film makers with a projection room hang a curtain over the screen, as this covers the screen when not in use and has the deceptive appearance of a window - which architecturally is a very clever solution.

There is another type of screen equally suitable for permanent installation. This is built into the ceiling like a roller blind, rolling up into a box which is either positioned on the ceiling or built into it. The screen is pulled down by a long hook, disappearing into the ceiling again after the performance. For those who desire every convenience the rolling up and down can be controlled by a button, the movement being operated by an electric motor.

Size of the Projection Screen

The above description of screens said

nothing about their size, being solely concerned with their composition and performance, which is of course related to price. The size is governed exclusively by the distance which is to lie between the projector and the screen. The opinion that a large picture is better than a small one is only partially correct. It is true that a large picture is good for large distances. When a film is shown, it is important that there is a certain relationship between the distance of the audience from the screen and the size of the projection. The best impression is achieved if the distance between the screen and the audience is about two and half times the length of the picture diagonal. A practical example of this: the correct screen size has to be found; the room is about 5m. long, and the plan is to purchase a screen which can be set up in different places; consequently the distance from wall to wall cannot be taken as a basis: room for the projection table must also be included, so that an average value of a distance of 4m. is arrived at:

Picture diagonal = approx. 1.60m.

2½ times this length = 4m.

Thus we have a basis for determining the size of the screen. Since the screens are usually square, a screen of 1.25 x 1.25m. would be approximately right for this room. The variable-focus lens on the projector can also be used to further compensate for slight differences.

This example shows in this case a larger screen would have been a mistake. Certainly the variable-focus lens can be used to enlarge the projected picture. but it is better used only to regulate it, since the picture would otherwise become rather too large and hence ill-defined.

Most screens are quadratic since they are also used for transparencies, and the format here must be quadratic on account of the varying vertical and horizontal shots. Anyone who does not want to project slides or who wants to purchase a screen especially for film projection, might purchase a rectangular screen. There are even models which have a black edge, which is not supposed to be a mourning edge, but to serve as a definite picture edge. The edge of the picture can easily appear rather jagged because of the dust which gathers at the edges, but this problem is eliminated by a black edging. One simply has to set the picture with the aid of the variable-focus lens so that it overlaps the black edge by a few centimetres, in order to guarantee a flawless picture edge. Screens with a black edge cannot of course be used for transparencies.

The most popular screen sizes are well known. Sizes with a side length of 1m. upwards are usual.

Projection surface	Distance of audience
100 x 100cm.	approx. 3m.
125 x 125cm.	approx. 4–5m.
150 x 150cm.	approx. 6m.
200 x 200cm.	approx. 8m.

Apart from this there are screens designed for permanent installation in all the desired sizes. A small theatre or gymnasium is essential to exploit the benefit of the larger sizes. In living rooms a screen of more than 2 x 2m. would seldom be of use.

ARRANGEMENT OF EQUIPMENT

The arrangement of the equipment is of course always to some extent dictated by one's personal situation. How the camera is set up, and in which position, is nearly always dependent on the size of the room. However, there are a number of elementary factors to be considered.

The lamp in the projector is designed to burn in a vertical position, which means that the projector must not be tilted too dramatically.

Although the accumulation of heat in the lamp remains unaltered. its position necessarily lessens the distance from the filament to the glass covering. An incorrect positioning of the lamp can occasionally result in the lamp overheating, because of the one-sided heating, and the bulb becomes soft and deformed.

An element of danger is added if the cables are not laid in an orderly manner. Mains cables, sound cables to the loudspeaker, etc. must be laid so that no one can trip over them in the darkness, since this might not only cause harm to a person, but it could also pull down the valuable equipment.

A tip for the arrangement of the equipment: some projection lenses do not have maximum focusing ability in the extreme wide-angle range (at the shortest focal distance). In this case, the setting should be avoided whenever possible, but otherwise the distance between the equipment and the screen can be to some extent increased. The effect is the same.

If possible the projector should be positioned so that it is accessible from above, in other words, not on a set of shelves, etc. Every projector possesses a built-in fan, which is only necessary to cool the lamp. Usually, it sucks the cold air in from the side and blows out the heated air upwards. If the side, whence the cold air is to be sucked, is blocked, this causes overheating, and the same applies if there is no outlet above the equipment. The projector should preferably be free on all sides, which also makes handling as easy as possible.

COMPILATION OF A FILM PRO-GRAMME

The choice and compilation of a film programme is of course above all dependent on the material available and on the nature of the audience.

One does not need a programme to show friends a film completed after a holiday. In this case, the guests can be given an initial impression of the holiday resort by means of books, postcards, maps, etc., and then the film can be presented as the climax. If the film itself offers sufficient visual and acoustic information about the country and its people, one might also turn directly to the film without pausing for an introduction.

If the programme is to consist of a number of films, their impression should intensify with each film. Obviously the best film is left to last. The film themes must also be arranged with due consideration of the interests of the audience. Every ciné-film maker will strive to ensure that his films contain no deficiences, that they are neatly edited and perhaps faultlessly scored. If silent films and sound films are included in one programme, a good sound film should be used for the finale.

The example shows how different effects can be achieved using the same letters but varying the lighting

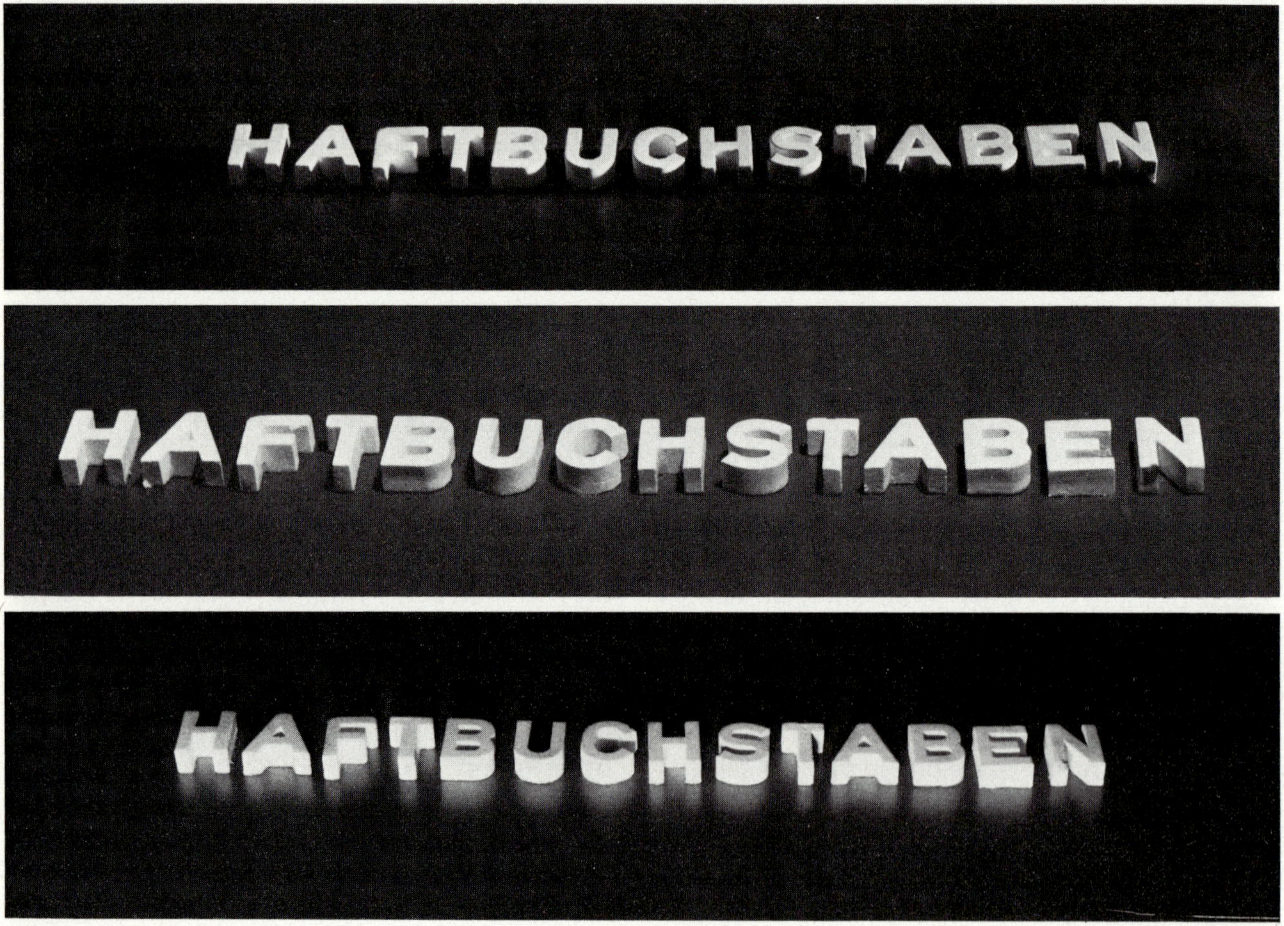

When compiling a programme, one should ensure that it is dominated by short films, and that a longer film is only shown in the first third. The actual projection is obviously of very great value to those watching the film, a point which should not be forgotten when showing films to friends and acquaintances. You were there, and have a personal memory of each scene, but generally, the audience is seeing the films for the first time. They probably have no relation to the film, unless they happen to have travelled with you. Experience shows that it is better not to show the uninitiated audience several films at once. The exaggerated personal content of most amateur films is of only peripheral interest to those not directly involved.

If the film library allows the composition of a programme which is both amusing and rich in variety, the guests might compile a chosen programme for themselves. This requires about ten films, from which four or five, depending on the length, are chosen by the guests. Then all those present are guaranteed their enjoyment.

Many ciné-filmers shy away from the idea of occasionally showing a bought film alongside their own, though there exists a very wide range of ready-made films, usually cuttings from cinema or television films. Many of the films are very well made, in a way no amateur could achieve, and a mixture of these productions with one's own can be extremely attractive.

Imagine a chidren's party, during which the mother or father shows a couple of Disney films as a surprise. For the children, this can be the climax of the party, and it will long continue to delight them; the adults can also enjoy a laugh over the funny figures.

The selection and composition of a film programme is of course only conceivable if the film collection is well ordered. We have already discussed in detail the best method of presenting films, which includes labelling and storing them. When a number of films have been shown it is extremely important that the right film is put away in the right cassette and returned to the right place, so that everything runs smoothly next time.

Finally we come to our last theme, which is a fitting way to close the book.

CARE OF THE EQUIPMENT

The equipment needed for ciné filming is all of a highly technical nature and naturally demands special care. The camera, projector, and the accessories occasionally form part of a 'large-scale operation', particularly in holiday time, when the camera is put to daily hard work, and again when the film is edited and scored, at which point the viewer and projector are much in demand.

As a rule, care of the camera takes priority with most ciné-filmers; psychologically this is understandable, but in practice it cannot be justified. The projector, viewer, splicer, and the other accessories, above all however the films, demand an equal amount of special and necessary care.

Although this care has already been alluded to in some of the chapters, the aim of this section is to discuss the topic as a whole, in order to stress its importance. Experience has shown that the care of the entire film equipment is not always taken sufficiently seriously.

CAMERA AND ACCESSORIES

The camera lays at the centre of the whole process. It is the piece of equipment most often in use, and hence given the most care and cleaning after use, but is this always done properly?

The first rule is to avoid carrying the camera in a hold-all or case. It is most carefully and safely packed in the bag which belongs to it. The original bag offers the best mechanical protection for the camera; the designers and manufacturers are best acquainted with the vulnerable points of the camera, and the bags are correspondingly made with added protection for the most sensitive areas.

Care of the camera also includes its inspection during filming. Sand might get into the camera at any time, or a finger print might appear on the front lens. Dust may enter the film gate when the film is changed. The batteries should also be checked regularly.

Cleaning the Optical System

The lenses in a camera are of glass and hence give the impression that they are easily broken. However this is not wholly true, since the lens in its brass mounting is not as unstable as is generally supposed. The front lens is indeed sensitive, but is well protected from all mechanical damage by means of a lens cover or a conversion red 1.5 filter. Of course this does not dispense with the need to remove any dust from all the moveable parts, or fingerprints from the protective filter. Such marks, particularly grease marks,can lead to a lack of definition in the picture. Unfocused photographs and films are frequently produced on holiday, simply because the use of suntan lotion has resulted in greasemarks on the lens.

A soft, fluff-free cloth (e.g. a clean handkerchief) or a special lens-cleaning paper are the most suitable means for cleaning the lens. Most of the marks can be removed without difficulty using these aids. A leather can only be used to clean the lens if it is not, as is often the case, full of dust. The dust, which gathers on the surface of the cloth while it is stored in the bag will have the effect of an emery board on the glass surface of the lens.

Sand is the greatest enemy of the camera, and consequently more than average care of the ciné camera is required on a seaside holiday. At best, one should check daily whether there is any sand in the filter screw or in any other moveable part of the camera.

If you realise, when adjusting the distance or the zoom lens that there is sand in the works, you should immediately try to remove it by blowing or repeated turning of the camera. On no account should the camera be cleaned with water. If the sand cannot be removed, a photographic dealer must be consulted, or the camera sent back to the manufacturers for inspection.

Salt water is a danger to any camera. A small splash on the front lens can affect its performance adversely. Salt water in the casing can be harmless, as long as it is removed immediately. If it dries there, a residue of salt may remain, but this can usually be wiped away later. Salt water can only cause serious defects if it reaches the revolving elements of the camera. However, if the camera falls in the sea, which is not impossible, there is little point in repair. A holiday by the sea with a camera is a source of great interest to the ciné filmer, but the technique of filming must include the observation of some safety precautions.

If certain parts of the camera are more difficult to operate than usual, it is often the result of a fall or bang. In this case, one should not attempt to put the matter to rights by using oil. Oil and grease can do much more harm than good, and at this point the camera should quite definitely be in the hands of a dealer.

The batteries are another danger point in any camera, since if they leak they can partially ruin their container or the casing. When changing the batteries, always check carefully to see whether the contacts are

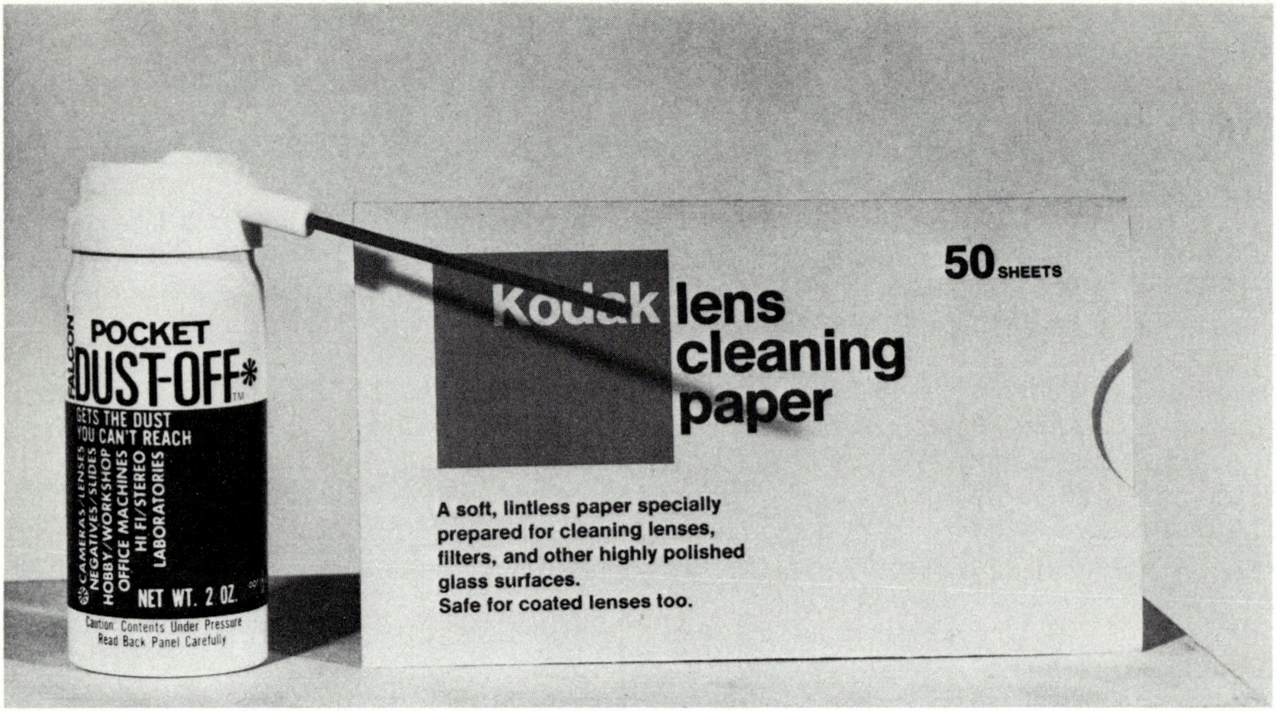

Care of the optical system:
aerosol with compressed air and lens-cleaning paper

uncovered, since even slight oxidation could result in the faulty operation of the camera. If filming is undertaken in a very humid atmosphere, the batteries should be taken out of the camera more often, and the battery compartment checked and perhaps cleaned. Prevention is better than cure!

Care of Accessories

Filters, close-up lenses, trick lenses, and other accessories are made of optical glass, which is considerably softer than normal window glass. Since it is more sensitive to mechanical damage, it requires greater protection. Consequently, the use of purses to protect these parts from scratches is to be recommended. The same applies for the care of these glass components as for the front lens of the camera. It is advisable to use lens paper, since this cleans the most thoroughly.

Bags and purses are usually made of leather and themselves require special attention. A colourless leather grease has proved useful for camera bags etc. A thin layer is applied and left a few days to be absorbed, then rubbed with a soft cloth, which is very important to prevent any grease marks getting on clothing or on the photographic equipment. If a bag gets soaked in the rain or chafed by rocks, it should be treated with grease.

Protection of Unexposed Film Material
This is very important on holiday and some reference should be made to it with regard to equipment care. X-ray security checks at the airport might in some cases damage the films, which is usually indicated at the luggage offices of most airports. Consequently the spare material should be kept at hand so that it can be produced at the control point. If the store of film is extensive, a specially produced film bag can also be used. This is made of a material which protects the films against the rays, and consequently should always be used, if the films have to be transported in a case.

PROJECTOR

Film projectors demand a different type of care from the camera. Since they possess a motor dependent on a mains current (110V. or 240V.), they also incorporate certain sources of danger, as with all equipment of this type. It is important to check that the electric lead from the projector and film viewer is in working order.

As already discussed, a projector becomes very hot due to the growing warmth of the lamp, but on the other hand, every electric motor requires lubrication for it to be able to function faultlessly. The warmth causes the liquid to evaporate from the grease, which will then become thick after a certain time, and the equipment becomes 'resinous'. In order to avoid this, after a certain number of hours of operation, which will be given in the equipment's instruction leaflet, a few drops of oil should be applied to certain places in the projector. The oiling points are usually made clearly visible by red spots, and will be detailed in the instruction booklet.

If the instructions suggest only one drop of oil at one point or another, this is to be taken literally; since one drop will indeed be sufficient for the given time. It can have bad results for both films and motor if too much oil gets into the motor. On the one hand the motor is smeared, and dust sticks firmly to it, on the other hand the film guide and film gate are soiled with the splashed oil. Even the film itself can acquire tiny oil splashes in this way, which can only be removed with great difficulty, if at all. It goes without saying that the camera lens, and above all the back lens, must be protected against oil.

One area of the projector needs regular care, namely, the film gate. Every time a film is shown it will carry dust which is deposited here. It must be removed before the next projection, since the heat will otherwise cause it to burn on to the film gate and it can scratch the film. This results in continuous marks at the edges of the picture, which produce a frayed edge on the screen.

Thus a small cause can have a great effect: it should never be considered too much trouble to remove the dust – this is best done regularly after each performance.

The cleaning of the film gate is best accomplished with a hard brush or paintbrush. Special picture-channel cleaners are also available for this purpose. In any case, the cleaning of the metal elements of the film gate is to be avoided. Even the most careful treatment would undoubtedly result in scratching or bending, since the film gate trap is made of very thin material.

It is important to undertake cleaning when the projector is switched off, in other words, has had a chance to cool. Obviously the equipment must be allowed to cool after each performance, before it is placed back in its case or cabinet. A projection lamp, when hot, is very sensitive to shaking, and for this reason it is very important, for the sake of the life expectancy of the lamp, that the projector is not moved during the showing, and not cleared away until the lamp is completely cool. Projection lamps are quite expensive; improper handling will reduce their life expectancy.

Since dust is attracted by warmth, it is good for the projector if it is also cleaned regularly inside, particularly near the lamp. The condenser and the other glass components become dull if the dust is allowed to remain on them too long, and this has a considerable effect on the picture quality.

If the projector should produce a fault, perhaps the film runs too slowly or unevenly, the best solution is to send the equipment to the manufacturer to be overhauled. Inappropriate intervention is only likely to increase the damage.

The film spools are delivered in boxes, not only to protect the films from dust, but also to ensure that the spool is not bent.

Sometimes an uneven running noise is produced during the presentation, if the wind-on spool on one side is too narrow for the film and grates as it turns. Previously, when metal spools were far more common, this happened far more frequently than with the modern, synthetic spools. If the spools are protected from one-sided pressure when stored, this grating in the projector can be avoided.

FILM VIEWER AND SPLICER

Both these pieces of equipment are used infrequently in comparison to the camera or projector, and perhaps it is for this reason that their care is sometimes neglected. In the chapter on film editing and montage a detailed account has already been given of why this equipment requires particular care, so a summary of this will suffice here.

It is inevitable that the dust mentioned so many times will gather at the film gate of the viewer during editing and montage. Since the film is passed through it a number of times, in order to examine the film and mark

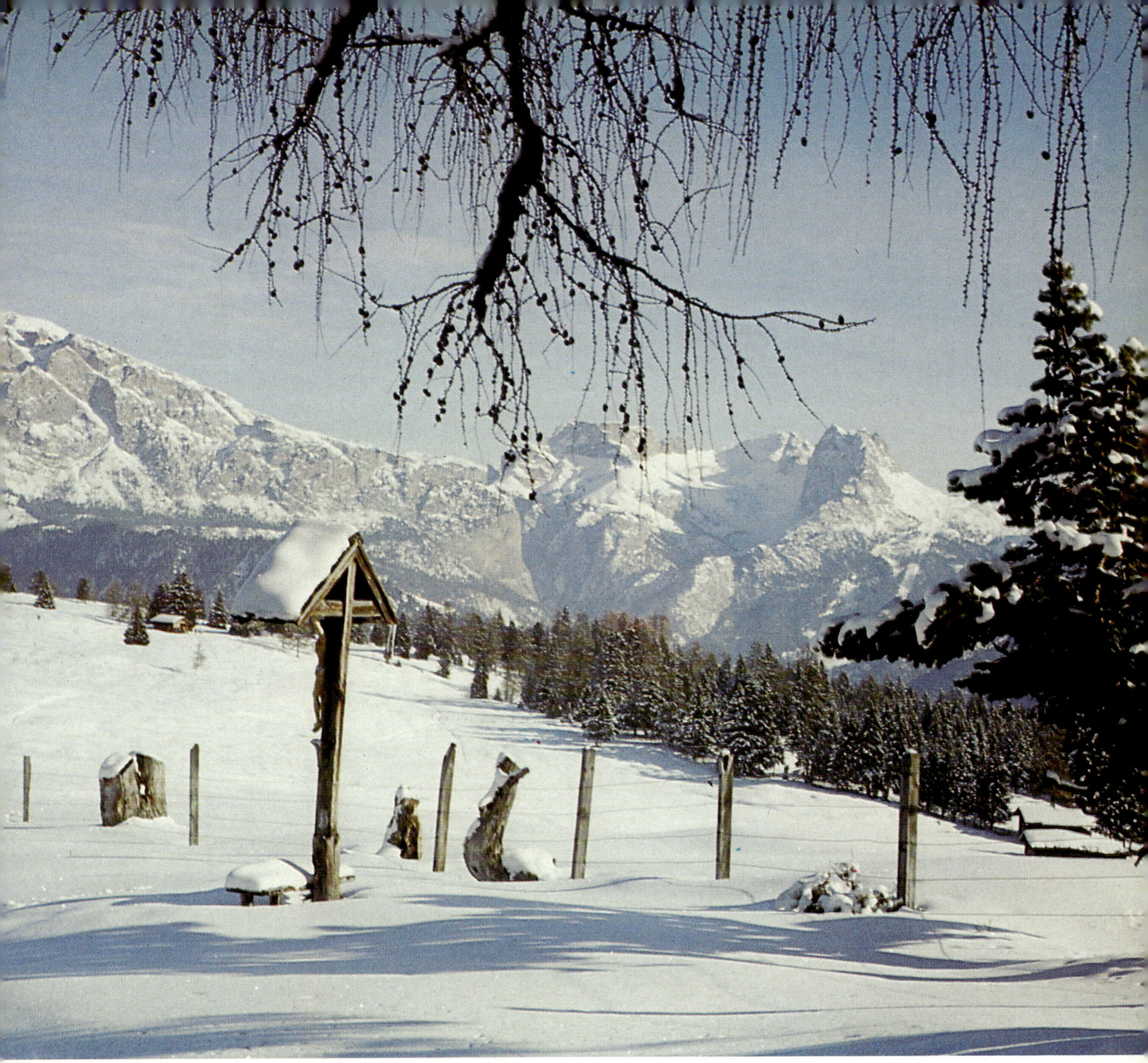

Plate 23: A slow pan away from the ski slope and the skiers to the undisturbed landscape conveys an idea of the charm of skiing

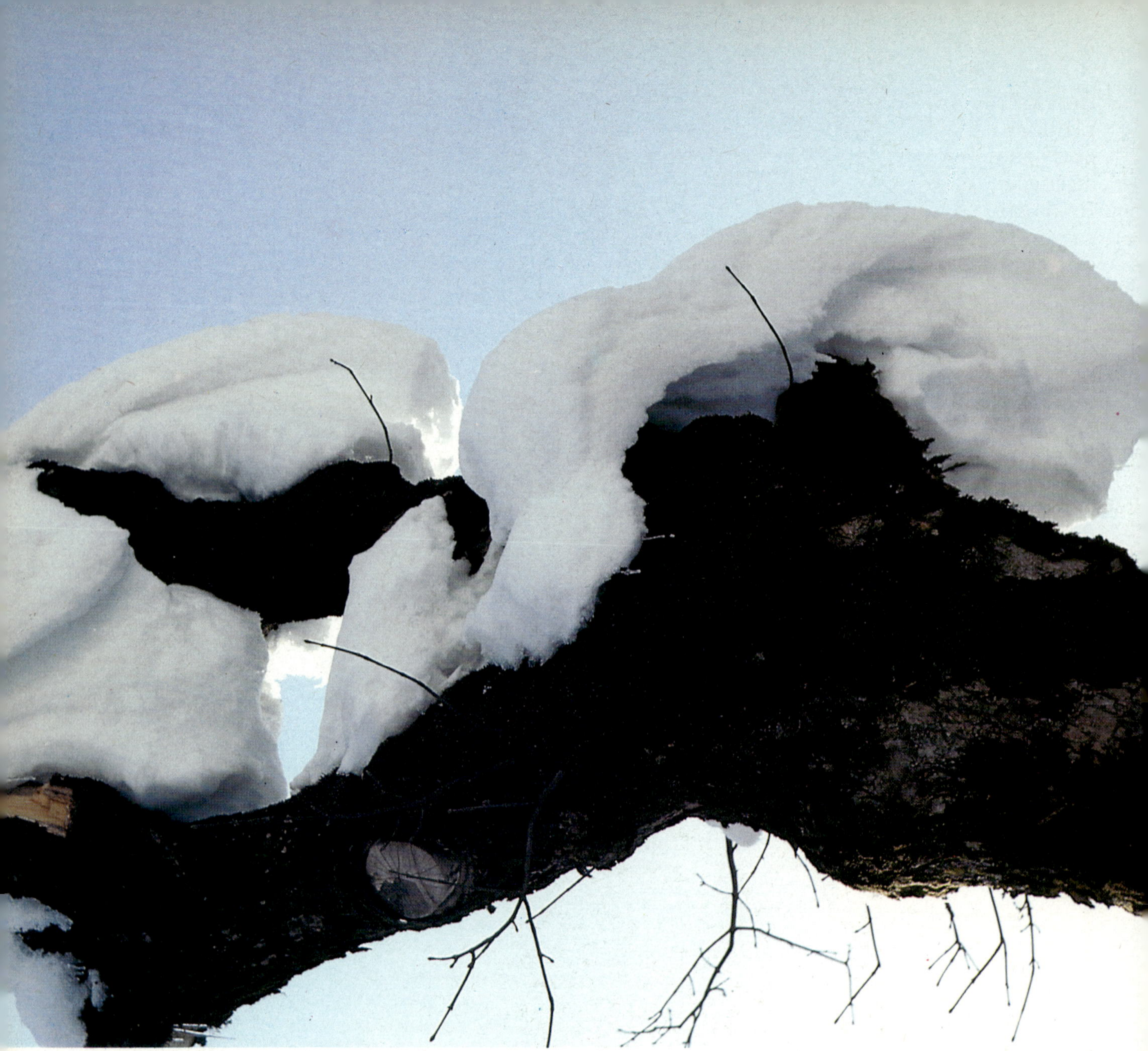

Plate 24: A frozen snow-covered branch says more about the cold than a shot of a thermometer

the right scenes, the dust which collects can produce some very bad scratches. Consequently the dust must be thoroughly removed after each editing, and the equipment stored in a cabinet, or wherever it can be best protected against dust. Indeed there is nothing worse for a ciné film than the effects of dust.

The axles of the film viewer must be lubricated after a certain number of working hours according to the instructions. Of course in most cases they are not electrically powered, but manual operation must function faultlessly.

If the film ends are trimmed in a splicer, this too must be cleaned after each use, since not only must the files work perfectly, but any film dust must be removed immediately. This can be done without any great difficulty, since the parts are easily accessible. ible.

The grinding wheels of an electrically powered splicer must be changed after a few years, and the batteries also require regular checking. Since the splicer derives its energy from the batteries, the same care must be applied here as with the batteries of a ciné camera. If the equipment has not been used for months, the batteries are best removed. Better safe than sorry.

THE FILMS

Storage of the films has already been discussed in detail with reference to the film library. Every film-maker knows that it is essential to clean the films. Films with a sound track should not be stored over or near a loudspeaker box or stereo system. The equipment produces magnetic fields which could affect, or completely or partially erase, the sound on the film. This equipment should not be used as storage space.

INSURANCE COVER

Finally a word on a theme which often does not seem relevant until it is too late: it concerns the protection of all the often very expensive ciné-film equipment.

Every film-maker should consider two possibilities: theft in the home or loss outside it, perhaps while travelling. Frequently neither a house policy nor a luggage insurance is found to cover film equipment.

In particular a normal luggage insurance does not always cover the risks to expensive photographic or film equipment. Many policies include a small-print appendix which allows optical equipment, cameras etc. only 10 or 20 per cent of the insurance amount. It is important to calculate the actual value of your equipment, and to establish how high the insurance must be to provide adequate cover against loss. This applies equally for house and luggage insurance. Many companies offer special insurance for such valuable equipment.

TABLES

Film Running Time

16 m/m		Super-8	2 x 8
18 frames			
1 m	7.3 sec.	13 sec.	14.5 sec.
15 m	1 Min. 49 sec.	3 Min. 16 sec.	3 Min. 39 sec.
30 m	3 Min. 39 sec.	6 Min. 32 sec.	7 Min. 18 sec.
60 m	7 Min. 18 sec.	13 Min. 4 sec.	14 Min. 34 sec.
90 m	10 Min. 57 sec.	19 Min. 36 sec.	21 Min. 51 sec.
120 m	14 Min. 36 sec.	26 Min. 13 sec.	29 Min. 7 sec.
24 frames			
1 m	5.5 sec.	10 sec.	11 sec.
15 m	1 Min. 22 sec.	2 Min. 17 sec.	2 Min. 44 sec.
30 m	2 Min. 44 sec.	4 Min. 54 sec.	5 Min. 28 sec.
60 m	5 Min. 28 sec.	9 min. 49 sec.	10 Min. 55 sec.
90 m	8 Min. 12 sec.	14 Min. 43 sec.	16 Min. 23 sec.
120 m	10 Min. 55 sec.	19 Min. 39 sec.	21 Min. 50 sec.

Running time of a short film of 15 minutes

	18 frames	24 frames
16mm	124 m.	164 m.
Super-8	69 m.	98 m.
Double-8	62 m.	82 m.

Film Speed

Comparison of DIN - ASA film speed
11 DIN - 10 ASA
12 DIN - 12 ASA
13 DIN - 16 ASA
14 DIN - 20 ASA
15 DIN - 25 ASA
16 DIN - 32 ASA
17 DIN - 40 ASA
18 DIN - 50 ASA
19 DIN - 64 ASA
20 DIN - 80 ASA
21 DIN - 100 ASA
22 DIN - 125 ASA
23 DIN - 160 ASA
24 DIN - 200 ASA
25 DIN - 250 ASA
26 DIN - 320 ASA
27 DIN - 400 ASA

DIN Grade = Rating of the light sensitivity of the filming material. (Deutsche Industrie Norm No 4512)
ASA Grade = Light sensitivity rating according to the American Standard Association.

Depth of field table
(figures given in metres)

Focal Distance in mm.	Distance Setting on the camera	Aperture			
		1·8	5·6	11	22
8	∞	1·90— ∞	0·66— ∞	0·38— ∞	0·23— ∞
	3 m	1·15— ∞	0·56— ∞	0·35— ∞	0·22— ∞
	1 m	0·71— 1·79	0·45— ∞	0·32— ∞	0·21— ∞
10	∞	2·84— ∞	0·96— ∞	0·52— ∞	0·29— ∞
	3 m	1·52— ∞	0·76— ∞	0·56— ∞	0·27— ∞
	1 m	0·78— 1·41	0·54—15·5	0·39— ∞	0·26— ∞
12	∞	4·05— ∞	1·34— ∞	0·71— ∞	0·38— ∞
	3 m	1·78— 9·98	0·97— ∞	0·60— ∞	0·35— ∞
	1 m	0·83— 1·25	0·62— 2·79	0·46— ∞	0·31— ∞
15	∞	6·29— ∞	2·05— ∞	1·06— ∞	0·55— ∞
	3 m	2·08— 5·43	1·26— ∞	0·82— ∞	0·48— ∞
	1 m	0·88— 1·15	0·71— 1·70	0·56— 5·45	0·39— ∞
20	∞	11·1 — ∞	3·59— ∞	1·83— ∞	0·92— ∞
	3 m	2·39— 4·02	1·67—14·1	1·17— ∞	0·72— ∞
	1 m	0·93— 1·08	0·81— 1·31	0·68— 1·87	0·53—13·0
25	∞	17·4— ∞	5·57— ∞	2·83— ∞	1·84— ∞
	3 m	2·58— 3·59	1·99— 6·08	1·50—17·6	1·18— ∞
	1 m	0·95— 1·06	0·85— 1·21	0·74— 1·52	0 59—31·9
30	∞	28 44— ∞	9 14— ∞	4 65— ∞	2 83— ∞
	3 m	2·72— 3·35	2·26— 4·44	1·83— 8·28	1·32— ∞
	1 m	0 97— 1·03	0·90— 1·12	0·83— 1·26	0·71— 1·71
40	∞	44·3 — ∞	14·2 — ∞	7·16— ∞	3·52— ∞
	3 m	2·81— 3·21	2·48— 3·77	2·12— 4 99	1·63—13·7
	1 m	0·98— 1·02	0·94— 1·07	0·88— 1 15	0·79— 1·36
48	∞	63·9 — ∞	20·5 — ∞	10·4 — ∞	5·13— ∞
	3 m	2·87— 3·15	2·62— 3·50	2·34— 4·18	1·92— 6·88
	1 m	0·98— 1·02	0·95— 1·05	0·91— 1·11	0·83— 1·23
60	∞	99·8 — ∞	3·19— ∞	16·1 — ∞	7·95— ∞
	3 m	2·91— 3·10	2·73— 3·32	2·52— 3·68	2·16— 4·73
	1 m	0·99— 1·01	0·97— 1·03	0·95— 1·06	0·90— 1·13

Depth of field table
(figures given in metres)

Focal Distance in mm.	Distance Setting on the camera	Aperture 1·8	5·6	11	22
70	∞	136·1—∞	43·75—∞	22·27—∞	11·14—∞
	3m	2·94—3·07	2·81—3·21	2·65—3·45	2·37—4·07
	1m	0 99—1 01	0 98—1 02	0 96—1 04	0 92—1 09
80	∞	169 —∞	54·0 —∞	27·3 —∞	13·5 —∞
	3m	2·94—3·06	2·83—3·19	2·68—3·39	2·42—3·88
	1m	0·99—1·01	0·98—1·02	0·97—1·03	0·94—1·05

(Figures relate to a circle of confusion of 0.02mm.)

PICTURE WIDTH FOR FILM PROJECTION

Focal Distance of the Projection Lens	Distance of Screen-Projector in Metres 2	3	4	5	6	8	10
Super-8							
12 mm	87	132	177	221	266	355	—
15 mm	70	106	142	177	213	284	—
20 mm	52	79	106	133	160	213	267
25 mm	42	63	84	106	127	170	213
30 mm	35	53	71	88	106	142	176
2 x 8							
12·5 mm	70	104	140	—	—	—	—
15 mm	58	87	116	145	175	—	—
20 mm	44	66	88	110	132	176	—
25 mm	35	52	70	87	104	140	—
35 mm	25	37	50	62	75	100	125
16 m/m							
35 mm	55	82	110	137	165	219	384
50 mm	38	58	77	96	115	154	269
70 mm	27	41	55	69	82	110	192

(Figures for picture width in centimetres)

FRAME SIZES OF CINÉ FILM

16mm	10.3 x 7.5 mm	film gate in the camera
Super-8	5.65 x 4.22 mm	
Double-8	4.9 x 3.6 mm	
16 mm	9.6 x 7.0 mm	film gate in the projector
Super-8	5.36 x 4.01 mm	
Double-8	4.5 x 3.3 mm	

Single frames per metre of film

16 mm	131 single frames
Super-8	238 single frames
Double-8	262 single frames

GLOSSARY

Acetate Film - Acetate is the most usual base material for the film emulsion. Nearly all film products are made of acetate material.

Action Viewer *see* **Film Viewer**

Adapter - Used to connect filters, cables, or lenses to screw-threads or sockets of varying sizes.

Animated Cartoon Film - Trick film with drawn figures, made mobile by virtue of the single-frame setting. Hundreds and thousands of drawings and single-frame settings are necesary for an animated cartoon. Each phase of movement must be portrayed by a sequence of numerous different continuous drawings. The animated film has been made famous by Walt Disney, past-master of the technique.

Aperture *see* **Diaphragm**

Artificial Light - Artificially produced light source for filming. Nowadays usually halogen light (3200°Kelvin). *See* **Film Lamp.**

Artificial-Light Film - Super-8 film is an artificial-light film. For daylight filming, a setting in the camera swings a filter into the stream of light. In Double-8 filming there are separate films for artificial light and daylight. A conversion filter (*see* **Conversion Filter**) is used for compensation.

ASA - American Standard Association. American film-speed rating. Shown on every film pack together with DIN rating.

Automatic Exposure Control - Only possible on cameras with a built-in exposure meter.

Automatic Prolonged-Exposure Control - Setting found on good-quality cameras. Measures individual exposures automatically, transporting the film onward after each exposure has been completed. The single exposures must be counted to find the length of the film scene. Some cameras have a single-frame counting mechanism for this purpose. *See* **Interval Timer, Single-Frame Setting.**

Automatic Release - Mechanical or electro-magnetic component, which automatically releases the film scene after a pre-running time and automatically switches off the camera.

B

Back Light - Shines on the subject from the opposite direction to the camera, thus the film is taken into the light (sun or headlamps).

Back-Light Correction - The exposure time (or the aperture) must be extended for shots taken in back light because of the shadows. This is either automatically controlled, or the backlight correction knob is used to open the aperture manually by one stop.

Back-Lighted Shot - Gives the subject contrast and luminosity. All the shadows advance towards the camera, heightening the impression of three-dimensional depth. A border of light around the subject contrasts it with the dark background.

Battery-Powered Tape Recorder - Powered by batteries and thus independent of a mains supply. Particularly suitable for life-sound recording, in conjunction with a ciné camera. Some tape recorders (and cassette recorders) of this type can be coupled with the ciné camera for synchronised sound recordings.

Bi-Fo Lens - Bi-focal close-up lens.

Black-and-White Film - Little used in Super-8 cameras. *See* **Colour Film**

Blend In - Method of blending a title into a film scene with a second shot. Can only be used in film systems where the film can be wound back in the camera (16mm. and Double-8 cameras).

Boom - Telescopic support for the microphone, used for life-sound recording. A boom brings the microphone nearer to the subject, and provides for the same recording direction without encroaching on the angular field of the camera.

Brightening - additional lightening by means of reflection.

C

Camera Buckle - Caused by a fault in the film's wind-on spool.

Camera Hold - Basis of this is the grip with built-in releaser. On many cameras built in as a 'revolver grip', otherwise obtainable as an accessory. If the camera is held by hand it

Flashlight shot of Thai musicians

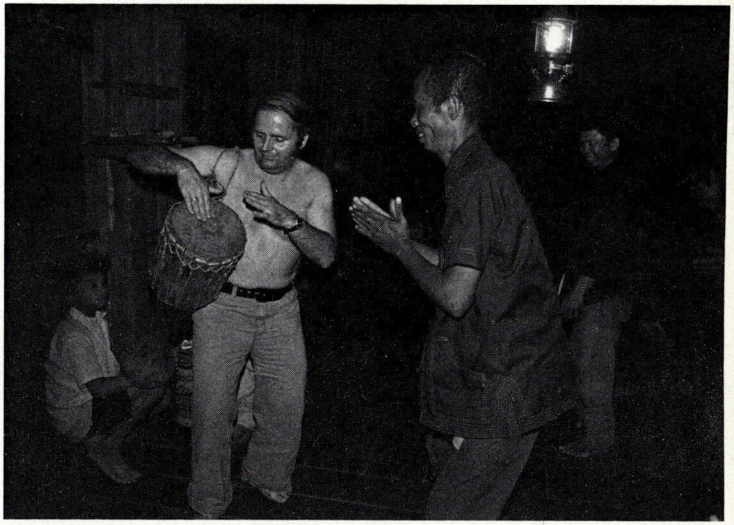

must be steady and not liable to wobble (if possible leant against the body). A shoulder pod or monopod is preferable, or best of all, a firm tripod. *See* **Tripod**

Camera Lens - Lens or group of lenses. In modern cameras a combination of different glass lenses of varying curvature, for which an electronic calculator has compared hundreds of values and corrected any optical faults. A distinction can be made between lenses with a fixed and lenses with a variable focal length: and then again between normal, wide-angle, and tele-range lenses. Each of these lenses can be composed from a combination of different lenses. *See* **Variable Focus Lens.**

Camera Position - Included in the detailed planning of the film in the script.

Camera Settings - Film scenes as stipulated in the script. Altered in accordance with the required dramatic effect and distinguishes between
full length - semi full length
close-up - medium close-up
large - full size.

Car Pod - Usually fixed to the windscreen with suction pads for shots from a moving car.

Cassette - Ciné film: light-proof casing of Super-8 film, inserted in the camera with the film. Still photography: container for films, inserted into the camera (types 110, 126). Sound recording: tape container for a cassette recorder. All cassettes facilitate the rapid and safe insertion or changing of film material.

Ciné Film - All types of film narrower than 35mm. film (normal film), i.e. 16mm; 9.5mm., and 8mm. systems.

Cinemascope - Wide-screen filming and reproduction. The picture is compressed by means of an anamorphic lens accessory during filming, and then rectified again during projection. Usually the ratio of the sides when presented is 1:2.

Clapper Board - Term used in professional filming, where the clapper board is filmed at each scene change, Double function:
1. The board gives the number of the scene and details required later for film editing.
2. As the two parts of the board (clapper) are clapped together at the beginning of each scene, they provide an acoustic signal which is recorded to aid the sound technician in his subsequent synchronisation of sound and film.

Close-Up Shot - Film taken in close-up range. *See* **Macro Shot.** Presents an enlarged image of very small objects. Effective method of enlivening a ciné film. Particularly favoured taking distance for shots of people and animals (easily achieved by means of a long focal-length setting). For close-ups in which the object to be filmed is at a closer proximity to the camera than the closest distance setting can accommodate, additional lenses are used, if no macro zoom lenses is available (*see* **Macro Zoom Lens**).

Colour Film –
a) Colour reversal film. Most ciné films are reversal films, i.e. films which are converted from negative to positive during development in the laboratory.
b) Colour negative film – Negative films, used almost exclusively in professional circles, if several copies need to be produced of one film.

Colour Filter *see* **Filter**

Colour-Correction Filter *see* **Conversion Filter**

The gentle rippling of the waves is an effective addition to film of a walk on the beach

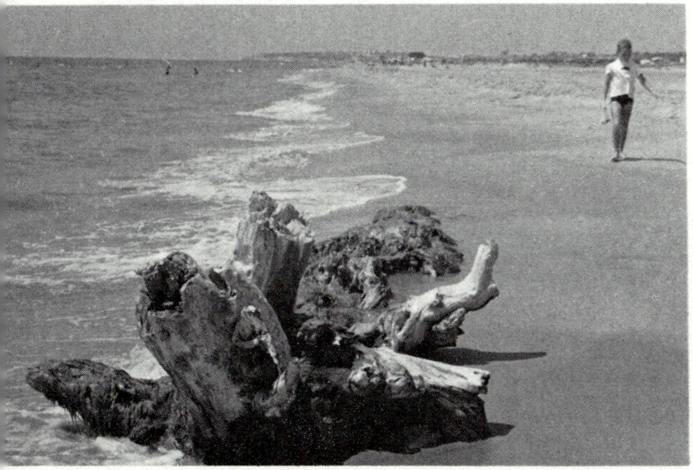

Colour Temperature – Term used in physics for the temperature of the light. The light colour is measured with a measuring instrument according to temperatures on the Kelvin scale: 1° *Kelvin* = Colour temperature of a shining body at 273°.
Low Kelvin grade = red light colouring
High Kelvin grade = blue light colouring
Artificial light, Kelvin grade = 3200° Kelvin
Daylight, Kelvin grade = 5600° Kelvin
Artificial-light and daylight films are regulated to these colour temperatures. Other temperatures ensue from mixed lighting and can be compensated for with a conversion filter.

Compendium – Serves as an adjustable lens hood in large cameras. Also provides a hold for filters, masks, etc in front of the lens of a ciné camera. Compendiums are used predominantly in professional circles, and for film tricks.

Condenser – Lighting system in optical equipment consisting of one or more converging lenses. Uesd in projection equipment, microscopes, and enlarging equipment.

Converging Lines – Perspective distortion. Always occurs when the camera is tilted during filming. Straight surfaces (e.g. architecture) can only be portrayed vertically if the plane of the film is parallel to the plane of the subject filmed. Otherwise converging lines occur.

Conversion Filter – Filter to accommodate the colour temperature of the type of film used. *See* **Filter.** Conversion filters exist in red and blue colours, both in varying gradations. The colour temperature (*see* **Colour Temperature**) of the light is established with colour-temperature measuring equipment, which gives an exact indication of which filter must be used to obtain optimum colour correctness. Exaggerated blue light colour can be subdued by reddish fiters, red colours with blue filters. Conversion filters can be combined. If, for instance, Red-7 is required, a 3 x and a 4 x filter can be imposed on each other.
Abbreviation: Red = CR filter, Blue = CB filter
The most usual types:
CR 1.5 = Skylight filter
CR 12 = Artificial-light film in daylight
CB 12 = Daylight film in artificial light. The aperture must be opened wider in accordance with the density of the filter (with an in-built exposure meter this occurs automatically).

Copy – Duplicate of a ciné film. In principle, copies can be made of all ciné films. Frequently however the copy reveals a considerable deficiency in the quality of focus and colour. The use of negative films is to be preferred. *See* **Colour Film.**

Crystal-Beaded Screen – Screen with microscopically small crystal beads sprayed on to the projection surface.

D

Daylight – Colour films are gauged on the colour temperature of the light from 5,400 – 5,600 Kelvin grades. Daylight corresponds to usual lighting outdoors. Electronic flash equipment produces a colour composition closely resembling that of daylight. In Super-8 equipment the camera must be set on the sun symbol in daylight, with Double-8 films the daylight-type film is used. *See* **Artificial Light.**

Daylight Screen – Projection screen for non-darkened rooms.

Depth of Field – The area for each setting in which the image is sharply focused. The depth of field is determined by the focal length used and the aperture setting.

Diaphragm – Mechanism regulating the intensity of light affecting the film by increasing or decreasing the diameter of the lens. The depth of field is also altered (*see* **Depth of Field**). Controlled automatically in most cameras, but can nearly always be operated manually as well.

DIN Rating - Rating for the light sensitivity of films. Higher DIN values mean greater general sensitivity. DIN = Deutsche Industrie Norm (German Industrial Norm) *See* **ASA**.

Dioptrics - Unit of measurement of the refractive power of a lens or an optical system, a reciprocal value of the focal length, measured in metres. The focal length is therefore dependent on the refractive power of the lens.
10cm. focal distance = 10 dioptrics
The effect of an additional lens is measured in dioptrics.
Close-up lens 1 = lens with 1 dioptric
Close-up lens 2 = lens with 2 dioptrics etc.
The higher the dioptrics of the lens, the nearer the taking position. *See* **Lens**

Direction - Precise instructions concering the creation of individual film scenes. Usually direction is given according to a script. The director gives the instructions, to which all the participants adhere. *See* **Script**

Dissolve - Connection of two film scenes by planned superimposition of frames. Dissolves are an elegant means of transition from one film scene to the next. In modern cameras it is possible to make a dissolve completely automatically. With manual dissolves the length of the film must be measured exactly. The exposure of the two superimposed pieces of film must correspond exactly.

Distortion - Lens fault of a wide-angle or variable-focus lens. Causes distortion in the form of straight lines inwards and outwards.

E

Editing – Part of film montage – *see* **Film Editing**

Effects Filter – Produces a particular colour effect, giving the subject a strange appearance (e.g. pop filter, chromofilter). *See* **Filter**

Ekta Sound – Sound-film system developed by Kodak. Records life-sound simultaneously with the film. All sounds are recorded on to the film sound strip (*see* **Single-Track System**) over an external microphone or one built into the camera.

Exposure – Amount of light required for a faultless shot. Too little light results in under-exposure (films too dark), too much light in over-exposure (films too bright). Under- and over-exposure are usually indicated by warning signals.

Exposure Correction – Essential when filters are used during filming. In cameras with internal measurement (light measurement through the optical system) the necessary alteration of the aperture occurs automatically, in the others manual correction is necessary. *See also* **Back-Light Correction**

Eye Piece – The lens in the lens sytem atuned to the eye, which facilitates direct observation of the intermediate image produced by the lens. Seen in the viewfinder of the ciné camera. In the eye piece the focus on the viewing surface is set in accordance with the eye, which is important to ensure correct focusing control on the ground-glass screen. If the eye piece is not adjusted correctly, while the object might appear in focus on the ground-glass screen, it will not be focused on the film.

A sunset is the most impressive back-light of all

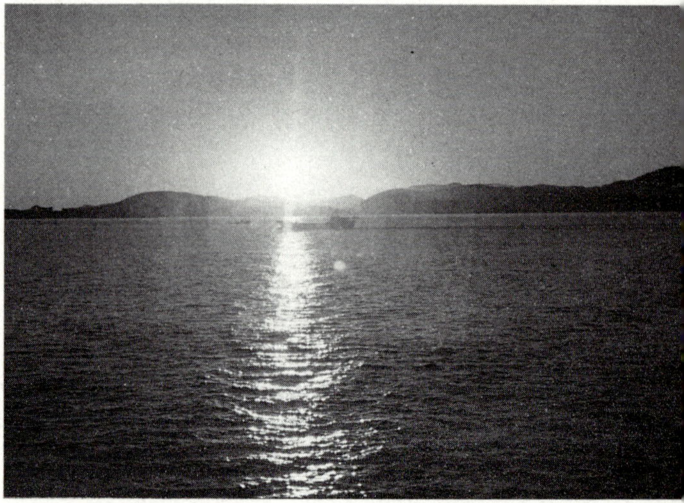

F

Fade-In – Converse of fade-out. The fully closed diaphragm is opened slowly to reveal a film scene. Fade-ins are often located at the beginning of a film or group of scenes.

Fade-Out – Closure of the aperture to the point of total darkness. Used to allow a film scene to die away harmoniously, at a variable slow pace. Fade-outs are both manually and automatically possible.

Film Cement – Adhesive for ciné films, usually acetate soluble. Used to join two pieces of film chemically. *See* **Polyester films,** which cannot be treated with this adhesive, since the cement does not dissolve into the film base.

Film Composition – Creation of a film. Formation and lighting of film subjects. Treatment of foreground and background. Determination of perspective (camera position) etc. Film composition dictates the sucess of a good film. *See* **Script**

Film Editing – Combining different film strips or parts of film in sequence and of a length which is dramatically correct. Produces a logically constructed film out of the available film material. *See* **Montage**

Film Feeder *see* **Film Transporter**

Film Lamp – Generates hard durable light. *See* **Artificial Light.** Source of light used in filming in dark rooms. Previously nitrophot lamps, now nearly all are halogen burners since they provide considerably more light and are much simpler to construct. Halogen lamps are produced to accept 240 (110) volts, for connection with the mains, or with a 12-volt transformer for battery powering. Battery lamps are employed relatively seldom, since the accumulator is big and heavy.

Film Material *see* **Colour Film, Black-and-White Film**

Film Montage *see* **Montage**

Film Music – Music composed especially for a film. Often very suitable for subsequent scoring of amateur films. However new or recent music is under copyright protection.

Film Speed – Light sensitivity of the film material. *See* **DIN** and **ASA**

Film Speed (Image Frequency) – Number of individual frames exposed per second in a ciné camera. Can be altered for trick shots (slow motion or time lapse). The most commonly used film speed for amateur films = 18 frames per second. *See* **Single-Frame Device**

Film Surface – Surface of the film exposed during filming. Usually marked in the ciné camera by a circle with a vertical line through it.

Film Title – Leader of a film. Gives details concerning the film theme, those involved, and the author. The title is the visiting card of the film, i.e. of the author, and can be produced in a wide variety of ways.

Film Transporter – Device for constant transport of the film in camera and projector. Usually there is a claw in the camera which grips in the film perforations and transports the film intermittently frame by frame. Similarly in the projector there are two sprockets which ensure even transportation to the film gate and from there to the wind-on spool. The film transporter is an important component of the ciné camera, since it guarantees visual continuity.

Film Viewer – Equipment for examining the ciné films during editing. The film can be observed and marked on a focusing screen of about 7 x 10cm. to 10 x 15cm.

Filter – Filters exist for black-and-white and for colour film material. Filters for black-and-white material are almost exclusively used in still photography, since there are hardly any black-and-white ciné films. The few common colour film filters provide for colour correction:
UV (Haze) Filter: subdues ultra-violet light. Used in mountainous settings and by the sea.
Skylight filter (Conversion Red 1.5): slightly pink colouring. Excludes the surplus blue element from the atmosphere, apparent in the light in strong sunshine.
A correction filter (*see* **Conversion Filter**) is used to subdue red and blue colours (artificial light and daylight). The conversion red 1.5 filter is the weakest of these.
Polarisation filter (Pol filter) can be rotated in its mounting and is used to polarise the light by means of varying settings in front of the lens, thus only light from certain directions is allowed to permeate through it. The pol filter avoids or diminishes the reflections in the subject. *See* **Polarisation.**
Grey filter: neutral grey filter, used only to subdue the light, has no effect on the colours. Used for filming in very bright lighting conditions (snow, sea, etc.), when the aperture would need to be further closed than the optical system allows. Grey filters come in varying gradations with extension factors of 2x, 4x and 6x.

Filter Adapter Ring – Connecting piece to compensate for varying screwing threads. *See* **Adapter**

Filter Factors – Engraved on the filter mount. Multiplied by the measured exposure time, in order to determine a faultless exposure value.

Fixed Focus – Fixed lens not allowing any distance setting. Has a fixed focal length (see **Focal Length**); distance is fixed on a middle value. Fix-focus lenses are not particularly light-intense and are only used in the simplest cameras.

Flare – Caused by the reflection of the individual lenses within the optical system. The greater the radius of curvature of the lens, the more frequently the flare occurs, chiefly with small apertures and in back-lighting. The flare shows a reflection or sometimes several reflections of the diaphragm in the picture.

Flash Light – Its only possible association with filming is in trick shots. Processes involving movement which are executed in darkness and over a long time span can be made visible by using flash light with the automatic single-frame device.

Flip-Over Title *see* **Title**

Focal Length – Distance between the optical centre of the lens when set at infinity and the focal point. The focal length is engraved on the lens together with the light intensity indicating the shortest distance from the centre of the lens surface to the film required for a focused image of an object at infinity. *See* **Depth of Field**

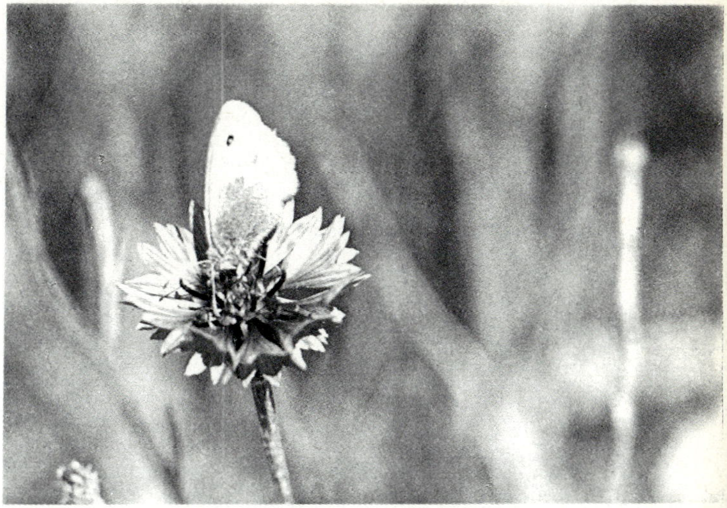

Close-up of a cornflower and a butterfly

Focal Point – The meeting point of all the rays of light passing through a convex lens.

Focus – Abbreviation = f., denotes the focal length of the lens, the numerical value of which is always engraved on the lens. *See* **Focal Length**

Foreground – Important component of many film shots. Landscapes are given a formative impression by the use of a striking foreground. Moreover, the size ratio of the foreground indicates proportions and gives the picture an impression of depth.

Frame Line - Interval between two pictures on a ciné film.

Framing Lever - Lever or switch on the film projector. Positions the picture correctly in the frame, if the frame line is visible at the top or bottom of the projected picture.

Frequency Range - Represents the number of sound cycles per unit of time. Sound film projectors and other sound reproduction equipment (tape, cassette, records) have different sound frequencies. Measured in Hertz (Hz) = cycles per second. Sound film projectors reach a frequency of about 30 - 11,000 Hertz, studio tape recorders up to 20,000 Hertz. Human audibility depends on age, is generally about 13,000 - 16,000 Hertz. (Concert pitch is at 440Hz.) *See* **Hertz, Heinrich**

Front Light - Lights the subject from approximately the same direction as the camera (sun or halogen lamp). All shadows advance from the camera, the greater the light source, the shorter the shadows.

G

Gradation - Measurement of whether a film has a hard or soft finish. Highly sensitive films = soft; less-sensitive films = hard.

Graduated Shutter Effect - Used in finished films to add a certain effect. Either the picture becomes gradually darker during projection, until it disappears, or, conversely, as a scene opens the picture appears gradually through the darkness, until it reaches the normal level of brightness. Thus a fade-in or fade-out effect is simulated. *See* **Trick Effects.**

Greased Plate - Piece of glass lightly smeared with grease. Used to effect in a trick shot, causing the end of a scene to blurr.

Grey Filter *see* **Filter**

H

Half Track - Sound track on a two-track tape recorder. Each sound recording occupies one half of the tape (half track) and runs in the opposite direction of the other recording. *See* **Tape Recorder, Soundtrack**

Halogen Lamp *see* **Projection Lamp**

Halogen Light *see* **Film Lamp**

Hertz, Heinrich (1857-94) - Discovered Hertzian waves which form the basis of modern radio techniques. Unit of measurment of the cycles named after him. *See* **Frequency Range**

I

Image Frequency *see* **Film Speed**

Impulse Cable - Connecting cable between the camera and the tape recorder or cassette recorder, relaying impulses from the camera to the tape, which regulates the synchronisation of picture and sound.

Impulse Equipment - Component of two-track scoring. The impulses are recorded on the tape and control the reproduction in the projector.

Indirect Lighting - Used predominantly for indoor close-ups (artificial light). The film lamps are directed towards the ceiling or a reflecting surface (screen), in order to avoid definite cast shadows. The amount of light near the lens is limited at the same time.

Indoor Shots - Films taken in enclosed spaces, usually with film lamps. In relatively light rooms, an XL lens with highly sensitive film can be used without artificial light.

Interchangeable Lens - The possibility of exchanging one lens in the camera for another. This possibility, widely used in still photographic cameras, is only present in a few ciné cameras and consequently it is not in most cases essential to the many uses of the variable-focus lens.

Interval Setting *see* **Pulse-Generating Device, Single-Frame Setting, Interval Timer.**

Interval Timer - Equipment for the automatic setting of single-frame shots at specific time intervals. The interval between the single frame settings can be up to 60 seconds long, and can be altered anywhere within these limits, but always at a constant rate. *See* **Single-Frame Setting.** Superior cameras usually possess a built-in interval setting. otherwise it can be obtained as an accessory.

Iris Diaphragm - Ring-shaped lens diaphragm with adjustable steel laminae. Positioned at a central optical point between two lenses. Has precise control over the intensity of light. Facilitates intermediary settings between the actual aperture values. Good-quality cameras usually have an iris diaphragm rather than the usual sector shutter for fade-ins and fade-outs. However the iris diaphragm must be equipped with its own motor on account of the greater friction which occurs. *See* **Sector Shutter**

K

Kelvin Grade (°K) *see* **Colour Temperature**

Do not forget to alter the setting when changing from indoor to outdoor shots among the temples (J. Klein)

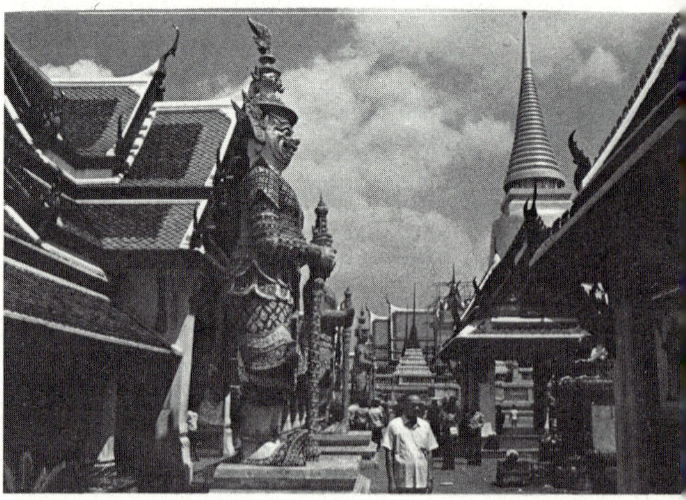

L

Leader – Normally a green film strip at the beginning of the film. *See* **Title**

Lens – Elementary component of the camera lens. There are convex lenses (converging lenses) and concave lenses (diverging lenses). The different lenses have varying powers of refraction. The camera lens is calculated according to the form and refraction of the lenses. A modern variable-focus lens consists of 15 to 20 lenses. The large number of lenses eliminates the element of image error inherent in each individual lens, so that a faultless image is produced. *See* **Dioptric.**

Lens Coating – Coating on all surfaces in and on the camera lens wherever air and glass come into contact. The coating is usually of a blue or blue-green colour and should prevent or minimise reflections within the lens system.

Lens Definition – Definition of a film scene is limited to a small area (a dot) in order to portray a striking subject particularly clearly. Achieved by
a) a wide-open diaphragm
b) a long focal length.

Lens Hood – Tube of metal, plastic, or other resilient material. Used for shots taken with side lighting, to prevent light reaching the taking lens and causing unwanted reflections. Has no effect on exposure.

Life Sound Recording – Sound-film recording on Super-8 film with sound track. The sound recording occurs as the film is taken by means of a microphone attached to the camera. The sound recording is made over a sound head built in to the camera. *See* **Ekta Sound, Original Sound.**

Light – Measured in waves and a requirement of every film shot. The varying lengths of the waves correspond to the varying light colours. The length of the waves can be measured by various methods. The most common is $1\mu = \frac{1}{1000}$ mm.

Lighting – Type of light used for photography and filming.
1. Daylight (predominantly blue light)
2. Artificial light (predominantly yellow light)

Double-8 films are suited either to one type of lighting or the other, Super-8 films only to artificial light. In Super-8 cameras, the film is modified for use in daylight by an in-built filter.

Mixing daylight and artificial light results in colour discrepancies; conversion filters of varying shades are used to compensate for this. *See also* **Conversion Filter**

Lighting Ratio - Also called lighting contrast. Indicates the relationship between the light intensities of various light sources, when the illumination of the subject consists of both main lighting and brightening light. Important for filming with artificial light.

Light Intensity - Ratio, engraved on the lens. The widest possible aperture that can be set. The smaller the figure given, the more light-intense the lens. Example: 1:1.8 means that the lens possesses a focal length which is 1.8 times as long s the widest effective opening of the diaphragm.

Lip Synchronisation - Absolutely simultaneous recording of film and sound. Movements and their associated sounds are recorded in synchronisation on two different bearers or the same bearer for sound and film, and reproduced simultaneously. Lip synchronisation is important for conversations and sounds where even a slight displacement would have a disruptive effect.

Low Light *see* **XL Lens**

M

Macro Shot - Film taken in magnifying range with a macro lens, possible with reflex viewfinder of a modern camera. Macro shots enlarge the object in a ratio of 1:1 to about 50:1. On account of the small depth of field of 1mm. or less, precise setting of the distance is essential for macro shots, stopping down to at least a middle aperture value.

Macro Zoom Lens - Variable-focus lens facilitating the setting of very short taking distances and allowing the taking of macro shots without an additional lens. Also permits attractive focus blending from ultra near to distant (zooms).

Magnetic Head - Small magnet in tape recorders, cassette recorders, or sound projectors. Records sound waves, transformed by the microphone into electrical impulses, on to the sound bearer. When reproduced, the electrical impulses are gathered by a sound head and transformed back to sound waves over an amplifier, which are made audible in the loudspeaker.

Magnetic Sound Process *see* **Tape Recorder**

Marginal Track *see* **Sound Track**

Microphone – Electroacoustic equipment which transforms sound waves entering it into electrical waves. Essential for all methods of life-sound recording.

Mixed Light – Mixture of daylight and artificial light. Can lead to colour displacement on ciné films and transparency films. To remedy this a conversion filter is employed. *See* **Conversion Filter.**

Mixer Unit – Equipment with which different types of sound recording (e.g. tape and microphone) can be transformed simultaneously (mixed) on to another sound bearer. Used for scoring magnetic sound films, so that sounds, music, and text are recorded in one phase of work.

Monopod *see* **Tripod**

Montage – The composition of the film material to form a film consisting of a sequence of planned scenes, after the film has been edited. *See* **Film Editing.** Montage involves the film viewer (*see* **Film viewer**) and splicer (*see* **Splicer**).

Motional Distortion –
a) If the movement of the subject is too fast the shot seems hesitant, because the interval between one shot and the next is too great.
b) The picture trembles because the camera has been panned too fast. Remedy: pan slowly or choose stationary camera position.

Mounting Title *see* **Film Title**

Multiple Exposure – Only possible with ciné cameras which allow back winding of the film. Back wind mechanism must be coupled with the single-frame setting. Thus, for instance, the blending-in of subtitles is facilitated

Mutiple Prism *see* **Trick Lenses**

Musical Accompaniment – Film music, played by a pianist in the time of the silent film, now provided by electronic sound carriers.

N

Natural Size – Image in a ratio of 1:1, i.e. the object taken is equal in size to its image on the film or negative.

Newsreel – Documentary film report of an actual event. Can be undertaken in private circles.

Nitrophot Lamp – Lamp used for photography and filming, artificial light of 3200°K. Nitrophot lamps have been largely superceded by halogen lamps. *See* **Halogen Lamp.**

Normal Film – Film of 35mm. width. Used in professional filming and still photographic cameras. The term 'normal' film originates from the time of the first 16mm. 'ciné films'.

Normal Focal Length – Normal focal length in Super-8 cameras is 15mm., in Double-8 equipment 12.5mm. The term 'normal' focal length originates from the time when lenses with a fixed focal length were in predominant use. *See* **Variable-Focus Lens.**

O

Optical Sound – Sound recording by an optical-electronic method (photographic reproduction of sound); a professional technique, not applicable to amateur-filming.

Optics – Originally the science of visible light. Collective term for all optical systems.

Original Sound – Sound recording taken as the film is shot, recorded by the life-sound process or on a tape recorder. When projected the original sound is presented together with the film, either on a sound track as life sound, or as a tape in the two-track process. Original sound can be transferred to the sound track by post scoring. *See* **Life Sound.**

Outdoor Picture – Collective term for all films and photographs taken in daylight, i.e. without artificial lighting. The daylight setting on the ciné camera will generally apply for outdoor pictures.

P

Panoramic Shot – Film shot encompassing a larger section than accommodated by the lens in the ciné camera. The camera must make a pan which takes in the whole width of the panorama, but is executed with extreme care. If the camera is turned too quickly, the picture will tremble on the screen. Explanation: the interval between one shot and the next is too great for a seamless image to be produced. Panoramic shots pose great difficulties for most film-makers.

Consider the effect of light and shadows when taking close-ups of people

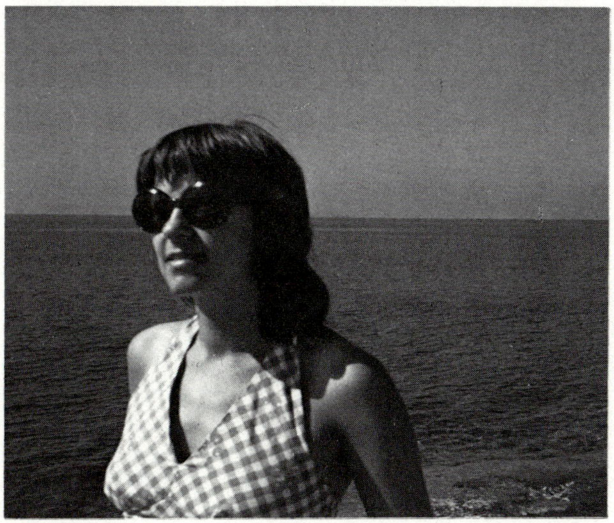

Panoramic Top – Tripod head, facilitating gentle movement for panoramic shots. Designed with a built-in motor or for manual operation. The motor requires about 100 seconds for a turn of 180°.

Pan Shot *see* **Panoramic Shot**

Parallax – Displacement of the image, i.e. the section of the scene seen in the viewfinder differs from the section apparent on the film. Only happens when the viewfinder image is not created by the taking lens itself. Parallax errors no longer occur in modern ciné cameras, since they are reflex cameras, and a characteristic of them is that the viewfinder and taking lens are identical.

Perforation - Row of holes on ciné and cinema films for even transportation of the film in the camera and projector (in 8mm. films, one perforation hole per frame). *See* **Film Transport.**

Perspective - Created by projection of the surroundings on a surface. The film perspective is the angle from which the camera captures the subject. There are various perspectives, producing very different effects. A distinction is made between linear and central perpectives, cylinder and globule perpectives. In film language we refer to worm's-eye view - from below to above, bird's-eye view - from above to below, normal perspective - at eye level. Alterations of perspective all add variety to a film.

Pilot Sound - Impulse sound in sound-recording processes in conjunction with a ciné camera, camera and tape recorder being electrically connected. Pilot sound ensures the parallel running of sound and film when projected.

Polarisation - Polarised light is directed light, the waves of which only move in one direction. Normal light moves in all directions. The light can be adjusted by means of a polarisation filter. *See* **Filter.**

Polyester Film - New type of film, using polyester as the film base. Polyester is thinner and less liable to break than the more commonly used acetate . *See* **Film Cement**

Post Scoring - Film scoring undertaken when all processes have been completed. Opposite of life-sound recording.

Projection - Presentation of a film or transparency using a projector. With film, 18 or 24 frames are projected on the screen per second.

This picture within a picture demands the use of a zoom

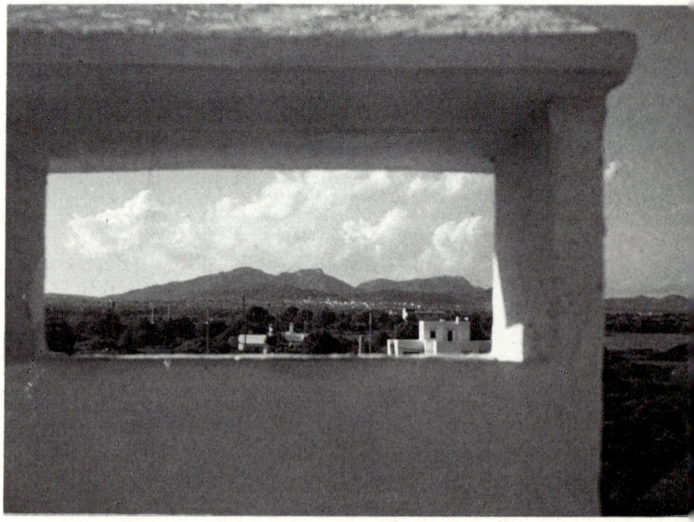

Projection Lamp –
a) High-voltage lamp
Lamp with normal mains voltage (240 or 110 volt). Oldest type, still used in old equipment. Obtainable in nearly all wattages from 50 watt to 1,250 watt. Other wattages are used in special circumstances.
b) Low-voltage lamp
Has a voltage considerably lower than the usual mains voltage (8 volt, 12 volt, 15 volt, 24 volt, etc.). Low-voltage lamps generally have the advantage that their light filament system is smaller that that of high-voltage lamps, and this approaches the ideal of a spot light source. The necessary transformer for the voltage is nearly always built into the projector.
c) Halogen lamp
The most modern piece of equipment in this sector. This extremely small lamp consists of a quartz flask, filled with iodide gas. Modern Super-8 projectors are fitted with this on account of its moderate warmth. The concave mirror is changed each time with the lamp, since the lamp is permanently connected to it. Halogen lamps in projectors are always low-voltage lamps.
Projection lamps should not be touched with bare hands and hot lamps should not be moved.

Projection Screen – Screen for the projection of transparencies or films. *See* **Crystal-Beaded Screen, Daylight Screen.**

Projector – Equipment for projection. Different equipment for silent films, sound films, and transparencies.

Pulse Generating Device –
a) Apparatus which transports impulses from the tape recorder to the film projector, guaranteeing absolutely parallel running of film and tape.
b) Impulse equipment, usually battery powered, sending release impulses to the camera. The interval from one single frame to the next can be adjusted, and thus it is possible to take extreme time-lapse shots almost completely automatically. *See* **Timer, Single-Frame Setting.**

R

Recording Head - sound head recording a magnetic impulse on the sound track or tape.

Red-Dot Setting - Red dots on the focal-length scale and distance scale combine to give the best possible depth of field for a snapshot. Setting most suitable for shots taken under time pressure. Exact setting is omitted. Requirement: relatively good weather, so that the automatic aperture is set to an average maintaining an equally average depth of field.

Reflected-Light Measurement *see* **Exposure Meter**

Reflex Viewfinder - Modern cameras nearly always possess a reflex viewfinder. The light rays from the path of the image-forming lens are intercepted by a barely visible reflecting system and projected on the ground-glass screen. Thus the reflex viewfinder has exact control over the section of the picture taken and its definition.

Releaser - Lever or button to induce transportation of the film. *See* **Automatic Release**

Remote Release - Electronic release; the film is released over long distances by means of a button or wireless control.

Rerecording - Recording of music from a tape on to a film or another tape. Requires a special rerecording cable.

Reverse Action - Backwind of a film projector, enabling the film to be wound back or projected backwards. For a dissolve, any ciné camera must be set briefly to backwind, in order to wind back the part of the film to be 'dissolved'. Some Double-8 cameras can wind the film back over great lengths (from the wind-on spool back on to the wind-off spool). With Super-8 film this is not possible.

Rotary Disk Shutter *see* **Sector Shutter**

Running Title *see* **Film Title**

S

Scene - Part of a film. The scene is that part of a film filmed without interruption. A sequence of movement is usually composed of several film scenes, often not combined until the montage work is done. *See* **Montage.**

Scene Length - Determined subjectively, but depends on the nature of the subject portrayed. There can be no general rule for scene length. A scene lasts on average about 5-8 seconds, but longer scenes or those lasting only a second are not a rarity. Alteration of the film length produces excitement or tranquility in the film.

Scene Transition *see* **Dissolve**
Fade-In
Fade-Out
Trick Effect

Scoring - Process by which a suitable acoustic accompaniment is added to an originally silent film.

Scoring Plan - Plan, according to which scoring is undertaken, e.g. a combination of various musical sounds and verbal commentary. Scoring plan is a part of the script. *See* **Script.**

Scoring Process *see* **Single-Track Process**
Two-Way Process
Life Sound

Script - Establishes the sequence of the film exactly including all instructions regarding composition, motifs, camera settings, and scoring. *See* **Film Composition**

Sector Shutter - Cameras normally possess a rotary-disk shutter, which is opened and closed throughout 180°. In the sector shutter

A striking foreground gives shape to the panorama shot (H. Reichert)

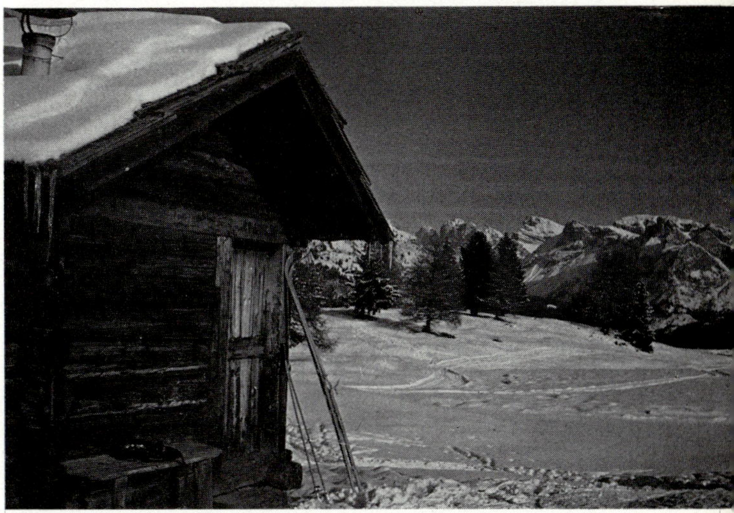

the open sector is also 180°, but the normal setting can be altered, by closing the sector by 90°, in order to film with only half the amount of light. A sector shutter can be closed progressively to achieve complete darkness. In practice this is a fade-out. *See* **Fade-Out, Iris Diaphragm.**

Sharp Focusing – Effected by the lens and regulated on a scale or in the camera's reflex viewfinder.

Shoulder Pod *see* **Tripod**

Single-Frame Setting – Trick setting on a ciné camera for the exposure of individual frames on the ciné film. Used for trick title shots, animated cartoons, and extreme-time-lapse shots. *See* **Film Speed**

Single-Track Process – Scoring method for ciné films of all types with a 0.8mm. wide sound strip, which is stuck on to the film. The strip records all the sounds, which are recorded and reproduced by the single-track projector. (Single track = Sound and picture on one strip)

Skylight Filter *see* **Conversion Filter**

Slow Motion – Presentation of quick movements at a slowed-down pace, in order to allow or improve their visiblity. More single frames are exposed during filming than are reproduced in the same amount of time during projection.

Example:
Filming = 54 frames per second
Reproduction = 18 frames per second
Slow motion = x 3.

Soft-Focus Lens – lens screwed in front of the camera lens in order to create a diffused image. The lens is used chiefly for portrait photographs, rarely in filming.

Sound Coupler – Coupling equipment for projector and tape recorder (or similar) in two-way recording process.

Sound-Effects Library – Collection of all sounds needed for film scoring, usually produced by the film-maker himself. The library must be catalogued, so that each sound can be located readily.

A sports report has its own laws (K. Briel)

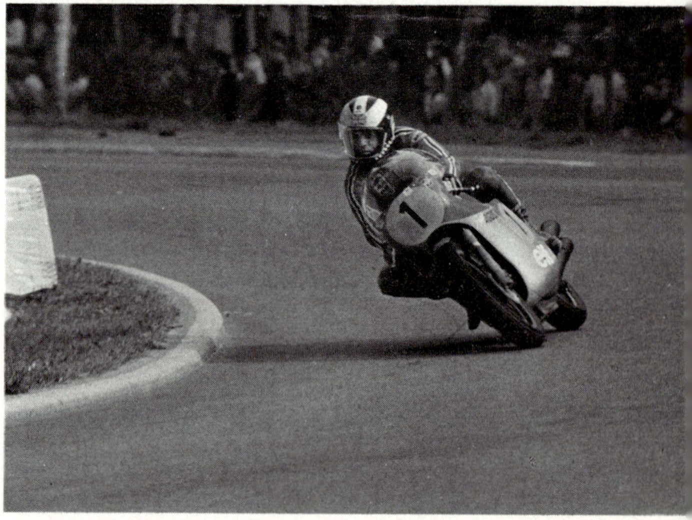

Sound-Effects Tape (Sound-Effects Record) – Manufactured product with the popular sound effects. Tapes and cassettes are less sensitive and more suitable for film work than records.

Sound Fading – Similar to a dissolve in filming. Two sound recordings are connected together seamlessly by being superimposed over a small area. Not successful with all music. Sound fading is accommodated in most film projectors by means of a trick setting.

Sound Film – Scored film. The system used to score is of no significance.

Sound-Film Interval – Usual distance from film gate to sound head. In every sound-film camera and most projectors this equals 18 frames.

Sound Head *see* **Magnetic Head**

Sound Library – Collection of music and sounds for scoring film. Many sounds can be produced by simple means. The sound library must be so arranged that all the desired sounds (tape or cassette) can be found quickly.

Sound Track – Strip of sound tape 0.8mm. wide added to the ciné film and on which the sound is recorded as with a tape. *See* **Single-Track Process.** For stereo sound, a sound track appears on both sides of the film (main track and compensatory track).

Splice – Weld in the film where it has been cut. A good splice is invisible and inaudible. If the splice is visible or audible when projected, it should be repeated. *See* **Film Editing.**

Splicer – Equipment used for joining different films or pieces of films. *See* **Film Editing.**
a) Wet splicer: Film cement (*see* **Film Cement**) is used for joining the film, both pieces of film being welded together chemically.
b) Dry splicer: Two pieces of film are bound on both sides with adhesive foil.
Editing cannot be omitted for a good film. A splicer is the most important tool the ciné-filmer possesses.

Spoken Text – Established text of film commentary for a tape or sound track.

Start Mark – Mark on the film and tape at the beginning of projection in two-way presentations. During filming and at each reproduction, the start marks on the film and tape must occupy the same position in the equipment.

Stereo Sound Recording – Sound recording on two separate sound tracks. Stereophonic film recording is only possible in post-scoring with sound projectors designed for this purpose. Stereophonic life sound has not yet been developed.

Stripping Machine - Equipment with which the amateur can supply his films with a sound-track. *See also* **Sound Track**

Subject Contrast - Contrast between the lightest and darkest parts of the film subject.

Swivelling Titles *see* **Film Title**

Synchronisation - Coupling of pictures and sound recordings made on separate equipment.

T

Taking Speed - 1. Of the ciné camera: number of individual frames exposed per second.
The following filming speeds normally apply:

for amateur films	18 frames per second
for professional films	24 frames per second
for television	25 frames per second

2. Of the sound-recording equipment: figure indicating the number of centimetres of tape which move past the sound head in one second. Normally 9.5 cm. on amateur equipment. Higher speeds imply high-frequency ranges.

Tape - Usually of synthetic material with a superimposed magnetic layer. For recording made by the magnetic-sound or needle-sound process (tape recorder).

Tape Recorder - Recording and reproduction equipment working in accordance with the magnetic-sound process. To record, the tape passes the poles of a sound head (electro-magnet) for reproduction it passes by a play-back head. Tapes can be erased magnetically with the erasing button and used as often as desired. Some equipment has varying running speeds, some is designed for two-track and some for four-track processes. For stereo recordings both tracks are recorded simultaneously, for mono recordings the tracks are generally recorded one after the other in opposing directions. *See* **Frequency, Magnetic Head.**

Tilt Top *see* **Tripod**

Time Lapse – Converse of slow motion. Very slow processes are made visible by being accelerated.

Film should not be used sparingly for scenes involving movement, as at the market

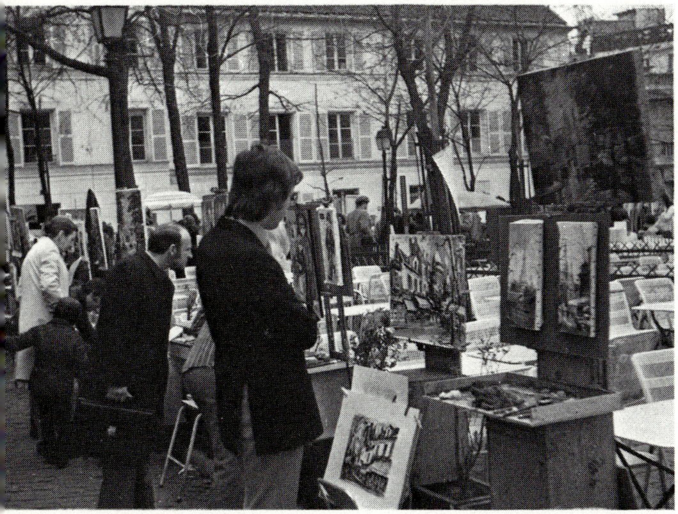

Example:
Filming = 2 frames per second
Reproduction = 18 frames per second
Time Lapse = x 9.

Timer – Pulse-generating device, usually built in to superior cameras in the form of an automatic single-frame device. Allows extreme-time-lapse filming. Thus for instance, shots can be taken at intervals of about 60 seconds. *See* **Pulse-Generating Device, Single-Frame Setting.**

Title *see* **Film Title**

Titler – Equipment for the production of film titles. Besides normal text titles, mounting titles, swivelling titles, flip-over titles, and titles on several planes can also be created.

Tracking Shot –
a) Readjustment of the variable-focus lens (zoom) during filming. Creates the impression that the camera either approaches the subject or moves away from it.
b) Camera is mounted on a mobile tripod and thus moved during filming. Method chiefly used in professional films.

Trailer – End of film. Usually consists of an end title or a ready made film strip. Is normally red, can be handled for rewinding. A film with the red strip at the front requires rewinding.

Trick Effect – Short printed film strip which can be stuck between two film scenes in place of a fade-in, fade-out, or dissolve, in order to avoid harsh editing. Trick effects come in various patterns, colour and black and white. *See* **Graduated Shutter Effect.**

Trick Lenses – Special-effect lenses, screwed onto the camera lens like a filter. Trick lenses include multiple prisms, bi-fo lenses, star filters etc. Not suitable for conventional film scenes, only employed occasionally to achieve a particular effect.

Trick Title *see* **Film Title**

Tripod – Apparatus which holds the ciné camera still during filming.
a) Three-legged tripod: tripod with a tilt top and three legs spread apart, which provide an absolutely firm hold. All the legs can be altered independently of the others.
b) Monopod: Lengthwise adjustable rod. Gives the camera a steady hold and prevents horizontal movement.
c) Shoulder pod: Body-held pod, pressed against the shoulder. Facilitates a steady hold of the camera.
d) Car pod: Fixed to the windscreen, facilitating steady filming in a moving car.

Two-Track Scoring – Scoring of a film on two sound tracks on each side of the film. One track is used for recording the music and sounds, the other for speech and commentary.

Two-Way Process – Scoring a film with two 'tapes'. Film strip and tape are in two separate pieces of equipment.

U

Underwater Filming - Film taken in water with a waterproof camera casing. Light underwater casings are only suitable for depths of up to about 10m. For greater depths one requires a film casing that can withstand the great pressure.

Unified Sound System - Coupling of the film projector and tape recorder by means of an accessory. Special fittings make this a possible method for nearly all projectors and tape recorders. Both pieces of equipment are controlled by impulses on the tape. After every fourth frame a new impulse reaches the projector, so that synchronisation of both pieces of equipment is guaranteed even for long films.

V

Variable Focus Lens - Film and still-photography lens with a variable focus length. Every variable-focus lens consists of three mutually independent lens combinations. Nearest the camera lies the base lens, only taken from its fixed position for macro shots in the macro setting. The position of the central component can be varied considerably and is used to adjust the focal length. The front portion serves to adjust the focus. The front part of the variable-focus lens is adjusted exactly by an indirect method. Figures indicating focal-length range and light intensity are engraved on the front ring of every variable-focus lens (e.g. 1:1.8, 7:56).

Viewfinder - Establishes in the camera the picture to be taken and allows it to be judged.
a) Direct viewfinder: Lies separate from the lens and produces parallax faults due to the displacement of lens and viewfinder,
b) Reflex viewfinder: Receives the image in the camera directly via the lens so that it cannot be different from the picture. *See* **Reflex Viewfinder.**

Viewing Angle – Field angle of the lens, measured diagonally across the picture. A Super-8 variable-focus lens has a viewing angle of 62° in the wide-angle range (6mm.), conversely on the telephoto setting (60mm.) it has a small viewing angle of only 7°.

Vignetting – Dark picture edges. Vignetting occurs if the image diameter of the lens used is not sufficient for the picture format, or it may be due to a tilted lens hood. If, for instance, a tele lens hood is used in the wide-angle setting of a variable-focus lens it may happen that the edges are concealed since the viewing angle of the lens is greater than the permitted opening of the diaphragm.

An impressive landscape can be used to lead from one part of the film to another (B. Bruns)

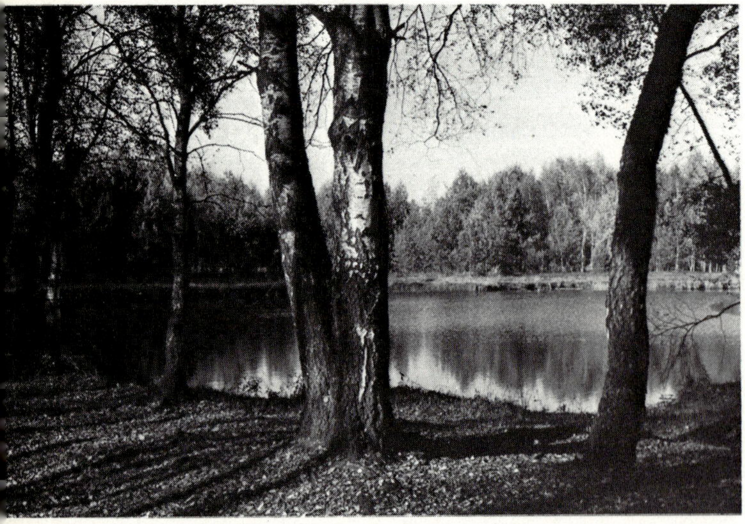

W X Z

Wide Screen *see* **Cinemascope**

Write-On Tape – Sound track with a rough backing which can be inscribed, in order to mark the sound insertions visibly on the tape.

XL Lens – **XL** = *ex*isting *l*ight, sometimes termed lowlight. Modern innovation allowing opening of the sector shutter up to 225° making it possible to film in poor lighting conditions (e.g. indoors). Used with highly sensitive Ekta 160 film, the normal room lighting is then adequate, providing the distances used are not too large. *See* **Sector Shutter.**

Zoom Lens *see* **Variable-Focus Lens**

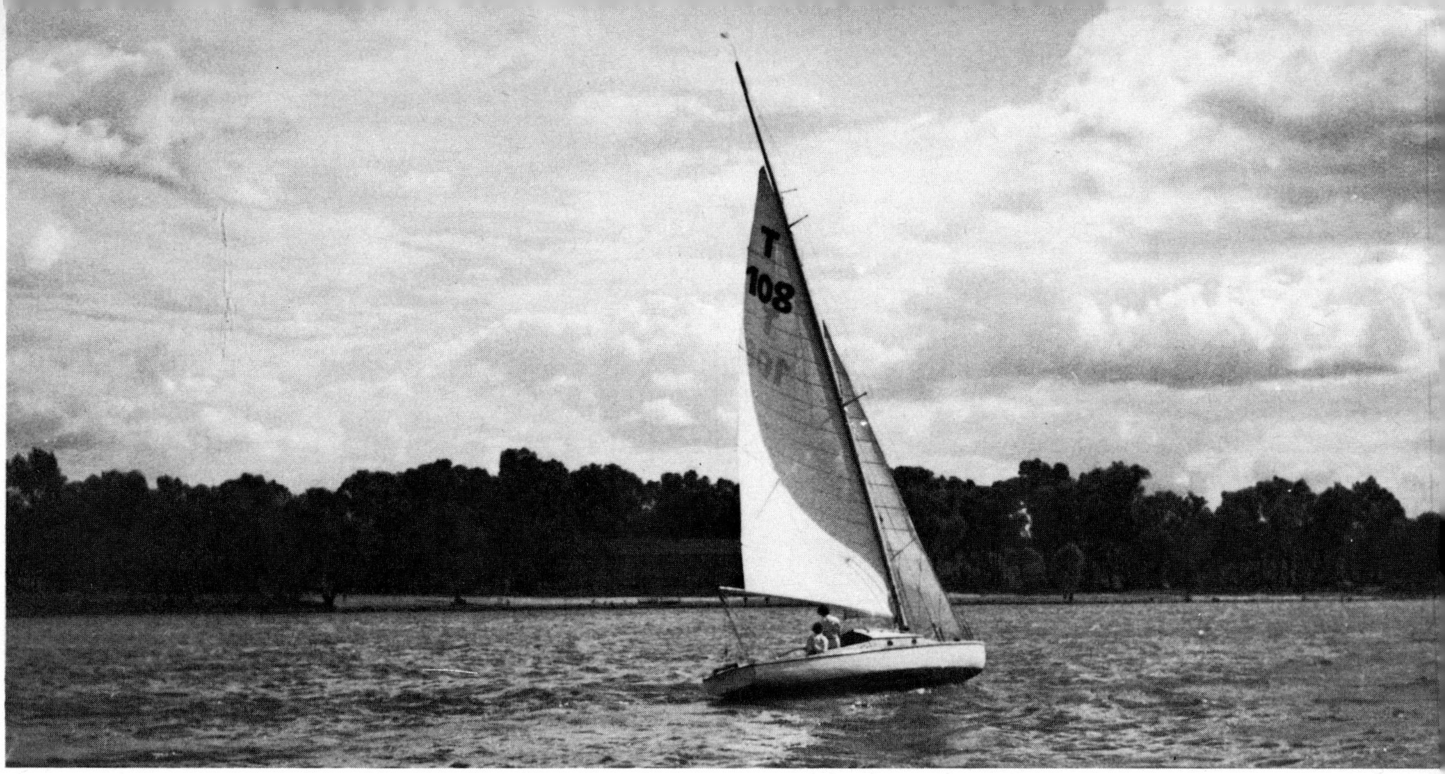

Contrasts in the film are very effective! Large and small ships (J. Schubert)

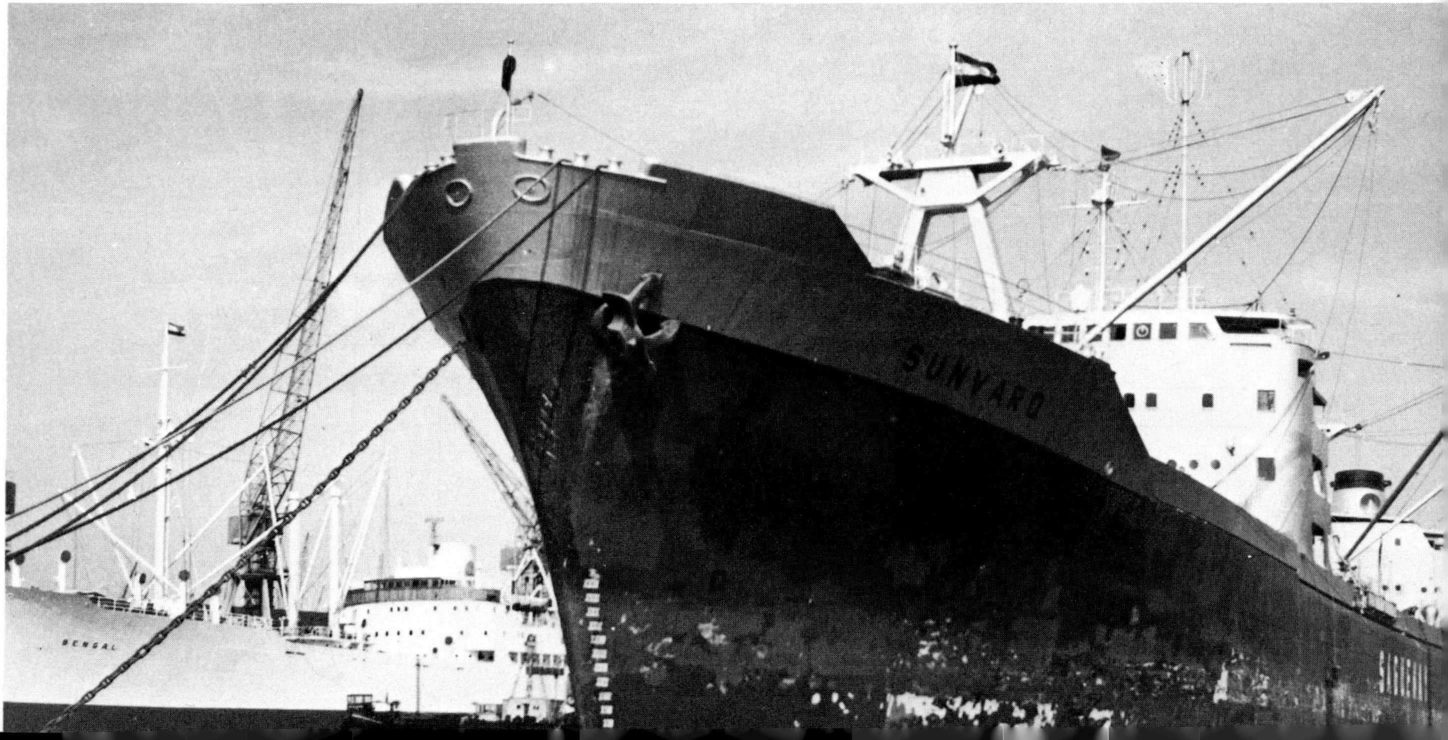